In The Post-Urban World

In the last few decades, many global cities and towns have experienced unprecedented economic, social, and spatial structural change. Today, we find ourselves at the juncture between entering a post-urban and a post-political world, both presenting new challenges to our metropolitan regions, municipalities, and cities. Many megacities, declining regions, and towns are experiencing an increase in the number of complex problems regarding internal relationships, governance, and external connections. In particular, a growing disparity exists between citizens that are socially excluded within declining physical and economic realms and those situated in thriving geographic areas. This book conveys how forces of structural change shape the urban landscape.

In The Post-Urban World is divided into three main sections: Spatial Transformations and New Geographies of Cities and Regions; Urbanization, Knowledge Economies, and Social Structuration; and Emerging Cultures in a Post-Political and Post-Urban World. One important subject covered in this book, in addition to the spatial and economic forces that shape our regions, cities, and neighbourhoods, is the social, cultural, ecological, and psychological aspects which are also critically involved. Additionally, the urban transformation occurring throughout cities is thoroughly discussed. Written by today's leading experts in urban studies, this book discusses subjects from different theoretical standpoints, as well as various methodological approaches and perspectives; this is alongside the challenges and new solutions for cities and regions in an interconnected world of global economies.

This book is aimed at both academic researchers interested in regional development, economic geography, and urban studies, as well as practitioners and policy makers in urban development.

Tigran Haas is Associate Professor of Urban Planning and Urban Design at KTH Royal Institute of Technology, Stockholm, Sweden, and Director of the Centre for the Future of Places (CFP) at KTH.

Hans Westlund is Professor in Regional Planning at KTH, Stockholm, Sweden, and Professor in Entrepreneurship, Jönköping International Business School (JIBS), Sweden.

Regions and Cities

Series Editor in Chief
Joan Fitzgerald, *Northeastern University, USA*

Editors
Ron Martin, *University of Cambridge, UK*
Maryann Feldman, *University of North Carolina, USA*
Gernot Grabher, *HafenCity University Hamburg, Germany*
Kieran P. Donaghy, *Cornell University, USA*

In today's globalised, knowledge-driven and networked world, regions and cities have assumed heightened significance as the interconnected nodes of economic, social and cultural production, and as sites of new modes of economic and territorial governance and policy experimentation. This book series brings together incisive and critically engaged international and interdisciplinary research on this resurgence of regions and cities, and should be of interest to geographers, economists, sociologists, political scientists and cultural scholars, as well as to policy-makers involved in regional and urban development.

For more information on the Regional Studies Association visit www.regional studies.org

There is a **30% discount** available to RSA members on books in the *Regions and Cities* series, and other subject related Taylor and Francis books and e-books including Routledge titles. To order just e-mail Joanna Swieczkowska, Joanna. Swieczkowska@tandf.co.uk, or phone on +44 (0)20 3377 3369 and declare your RSA membership. You can also visit the series page at www.routledge.com/ Regions-and-Cities/book-series/RSA and use the discount code: **RSA0901**

In The Post-Urban World

Emergent Transformation of Cities and
Regions in the Innovative Global Economy

**Edited by Tigran Haas and
Hans Westlund**

Routledge
Taylor & Francis Group

LONDON AND NEW YORK

First published 2018 by Routledge

2 Park Square, Milton Park, Abingdon, Oxfordshire OX14 4RN
711 Third Avenue, New York, NY 10017

Routledge is an imprint of the Taylor & Francis Group, an informa business

First issued in paperback 2018

British Library Cataloguing in Publication Data
A catalogue record for this book is available from the British Library

Library of Congress Cataloging in Publication Data
Names: Haas, Tigran, editor. | Westlund, Hans, editor.
Title: In the post-urban world : emergent transformation of cities and
regions in the innovative global economy / edited by Tigran Haas and
Hans Westlund.
Description: Abingdon, Oxon ; New York, NY : Routledge, 2018. |
Includes bibliographical references and index.
Identifiers: LCCN 2017026351| ISBN 9781138943926 (hardback) |
ISBN 9781315672168 (ebook)
Subjects: LCSH: Urbanization–History–21st century. | Cities and towns–
History–21st century. | Urban policy. | Regional planning.
Classification: LCC HT361 .I477 2018 | DDC 307.7609/05–dc23
LC record available at https://lccn.loc.gov/2017026351

ISBN: 978-1-138-94392-6 (hbk)
ISBN: 978-1-138-39415-5 (pbk)

Typeset in Times New Roman
by Wearset Ltd, Boldon, Tyne and Wear

"The editors claim that the difference between the 'urban' and 'non-urban' is increasingly blurred and new conceptions of poly-centric city regions are emerging, which are the themes of this important book. It offers innovative suggestions on how to enhance local resilience as well as examples of successful adaptation strategies. Internationally renowned authors have contributed essays on urban solutions and how to make cities more sustainable, resilient and socially inclusive. This book is an informative, comprehensive and up-to-date account which will be of considerable use to its readership. An important resource and I recommend it highly."

Professor Steffen Lehmann, Director of the Cluster for Sustainable Cities and Professor of Sustainable Architecture, University of Portsmouth, UK

"By providing an insight into the complexities of changes of cities' internal spatial transformations and extensions to new types of city regions, on the one hand, and the global networks of these 'post-metropolitan' regions, on the other, this book offers an elegant and stimulating analysis of a new urban paradigm."

Roberta Capello, Professor of Regional Economics at Politecnico of Milan, Italy

"This book represents not only an impressive collection of long-awaited statements on post-urban cities by world leading thinkers in the most vibrant field of regional studies, but also a major contribution to post urban policy discourses for policy makers in global knowledge society. The post-urban dynamisms, most typically characterized by re-urbanization, densification of city regions, region enlargement, downgrading of intracity relations and upgrading intercity communications, are expressions of the dissolution of conventional frames of references on urban development: the urban-rural dichotomy and the urban-suburban dichotomy. The message is really striking and innovative. Focusing on the transformation of cities, each chapter addresses the basic features of the emerging post-urban world and policy implications for future. This book will appeal to academics in the fields of regional studies, economics, geography, sociology and engineering. It will also be of interest to policymakers and professionals in the fields of urban development and regional policies on different spatial scales."

Professor Kiyoshi Kobayashi, Graduate School of Management, Kyoto University, Japan

Contents

Figures

Tables

Contributors

Patrick Adler is a Research Associate at the Martin Prosperity Institute, Rotman School of Management, University of Toronto in Canada and Research Fellow and Teaching Associate at the University of California, Los Angeles (UCLA).

Julian Agyeman is Professor of Urban and Environmental Policy and Planning at Tufts University, Medford, Massachusetts and a Visiting Professor at the School of Urban Planning at McGill University, Montreal. He is the co-editor of *Just Sustainabilities: Development in an Unequal World* (MIT Press, 2015).

Michael Batty is Professor of Planning in the Bartlett School at University College London (UCL) where he is Chairman of the Bartlett Centre for Advanced Spatial Analysis (CASA). His latest book is *The New Science of Cities* (MIT Press, 2013).

Laura Burkhalter is an architect and environmental designer, Los Angeles, principal and founder of Laura Burkhalter Design Studio Inc., and founder and director of Institute for Bionomic Urbanism (IBU).

Manuel Castells is University Professor and the Wallis Annenberg Chair in Communication Technology and Society at the University of Southern California (USC), Los Angeles. He is also Professor Emeritus, University of California, Berkeley, and Professor of City and Regional Planning and of Sociology.

Susan Fainstein is a Senior Research Fellow in the Harvard Graduate School of Design (GSD), Massachusetts, and also the Professor Emeritus of Urban Planning. Her book *The Just City* was published in 2010 by Cornell University Press.

Kyle Farrell is a Doctoral Fellow in the Department of Urban Planning and Environment at KTH Royal Institute of Technology, Stockholm, Sweden and Fellow at the Centre for the Future of Places (CFP) at KTH.

Richard Florida is a professor and head of the Martin Prosperity Institute, Rotman School of Management, University of Toronto. His latest book is *The*

New Urban Crisis: How Our Cities Are Increasing Inequality, Deepening Segregation, and Failing the Middle Class – and What We Can Do About It (Basic Books, 2017).

Carl B. Frederick is a postdoctoral research fellow in the Saguaro Seminar at the Harvard Kennedy School, John F. Kennedy School of Government, Harvard University, Massachusetts.

Edward L. Glaeser is the Fred and Eleanor Glimp Professor of Economics in the Faculty of Arts and Sciences at Harvard University, Massachusetts. His latest book is *The Triumph of the City: How Our Greatest Invention Makes Us Richer, Smarter, Greener, Healthier, and Happier* (Pan, 2012).

Tigran Haas is the Associate Professor of Urban Planning & Urban Design at KTH Royal Institute of Technology, Stockholm, Sweden, and Director of the Centre for the Future of Places (CFP) at KTH. His latest book is *Emergent Urbanism: Urban Planning & Design in Times of Structural and Systemic Change* (co-edited with Krister Olsson, Ashgate-Routledge, 2014).

Paul L. Knox is the University Distinguished Professor and Senior Fellow for International Advancement, the College of Architecture and Urban Studies, Virginia Tech. His latest books are *Atlas of Cities* (Princeton University Press, 2014) and *London: Architecture, Building, and Social Change* (Merrell, 2015).

Karima Kourtit is a postdoctoral research fellow at KTH Royal Institute of Technology, Stockholm, Sweden, School of Architecture and the Built Environment, Department of Urban Planning and Environment.

Nina-Marie Lister is the Graduate Programme Director and an Associate Professor in the School of Urban and Regional Planning, Ryerson University, Toronto, Canada. Her latest publication is *Projective Ecologies* (with Chris Reed, ACTAR Press, 2014).

Duncan McLaren is a freelance environmental researcher and advisor and former Chief Executive of Friends of the Earth Scotland. He is Director of McLaren Environmental Research and Consultancy. He is the co-editor of *Just Sustainabilities: Development in an Unequal World* (MIT Press, 2015).

Rahul Mehrotra is Principal of architecture firm RMA Architects of Mumbai, India and is Professor of Urban Design and Planning, as well as the Chair of the Department of Urban Planning and Design at the Harvard Graduate School of Design (GSD), Massachusetts.

Michael Neuman is Professor of Sustainable Urbanism, Faculty of Architecture and the Built Environment, University of Westminster, London, Principal of M. Neuman Consultancy, and was Professor of Sustainable Urbanism, Faculty of the Built Environment, University of New South Wales, Sydney, Australia.

Peter Nijkamp is the Professor Emeritus of Regional Economics and Economic Geography at the Vrije Universiteit, Amsterdam, the Netherlands, a fellow of the Tinbergen Institute, and Guest Professor at KTH Royal Institute of Technology, Stockholm, Sweden, Department of Urban Planning and Environment.

Nadia Nur is Senior Researcher at Roma Tre University and Postdoctoral Fellow at the Department of Architecture (Roma Tre University) and Urban Studies in Rome, Italy.

Jessie P. H. Poon is Professor of Geography at the Department of Geography, University at Buffalo, The State University of New York. She is the editor, with Peter Nijkamp and Kenneth Button, of *Highlights in Regional Planning* (Edward Elgar, 2006) and with David L. Rigby of *International Trade: The Basics* (Routledge, 2016).

Robert D. Putnam is the Peter and Isabel Malkin Professor of Public Policy at Harvard University, Massachusetts. He has written 14 books, including *Bowling Alone: The Collapse and Revival of American Community* (Simon & Schuster, 2000) and recently *Our Kids: The American Dream in Crisis* (Simon & Schuster, 2016).

Saskia Sassen is the Robert S. Lynd Professor of Sociology at Columbia University, New York and the Centennial Visiting Professor at the London School of Economics (LSE). Her latest book is *Expulsions: Brutality and Complexity in the Global Economy* (Harvard University Press, 2014).

Richard Sennett is the Centennial Professor of Sociology at the London School of Economics (LSE) and University Professor of the Humanities at New York University and the Chair of Theatrum Mundi. His latest book is *Together: The Rituals, Pleasures, and Politics of Cooperation* (Yale University Press, 2012).

Jennifer M. Silva is Assistant Professor of Sociology at Bucknell University, Lewisburg, Pennsylvania. She is the author of *Coming Up Short: Working-Class Adulthood in an Age of Uncertainty* (Oxford University Press, 2013).

Kaisa Snellman is Assistant Professor of Organizational Behaviour at INSEAD (a graduate business school with campuses in Europe (Fontainebleau, France), Asia (Singapore), and the Middle East (Abu Dhabi)) where she teaches courses in organizational behaviour and organizational theory.

Edward Soja (1940–2015) was the Distinguished Professor Emeritus of Urban Planning, Luskin School of Public Affairs at the University of California, Los Angeles (UCLA) and at the London School of Economics (LSE). His last book was *Seeking Spatial Justice* (University of Minnesota Press, 2010).

Emily Talen is Professor of Urbanism at the University of Chicago, Division of Social Sciences. She was also a professor at Arizona State University and

University of Illinois at Urbana-Champaign. Her latest book is *Retrofitting Sprawl: Addressing Seventy Years of Failed Urban Form* (University of Georgia Press, 2015).

Fran Tonkiss is the Professor of Sociology and Deputy Head of Department at the London School of Economics (LSE) and the former Director of the LSE Cities Programme. Her latest book is *Cities by Design: The Social Life of Urban Form* (Polity, 2013).

Felipe Vera is a practising architect and urbanist and currently is Faculty Instructor in Urban Planning and Design at the Harvard Graduate School of Design (GSD), Massachusetts.

Hans Westlund is Professor in Regional Planning at KTH Royal Institute of Technology, Stockholm, Sweden and Professor in Entrepreneurship, Jönköping International Business School (JIBS), Sweden. His latest book, with Johan P. Larsson, is *Handbook of Social Capital and Regional Development* (Edward Elgar, 2016).

Fulong Wu is Bartlett Professor of Planning at University College London (UCL) and Bartlett Chair of Planning at The Bartlett School of Planning, Faculty of the Built Environment. He has recently published *Planning for Growth: Urban and Regional Planning in China* (Routledge, 2015).

Wei Yin is a Doctoral Fellow in that Department of Geography at SUNY – The State University of New York, Buffalo.

Preface

In the last few decades, many global cities, towns, and municipalities have experienced unprecedented economic, social, and spatial structural change. Today, we find ourselves at the juncture between entering a post-urban and a post-political world, both presenting new challenges to our metropolitan regions, municipalities, and cities. Specifically, these challenges are of a spatial, economic, demographic, ecological, cultural, and social nature. Megacities and many declining regions and towns are experiencing an increase in the number of complex problems regarding internal relationships, governance, and external connections. In particular, a growing disparity exists between citizens that are socially excluded within declining physical and economic realms and those situated in thriving geographic areas.

Throughout this book, the authors discuss from different theoretical standpoints, as well as various methodological approaches and perspectives, the challenges and new solutions for cities and regions in an interconnected world of global economies. These solutions are the result of deliberate policy, planning, and development measures, as well as a complex product of interconnected forces. Such forces are derived from economic, social, and spatial processes of structural change, as well as citizen input and activities. The chapters of this book are assembled under three main themes, highlighting this complex of interactions and the solutions for future challenges, in addition to raising several important questions. One important motif is that in addition to the spatial and economic forces that shape our regions, cities, and neighbourhoods, social, cultural, ecological, and psychological aspects are also critically involved. Additionally, the urban transformation occurring throughout cities with respect to economic, social, and spatial structural change is thoroughly discussed. Overall, this book conveys how forces of structural change shape the urban landscape.

Chapters are written by today's leading urban minds and cover cutting-edge topics in their respective fields and ongoing research themes. For the first time, this book assembles an incredibly diverse, yet interconnected, group of world-class researchers. Moreover, a combination of their latest interdisciplinary thoughts on regional science, urban development, economics, social and urban theory, and ecology are presented, specifically regarding the major challenges facing metropolitan regions. Furthermore, such a diverse mixture of topics and perspectives highlights how forces of structural and transformative global and local change are shaping the current urban landscape. The book is divided into three main sections, each consisting of seven chapters: (1) Spatial transformations and the new geography of cities and regions; (2) Urbanization, knowledge economies, and social structuration; and (3) Emerging cultures in a post-political and post-urban world.

Acknowledgements

This book is the first product of the newly established Centre for the Future of Places (CFP) at the School of Architecture and the Built Environment, KTH Royal Institute of Technology in Stockholm, Sweden. The mission of the centre is to become an international hub for research on cities, doing studies on micro, meso and macro perspectives, but also to act as a clearing house for new ideas and proposals on how cities should be planned, designed, and retrofitted best to meet both today's and tomorrow's challenges, with the specific focus on public places and urban spaces. The CFP has been established to promote sustainable urban development by shifting the urban discourse from objects to places in order to promote healthy and livable cities within the disciplines of urban planning and urban design. Tigran Haas and Hans Westlund would like to extend their deepest gratitude to the Axel and Margaret Ax:son Johnson Foundation, especially Peter Elmlund and Kurt Almqvist, for kindly supporting the CFP and therefore this project as well. We are particularly grateful that the foundation has chosen to facilitate scientific research in general and, in particular, to benefit the liberal arts and the (applied) social sciences as well. The editors would also like to thank the great staff of Routledge and all their kind assistance in the process of assembling, designing, and executing this anthology, especially Robert Langham, Lisa Thompson, Eleanor Best, Laura Johnson, and Penny Harper. We have benefited greatly from the comments and suggestions of the peer reviewers. A special word of thanks and appreciation goes to Ms Jing Jing for fantastic and swift editorial assistance.

In addition, we would like to thank Professor Manuel Castells, Professor Saskia Sassen, and Professor Edward Glaeser for their early encouragement for the idea we had for the book project. Last but not least, we would like to thank all the authors in this book for their fantastic contributions and for giving us their valuable time on this project. We are very grateful for that. Finally this is an opportunity to remember the late Professor Edward Soja, who is one of the authors in the book.

Introduction

In the post-urban world

Hans Westlund and Tigran Haas

The complexities of contemporary global urban, political, economic, and environmental issues are evident. It is not hyperbole to say that human beings are now confronted with the greatest challenge that we have ever faced; in fact, it is a matter of life and death. The planet has recently been experiencing a convergence of natural and man-made crises that are unprecedented in our lifetime. We are also facing the consequences of accelerating and rapid urbanization, the scarcity of natural resources and their mismanagement, the impact of major errors in our responses to disasters, and the increasing demand for and complexity of greatly expanding transportation flows (Haas, 2012). Our societies have also undergone rapid and radical shifts in terms of age and class, increasing inequities between the rich and poor and intense demand for affordable and high-quality housing. All of these major challenges require immediate solutions from architects, urban planners, urban designers, landscape architects, and urbanists; actually, we need the combined efforts of all good people who are concerned with the physical condition and future of our cities. We need these professionals and experts to contribute their most imaginative, pragmatic, resilient, innovative, and just solutions.

Mankind has spent almost its entire history in what we nowadays call countryside. Cities emerged as small islands in 'oceans of countryside' when agriculture had become efficient enough to feed also a non-farming population. With the exception of a few cities with strong management and transportation systems (such as ancient Rome) most cities, by today's standards, remained small until the Industrial Revolution. It has been estimated that the urbanization rate in the world in 1800 was not more than 3% (Raven, Hassenzahl, & Berg, 2011). Edward L. Glaeser has pointed out that cities with a million inhabitants before the year 1800 were all capitals of empires and the reason that they could reach that size was that they were the best governed cities in the world.

The industrial revolution would change the urban-rural balance forever. Industrialization meant urbanization, either by growth of existing cities or by emergence of new urban agglomerations. But urbanization also meant increased demand for rural products, such as food, building material, firewood, and not least: raw material for the new industries. In this way, industrialization also triggered the development of rural areas – but not enough, so for millions of Europeans emigration to America was the opportunity to a better life.

The industrial crisis of the western world in the 1970s marked a transformation of the world economy. The old, industrial-manufacturing economy took a significant step back and a new economy, based on the technological shift from mechanical to digital technology, the knowledge economy, started to rise.

The expansion of the knowledge economy is strongly intertwined with the globalization that was spurred by technologic development as well as political/institutional decisions. On the one hand: the digitalization of banks and the international financial system meant in itself a globalization of the financial sector and that national governments no longer could control financial flows across national boundaries. On the other hand: the economic reforms of China in 1978, the fall of the iron curtain in 1989, and the transformation of the European Economic Community (EEC) to the European Union (EU) in 1993 and its subsequent enlargement, were some of the important political/institutional steps in the world's globalization.

The knowledge economy's integration with globalization has brought enormous changes to the world. This book focuses on one of many aspects of these changes, namely the *transformation of cities* that has occurred in the wake of the global knowledge economy's breakthrough. This is certainly not the first book that addresses these issues. However, it is the first book that simultaneously addresses cities' internal spatial transformations and extensions to new types of city regions, and the global networks of these, in the words of Edward Soja, 'postmetropolitan' regions. Combining these two aspects, our conclusion is that we are entering a *post-urban world*.

The industrial crisis of the 1970s was not only a result of rising oil prices, but also of the emergence of new competitors in some of the core industries of the western world: steel and engineering industries, including even such an advanced industry as the automotive industry. The breakthrough of the knowledge economy saved the western nations from economic stagnation but it did not save all regions from the negative sides of this transformation. Some cities and regions were winners and some were losers. However, at national levels the breakthrough of the knowledge economy was strong enough to prevent protectionist policies in favor of the declining sectors. This opened up for the rapid industrialization of China and other developing countries – and with that, the most rapid urbanization that the world had experienced.[1]

A first feature of the post-urban world is that while the crisis of the 1970s was accompanied by counter-urbanization in many of the developed countries (Beale, 1975; Champion, 1992), the following decades have mainly been characterized by *re-urbanization*. In contrast to the traditional urbanization that consisted of migration from countryside to cities (and often within the same region) this re-urbanization of the western world has been based on other sources:

1   migration from declining manufacturing cities and regions to expanding knowledge – and service sector cities and regions – or from the centers of declining manufacturing cities to suburbs;

2 upward migration within the national urban hierarchies, i.e., from smaller urban settlements to bigger ones, and;
3 increasingly, on immigration from low-income, or war-affected countries.

Another strong tendency in the current wave of urbanization is *densification* of city regions, in particular densification of suburbs. Edward Soja discussed the transformation of big cities from dense centers with sprawling low-density suburbs, to polycentric city regions with relatively high density all over.

> Where this process is most pronounced, the longstanding urban-suburban dualism of metropolitan urbanization has almost disappeared, as the age of mass suburbanization shifts to one of mass regional urbanization, a filling in so to speak, of the entire metropolitan area.
>
> (Soja, 2011, p. 684)

The result is according to Soja a 'postmetropolitan' region; a new spatial framework in which the idea of place is weakened and the limits between what is urban and what is non-urban are blurred and tend to dissolve.

A third important trend is the '*region enlargement*' in the form of spatial extensions of labor markets due to improved transportation infrastructure and public transportation, among others in the form of upgraded and more frequent commuter trains. This enhancement of the transportation infrastructure and its traffic has both contributed to the abovementioned densification of the suburbs as well as to extended commuter traffic and thus larger labor markets. This means that the city regions have not only been densified within a given area, but also 'sparsified' when more distant centers (and their suburbs and adjacent rural areas) have become integrated in the metropolitan transportation networks.

The fourth and last trend of the emerging post-urban world that we want to highlight is *the downgrading of the relations between city regions and their hinterlands and the upgrading of their networks to other city regions* that has emerged with the expansion of the knowledge economy. One of the most important differences between the knowledge economy and its predecessor is that human capital has replaced raw materials and physical capital as the main production and location factor. The large, diversified labor markets of city regions have become a key location factor for both businesses and labor. The more peripheral cities, towns, and rural areas suffer of lack of sufficient concentrations of the now most important production factor, human capital, which means that their labor markets remain small and the knowledge economy has difficulties to develop there. With the decreased relative importance of raw materials, these areas have less and less to offer the city regions. Instead, the city regions' exchange mainly takes place with other city regions, whose import and export markets are much larger than those of their peripheral hinterlands. From the countryside's perspective this means a division in two parts: one city-close part that is being integrated in the extended city regions, and one peripheral part that is less and less needed in the knowledge economy. These changes are expressions of that neither the city nor the countryside is what it was and that a stage that we can call post-urban has occurred.[2]

The four features of the post-urban world that were sketched above are expressions of the dissolution of two dichotomies that have formed much of our thinking on urban development: the urban-rural dichotomy and the urban-suburban dichotomy. Both these dichotomies were based on the well-grounded perception that the urban was something fundamentally different from the rural and the suburban, respectively. This is no longer the case. The emergence of city regions – where small towns as well as rural and natural areas are included, while other, more peripheral rural areas and smaller cities end outside the positive influence fields and gradually fade away – means that the traditional urban-rural dichotomy is being dissolved. The emergence of densified, multi-nuclear city regions also signals that the dichotomy between dense city centers and sparse suburbs wither down. This latter process has been denominated as 'postmetropolitan' by Edward Soja. Together, these two processes have formed the base for the post-urban world.

Aside from these features of the post-urban world, some of the leading ideas and discussions in the global urban age of development have and are still associated with cities: the *concept of global cities* (Sassen, 2005) *rise of the creative class* (Florida, 2003), *the network society* (Castells, 1996), *city of bits* (Mitchell, 1995), and ultimately the *triumph of the city* (Glaeser, 2011) and *well-tempered city* (Rose, 2016). These discourses see a plethora of structural transformations and emerging patterns that are either in place, happening, or in the continuous 'becoming.' Creativity is becoming a more important part of the economy as cities hinge on creative people, i.e., they need to attract creative people's human capital which generates growth and therefore the cities are engines of growth and economic prosperity when they exemplify this 'creativity.' We are witnessing a major flow of social and economic dynamics of the information age, virtual places as well as physical ones, and interconnection by means of telecommunication links as well as by pedestrian circulation and mechanized transportation systems. The new network society becomes structured around networks instead of individual actors, and works through a constant flow of information through technology. This is closely connected to the ongoing miniaturization of electronics, the commodification of bits, and the growing domination of software over materialized form. The emphasis on the formation of cross-border dynamics through which cities begin to form strategic transnational networks is seen in the case of global cities; the dynamics and processes that get territorialized are global. The celebration of the city becomes an impassioned argument; the city's importance and splendor, humanity's greatest creation, and our best hope for the future is bestowed with the key role in addressing the important issues in these challenging and crises-ridden times, Ultimately, the cities will be those battlegrounds where the environmental, economic, political, and social challenges of the 21st century will be addressed and ultimately fought (or lost).

The post-urban world can also be deducted from a philosophical framework. The transformation of the urban-rural relations can be described in a Hegelian dialectical framework, in which a thesis is being met by an antithesis and the two eventually are transformed into something new and 'higher': a synthesis.[3] In this framework, the rural forms the original thesis and the urban emerges as the antithesis. Over the centuries the rural thesis and the urban antithesis act as the two main poles of spatial interaction. The industrial revolution means a substantial shift of balance between the two poles in favor of the urban. With the emergence of the knowledge economy it is clear that a synthesis has arisen: the big cities have incorporated surrounding towns and countrysides and transformed them to parts of multifunctional city regions that are connected in global city networks. Outside are the remote parts of the former hinterlands that, in the words of Lefebvre (2003, p. 3), slowly "are given over to nature." The urban-rural dichotomy has ceased to exist and a synthesis has emerged where neither the city nor the countryside are what they were. A world with these new spatial relations is a *Post-Urban World*.

The contents of the book

Part I: Spatial transformations and new geographies of cities and regions

In Chapter 1, Edward L. Glaeser makes a broad overview of urbanization and its links to agricultural and industrial development in various parts of the world. He discusses explanations to the urbanization without growth that characterizes many countries in current Sub-Saharan Africa. He then turns to the positive and negative consequences of massive poor world urbanization. While there are upsides, there are also downsides that imply a need for effective urban governance to address the negative externalities that occur in dense neighborhoods. Glaeser suggest that developing world cities have a tradeoff between disorder and dictatorship, and that urbanization may lead to either more demand for governmental control or more demand for freedom. He concludes that cities have the capacity to build a socially linked cluster of educated people of trade. That cluster has an interest in stable government, rule of law, and economic freedom. The great hope is that over time cities will build the civic capital to greatly improve the governments of the poorest nations.

In Chapter 2, Richard Florida and Patrick Adler summarize the key findings of a larger research project on the shape and form of the increasingly divided city and the patchwork metropolis. The project mapped neighborhood locations of three major classes across many of America's largest metro areas and their core cities. The most striking pattern is the sheer extent of class division in the modern city and metropolis. This new divided city and patchwork metropolis marks a significant change in American living patterns. Just as the rise of the knowledge economy split the job market into high wage knowledge work and lower wage service positions, middle class neighborhoods have also been hollowed out as the geography of cities and metropolitan areas becomes increasingly divided between high and low income neighborhoods. Cities and metropolitan areas have been cleaved into isolated, class-based, economically segregated islands, in which either the advantaged or the disadvantaged clearly predominate. The old, stark divide between city and suburbs has given way to a new pattern of class division and geographic separation that spans them both.

In Chapter 3, Rahul Mehrotra and Felipe Vera are looking at the contemporary landscape of cities, arguing that today's urbanism seems to be suspended in a constant negotiation between two contrasting situations. The first derives from the assumption that development is about accumulation. This generates a common anxiety that drives cities with capital investments, producing what can be referred to as a 'hyper-city.' Architecture, as the basic unit of urbanism, seems to be obsessed with the idea of the city as the centralizing spectacle often driving the inherent impatience of capital. The second one is an expanded version of the idea of the kinetic city under the rubric of ephemeral urbanism which presents a compelling vision that enables a better understanding of the blurred lines of contemporary urbanism – both spatial and temporal – and the influence of people in shaping spaces in urban society. The authors conclude that urban design must find a way to return to this space of human 'action,' with meaningful political intervention in these landscapes that fall under the realm of ephemeral urbanism. Finally the ephemeral, as Mehrotra and Vera see it, will truly offer a productive and creative force that serves the imagination as well as construction of a more nuanced and inclusive urban space.

In Chapter 4, Michael Batty argues that the contemporary city is a constellation of networks and flows which although continuing to underpin urban form, are tending to destroy the idea that form follows function. Therefore, we cannot generate a proper understanding of the city by focusing on location alone but we need to think of locations as aggregations of interactions, of flows which determine the physical networks which make such interactions possible. This is an old argument that has been central to urban analysis since the beginnings of the industrial revolution but as the world moves into its post-industrial digital era, it is ever more important to see cities as functioning through multiple networks where distance is increasingly less important than in the past. Batty describes how various visualizations of networks and flows give us a quick picture of the complexity of cities and then suggests how we might measure this complexity. He concludes with some speculations as to how the multiplexing of networks is rapidly becoming the dominant paradigm for interpreting how 'form ever follows function.'

In Chapter 5, Hans Westlund takes his starting point as the writings of Lefebvre, Soja, and Hägerstrand and discusses different aspects of the urban transformation to a post-urban world. The notion of a post-urban world leads not only to a wide range of issues on the future of integrated city regions and their internal and external networks. The fact that neither the urban nor the rural is what it was, also leads to questions on the future of urban-rural relations. Westlund's chapter starts with an overview of how urban-rural relations have been interpreted in spatial theories from the pre-industrial era and onwards. It thereafter discusses urban-rural relations in the knowledge economy and the dissolution of the urban-rural dichotomy in the post-urban world. Finally, possible development strategies for the peripheral countryside to avoid turning back 'over to nature' are discussed.

In Chapter 6, Paul L. Knox writes that global cities, particularly those in the West, are being quietly recast through coalitions and partnerships of real estate, finance, construction, and professional interests: 'regeneration machines' that draw on international capital and markets while engaging locally in tactical politics around land-use regulation, policy, and decision-making. These regeneration machines are a product of the reflexive neoliberalism of national and metropolitan governments and of the increasingly international dimension of inter-urban competition. Knox discusses the consequences of the reflexive neoliberalism on planning and architecture, with particular focus on London.

In Chapter 7, Richard Sennett turns to the relation of social life to physical design. In this chapter on the novel concept and construct of the Open City he explores what shape cities should have to admit the complexities and conflicts of the people who live together, in a particular way. Sennett focuses on edge conditions within the city, distinguishing between borders and boundaries, exploring the design of porosity and mixture of people who differ from one another. The nuanced discussion centers also around borders, i.e., in the realm of human culture, territories consist similarly of boundaries and borders – in cities, most simply, there is a contrast between gated communities and complex, open streets. But the distinction cuts deeper in urban planning. Sennett's open and closed, once set in the context of a modern city, deviate from the idea of balance between closed guidance and open imagination. In sum, we can define an open system as one in which growth admits conflict and dissonance.

Part II: Urbanization, knowledge economies, and social structuration

In Chapter 8, Jessie Poon and Wei Yin document the role of human capital in the USA's Rustbelt cities' resurgence. Employing a comparative analysis with Sunbelt cities, they point to a variegated landscape where certain old industrial cities have managed to build or retain a stock of human capital despite profound shifts in the geography of production. Skill ratios of Rustbelt cities are comparable to their Southeastern counterparts today whereas this was not the case in 1980. The confluence of real estate affordability and good schools has attracted talented individuals to stay or relocate to other metropolitan cities within the region, and encouraged new skilled immigrants to settle there.

In Chapter 9, Kaisa Snellman, Jennifer M. Silva, Carl B. Frederick, and Robert D. Putnam focus on the 'engagement gap' among young people. Since the 1970s, upper-middle-class students have become increasingly active in school clubs and sport teams, while participation among working-class students has veered in the opposite direction. These growing gaps have emerged in the wake of rising income inequality, the introduction of 'pay to play' programs, and increasing time and money investments by upper-middle-class parents in children's development. The authors stress that these trends need to be taken into account in any new initiative to monitor mobility and that these trends also present a challenge to the American ideal of equal opportunity insofar as participation in organized activities shapes patterns of social mobility.

In Chapter 10, Kyle Farrell and Tigran Haas analyze global city policy, most recently reflected in the *Third United Nations Conference on Housing and Sustainable Urban Development* (Habitat III). The findings highlight a shift in emphasis from an approach to city-building focused on the quantitative supply of urban amenities, towards a growing trend that promotes livability and the importance of enhancing quality of life in cities. At the heart of this shift, is the growing recognition of a public space mandate. Unlike other infrastructure, public spaces afford a human element to the city; offering an opportunity for residents to improve their health, prosperity, quality of life, and overall to enrich their social relations and cultural understanding. Although key decisions have already been taken in the policy arenas of 2015 and 2016, the future of cities is still in the hands of the stakeholders that comprise them. Farrell's and Haas's conclusion is that any attempt to establish a public space agenda that does not place the citizens at the center of it will face severe constraints in their attempt to build livable cities.

In Chapter 11, Fulong Wu discusses the circumstance that Chinese cities are emerging in multiple senses: They have created new physical spaces to accommodate the fast urbanization of the country but have also developed new properties and characteristics along with urban transformation. The novelty created by emerging cities in China is not easily covered by Western urban theory. His chapter examines the dynamism of Chinese urban transformation, especially political economic changes vis-à-vis so-called neoliberalism, and spatial outcomes as diverse and contrasting spaces of formality and informality. In contrast to an ideology of free market dominance, Chinese local development shows a hybrid form, combining the features of the developmental state with instruments created in the market. Pragmatism is adopted to legitimize the state as a key driver for economic growth. Finally, Wu discusses the implications of his findings for global urban studies.

In Chapter 12, Karima Kourtit and Peter Nijkamp take their point of departure in the emerging 'urban century,' in which cities are functioning as centripetal and centrifugal force fields of new and complex spatial developments in the global 'post-urban world.' The emerging digital technology offers unprecedented opportunities for reinforcing the position of urban areas through dedicated marketing and strategic planning tools. The chapter highlights the strategic importance of modern interactive digital information tools for building a sustainable urban future. The chapter introduces and illustrates 'urban Facebooks' as important and effective mechanisms for interactive and participatory urban planning, geared towards an 'urban facelift.' Various examples of the use of this new planning tool in several European cities are given, based on a systematic typological approach. It concludes that the use of digital 'urban faces' offers many novel opportunities for strategic urban planning in a 'post-urban world.'

In Chapter 13, Edward Soja, in line with the general theme of this book, argue that we are witnessing an unprecedented period in which the urban and the regional, formerly quite distinct from one another, are blending together to define something new and different. Never before have regional approaches been more important in urban research, and urban emphases more influential in regional development theory and planning. His chapter identifies eight challenging themes for innovative critical and comparative regional research: the new regionalism; the generative power of cities and regions; regional urbanization; the end of the metropolis era; extended regional urbanization; multiscalar regionalism; regional governance and planning; and seeking regional democracy. In Soja's view, each of these themes is stimulated by new spatial insights and brimming with innovative research possibilities.

In Chapter 14, Fran Tonkiss discusses issues of knowledge, inequality, and the city. She draws attention to the double life of knowledge as private asset and as collective good which has implications for the structuring of inequalities in cities and for attempts to promote greater urban equity, and social and economic inclusion. The discussion focuses on one of the primary ways in which knowledge is distributed in contemporary cities: through the sorting of skill in urban labor markets. Furthermore Tonkiss points to the so-called socializing of knowledge in relation to information and the open-source city. The discussion ends with problematizing the idea of the informational role of the city which points towards an entry into the informational age, where presumably cities will flourish instead of dying out. For Tonkiss the question remains who and how many will be able to flourish in it?

Part III: Emerging cultures in a post-political and post-urban world

In Chapter 15, Laura Burkhalter and Manuel Castells fundamentally, through a proposed urban paradigm, call for and put life at its center. The aim is to propose that there are other ways in which humans may co-inhabit in geographic vicinity creating a certain density and size, considered a metropolitan region or city. What Burkhalter and Castells are calling for is a fundamental revisit of the validity of those building blocks and the possibility that another type of city is possible. The focus is on People Centered Infrastructural Possibilities with the creative city and sharing economy as its spearheads. This is done through the means of community-based self-determination and citywide connective, people-centric infrastructure and parks, the expressions of the polycentric city, can become as pluralistic, creative, and diverse as life itself. They point to the importance of the intrinsic interrelationship of density and a multimodal transportation system, the issue of urban self-reliance in the spectra from shopping malls to urban farming and the focus on people-centered land use patterns. Finally the authors draw attention to the idea of intelligent, informed urban growth, where regulations need to be intention based and inherently adaptive and flexible, so that they continue to evolve alongside the growing empirical data and intelligence as well as the constituents' changing needs and demands.

In Chapter 16, Saskia Sassen focuses on a trend that has emerged with great force and a capacity to privatize cities and displace large numbers of workers and enterprises that may long have lived and operated in these cities. It is the large-scale buying of buildings by national and foreign private and corporate entities, and their transformation mostly into high-end expensive properties. She suggests that much of this built density does not contribute to the urbanity of a city center. Indeed, at its most extreme, there is a de-urbanizing of the city. In the light of this development, Sassen raises some provocative questions on the future of cities: Might urbanity be shifting partly to the neighborhoods – places often seen as parochial and homogeneous? Is the center of the city becoming de-urbanized even as it raises its density? Would the dense but de-urbanized urban core actually be the non-city? That is to say, what used to mark the limits or edge of the city is now at its center, so that entering that corporate center means exiting the city?

In Chapter 17, Susan Fainstein observes that the term resilience has become the popular formulation for plans that deal with preparedness for disaster. For her it implies adaptation rather than returning to a pre-crisis state. Its use has been extended from environmental events to social and economic crises and its fault is that it obfuscates underlying conflict and the distribution of benefits resulting from policy choices. This chapter examines how resilience is currently being defined, and also discusses the way in which it obscures power relations. Fainstein points out that the development of resilience policies is cloaked in complicated models showing complexity and indeterminacy. Marxist analysis provides insights that cut through the failure of these models to assign agency, but it does not offer approaches short of revolution to assist present-day planning. Susan Feinstein's enlightening conclusions of the chapter present strategies that can lead to greater justice in planning to cope with the impacts of devastating events.

In Chapter 18, Emily Talen delves into the complex matter of explaining and valuing neighborhood social diversity and metropolitan segregation where she notes that the story of 20th-century urbanism is a story of manifest social division. When it comes to socially mixed neighborhoods, there could be more nuance, sensitivity, and adjustment, writes and analyzes Talen. The desire for social mix varies widely depending on cultural background. We need to learn from our decades of attempting to create mixed neighborhoods and refine accordingly. In that sense proximity alone does not achieve a plural, integrated society. People in a diverse setting find other, non-spatial ways of maintaining social distance. Talen observes that the social mixing debate need not devolve into dismissals of "spatial solutions to poverty," as if place and the opportunities it affords are irrelevant – where the physical neighborhood is seen as no longer mattering.

In Chapter 19, Michael Neuman and Nadia Nur through their analysis reveal that the engagement with the neighborhood is fundamental for the resistance to the city government and the resilience of the self-managed spaces. The chapter highlights the response of activist citizens in one city, Rome, Italy, to the multiple crises confronting them. Attitude toward civic engagement and self-determination gained in the era of post-war democracy is now turning into a powerful tool for constructing a radically alternative politics. This is being expressed by new social movements that the chapter analyzes, Scup!, being the first and Communia the other. The chapter draws attention to the fact that the networks within which Scup! and Communia are composed, are made up primarily by other occupied spaces, social centers, associations, and collectives that join common projects with the aim of shaping a pathway for reappropriating urban spaces in order to transform them into 'commons.' Their conclusions point to the fact that the network seems not to want to reject institutions or representative democracy as a whole. Instead, as Neuman and Nur argue and show, it has introduced important new practices where politics can be understood in a more proactive and participative way.

In Chapter 20, the emergence of a new direction and emphasis ecology represents another significant and concomitant shift with a change in urbanism and the reality of climate change. Lister observes clearly that there is an important connection between stability, change, and resilience – a property internal to any living system and a function of the unique adaptive cycle of that system. The author asks key questions such as: What does design for resilience look like? What tactics do post-urban planners and designers need to engage in for attaining resilience? Resilient systems are defined by diversity and by inherent but irreducible uncertainty. The author concludes by stating that activating resilience requires a subtle and careful approach to design: one that is contextual, legible, nuanced, and responsive, one that is small in scale but large in cumulative impact. Lister points out that in designing for change with this sensibility, we have begun to cultivate a culture of resilience and the adaptive, transformative capacity for long-term sustainability – thriving beyond merely surviving – with change in the post-urban landscapes that now define us.

In Chapter 21, Duncan McLaren and Julian Agyeman show a path towards sharing cities for a smart and sustainable future, exploring in the chapter the contemporary terrain, contestations, and transformations of sharing in cities and seek to explain how these might be harnessed to rebuild social cohesion in forms suited to a globally interconnected, post-modern, intercultural world. Through nuanced analyses the authors outline the breadth of sharing practice, its evolutionary roots, and historic emanations in cities. After that they describe and theorize current transformations in sharing from traditional evolved communal forms, to intermediated commercial forms. What follows is the discussion that identifies forms of urban sharing beyond the commercial, highlighting the focus on urban commons in concepts such as social urbanism. The authors highlight the ways in which social inclusion and interculturalism, including recognition of and respect for counter-cultures, are central to the shift in values and norms implied in the sharing paradigm. They explore the new and revived forms of collective politics that become possible in a sharing city. Finally, they point out some of the practical steps necessary to build genuinely smart and sustainable sharing cities. For them the sharing city is a new paradigm for cities, opening a genuine third way between state and market.

Notes

1 It should be underlined that the current, rapid urbanization of developing countries is not only caused by industrialization.
2 For a further discussion on the change of urban-rural relations, see Westlund (2014) and Westlund's chapter in this book.
3 The German philosopher Georg Wilhelm Friedrich Hegel (1770–1831) is generally seen as the father of this framework. It has been claimed that Hegel considered the thesis-antithesis-synthesis framework a "lifeless schema" and that he did not use it in his works. Instead, the framework should have come from Kant and Fichte (Mueller, 1958). However, this claim does not seem to have been accepted by the mainstream interpretations of Hegel's dialectics.

References

Beale, C. L. (1975). *The revival of population growth in non-metropolitan America*. Economic Research Service, publication 605, US Department of Agriculture, Washington, DC.

Castells, M. (1996). *The rise of the network society: The information age: Economy, society, and culture* (Vol. 1). New York: John Wiley & Sons.

Champion, A. G. (1992). Urban and regional demographic trends in the developed world. *Urban Studies, 29*, 461–482.

Florida, R. (2003). Cities and the creative class. *City & Community Journal, 2*(1) (March). American Sociological Association, 3–19.

Glaeser, E. (2011). *The triumph of the city: How our greatest invention makes us richer, smarter, greener, healthier and happier*. New York: Pan Macmillan.

Haas, T. (Ed.). (2012). *Sustainable urbanism and beyond: Rethinking cities for the future*. New York: Rizzoli.

Lefebvre, H. (2003). *The urban revolution*. Minneapolis: University of Minnesota Press (French original first published 1970).

Mitchell, W. J. (1995). *City of bits: Space, place, and the infobahn*. Cambridge, MA: MIT Press.

Mueller, G. E. (1958). The Hegel legend of 'thesis-antithesis-synthesis.' *Journal of the History of Ideas, 19*(3) (June), 411–414.

Raven, P. H., Hassenzahl, D. M., & Berg, L. L. (2011). *Environment* (8th ed.). New York: John Wiley & Sons.

Rose, J. (2016). *The well-tempered city*. New York: Harper Wave.

Sassen, S. (2005). The global city: Introducing a concept. *Brown Journal of World Affairs, XI*(2), 27–43.

Soja, E. W. (2011). Regional urbanization and the end of the metropolis era. In G. Bridge & S. Watson (Eds.), *The new Blackwell companion to the city* (pp. 679–689). Oxford: Blackwell.

Westlund, H. (2014). Urban futures in planning, policy and regional science: Are we entering a post-urban world? *Built Environment, 40*(4), 447–457.

Part I

Spatial transformations and new geographies of cities and regions

1 Urban transformations and the future of cities

Edward L. Glaeser

Introduction

For over 100,000 years, our species existed as low-density hunter-gathers. For the past 10,000 years, humans lived as rural farmers and as late as 1900 only 15% of humanity lived in cities. In the shockingly short time of a century, the human experience has transformed itself dramatically, so that we are now an urban species. In the West and in East Asia, urbanization has been associated with rapidly rising incomes, but a surprising number of mega-cities have emerged in countries like the Democratic Republic of the Congo that are still extremely poor.

In the second section of this chapter, I discuss the three trends that have come together to make humankind an urban species. In the wealthy West, many cities have enjoyed a remarkable resurgence as former industrial cities have retrofitted themselves as centers of knowledge creation and business services. In some cases, particularly in Europe, these wealthy cities have also succeeded as centers of consumption as well as production. In East Asia, urbanization has been part of a collective process of rapid industrialization and development that echoes the earlier Western industrial revolution, but on steroids.

Sub-Saharan Africa today and Latin America during the 1960s experienced urbanization without growth (Fay and Opal, 2000; Gollin, Jedwab, & Vollrath, 2016). In the second section, I discuss two competing explanations for this phenomenon. The *centralized power hypothesis* argues that urbanization in these poorer places reflects political power that has expanded within the capital and that has attracted migrants for rural areas (Ades and Glaeser, 1995). The *agricultural trade hypothesis* argues that today's poorer countries have a comparative disadvantage at farming and consequently have specialized in more urban tasks (Glaeser, 2014). The second section suggests that the agricultural trade hypothesis may explain why poorer countries have urbanized, but that the centralized power hypothesis explains why this has produced mega-cities (Davis and Henderson, 2003).

In the third section, I turn to the positive and negative consequences of massive poor world urbanization. The most obvious upsides of urbanization are economic. Agglomeration economies imply that mass urbanization should lead to short-term increases in productivity; more suggestive evidence hints at the possibility of dynamic benefits if cities increase the speed of economic growth. Cities may engender longer-term growth directly, by increasing the flow of knowledge and the production of new ideas, and indirectly, by facilitating investment in physical and human capital.

The downsides of density weigh against these benefits. Urban crowding leads to traffic congestion and the spread of contagious disease. Urban proximity may also abet crime and it is more expensive to build in dense urban areas. These downsides imply a need for effective urban governance to address the negative externalities that occur in dense neighborhoods.

The fourth section turns to the governance problem in cities, which I separate into policy and politics. The technocratic approach to governing mega-cities emphasizes better policies, such as regulations that nudge slum dwellers to adopt clean water and sewerage, or congestion pricing. But these policies cannot happen as long as governments are weak and unwilling to act in the public interest. Consequently, I also discuss the political development of developing world mega-cities.

One question is whether privatization or independent public agencies can meaningfully improve the quality of city life. There are examples of benign privatization and benign parastatals, but also examples of massive corruption and indolence. I follow Djankov, Glaeser, La Porta, Lopez-de-Silanes, and Shleifer (2003) and suggest that developing world cities have a tradeoff between disorder and dictatorship, and that urbanization may lead to either more demand for governmental control or more demand for freedom. Finally, I discuss the "Boston Hypothesis," raised by Glaeser and Steinberg (2017) which suggests that cities will improve their own governments through democratic revolution and peaceful reform. While urban concentration does make regime change more likely, it is less clear that stable democracies will naturally emerge from even successful uprisings.

The urbanization of humankind

In 1910, when my grandparents were young, less than one-third of Europeans lived in cities with more than 5,000 inhabitants. The only countries on earth that were mostly urban were Belgium, the Netherlands, and the United Kingdom (Bairoch & Goertz, 1986). The United States became a predominantly urban nation only in 1920, when its per capita income level was above $8,000 in 2016 dollars. By 1967, when I was born, Europe and North America were overwhelmingly urban and Latin America was also rapidly urbanizing, but Africa and Asia were still overwhelmingly rural. In that year, fewer than 36% of humans were urban. Today, 54% of humanity is urban and poor countries, as well as rich ones, enjoy the benefits and experience the costs of dense cities.

This change is without precedent. Throughout almost all of history, the experience of humankind has been non-urban. We evolved along the hot banks of the Awash River in the Afar Triangle in modern Ethiopia. We needed abundant land to survive as hunter-gatherers and so we spread globally over hundreds of thousands of years.

About 10,000 years ago, the Neolithic Revolution enabled our ancestors to produce significantly more calories from a fixed amount of land. That meant that humans could become more sedentary and villages began to emerge, such as Catalhoyuk in Southern Anatolia. The first cities appeared in the fourth millennium before the Common Era in Mesopotamia (Smith, Ur, & Feinman, 2014), unsurprisingly near the heartland of the first agriculturalists. Agricultural productivity enabled urbanism then, as it would throughout almost all of human history.

Politics and trade seem to have been the forces that brought humans together into urban areas. Memphis grew great as the capital of ancient Egypt and housed perhaps 60,000 people four millennia ago, making it the world's largest city. Tyre emerged as a trading powerhouse selling its purple dye throughout the Mediterranean. Commercial and imperial cities have coexisted ever since, but before 1800, the true urban giants were almost always the capitals of great empires.

Rome, Xi'an, Baghdad, Kaifeng, Hangzhou, Istanbul, and Beijing may have all reached one million inhabitants before the industrial revolution.[1] While their level of economic development was low by modern standards, these were all the capitals of great empires. Empires typically become great through public capacity in conquest and administration, and consequently these cities were governed by the strongest states of their time.

Julius Caesar might not have had access to electronic road pricing, but he was able to ban wheeled vehicles from Rome during daylight hours. Xi'an had an amazingly sophisticated set of sanitary canals. Kaifeng built great towers for spotting and responding to fires. The downsides of density were mitigated by public competence.

Smaller, commercial cities began to reappear in Europe during the Middle Ages. By 1300, Florence, Genoa, and Venice each had about 100,000 inhabitants. In the north, the trade and weaving center of Bruges had a population of 50,000. As trade moved from the Mediterranean to the Atlantic, northern powerhouses such as Antwerp, Amsterdam, and London emerged. Similar trading hubs, such as Boston, New York, and Philadelphia would appear on the other side of the Atlantic.

The great watershed in urban growth occurred during the industrial revolution, which was preceded by revolutions in agriculture and transportation. The productivity of agricultural land rose dramatically during the 18th century due to crop rotation, the Dutch plough (borrowed from the Chinese during the 17th century), and the spread of the potato (Nunn and Qian, 2011). An explosion of English canal building made it easier to move food over space. Urban expansion during English industrialization was only possible because these earlier advances had made it possible to feed so many urbanites.

Industrialization then acted as a pull on former farmers and their children who were able to find work in urban textile mills and car factories. The earliest factories were typically located near water sources that lay outside of older urban cores, such as the Merrimac River in Massachusetts or the Cromford Sough in Derbyshire. Continuing improvements in steam engine efficiency meant that industrial production could be powered by coal, rather than water, and could therefore be urbanized, albeit at a cost in urban air quality. Factories located in cities like Detroit, Manchester, and Gothenburg, because of access to ports and later rail lines, enabled industrial supplies to be readily shipped in and finished products to be shipped out.

In a sense, heavy industry was always a strange match for urban density. Factories are space intensive, and they produce pollution that makes a city less attractive as a place to live. During the era of Henry Ford, factories became massive self-contained units and it was hard to see why such entities benefitted from proximity to other urbanites. Ford himself moved his operations from downtown Detroit to the enormous, suburban River Rouge complex during and after World War I. After World War II, heavy industry fled big cities far more dramatically and many cities experienced depopulation along with deindustrialization.

The mid-20th century belonged to the automobile and the air conditioner, and America built endless acres of Sunbelt sprawl. As richer urbanites fled to California or at least to Westchester, city populations began to decline during the 1950s. By the 1970s, almost all of America's older colder cities seemed like they were headed for the trash heap of history. Seattle seemed as doomed as St. Louis. New York's prospects looked no better than those of Detroit.

But then something unexpected happened. In the 1990s, many city populations stabilized in the wealthy West, and some cities started experiencing robust growth after 2000. Some older cities, including New York, London, Paris, and Frankfurt, became places of extraordinary wealth. High housing prices signaled the demand for urban lifestyles.

The growth was not uniform. Skilled cities were far more successful than unskilled cities, both in terms of population and income growth (Glaeser & Saiz, 2004). The success of Seattle relative to Detroit can be readily explained by the fact that 57.5% of Seattle's adults have a college degree or more, while only 13.1% of Detroit's adults are so well educated. Entrepreneurial human capital, at least as measured by average establishment size or the share of employment in new establishments, is also a potent predictor of urban employment growth (Glaeser, Kerr, & Kerr, 2015).

One interpretation of these facts is that globalization and new technologies did initially disperse urban populations, but these forces also increased the returns to human capital and innovation. Literally hundreds of studies have confirmed the rise in returns to skill since the 1970s (e.g., Goldin & Katz, 2009). Cities, like schools, have the capacity to build skills, because cities enable workers to learn from the people around them (Glaeser, 1999). Declining costs of electronic communication can lead to a more interactive society that ultimately favors urban density (Gaspar & Glaeser, 1998). The dependence of so many Western cities on financial services is perhaps unsurprising since the returns to better information are so high in that sector.

Western cities have also thrived as centers of consumption as well as production (Glaeser, Kolko, & Saiz, 2001). As city streets have become safer, prosperous people are willing to pay a premium to enjoy urban amenities, including museums, restaurants, and quirky urban shops. The rise of the consumer city is demonstrated by the correlation between urban amenities and city growth and by the rise of reverse commuters: people who are willing to pay the high cost of urban living despite working in a suburb. The increasing importance of urban amenities helps explain why urban housing prices have often risen more than urban wages.

Indeed, one reasonable view is that in the 21st century, the best local economic development strategy is to attract and train smart people and then get out of their way. Attracting smart people depends on quality of life, which can lure young people to Milan or repel them from older rustbelt cities. The enduring success of London, Stockholm, and San Francisco partially reflects the appeal of these cities as places to live as well as places to work.

Urbanization in East Asia

The growth of East Asian cities seems almost like a replay of the Western industrial revolution run at fast forward. High levels of agricultural productivity meant that Japan was more highly urbanized than France, Germany, or the United States in 1850. The country's urban population was particularly centralized in the capital city partially because political power was so centralized in the hands of the Tokugawa Shogunate. When Japan opened itself to the West after the Meiji Restoration, industrialization occurred quickly and urbanization grew, and by 1950, three-quarters of the Japanese population were urban.

By contrast, Korea was an overwhelmingly rural nation at the start of the 20th century. During the 1930s, Korea's Japanese masters promoted the growth of war-related industries and Seoul started expanding. Yet Korea's urbanization rate only reached 14% at the end of World War II. The bombing of Korea's cities, especially Seoul, during the Korean War helped ensure that Korea's urbanization rate remained close to 30% in 1960.

But then over the next 40 years, Korea's urbanization rate soared from 30 to 90%, an almost unbelievable change. While U.S. and European urban systems were dispersed, partially because 19th-century cities needed to be close to natural resources, Korea's urbanization was dominated by the expansion of Seoul, which is now larger than New York City. Korea has few natural resources other than the wits of the Koreans themselves, and consequently, manufacturing could be highly centralized. The region around Seoul contains 24 million people and is one of the largest metropolitan economies in the world.

Korea's urbanization was driven by a dramatic rise in government-supported export-driven industrialization, which moved up the technology ladder swiftly. This movement is typified by Samsung's moves from sugar refining (a classic premodern urban industry) to textile production during the 1950s and then into electronics during 1960s. Today, the Seoul-based behemoth is a global technology leader. South Korea has moved relatively easily from industrial to post-industrial economy because the government invested so heavily in human capital, meaning that Seoul is far more like Seattle than like Detroit.

China's urbanization has been even larger and more dramatic in scale. Despite a long history of Chinese mega-cities, China was only 13% urban in 1953. Thirty years later, the country was only 21% urban, but as China's economy expanded enormously under Deng Xiaoping and his successors, unprecedented urban growth occurred. The expansion of China's urbanization rate – 30 percentage points over 30 years – appears far less dramatic than the growth in the rate seen in South Korea. The key difference is that Korea's urbanization involved tens of millions, while China's urbanization involves hundreds of millions of people.

The scale may be unprecedented, and China has many unique characteristics, but the overall pattern is similar to that seen in South Korea, Japan and the 19th-century West. China's real agricultural productivity rose by 5.1% annually from 1985 to 2007. More productive farms and rising agricultural imports were able to feed millions of workers who moved to urban factories. Just as in Korea, Chinese producers moved from basic products, including garments, to more sophisticated industrial outputs. Urbanization and economic growth moved closely together.

Urbanization without growth in Latin America and Africa

The Western path of urbanization was slow and tightly linked to both agricultural productivity improvements and industrialization. The East Asian path towards urbanization was fast, but also tied to rapid industrialization and economic growth. The path to urbanization in Latin America and Sub-Saharan Africa was different. In both countries, urbanization occurred before industrialization and, in some countries, with little evidence of agricultural productivity growth.

Latin America moved first. According to U.N. population estimates, the Latin American and Caribbean region was 41% urban in 1950 and exceeded the 50% threshold in 1961. Today, 79.5% of the region is urban, making it the second most urbanized region of the world after North America. The urbanization rate in South America was over 83% in 2014, making it the most urbanized continent on the globe.

A remarkable feature of Latin American urbanization is that it occurred when Latin America was still reasonably poor. For example, Mexico became 50% urban in 1960, when its per capita income was $340 in current dollars, or $2,700 dollars in 2016 dollars. Brazil was more than 50% urban by 1964, when its per capita income was only $2,000 in 2016 dollars. Latin America became urban long before it was either rich or industrialized, which was noted by a number of scholars at the time (e.g., Arriaga, 1968; Browning, 1958).

Why did Latin America urbanize before it industrialized? Perhaps the simplest explanation is the combination of agricultural productivity and trade. Relative to the calories needed for survival, almost every urban product is a luxury good. Large urban populations need to be able to eat, and that constrained the growth of cities in the European past. Over the course of the 19th and 20th centuries, agriculture became far more productive in both the north and in Latin America. The Green Revolution particularly enabled the expansion of food production in the global south. Food surpluses then enabled urbanization at far lower levels of overall wealth.

The most tangible evidence for rising agricultural productivity is declining agricultural prices. The dollar per bushel paid to Iowa farmers dropped by 50% in real terms between 1925 and 1960; the price of soybeans dropped by 65% over the same years.[2] In the decades after 1940, Mexico and Brazil also imported American agricultural technology through the Green Revolution.

In the Mexican case, low food prices were also maintained through price controls starting in World War II, which effectively subsidized urbanization at the expense of agriculture. In 1944, for example, selling prices for corn were capped at 242 pesos per ton, which required a subsidy of 60 pesos per ton (Ochoa, 2000). In 1962, Mexico created a national food parastatal that managed national purchases of commodities like corn, and provided food at subsidized rates to consumers. Cheap food made Mexican urbanization possible.

Brazil was even poorer than Mexico when it hit the 50% urbanized mark, but Brazil's farms, like those of later African urbanizers, didn't need to feed the country's growing mass of urbanites. As Porcile (1995) describes, Argentina was cut off from its traditional export markets by World War II and conflicts with the U.S. Argentina sought new markets for its abundant wheat, and that led it to Brazil. Brazil began importing large quantities of wheat during the 1940s, almost entirely from Argentina. After 1950, the U.S. also became a significant supplier of wheat to Brazil.

Increasingly, developing world cities are open economies, and in an open economy, agricultural productivity is not necessary to support urban life. When economies are open, agricultural weakness leads to urbanism, not agricultural strength, because economies specialize in the sectors where they enjoy a comparative advantage (Glaeser, 2014). Consequently, when African countries opened to world trade, their weak agricultural sectors naturally led them to urbanize rapidly, following the Brazilian model.

In the case of Mexico and Brazil, significant oil revenues came after mass urbanization, but natural resource wealth further bolstered the strength of cities. Natural resource production sometimes directly generates jobs in cities, but more often natural resource wealth is used by developing world countries to provide government jobs, typically located in the capital city, and sometimes urban amenities. Rio de Janeiro's fiscal problems in 2016 partially reflect a shortfall of oil-related revenue.

Natural resources have played an outsized role in African urbanization precisely through this public sector channel. Oil and minerals, including gold and diamonds, are the primary exports of many African countries, including the Democratic Republic of the Congo, Ghana, Nigeria, Zambia, and Zimbabwe. These resources pay for public sector jobs in the capital city, which then lead to a demand for services that are provided by rural-urban migrants. The cities are poor, but still attractive for many given the extreme poverty of the alternative: subsistence agriculture.

Density and dictatorship

Natural resource wealth funds developing world governments, and often those governments can be either unstable or dictatorial. In either case, there is a tendency to allocate national resources towards the proximity of the capital. The flow of resources to the capital then attracts a flood of population who flee rural poverty.

The simplest political cause of urbanization occurs because dictators often spend where they live. Sometimes, they spend to beautify their palaces and environs. Sometimes, they spend in response to the influence of local courtiers and lobbyists. The flow of funds to connected locals then makes its way down the food chain as service providers cater to the fortunate few who benefit directly from the sovereign's largesse. This is a model of imperial capitals throughout history, from St. Petersburg to Nineveh.

The second channel is slightly more strategic. An unstable regime has more to fear from local unrest than from unrest in the far-flung hinterland. Consequently, the regime channels resources to the capital to buy local peace and these resources then attract more people to the capital. While a far-seeing autocrat may recognize the downsides of attracting more people to the capital, and may even remove himself to a safer, more remote spot despite this effect, typically there will still be a tendency to favor the residents of the capital.

Both of these channels predict excess urbanism in places with dictatorship or instability, but the urbanism should primarily take the form of a bloated primate capital. Such primates are indeed more common in dictatorial or unstable regimes (Ades & Glaeser, 1995). This theory does not explain a more general growth in urbanism in the poorer parts of the world on its own (Davis & Henderson, 2003).

The consequences of massive urbanization

The cities of Sub-Saharan Africa, like the Latin American cities during the 1960s, are less productive than outsiders might hope. Yet there is little reason to think that they are causing economic harm. Wages are higher in cities in wealthy and poor countries alike, and firms locate in big cities for a reason.

The primary concerns about urbanization in Africa relate to quality-of-life issues, including health and pollution, not productivity. Opponents of urbanization correctly understand that there are downsides to density. Crowding into dense cities can facilitate the flow of contagious diseases, or create air and water pollution that inculcates illness. Traffic congestion gets worse when more people drive on city streets. Crime can also be facilitated by urban proximity.

The case for urbanization depends on the benefits of city size exceeding the costs, and the costs in turn depend on the quality of government. Effective governments, like that of Singapore, are able to address traffic congestion with electronic road pricing and good public transit. They can address contagious disease with good water systems and sewerage, and crime with effective law enforcement. Weak governments can fail along many dimensions, making city life far worse. The urbanization of the poor world makes the weaknesses of their public sectors more obvious as well as more costly.

Contagious disease can be the most significant downside of urban density. Plagues once ravaged the great cities of the West and contagious diseases, like AIDS, can still be disproportionately urban. Cities facilitate the flow of bacteria, but this downside can be mitigated with public health investments and effective medical responses to disease, such as vaccination. Cholera continues to kill in African cities, but the numbers of the dead are far lower than in the 19th-century cholera outbreaks because the available medical responses are so much more effective.

The problem of delivering water and sewerage services requires a robust combination of infrastructure spending and regulation. The engineering aspects of water and sewerage infrastructure are well understood and, for a price, wealthy world engineering companies are happy to build sewage treatment plants and water mains. Naturally, the costs of sanitation can be quite high relative to GDP in the world's poorest cities.

Moreover, building the primary infrastructure is not enough. Individual customers need to be connected to the infrastructure and typically this means that they need to pay something for the connection. Yet many poorer urbanites are not willing to pay a $1,000 connection fee for water or sewerage and consequently, a last-mile problem is common in many poor world cities. That problem also appeared in 19th-century New York, where cholera epidemics continued for 25 years after the opening of the Croton Aqueduct because poorer New Yorkers were unwilling to pay the connection fees.

Ashraf, Glaeser, and Ponzetto (2016) provide a framework analyzing the last-mile problem. One method of inducing adoption is to subsidize it heavily, but this leads to public waste. A second method is to follow 19th-century New York's example and penalize people who don't connect, but that approach can lead to abuse and extortion. For a broad set of parameter values, the model suggests that the right approach is to combine weak penalties, small enough so that the innocent are not extorted, with subsidies. This chapter also emphasizes that enforcing such regulations is particularly hard in developing world cities that don't have well-defined property rights.

In the case of transportation as well, it is hard to imagine taming the congestion of Djakarta or Bangkok with infrastructure alone. Extra roads will generate more driving (Duranton & Turner, 2011), which can be avoided if congestion charging induces drivers to internalize the social costs of their actions. If congestion pricing revenues are used to fund public transportation options, especially buses, then poorer urbanites will particularly benefit from such policies.

High housing costs naturally result from the high cost of urban land. Taller buildings create a natural way of squeezing more urban space into a fixed footprint of land, but building up is usually more expensive than building out. While high housing costs are inevitable, in much of the world land use regulations make housing more expensive than it should be.

Cities throughout the world regulate land usage, maximum heights, and other aspects of building. In some cases, these regulations are perfectly sensible. The downsides of locating large-scale, polluting industries in heavily residential districts should be obvious. Building codes that help ensure that buildings burn less often also seem quite justifiable. But while some building codes are sensible, in most of the world, land-use regulations are adopted with almost no serious cost-benefit analysis.

India remains one of the more extreme examples of excessive land-use restrictions. Mumbai has labored under floor area ratio (FAR) restrictions that make it hard to provide more than 1.25 stories on average. Such restrictions mean that it is difficult to provide enough residential space in central locations. When skyscrapers are built, they must be dispersed to accommodate FAR rules, and consequently it is hard to create a walking city. If buildings of various forms do generate measurable negative externalities to the city as a whole, then the most sensible approach is to impose development taxes that charge the builders for the social costs of these new structures.

While policy analysts often have minor disagreements, there is no shortage of policy tools for addressing the downsides of density. The larger question is whether the governments of developing world cities are actually capable of implementing those policies. I turn to the problems of implementing public policy in the developing world next.

Towards governing the post-urban world

Technocratic solutions exist for problems such as traffic congestion and water pollution. Yet it is unclear whether governments have the political will to embrace these solutions or the public capacity to implement solutions that have been embraced. For example, congestion pricing requires the political strength to implement a policy that will be wildly unpopular among the most frequent drivers and have enough public sector strength to actually collect charges from motorists.

In some cases, the public sector challenge is to take actions – such as collecting congestion fees. In other cases, the public sector charge is to stop private actions, such as driving on dedicated bus lanes. Developed and developing world city governments often have problems with both tasks.

Public vs. private vs. parastatal

One common proposal is that public-private partnership can enable governments to borrow capacity from private companies. Even if the public sector is incapable of building and operating a toll road, presumably there exists a private sector firm that can do it. Private-sector firms do have stronger incentives and the ability to hire and reward global talent. Unfortunately, they also have the incentives and ability to corrupt government officials. Engel, Fischer, and Galetovic (2014) documents the myriad challenges with implementing public-private partnerships. While the Chilean experience has been generally positive, in countries with weaker institutions, the track record shows more corruption than competence.

The problem of corruption is particularly severe when the service needs to be subsidized with tax revenues. The private provider has a strong incentive to lobby and bribe in order to achieve a larger subsidy. There are numerous examples of cases in which a private provider has successfully renegotiated and obtained a more generous subsidy.

Nineteenth-century Americans recognized the graft and service quality problems that can occur with private provision of public services. They moved towards the model of independent public agencies, such as the Port Authority of New York and New Jersey, which was once hailed as a model public competence. In principle, independent public authorities can operate free from politics and public sector rules that restrict performance-related pay or firing underperforming workers.

Yet independent government agencies, often called parastatals, can be less functional in the developing world today than they were in U.S. history. Typically, the early leaders of these agencies in the U.S. had a distinct public profile and their performance ensured both public acclaim and private sector opportunities. In many developing world cities, there are few lucrative private sector opportunities, and so parastatals work primarily to ingratiate themselves with political leaders. Consequently, the independent agency can be worse than direct private provision, since public leaders can use the agency as a source of patronage, while simultaneously claiming that they have nothing to do with its budgetary woes and low service quality.

The tradeoff between dictatorship and disorder

Moving to private or parastatal provision is not a panacea for poor public-sector quality. What can help improve the competence and incorruptibility of the public sector?

The U.S. experience emphasizes competing political entities that monitor each other. New York's typically Republican state government would happily conduct corruption investigations of New York's typically Democratic city government. New Deal spending at the city level meant that the federal government imposed accounting standards that appear to have reduced local corruption. The U.K. experience combined strong civil service reform, which isolated bureaucrats from political pressure, with sufficiently high quality legal institutions so that official misconduct would be punished.

These experiences are certainly valuable in the developing world, but U.S. or U.K. institutions are not easy to implement quickly. Perhaps Singapore provides a better model of a quick move from corruption to competence in a developing world context. The Singapore model under Lee Kwan Yew combined high salaries for public officials with draconian penalties for even the appearance of corruption. Centralized control of the system made implementation far easier. In essence, Singapore's experience suggests that competence can replace corruption quickly if there is a highly empowered leader who actually wants to improve government.

Naturally, the great danger with empowering a leader is that the leader may do more damage himself. This highlights a fundamental tradeoff in institutional tradeoff: dictatorship versus disorder. A highly empowered leader will have more capacity to crack down on the downsides of density, including crime and traffic congestion. But that leader will also have the capacity to restrict trade or extract rents for his own private purposes.

Djankov et al. (2003) argue countries can choose along an institutional possibilities frontier (IPF) between the amount of losses from private abuse, which they call disorder, and the amount of losses from public abuse, which they call dictatorship. Countries can choose more or less dictatorship by setting up checks and balances or eliminating them, but they cannot reduce the levels of losses from both private and public abuse.

What does urbanization imply from the ideal tradeoff between dictatorship and disorder? In the economic realm, urbanization increases the capacity for trade, which makes public rules that restrict trade more costly. The burghers of the 16th-century Netherlanders, like the merchants of 18th-century Boston, were unhappy with rules imposed by their royal overlords. However, the negative externalities in cities can also make a firm hand more appealing. The popular appeal of Philippine strongman Rodrigo Duterte partially reflects the promise of this former mayor to tame the downsides of density.

In a sense, the urban desire for both economic freedom and some social control may help us to understand why urbanization in East Asia has not uniformly produced democracy. Singapore is, perhaps, the most extreme example of a state that allows broad latitude in economic affairs while maintaining strict controls over social matters, including forced integration of public housing to reduce the possibility of racial conflict. China's post-Deng leaders can also be seen as following such a mixed approach.

The Boston hypothesis and civic capital

The institutional possibilities frontier may be stable at a point in time, but it can surely evolve over time. Djankov et al. (2003) suggest that higher levels of human capital may create civic capital that shifts the curve inward, and reduces the costs of both public and private abuse. The link between education and governmental quality reflects the greater capacities of a more educated citizenry and, in particular, their greater ability to communicate with one another.

It is also possible that urbanization will generate civic capital and reduce the social costs from both democracy and disorder. One channel is that urbanization itself generates human capital, because people learn from those around them. Alfred Marshall may have focused on learning "the mysteries of the trade" in cities, but it is also presumably possible to learn how to be an effective citizen.

Another possibility is that cities specifically lower the costs of organizing which enables the collective action needed to force governmental change. In some cases, urban organizations can be apolitical entities that turn to political functions, such as labor unions or the Weavers' Guild of Medieval Bruges. In other cases, urban organizations can be specifically political and meant to produce change, such as "Sons of Liberty" who cropped up in America's colonial cities before the revolution or the Committee of Seventy which took on New York City's corrupt Boss Tweed.

A particularly interesting possibility is that cities enable the creation of bonds across ethnic lines, which are necessary for really effective political change. Perhaps small villages can coordinate a small, homogeneous community, but to effectively thrive in heterogeneous cities, you need the ability to bridge across ethnicities and social groups. That ability can help turn a small protest into a mass movement.

There are also downsides of urbanization for political mobilization. Urban proximity may make it easier for leaders to spy on their people or to control their behavior. The benefits of urban bridging presumably disappear when groups are rigidly segregated into ethnic ghettos.

Consequently, it remains a hypothesis that developing world cities can lead to democracy and government, as Boston's urbanity did in 1776. The future is unclear, but the cities of the West achieved large political impact, and it is hard to be optimistic about the political future of places that are poor and rural. It is at least plausible that cities will eventually tame their own demons by eventually upgrading the quality of government.

Conclusion

The world is urbanizing rapidly and this creates both opportunities and challenges. Global trade in food, and improvements in agricultural productivity such as the Green Revolution, have helped the rise of poor-world urbanization. The consequence of this trend is that massive cities have emerged in places that are both poor and poorly governed.

It can be tempting to look at the dysfunction of Kinshasa or Port-au-Prince and think that poor-world urbanization is a terrible mistake. Certainly, the negative externalities that afflict cities when government is weak can be terrible. Yet, while these downsides are real, there are also upsides to cities that extend beyond the economy.

Cities have the capacity to build a socially linked cluster of educated people of trade. That cluster has an interest in stable government, rule of law, and economic freedom. The great hope is that over time cities will build the civic capital to greatly improve the governments of the poorest nations.

Notes

1 My selection of these six cities is based on their inclusion in at least two of the lists created by Chandler (1987), Modelski (2003), and Morris (2010). In all cases, ancient population estimates are subject to considerable uncertainty.
2 www.extension.iastate.edu/agdm/crops/pdf/a2-11.pdf.

References

Ades, A. F., & Glaeser, E. L. (1995). Trade and circuses: Explaining urban giants. *The Quarterly Journal of Economics, 110*(1), 195–227.

Arriaga, E. E. (1968). Components of city growth in selected Latin American countries. *The Milbank Memorial Fund Quarterly, 46*(2), 237–252.

Ashraf, N., Glaeser, E. L., & Ponzetto, G. A. (2016). Infrastructure and development infrastructure, incentives, and institutions. *The American Economic Review, 106*(5), 77–82.

Bairoch, P., & Goertz, G. (1986). Factors of urbanisation in the nineteenth century developed countries: A descriptive and econometric analysis. *Urban Studies, 23*(4), 285–305.

Browning, H. L. (1958). Recent trends in Latin American urbanization. *The Annals of the American Academy of Political and Social Science, 316*(1), 111–120.

Chandler, T. (1987). *Four thousand years of urban growth: An historical census*. Lewiston, NY: Edwin Mellen Press.

Davis, J. C., & Henderson, J. V. (2003). Evidence on the political economy of the urbanization process. *Journal of Urban Economics, 53*(1), 98–125.

Djankov, S., Glaeser, E., La Porta, R., Lopez-de-Silanes, F., & Shleifer, A. (2003). The new comparative economics. *Journal of Comparative Economics, 31*(4), 595–619.

Duranton, G., & Turner, M. A. (2011). The fundamental law of road congestion: Evidence from US cities. *The American Economic Review, 101*(6), 2616–2652.

Engel, E., Fischer, R. D., & Galetovic, A. (2014). *The economics of public-private partnerships: A basic guide*. Cambridge, U.K.: Cambridge University Press.

Fay, M., & Opal, C. (2000). *Urbanization without growth: A not so uncommon phenomenon* (Vol. 2412). Washington, DC: World Bank Publications.

Gaspar, J., & Glaeser, E. L. (1998). Information technology and the future of cities. *Journal of Urban Economics, 43*(1), 136–156.

Glaeser, E. L. (1999). Learning in cities. *Journal of Urban Economics, 46*(2), 254–277.

Glaeser, E. L. (2014). A world of cities: The causes and consequences of urbanization in poorer countries. *Journal of the European Economic Association, 12*(5), 1154–1199.

Glaeser, E. L., Kerr, S. P., & Kerr, W. R. (2015). Entrepreneurship and urban growth: An empirical assessment with historical mines. *Review of Economics and Statistics, 97*(2), 498–520.

Glaeser, E. L., Kolko, J., & Saiz, A. (2001). Consumer city. *Journal of Economic Geography, 1*(1), 27–50.

Glaeser, E. L., & Saiz, A. (2004). The rise of the skilled city. *Brookings-Wharton Papers on Urban Affairs, 5*, 47–94.

Glaeser, E. L., & Steinberg, B. M. (2017). Transforming cities: Does urbanization promote democratic change? *Regional Studies, 51*(1), 58–68.

Goldin, C. D., & Katz, L. F. (2009). *The race between education and technology*. Cambridge, MA: Harvard University Press.

Gollin, D., Jedwab, R., & Vollrath, D. (2016). Urbanization with and without industrialization. *Journal of Economic Growth, 21*(1), 35–70.

Modelski, G. (2003). *World cities: 3000 to 2000*. Washington, DC: FAROS 2000.

Morris, I. (2010). *Social development*. Unpublished manuscript, accessed online at ianmorris.org/docs/social-development.pdf.

Nunn, N., & Qian, N. (2011). The potato's contribution to population and urbanization: Evidence from a historical experiment. *The Quarterly Journal of Economics, 126*(2), 593–650.

Ochoa, E. C. (2000). *Feeding Mexico: The political uses of food since 1910*. Wilmington, DE: Scholarly Resources.

Porcile, G. (1995). The challenge of cooperation: Argentina and Brazil, 1939–1955. *Journal of Latin American Studies, 27*(01), 129–159.

Smith, M. E., Ur, J., & Feinman, G. M. (2014). Jane Jacobs' "cities first" model and archaeological reality. *International Journal of Urban and Regional Research, 38*(4), 1525–1535.

2 The divided city and the patchwork metropolis

Richard Florida and Patrick Adler

Introduction

Urbanists and geographers have long been concerned with the factors that shape and structure our cities and metro areas. Our basic understanding of the structure of cities comes from the Chicago School of urbanism. Beginning in the 1920s and 1930s, Park, Burgess, and their associates at the University of Chicago developed a series of basic models of urban and metropolitan form based initially on "concentric zones" (Park, Burgess, & McKenzie, 1925). They later advanced two additional models, a "sector model" and a "multiple nuclei" model (Harris & Ullman, 1945; Hoyt, 1939). In their most basic and simplified form, those models portray an urban core occupied by commerce, industry, and the residential locations of the disadvantaged and the working classes surrounded by more affluent middle and upper class suburbs. For more than a century then, the geographic division between city and suburb was also America's overarching class divide. The upper and middle classes lived in the suburbs; the poor lived in less advantaged cities or in undeveloped rural places. This outward-oriented suburban pattern reached its pinnacle in the 1980s, captured by the so-called "edge city model," where suburban office parks and malls outside the city center replicated the functions of the old central business district (Garreau, 1992).

Urban form has undergone something of a shift in the past couple of decades with the back-to-the-city movement led mainly by the young and the affluent. Ehrenhalt has dubbed the new urban morphology "the great inversion," where businesses and affluent populations head back to downtown areas, while poverty and working class populations move out to the suburbs (Ehrenhalt, 2012). A detailed study of Toronto by Hulchanski and his colleagues mapped the new class compositions and changing structures of Toronto's neighborhoods. They found middle class neighborhoods were disappearing and the affluent were clustering near the urban core and along transit lines, while the poor and working classes were pushed out to the suburbs (Hulchanski, 2010).

Beveridge compared the changing patterns of urban development and form in Chicago, Los Angeles, and New York City and found evidence for both the return to the city movement – in New York and Chicago and in continued outward oriented growth in Los Angeles (Beveridge, 2011). Delmelle examined patterns of neighborhood change in Chicago and Los Angeles from 1970 to 2010 and found evidence of gentrification in urban Chicago, but much less in Los Angeles where the affluent and elite tended to be located in upscale suburbs and along the coast (Delmelle, 2016).

This chapter summarizes the key findings of a larger research project on the shape and form of the increasingly divided city and the patchwork metropolis (Florida, Matheson, Adler, & Brydges, 2014). The project mapped neighborhood locations of three major classes across many of America's largest metro areas and their core cities.

Mapping the divided city and metropolis

Class remains an inescapable presence in America, cross-cutting almost every aspect of the social structure from education and employment to income, politics, and health. We define class based on the work people do and the occupations they are engaged in (Florida, 2002, 2012). About a third of the U.S. workforce belongs to the growing knowledge-based creative class, which includes researchers, scientists, academics, designers, entrepreneurs, entertainers, artists, and others who work with their minds. Just 20% are members of the blue-collar working class, which includes factory workers, tradespeople, and other skilled, often unionized workers, down from almost 40% of the workforce at the mid-point of the last century. The largest and fastest-growing class, which accounts for about half of the work force, is the service class, whose members toil in routine, low-skill, low-pay jobs like food preparation, janitorial work, health aides, and retail trade.

The maps in this chapter plot the neighborhood location of these three major classes by Census tract level based on data from the 2010 American Community Survey (United States Census Bureau, 2012). Neighborhoods are shaded based on the class that has a plurality of residents. The maps also identify four key factors that tend to shape to location the advantaged knowledge and professional workers that make up the creative class, thus structuring the divided city and metropolis. The first factor is proximity to the urban core. We operationalize this as the area within two miles of the center city's city hall as per the Census Bureau (Wilson, Plane, Mackun, Fischetti, & Goworowska, 2012). The second factor is proximity to knowledge-based institutions, including universities, government laboratories, and think tanks. Knowledge-based institutions directly employ large numbers of science and technology, creative and professional workers, and also act as magnets to attract these individuals. The third factor is proximity to transit. A number of studies have shown the increasing preference of knowledge workers for locations close to transit (Duncan, 2011). We map light-rail and subway lines, but do not map the location of rapid bus service or of tram or funicular railways. The fourth factor is natural amenities. Here again, research has shown the clustering of highly educated and creative workers around natural amenities as well as the higher prices of housing around these amenities (Clark, 2004; Glaeser, Kolko, & Saiz, 2001). We map major parks and green spaces including national parks, forests, and monuments, state designated parks and forests as well as county and local parks.

Based on this, we identify three types of patterns present in the divided city and metropolis: "Core-Oriented," "Class Bloc," and "Fractal." We now discuss each in turn.

Core-Oriented

In Core-Oriented metros, we find a large concentration of the creative class at or around the core. Still, this pattern does not completely correspond to an inverted pattern, as the advantaged creative class extends considerably into the suburbs as well. Figures 2.1 through 2.4 show the pattern for four metros that illustrate the Core-Oriented pattern: New York, Chicago, Boston, and San Francisco.

New York

In New York, the advantaged creative class has colonized the urban core from Manhattan into Brooklyn. It extends out from there into a broad band of suburbs from Long Island to New Jersey and Connecticut as well. The less advantaged service class is located in between the core and the outer suburbs, especially in New Jersey.

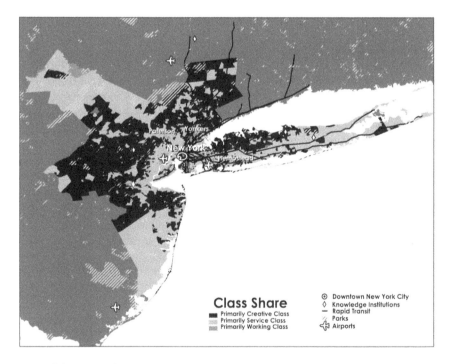

Figure 2.1 New York.

In the city itself, the creative class is highly clustered and concentrated in Manhattan, from the southern tip of the Financial District through Tribeca, SoHo, the Village, Chelsea, Midtown, and the Upper East and West Sides. For all the talk of gentrification in Brooklyn, the creative class is confined almost completely to the northern part of the borough, though it is beginning to stretch out from there. The service class is mostly clustered in the city's outer boroughs. There are just a few majority working class locations left in the region, mostly in and around Newark, Elizabeth, Paterson, and Passaic in New Jersey.

Chicago

In Chicago, the creative class hugs the lakeshore around downtown and then extends northward through Evanston, home of Northwestern University. In fact, the creative class has taken over many of the older industrial and warehouse

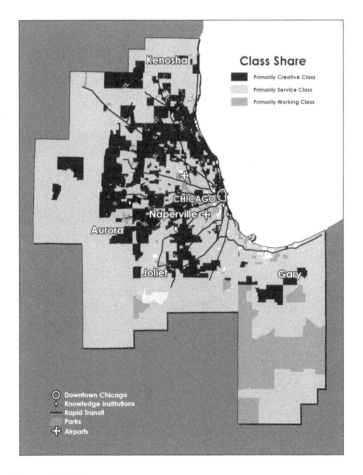

Figure 2.2 Chicago.

districts of the Chicago School's infamous zone in transition. In the city itself, the creative class is highly concentrated along the shore of Lake Michigan, from the Loop to Wrigleyville in the north and south to the Hyde Park area surrounding the University of Chicago. From there it wraps around in a crescent-like configuration toward Naperville.

Instead of affluence moving outward, the less advantaged service class occupies the way-off fringes of the region, as well as the areas between the urban and suburban creative class clusters. But disadvantage also remains in the city itself. Nine of the 10 neighborhoods with the highest service class concentrations are in the city proper. Few working class districts remain in this once great industrial city with its huge factory districts. The region's remaining working class neighborhoods are now located outside the city in far off Joliet and Gary.

The San Francisco Bay Area

The San Francisco Bay Area (which spans the three large cities of San Francisco, Oakland, and San Jose) is dominated by the advantaged creative class, which occupies large swaths of territory around the city's downtown, around the University of California in Berkeley, in Marin County in the north, and in the southeast and southwest around Stanford University and Silicon Valley. The

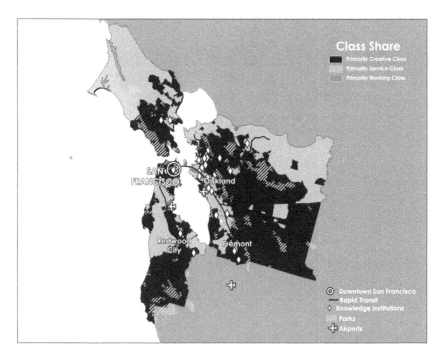

Figure 2.3 San Francisco.

creative class occupies much of the city of San Francisco itself, especially in and around its gentrified urban core, which has become home to startups and high-tech companies. The creative class is also heavily concentrated in the East Bay, which is home to 6 of the 10 neighborhoods with the largest creative class concentrations.

Regionally, the class divide takes on a fragmented pattern. There are large service class districts at the far peripheries north of Marin and east of Oakland, in a long band running from Oakland to Fremont, in Menlo Park, and in East Palo Alto in the heart of Silicon Valley. This pattern can also be seen in the city itself, where service class clusters surround some of its most affluent and advantaged neighborhoods. Alongside its considerable creative class, the city of San Francisco is home to 8 of the 10 neighborhoods with the highest service class concentrations in the Bay Area – six of them within a 1.5 mile or so circle encompassing Chinatown and the Tenderloin. Virtually no working class districts can be seen on the map.

Boston

The advantaged creative class dominates Greater Boston, stretching out from the downtown core in large wedges to the north and southwestern suburbs and along the southeastern Atlantic coast. The creative class is tightly clustered in and around downtown Boston, from the Financial District and Faneuil Hall to upscale Beacon Hill and Back Bay; the South End, the heart of the city's gay community; and the Fenway-Kenmore area.

Following a pattern identified half a century ago by the historian Sam Bass Warner, the city and metro have been powerfully shaped by their transit infrastructure (Bass Warner, 1962). The Red Line passes through Cambridge, which has transformed from an industrial city into a full-blown knowledge cluster with huge concentrations of the creative class (a whopping two-thirds of its residents are members) and which attracts more than a billion dollars in venture capital. Large creative class concentrations also stretch west into the suburbs across Belmont, into the historic colonial towns of Lexington and Concord, and the upscale suburbs of Newton, Wellesley, and Sudbury – most of which are connected to the core of the city by transit or commuter rail. Substantial creative class clusters are also located along the region's Route 128 high-tech corridor. There are also considerable creative class concentrations in the affluent communities that line the northern coastline, like Manchester-by-the-Sea, Swampscott, and Marblehead. Three of the region's ten leading creative class neighborhoods are in Boston proper, and four are in Cambridge. The remaining three are in suburban Newton, which sits on the Green line close to Boston College.

The service class is located in a tight band outside downtown Boston, continuing north past Marblehead and south to Quincy along the coast, forming two big clusters at the northern and southern fringes of the metro. Nine of the ten most concentrated service class neighborhoods are in Boston proper, mainly in

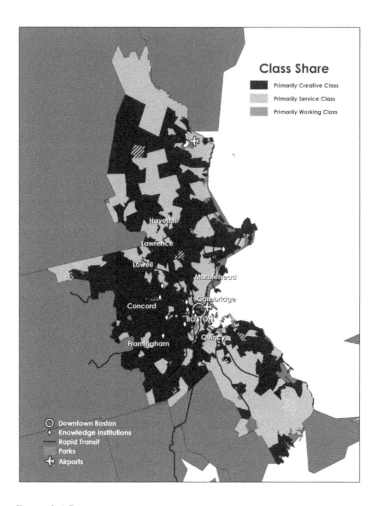

Figure 2.4 Boston.

South and East Boston around historically black Roxbury and near Logan airport. Slightly less than 15% of the region's workers belong to the blue-collar working class, well below the national average – and a stark change from half a century ago, when Boston was a pre-eminent manufacturing center.

Class Blocs

In the Class Bloc model or type, the metro is essentially split into separate locations for creative class and the service class. The advantaged class is weighted more heavily to the suburbs than the core. Figures 2.5 and 2.6 show the pattern for two metros that illustrate the Class Bloc pattern: Atlanta and Dallas.

Atlanta

Atlanta's creative class occupies the areas north and east of the core from downtown through Midtown and Buckhead in the city to the upscale suburbs to the north. The southeast is nearly all service class, with just a few creative class islets. The working class is pushed to the far outskirts of the region.

The city's class divide follows a similar, but even more pronounced pattern. The creative class dominates the entire northeastern quadrant of the city. The neighborhood with the highest creative class concentration is Druid Hills, a bucolic late 19th- and early 20th-century planned community that crosses out of Atlanta proper into DeKalb County. The service class is pushed to the periphery of this large creative class cluster and occupies the entire Southwest of the city. Seven of the region's top ten service class locations are located within Atlanta's city limits. Many of these neighborhoods are poor and black, with the geography of racial segmentation overlaying that of class. The working class occupies the far corners of the metro. Two of its leading working class districts are in Forest Park, a minority majority town some 10 miles south of the city, where some 30% of the population lives below the poverty line.

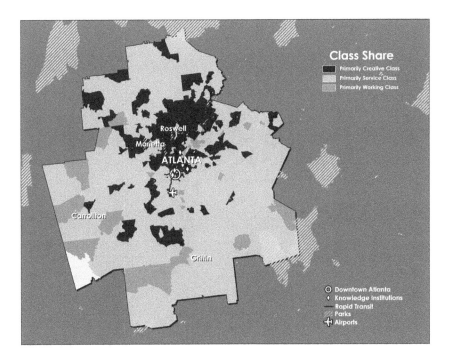

Figure 2.5 Atlanta.

Dallas

The region's class divide takes shape around a north-south axis. Six of the metro's ten creative class neighborhoods are located in the affluent northern suburbs of Plano, Frisco, and Irving. The region's southern tier is almost entirely service class, interspersed with a few creative class clusters. The working class is clustered at the far outskirts of the region. The city's class divide follows a similar north-south axis, demarcated by Interstate 30 and the impressive steel and glass skyline of Dallas's downtown core. There is also a less pronounced east/west divide along the Trinity River just south of downtown, separating the working and service class.

Fractal

The Fractal pattern is less well-organized than the other two types. The advantaged class occupies islands that are spread throughout the metro. Figures 2.7 and 2.8 map the pattern for two metros that illustrate the Fractal pattern: Los Angeles and Houston. In Los Angeles, this pattern appears to be structured at least in part by proximity to the waterfront. Both metros are car-oriented regions that reached their current population rank after World War II. Their reliance on freeways and their sprawling geographic scope helps to structure their disorganized, fractal pattern.

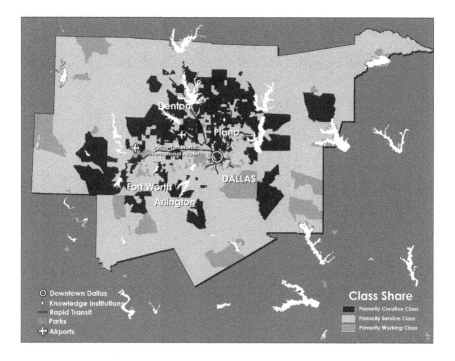

Figure 2.6 Dallas.

Los Angeles

Unlike London and New York, Los Angeles's creative class is arrayed along its magnificent coastline, stretching from Malibu in the north to Irvine, Laguna Beach, and Dana Point in the south, expanding significantly eastward in both the north and south. A major creative class cluster stretches from Hollywood, Bel Air, and Westwood, where UCLA is located, out to Venice; a second can be seen around Pasadena, home to Caltech and the Jet Propulsion Laboratory; and a third around the University of California at Irvine in the southeast. A much smaller, budding creative class cluster can be found around the old lofts, factories, and multi-story buildings downtown, which has become a major hub for artists and art galleries, some of them recently relocated from New York.

The service and working classes occupy the proverbial hole-in-the-donut, a large expanse more or less at the center of the metro, as well as the farther-out

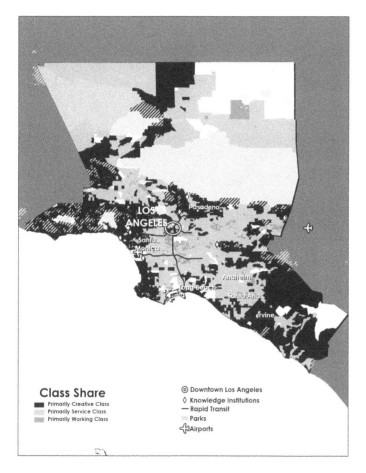

Figure 2.7 Los Angeles.

fringes. There is an enormous service class concentration between Santa Monica in the west and Pasadena in the east that stretches all the way south to Anaheim and Santa Ana; two additional big clusters in the metro's northern and northeastern corners; and also in the inner city neighborhoods between Hollywood and downtown. Los Angeles's once thriving working class neighborhoods have mostly disappeared, with a few specks on the map at the center, in the northeast near Burbank, in the south around historically black Compton, and around the huge port of Long Beach.

Houston

Houston's class divide takes the form of several interspersed rings, with a large service class bloc located in between the creative cluster in and around downtown and another one out in its suburbs. The advantaged creative class is located in a wide band that loops around the center of the city and metro toward Sugar Land in the southeast and the Woodlands to the northeast, with a small cluster in and around the urban core. Interestingly, nine of the metro's top ten creative class neighborhoods are in the city proper. Seven are located in the upscale area around Rice University and medical center. There is another creative class cluster near the Johnson Space Center in Clear Lake.

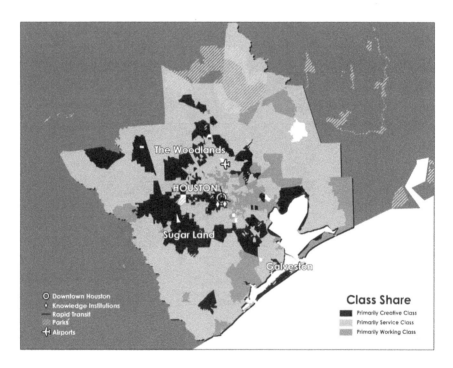

Figure 2.8 Houston.

Nine of the ten neighborhoods with the largest service class concentrations are also located in this band: five in the distressed southeast and southwest areas of the city, two in neighborhoods near George Bush Intercontinental Airport, one in the northern outpost of Westchase, and one in the northeastern area of the city. The rest of the service class is pushed much further out to the far fringes of the metro. The working class, which has a considerable presence in Houston compared to most of the metros we've mapped, is concentrated in districts to the south and north of downtown and around the Port of Houston.

Conclusion and discussion

As we have seen, the divided city and metropolis takes on three basic patterns. (In reality, of course, cities and metros frequently share elements of all of these three archetypes.)

In the first, the advantaged creative class effectively recolonizes the urban center, radiating out into the suburbs, pushing the service and working classes into the leftover spaces in the core and mainly out to the suburban and ex-urban fringes.

In the second, the city and metropolis are essentially cleaved in half, with the advantaged creative class and disadvantaged service class occupying entirely separate blocs of the city. The advantaged class is more heavily weighted to the suburbs, though it does in some cases cross over into the city.

In the third, the advantaged class is strung out in a series of islands, archipelagos, or even tessellations spread out across the city and suburbs.

The most striking pattern to emerge from this research is the sheer extent of class division in the modern city and metropolis. The analysis finds a clear pattern of geographic class division across all metros examined. Although the pattern is expressed differently, each has pronounced clusters of the creative class in and around the urban core. The service class surrounds these creative class clusters and is also pushed towards the peripheries of these cities and regions. There are very few remaining working class clusters; the ones that do remain are also largely pushed to the peripheries.

The research further identifies four principal axes of cleavage across the divided city and metropolis.

The urban core: The urban core has become a key axis of the class geography of the modern metropolis. Its transformation to a locational center for the creative class is a striking reversal from its former role as a center for industry, commerce, and shopping and its subsequent abandonment in the 1960s and 1970s.

Transit: In virtually all of the metros examined, we find evidence of creative class clustering around major mass transit arteries. Transit provides a way for knowledge and professional workers to access the core without having to bear the opportunity costs of commuting by car, while enhancing their productivity by allowing them to work and interact while in transit.

Knowledge Institutions: In each metro, there are substantial clusters of the creative class around major universities and research facilities. This represents a shift from the past, when universities functioned as more transitory stopping points for students to gain knowledge and degrees en route to their professional lives and careers. Many of the universities that were located in the downtowns of big cities were surrounded by blight and disadvantage, though some of these neighborhoods did retain higher and middle income residents, mainly professors and health care workers employed at universities and medical centers.

Natural amenities: Natural amenities comprise a fourth and final clustering force. Of particular importance is location along waterfronts. In many cases, waterfronts are reclaimed from industrial uses and provide the additional advantages of close proximity to the urban core and an abundance of warehouse buildings that can be repurposed as loft offices and housing.

These axes of cleavage are frequently interrelated and overlap with one another. The urban cores of many cities and metros grew up beside natural harbors and navigable lakes and rivers. Many older universities and colleges originally grew up in city centers as well. The rise of the new class-divided city and metropolis is not a mechanical response to these four axes, but a gradual consequence of ongoing historical and economic processes.

The patterns we identify differ from both the traditional outward-oriented Chicago School models and are more complex than the inward-oriented model of the "great inversion." Instead, we find class divides that span both city and suburb. We refer to this ubiquitous juxtaposition of concentrated advantage and concentrated disadvantage as the *patchwork metropolis*. We further find that the evolving class divides of the patchwork metropolis are shaped and structured by the locational choices of the advantaged class. In city after city, metro after metro, the affluent have colonized the most economically functional and desirable places – in and around the urban core, along transit routes, close to universities and knowledge-based institutions, and along waterfronts and other natural amenities. The less advantaged classes are shunted into the spaces left over or in between – either traditionally disadvantaged areas of the inner city or the far fringes of the suburban and ex-urban periphery.

This new divided city and patchwork metropolis marks a significant change in American living patterns. While there have always been affluent neighborhoods, gated enclaves, and fabled bastions of wealth, the people who cut the lawns, cooked and served the meals, and fixed the plumbing in the big houses used to live nearby – close enough to vote for the same council people, judges, aldermen, and members of the board of education. Even if the gentry's children went to Choate and Exeter, they paid local taxes that supported local schools and other services. When they were drafted into the military, the children of the poor and the children of the rich served side by side.

Today, this is no longer the case. Just as the rise of the knowledge economy split the job market into high wage knowledge work and lower wage service positions, middle class neighborhoods have also been hollowed out as the geography of cities and metropolitan areas becomes increasingly divided between high and low income neighborhoods. Our cities and metropolitan areas have been cleaved into isolated, class-based, economically segregated islands, in which either the advantaged or the disadvantaged clearly predominate. The old, stark divide between city and suburbs has given way to a new pattern of class division and geographic separation that spans them both.

References

Bass Warner Jr., S. (1962). *Streetcar suburbs: The process of growth in Boston 1870–1900*. Cambridge, MA: Harvard University Press.

Beveridge, A. A. (2011). Commonalities and contrasts in the development of major United States urban areas: A spatial and temporal analysis from 1910 to 2000. In M. P. Gutmann, G. D. Deane, E. R. Merchant, & K. Sylvester (Eds.), *Navigating time and space in population studies* (pp. 185–216). Netherlands: Springer.

Clark, T. N. (Ed.). (2004). *The city as an entertainment machine* (Vol. 9, *Research in urban policy*). London: Elsevier.

Delmelle, E. C. (2016). Mapping the DNA of urban neighborhoods: Clustering longitudinal sequences of neighborhood socioeconomic change. *Annals of the American Association of Geographers, 106*(1), 36–56.

Duncan, M. (2011). The impact of transit-oriented development on housing prices in San Diego, CA. *Urban Studies, 48*(1), 101–127.

Ehrenhalt, A. (2012). *The great inversion and the future of the American city*. New York: Vintage.

Florida, R. (2002). *The rise of the creative class: And how it's transforming work, leisure, community and everyday life*. New York: Basic Books.

Florida, R. (2012). *The rise of the creative class – revisited: 10th anniversary edition – revised and expanded* (2nd ed.). New York: Basic Books.

Florida, R., Matheson, Z., Adler, P., & Brydges, T. (2014). *The divided city: And the shape of the new metropolis*. Toronto: Martin Prosperity Institute. Retrieved June 28, 2017, from http://martinprosperity.org/content/the-divided-city-and-the-shape-of-the-new-metropolis/.

Garreau, J. (1992). *Edge city: Life on the new frontier*. New York: Anchor Books.

Glaeser, E. L., Kolko, J., & Saiz, A. (2001). Consumer city. *Journal of Economic Geography, 1*(1), 27–50.

Harris, C. D., & Ullman, E. L. (1945). The nature of cities. *The Annals of the American Academy of Political and Social Science, 242*(1), 7–17.

Hoyt, H. (1939). *The structure and growth of residential neighborhoods in American cities*. Transportation Research Board. Retrieved June 28, 2017, from https://trid.trb.org/view.aspx?id=131170.

Hulchanski, J. D. (2010). *The three cities within Toronto: Income polarization among Toronto's neighbourhoods, 1970–2005*. Toronto: Cities Centre, University of Toronto.

Park, R. E., Burgess, E. W., & McKenzie, R. D. (1925). *The city*. Chicago: University of Chicago Press.

United States Census Bureau. (2012). *5-Year 2010 American community survey*. Retrieved May 2, 2015, from www.census.gov/acs/www/data_documentation/summary_file/.

Wilson, S. G., Plane, D. A., Mackun, P. J., Fischetti, T. R., & Goworowska, J. (2012). Patterns of metropolitan and micropolitan population change: 2000 to 2010. *2010 census special reports*. Washington, DC: US Census Bureau.

3 Ephemeral urbanism

Looking at extreme temporalities

Rahul Mehrotra and Felipe Vera

Looking at the contemporary landscape of cities, one could argue that today's urbanism seems to be suspended in a constant negotiation between two contrasting situations. The first derives from the assumption that development is about accumulation. This generates a common anxiety that drives cities with capital investments, producing what can be referred to as a "hyper-city." This phenomenon is manifested in the form of settlements that exacerbate formal urban attributes. In this more traditional context, architecture and urban design emerge as almost a purely material exercise, often disconnected from the social implications of urbanism. Architecture, as the basic unit of urbanism, seems to be obsessed with the idea of the city as the centralizing spectacle often driving the inherent impatience of capital. Currently, this is the most predominantly practiced disciplinary focus. The second situation in debates about urbanism is derived from the idea that there is a more elastic, and perhaps weaker, expression of the urban condition, referred to as a "kinetic city" (Mehrotra, 2008). This completely different observation of urbanity considers the city in a state of constant flux. This continuous, kinetic quality is characterized by physical transformations that shift the very fabric of the typical notions of accumulation and its relationship to development. Furthermore, the kinetic city cannot be understood as a two-dimensional entity. Instead it is multifaceted, a three-dimensional conglomeration of incremental development, perceived as if in motion. Here the city is a place where conceiving functional arrangements is more important than the construction of the architectonic body, where openness prevails over rigidity and flexibility is valued over rigor. It is a city that is premised on detachment. In this context, sustainability relies more on the city's capacity to deconstruct, disassemble, reconfigure, and reverse previous iterations.

This reading of the city as the kinetic city presents a compelling vision that potentially allows us to better understand the blurred lines of contemporary urbanism and the changing roles of people and spaces in urban society. The increasing concentrations of global populations exacerbate the inequalities and spatial divisions of social classes. From this perspective, an equitable application of urbanism can address the increasingly inequitable economic conditions that are prevalent in densely populated environments. In a way, the kinetic city is a home to an emergent population that is excluded from normative transnational networks of commerce and civil interaction. This is not to say that the kinetic city is merely for the impoverished. Rather, it is a temporal articulation and occupation of space, creating a richer sensibility of spatial reasoning that includes formally unimagined uses in dense urban conditions. In many ways the kinetic city is reliant upon an indigenous urbanism that has a particular "local" logic that reacts to people's needs, in relation to the place they inhabit. Understanding the idea of how to operate in a kinetic city is specific to certain contexts of rapid growth and that are in a state of unresolved or perpetual flux. Therefore, in an attempt to embrace more extreme conditions, to make this reading resonate more broadly and productively the notion of the kinetic city could be expanded from "kinetic" to "ephemeral," and from merely "city" to the more encompassing, "urbanism." By reformulating the categories the new focus would potentially shift from the notion of the kinetic city as a means to describe some specific local conditions, to that of "ephemeral urbanism" more broadly. This reformulation offers a more accurate acknowledgment of the temporary nature that is expressed when describing a city as kinetic. It becomes a conceptual instrument that encompasses a range of alternative forms of urbanism across more diverse geographies. For example, it offers an approach to urbanism where density is not the overriding criteria and conditions within and outside the boundaries of the city are simultaneously negotiated to build more meaningful, productive, and inclusive urban expressions.

Today, urban environments face ever-increasing flows of human movement as well as an accelerated frequency of natural disasters and iterative economic crises that dictate the allocation of capital towards the physical components of cities. As a consequence, urban settings are required to be more flexible in order to be better prepared to respond to, organize, and resist external and internal pressures. At a time in which uncertainty is the new norm, urban attributes like reversibility and openness appear to be critical to a more sustainable form of urban development. Therefore, in contemporary urbanism around the world, it is clear that in order for cities to be sustainable, they need to resemble and facilitate active fluxes in motion, rather than be limited by static, material configurations.

This expanded version of the idea of the kinetic city under the rubric of ephemeral urbanism presents a compelling vision that enables a better understanding of the blurred lines of contemporary urbanism – both spatial and temporal – and the influence of people in shaping spaces in urban society. Thus to engage in this discussion the exploration of the temporary landscape opens a potential space for questioning the idea of permanence as a univocal solution to various urban conditions. One could instead argue that the future of cities depends less on the rearrangement of buildings and infrastructure, and more on our ability to openly imagine more malleable technological, material, social, and economic landscapes. From these settlements, we can learn how to look towards an urbanism that recognizes and more deftly handles the temporary and elastic nature of contemporary and emerging built environments. These effective strategies for managing change have the potential to be essential elements in the construction of contemporary urban environments. The challenge is then to learn from these extremely kinetic conditions in order to manage and negotiate the layers of urbanism while accommodating emergent needs of large, often-neglected parts of any urban society. The intention is for the evidence included in the following pages to serve as inspiration for a more flexible urban design, more in line with emergent realities, enabling us to deal with more complex scenarios.

Temporary cities have a great deal to offer in the study and application of urbanism. However, given their heterogeneous nature it is difficult to organize a cohesive terrain of scholarship from which to move into mainstream application. Temporary cities, unlike more permanent ones that have a range of elements that simultaneously support their continuity, are usually structured around a central purpose. This *modus operandi* is not only the central force that defines an ephemeral city's dimensions and complexity, but also the life cycle of the settlement, its material composition, and its place in the cultural memory of its society. Following this line of thought, it is possible to categorize ephemeral cities in clusters of cases configured in diverse taxonomies, fused by their common characteristics of temporality. Similarities such as the time sequence of deployment processes, supportive institutional structures, and morphological geometries are among many other possible attributes that could be articulated for each taxonomy.

These varied taxonomies could be a useful way to organize cases that are differentiated through variables such as length, size, metabolism, perceived levels of risk, patterns of spatial use, grid morphology and complexity, technology, logistical implementation, etc. They respond to particular conditions and contexts while sharing the certainty – or at least the expectation – of a date of expiration. Thus they challenge us to develop tools for intervening and thinking about nonpermanent configurations as a legitimate and productive category within the discourse on urbanism. In fact, they represent an entire surrogate urban ecology that grows and disappears on an often extremely tight temporal scale. When temporal urban landscapes are seen as the expression of a distinctive form of urbanism a potentially productive dialogue is established between ephemeral settlements. These settlements span a diverse range, from refugee camps to weekend long festivals along with other temporal urbanizations configured for celebration.

Andrea Branzi's 10 recommendations for the construction of a "New Athens Charter" offered critical provocations for the radical rethinking of the urban as a more inclusive and less Eurocentric project. Of his 10 recommendations, the third seems to point directly to the construction of a new concept of time in a city that should be thought of as a place for "cosmic hospitality" in which designers could encourage "planetary coexistence" between "man and animals, technology and divinities, living and dead." In doing so, a model for the city could be found that is "less anthropocentric and more open to biodiversity, to the sacred, and to human beauty" (Branzi, 2015). Religion as taxonomy of ephemeral urbanism seems to advance this line of thinking, proposing temporary reconfigurations of the urban that are, in a way, short glimpses of this very city model.

In this sense, ephemeral landscapes of religion are constituted by cases in which the urban space is modified, totally transformed, or even created in order to facilitate the practice of faith. These cases present thoughtful strategies for ephemeral configurations deployed to celebrate religious beliefs. Some of the cases such as the Qoyllur Rit'I in Peru go as far as generating temporary megacities from almost nothing. Others convert streets into open temples, such as the light constructions made annually to host the Durga Puja in Kolkatta, while others transform massive regional infrastructures into a procession path, as in Lo Vasquez, Chile.

These cases challenge the pace at which the generic city is progressively constructed, showing us how the intensity of the events stretches the physical and symbolic boundaries of the everyday functional spaces. In recent years, for instance, there has been an extraordinary intensification of pilgrimage practises, which has been translated into a need for larger and more frequently constructed structures for hosting massive gatherings. Extreme examples of temporary religious cities are ephemeral constructions set up for the Hajj, as well as a series of temporary cities constructed in India for hosting celebrations such as the Durga Puja, Ganesh Chaturthi, and Kumbh Mela – a religious pilgrimage that, according to official figures, supports the congregation of more than 100 million people. Many attributes of the ephemeral can be extracted from these cases. Conditions of appropriation, transformation, reversibility, reactivation, demarcation, and other strategies are deployed in the construction of these temporary environments. Lessons can be taken from the ephemeral functionality of these places that challenges the idea that the city is a stagnant artifact, built upon mechanisms perceived as being permanent.

Many of these cases, especially those that are about the deployment of cities, can only happen because they consider the possibility of their own deconstruction in advance. These landscapes can be as intense as they are because in each of these cases the reabsorption of such reconfigurations is considered. A paradigmatic case that illustrates the importance of reversibility is the ephemeral megacity for the Kumbh Mela. This is the biggest ephemeral city in the world and leaves almost no trace on the ground after its disassembly. Occurring every 12 years, the Kumbh Mela is the largest religious gathering in the world, resulting in the largest deployment of a temporary city on the planet. It is located adjacent to the city of Allahabad, India, at the confluence of the sacred rivers, the River Ganges and River Yamuna. The event unites people from all over the globe through the ritual of bathing in the holy waters of the *Sangam* (or confluence), in the exact spot in which these two sacred rivers, along with a third mythical river, the *Saraswati*, converge. For 55 days, the floodplain of the river becomes a completely functional religious city requiring huge infrastructural investments. A series of functional elements of a more permanent city are rapidly replicated – roads, pontoon bridges, tents of various sizes, and several typologies of social organization. The aggregation of units converges in an endless texture of cotton, plastic, plywood, and several other materials, organized by an infrastructural grid of roads, electricity, and waste management. The city is equipped to facilitate

7 million residents with an additional flux of 10–20 million, who come for cycles of 24 hours on the main bathing dates.[1] The grid and the allocation of land are determined by a negotiation process between institutions and dwellers, defining the general structure of blocks and locations based on previous iterations, leaving the interior organization of the camps for each community to determine. The same city re-emerges every 12 years, expressing in its formal configuration particular structures of power, hierarchical organizations, and relational connections between old and new dwellers. This massive operation generates both urban form and value by resembling its previous version.

In the same way that religious ephemeral settlements are a means for what a society perceives as valuable and memorable, other ephemeral forms play similar but secular roles. Temporal celebratory landscapes are also ways to provide space and place to the conservation of social traditions, enhancing the values of cohesion, and allowing for interactions in the form of cathartic gatherings. In this way, additionally to ephemeral settlements fostering the encounter with the sacred, many other impermanent landscapes appear for the support of the celebration of the mundane, inside and outside the city. Sacred ephemeral landscapes open opportunities for inverting hierarchies and making horizontal social relationships in the city. They also transform thresholds, softening them. Both things are achieved by the implantation of a major common purpose that unifies differences.

Celebratory ephemeral manifestations achieve the same effect as they provide heterotopic spaces in which one can usually see the dissolution of social predetermination and a diversity that is not normally achieved in the everyday city. Nonreligious cultural celebrations have historically been places of social intensity and cultural expression. Many settlements regularly pop up around the globe, creating "contact zones" for groups of people that would otherwise not interact with or even find each other. These structures are well expressed in the softer, secondary layers that penetrate the permanent city, as in the case of Latin American carnivals and street parties or the massive artistic performances that activate urban spaces, or even in the form of discrete settlements outside or adjacent to urban centers all around the world. Music festivals such as Exit in Serbia, Coachella in California, and Sziget in Budapest, motivate the construction of extended ephemeral settlements that for short periods of time congregate large groups of people. They range from relatively small gatherings, like Burning Man in Nevada or Fuji Rock in Japan, which attract around 40,000 people, to events like Glastonbury in England, the Roskilde Festival in Denmark, and Rock Werchter in Belgium, which draw in around 350,000 people overall. Temporary celebratory landscapes are disruptions to the "business as usual" condition of the city. They open the way for very intense short-term interactions that physically transform the urban space, allowing for cultural expression in perhaps its most radical condition. In these contexts the individual and the community are placed at the center through great strategies for social and spatial binding. The permanent city becomes secondary to the idea of a shared and cultural connectivity.

There are other forms of the temporal in which architecture and urban design work in completely opposite ways to that of ephemeral cities of celebration. This is a neutralizing urbanism that disposes of grids and units as well as any expression of identity, reducing life to its more basic and "bare" condition. These are, for instance, ephemeral landscapes of refuge, a taxonomy that seems to have been increasing in scale and frequency in recent years. Examining this classification of ephemeral urbanism is fundamental for understanding the same contemporary condition of more permanent cities. The reason for this is that as the need for refugee camps increases, permanent cities begin to mimic the operative modalities of these camps. Taking this argument further, referring to the bio-political camp in its more radical condition, that of the concentration camp, Giorgio Agamben argues that it is essential to "recognize the structure of the camp in all its metamorphoses" not only because of the need for major emphasis on the temporal dimension of cities but also because, "Today, it is not the city but rather the camp" that is "the fundamental bio-political paradigm of the West" (Agamben, 1998, p. 181).

We can refer to refugee camps as products of a form of urbanism that emerged during what the ethnologist Michel Agier called, "The management of the undesirables" (Agier, 2011). His comment was stated in response to the political tensions that contributed to the displacement of people all over the world. The refugee camps located on the Ivory Coast that accommodate more than 900,000 people – coming largely from Liberia but also from other adjacent locations – provide some of the most extreme examples. The most striking cases, however, are those of Dabaad in northeastern Kenya. These camps have been in existence for two decades and presently accommodate approximately 500,000 people. The Breidjing camps in Chad (home to 200,000 people) and several camps in Sri Lanka (which collectively house 300,000 people) act as further examples of this type of provisional response. Surprisingly, these camps only hold a small fraction of the 59.5 million people that are currently displaced around the world and living in temporary accommodation, according to the United Nations High Commissioner for Refugees (UNHCR, 2015).

These cases demonstrate some of the contradictions of the ephemeral city that might aspire to be transitional, but may actually turn into an unaccepted permanent solution, built with components not meant for permanence. For instance, Daabad – located in the Garissa County of eastern Kenya, on its border with Somalia – has been in operation since the early 1990s. It hosts about half a million refugees, most of them arriving from Somalia, a number that is still increasing. With these figures, Dadaab surpasses most cities in Kenya, being one of the largest settlements in the country and the most expansive refugee camp in the world, and increases on a daily basis. According to UNHCR, nearly a thousand people arrive every day by foot from Somalia and Ethiopia. The level of urbanization is actually much more developed than one might think by merely looking at the online images of tents aligned in the desert. The settlement contains an airstrip, as it also functions as a base for UNHCR operations.

On the other hand, very light but highly influential layers of territorial control dynamics are deployed to support military activities. Ephemeral military landscapes actually appear inside and outside countries as national or transnational operations of protection, control, and aggression. The scales of capital, people, and the spatial consequences of these operations are humongous. They have life cycles that go from very short and compressed time frames (2–3 years), as is the case of Sharana Base and John Pratt Camp, both in Afghanistan; to bases built with a longer duration in mind (about 8–15 years) as seen in the cases of Operating Base Lightning (Afghanistan), Forward Operating Base Al Asad (Iraq), Camp Monteith (Kosovo), Camp Julien, (Afghanistan), and Camp Doha (Kuwait). Doha is the longest in-operation base included in this publication. The engagement they have with the territory in which they are inserted is as minimal as possible given the complexity of territorial deployments when operating from far away. Bases are often perceived as outsiders, and their occupants move lightly throughout regions seeking occasional connection or isolation depending on their needs.

Temporary military landscapes have a huge impact on permanent territories and cities, drastically transforming processes of urban development. In a way, ephemeral military settlements produce disruptions in the territory by changing the drivers of growth while juxtaposing the temporary and the permanent in antagonistic ways. Military activity inflicts corrosion on sites, disrupting current conditions and bringing the same uncertainty of life to the quotidian experience. The ephemeral in this case has three faces. The first is that of the light construction of the military settlements; the second is the destruction inflicted on the places in which they operate; and the third is the temporary response to those who suffer from the consequences of military activities. The ephemeral military conditions create an inescapable context of pain and fear as a by-product of the camp in its more radical expression.

As an extension of this type, the landscapes of strife deal with disaster, which impacts the built environment with the displacement of people and even with the managing of death. The temporary response is often focused on managing post-disaster contexts, as territories in which disasters happen remain full of tensions related to issues of land, economy, the augmented vulnerability of different groups within the society, and the urgent need to start planning for relief and recovery in a sustainable way. Unlike other forms of the ephemeral, responses to natural and manmade disasters problematize the question of permanence in a much more complex way. While, for instance in a refugee camp, impermanence is questionable and dependent upon a multitude of factors. Outsiders or the military typically decide the location and conditions of the settlement. This creates anxiety and conflict over empowerment and control. Because of this, protection is what drives the ephemeral in landscapes of strife. The construction of temporary settlements is the need for shelter and the re-establishment of broken relationships in the territory. In this way, ephemeral settlements serve as short-term reconstruction efforts that are key parts of planning to reduce vulnerability and enhance resilience. The United Nations Relief Coordinator (UNDRO) has often referred to the logistical challenges that temporary responses pose to relief strategies in the wake of disasters. They define different stages in which the material response progressively acquires thickness. This definition applies to the first-day emergency response (which is measured in hours and days), the building of places for early recovery (projected in terms of months), and then the construction of more resilient settlements (conceived in terms of years). In this case, the parallel between temporary urban thinking and the material condition for the response is inevitable, as the biggest problem is that relief strategies are often generated by the lack of coordination between temporal and spatial thinking.

The question of disaster management has historically been focused on the standard of shelter and the efficiency of the response. Today the discussion is much more nuanced. The intention for the ephemeral response to actually be transitory is not always achieved. We often see cases in which people quickly leave the temporary accommodation in an attempt to return to the place that was previously devastated. The self-relocation of communities back into vulnerable places often happens after flooding disasters and is one of the challenges that is faced regularly. The tension between the top tier of the managing structure and people's aspirations creates a tension between what is feasible, reasonable, and what is actually done. Therefore, ephemeral landscapes of strife are less about deployment and disassembly, and more about the negotiation between people and institutions for reconciling the capacity of communities for the managing of their own crises, and the impulse of the top-down structures for managing crises in pragmatic yet unsustainable ways.

The idea of the camp as a structure for the "management" rather than "enabling of life" is also present in other taxonomies of ephemeral urbanism. One of the clearest examples of this could be found by looking at the range of temporary cities built for the exploitation of natural resources in mining, oil extraction, and forestry. The scope of extractive activities, like the ones in operation at camps that have more than 10,000 temporal dwellers – the Yanacocha mine in Peru, the Maritsa Iztok Mines in Bulgaria, the Motru Coal Mine in Romania, and Chuquicamata in Salvador, as well as the Pelambres sites in the north of Chile – generate completely different sorts of temporary settlements. Additionally, the complexity of dealing with environmental consequences and incredibly large-scale operations that constantly modify the topography of a temporary landscape at a territorial scale presents a huge design and management challenge.

In these cases, the life cycle of temporary cities aligns with the duration of the extractive activity and the presence of the resource. Therefore, most of these settlements are developed knowing that they have a predictable expiration date. This is a form of urbanism at the service of global economic flows, which determine the patterns of growth in relation to the demand for commodities based on access to natural resources. A considerable portion of the urban development happening in countries with commodity-based economies is defined by human occupation linked to extractive practices. These practices are sometimes connected to existing communities in which resources are present or preexisting infrastructure is utilized. In this sense, ephemeral landscapes of extraction are a by-product of the extractive activity, which being local in its operation is determined by global needs and aspirations. They emerge as highly efficient systems that maximize productivity, optimize processes, and produce automatized and standardized results.

As other ephemeral settlements, the extractive camp has the capacity to be constructed within a short period of time. It can also be deconstructed at the same speed, simply by inverting the constructive process. The camp as a configuration of settlements allows spaces to actively respond and react to the flows of people, transportation, goods, and communication while facilitating efficiency to the extent possible for the basic need of the urban space. However, within the camp paradigm, lightness goes beyond the domain of the material conditioning and political institutions as well as the society itself. Material lightness is often accompanied by the thinness of institutions, the predominance of the private, and the tendency to eliminate any element which does not serve efficiency and productivity. Are camps, or cities – in the contexts of natural resource extraction – really always meant to be consumers, destined for obsolescence and disappearance? Accepting this condition forces us to contend that settlements supporting extractive territories are destined to not be cities. Rather they are merely camps struggling to fulfill their aspirations of becoming cities. This is an aspiration that is rarely – if ever – accomplished, perhaps because camps (or camp-like cities), with regards to extraction, are inherently by-products of consumption practices.

Consumption, however, in other contexts can be an important activator of urban life and play a key role in community formation as also sometimes functioning in making society more politically meaningful, representative, and democratic through temporary uses of the urban space. We now focus on impermanent spaces that emerge not in urban configurations supporting the extraction of resources but in the spaces that support the exchange of production with the resources we extract. This leads to the construction of a category of ephemeral landscapes of transaction. These landscapes are a series of impermanent responses and provoke us to think about the role of transaction in the construction of the urban landscape. These are cases with much more accelerated time durations than landscapes that are constructed for extraction. Unlike the hundreds of years that we see in the assembling and disassembling or reabsorption of settlements supporting extraction, transactional spaces are often resolved in much more accelerated time spans, emerging and disappearing in a week, a day, an hour, or even in the sequential iterations of a few minutes.

Therefore, the landscape of ephemeral-transactional spaces is composed of cases that adapt space for transactions through a series of different strategies that respond to market fluctuations or emergent opportunities. The most obvious manifestation of this is the phenomenon of off-street vendors and other forms of mobile/flexible goods suppliers that have become ubiquitous in cities around the globe. As a more fluid response for transactional spaces and practices, ephemeral solutions provide the systemic robustness and often help to soften thresholds between diverse groups present in the urban space. The cases could cover a plethora of strategic approaches of temporary space occupation that goes from a more traditional and controlled linear occupation of streets, to farmers markets, to much more complex responses of infrastructural networks that support trade. These take the form of extreme clusters of vendors in isolated areas, unusually reversible infrastructure, unexpected juxtaposition of uses, and a series of responses that allow ephemeral landscapes of transaction to combine with more permanent or institutionalized frameworks within the city.

Landscapes of transactions work at very different scales. Starting with the street hawker who incrementally constructs his own flexible space for trans-actions, to the massive grounds, that allow in one large space the presence of many small sellers, giving space to an unusual economic diversity. This happens in cases like La Salada in Argentina. La Salada is an informal flea market where vendors sell mostly textiles. Twice a week, this ephemeral space for transactions triggers a powerful economy in which many home-based manufacturers sell their products to wholesalers who come from across the country. The market borders the Matanza River, occupying empty warehouses located on the riverbank. It is the largest market in Argentina, generating twice the profit than that of a regular shopping center of the same scale, and employing about 6,000 people including security, maintenance, and administrative staff. In this way, the ephemeral occu-pation of space is really an important component of the local economy. Inter-national borders are immaterial limits that often foster the emergence of ephemeral landscapes of transaction. The same pluralistic expression that is created by a field condition hosting many small traders is also what we find in Ciudad del Este, a big market zone located between Paraguay, Brazil, and Argentina, at the confluence of the Iguassu and Parana rivers.

These cases provoke us to think about urbanism is a different way. The city clearly needs to find alternative ways to give space to a more pluralistic economy, allowing flexible functional occupations to generate micro operations that activate the urban landscape. Referring to this, Martha Chen advocates,

> What is needed, most fundamentally, is a new economic paradigm: a model of a hybrid economy that embraces the traditional and the modern, the small scale and the big scale, the informal and the formal. What is needed is an economic model that allows the smallest units and the least powerful workers to operate alongside the largest units and most powerful economic players.
>
> (Chen, 2012)

The range of potential cases in this taxonomy might help us to find the agency of urban design and planning for intervening in such conditions. The factors that allow home-based producers to be inserted in global value chains has to do with controlling barriers of entry, and securing them in relation to risk. In this regard, design and planning policies act in tandem with spatial paradigms to support these conditions. Simple operations might allow street vendors to coincide and even improve the way in which big retailers and wholesalers do business. The gathering of evidence on a massive scale and the fundamental functionality of ephemeral landscapes affect contemporary cities in both developed and emergent economies.

This should influence us to include their attributes into the urban imaginary. In this regard, Chen's insightful commentary propels us towards this imagination: "Some years ago, the world embraced biodiversity – and still does. Today, the world needs to embrace economic diversity. Both are needed for sustainable and inclusive development" (Chen, 2012).

The temporary has increasingly provided a strategic set of tools for designing the city by posing as surrogate ecology for cities, some of which have not registered in the business-as-usual discussion about urbanism. The ephemeral expresses itself in highly diverse manners and is deployed across a huge range of scales, from the small infill within the preexisting and more permanent city, to the construction of ephemeral megacities hosting millions of people. Here, the urban landscape does not necessarily adhere to its traditional quest for permanence, but it is rather a pulse, assembling and disassembling itself in a reversible manner according to needs and opportunities, market demands and resources, and the restrictions and aspirations of its inhabitants. Its scope therefore goes far beyond the problems of a material nature, since it can be conceptualized as a diverse paradigm in the production of space. One that in its least radical and more visible expression is an enabler of critical, social, and economic processes in the city that shed light on alternative strategies of development. This is true when referring to transactions, celebrations, or even ephemeral religious landscapes. They support all sorts of processes within and outside the city, in which impermanence seems to be a precondition. This is clear when we refer to cases of strife, when it works as a transitory enabler for construction and reconstruction of the city, or when we find the temporary as main physical response for the support of celebratory practices.

Examples of ephemeral landscapes, as for instance those of celebration, religion, or transaction, present us with a bottom-up condition that leads to the unfolding of "action" in the city. The ephemeral enables "action" as it has the power to transform and activate spaces. The many forms of the ephemeral, which of course exceed the cases mentioned in this chapter, support the functioning of the contemporary metropolis as the place of specialized and unexpected relations. The ephemeral paradigm of space coexists with the robust attributes of the permanent, allowing for the creation of a more fluid occupation of the territory. In the context of ephemeral urbanism, extraction, refuge, and the military are linked in the way that the spatial categories they represent express the temporary as an absolute and multidimensional condition evolved from mechanisms of control, management, and in a way, of contemporary modalities of conquest. This implies a highly efficient system that maximizes productivity, optimizes processes, and produces automated and standardized results. It is the perfect embodiment of the paradigm, one that does not allow for accumulation and that goes to the other extreme, becoming a site of passage dominated by efficiency. Indeed, it is efficiency that drives the layout of these sites and the organization of logistics and the spatial configuration. It is the same efficiency that constructs the conditions for life itself to thrive, for "action" to retreat to become a secondary human activity.

The space, in which the efficiency matrix subjugates "action," blurs the indistinctive threshold of what is juridical and ethically acceptable. It is in this context that we are challenged by the need to develop tools for intervening and thinking about these non-permanent configurations. Tools that will propel us to establish a productive understanding of the aspirations that define the patterns of growth and use and the emerging form of occupation in the broader global territory. Urban design must find a way to return to this space of human "action," with meaningful political intervention in these landscapes that fall under the realm of ephemeral urbanism. Ephemeral urbanism can then be both the problem, when it adopts an absolute condition under the camp paradigm; or the solution, when it emerges in coexistence with permanent aspirations of a thick social fabric. Then the ephemeral will truly offer a productive and creative force that serves the imagination as well as construction of a more nuanced and inclusive urban space.

Note

1 For a more detailed description see Mehrotra and Vera (2013).

References

Agamben, G. (1998). The camp as nomos. In D. Heller-Roazen (trans.), *Homo sacer: Sovereign power and bare life.* Stanford, CA: Stanford University Press.

Agier, M. (2011). *Managing the undesirables.* Malden, MA: Polity.

Branzi, A. (2015). *From radical design to post-environmentalism.* F. Vera & J. Sordi (Eds.). Santiago: ARQ Ediciones.

Chen, M. A. (2012). The informal economy: Definitions, theories and policies. *Women in informal economy globalizing and organizing: WIEGO Working Paper, 1.* Retrieved June 28, 2017, from http://wiego.org/sites/wiego.org/files/publications/files/Chen_WIEGO_WP1.pdf.

Mehrotra, R. (2008). Negotiating the static and kinetic cities: The emergent urbanism of Mumbai. In A. Huyssen (Ed.). *Other cities, other worlds: Urban imaginaries in a globalizing age* (pp. 113–140). Durham, NC: Duke University Press.

Mehrotra, R., & Vera, F. (2013). Reversibility. *FunctionLab, 720*(04). Retrieved June 28, 2017 from http://functionlab.net/wp-content/uploads/2014/06/720_Reversibility.pdf.

UNHCR (2015). *World at war: UNHCR global trends: Forced displacement 2014.* Retrieved February 15, 2016, from http://unhcr.org/556725e69.pdf.

4 Cities as systems of networks and flows

Michael Batty

Cities are places where populations cluster to engage in economic exchange usually around a central market which represents an efficient point of distribution in a wider hinterland where various goods are produced. Our cities still manifest this age-old role where central business districts (CBDs) and retail centres are the modern day equivalents of the market place and where multiple transport networks of both a physical and ethereal kind serve to tie people together to share the fruits of their labours through contemporary production and social processes. Although networks underpin this rational for cities, the dominant focus for the last century or longer has been on searching for patterns in the location of different activities with populations defined largely by radial routes and concentric rings that still dominate the morphology of the contemporary city. Location has taken pride of place to interactions or networks, largely because it is easier to see a pattern in location and because cities, certainly until the industrial revolution, manifested very close associations between the networks of distribution that defined their roles in exchange and the patterns of location that emerged to support these networks.

Yet focusing predominantly on location gives an entirely false sense of what cities are all about. Although most cities still have well-defined central cores that function to tie economic and social activities together, the networks that sustain these cores are becoming ever more complex, diversified, and diffuse. In a world that is fast globalising, it is no longer possible to trace the ramifications of the networks that support our cities in the simpler local manner which defined an earlier world. For example, even though world cities still have very strong CBDs, the amount of activity in such cores is often considerably less than in the rest of the city. Even in a strongly monocentric city like London which has about 4 million jobs in its administrative area, only half of these are located in its extended CBD with the other half scattered around the rest of the metropolis. If we then add to this the amount of traffic which criss-crosses the metropolis and then consider the vast amounts of electronic information that are transmitted daily through the city from all over the globe, then trying to understand the functioning of the city purely on the basis of its patterns of location poses enormous limits on our understanding. It is imperative that we move well beyond an understanding that is primarily locational.

Location then in cities is no longer and probably never has been the essential focus: it is interactions between locations – actions that involve two or more locations. Locations can be seen as aggregations or agglomerations of interactions, clusters of people for example who work in a location but live elsewhere, retail customers who shop in a centre but live elsewhere, clusters of commodities that are delivered to centres of production from a more remote and wider hinterland, and so on. Add to this the myriad of flows that involve the transfer of electronic information and it is easy to see how complex such a constellation of urban functions might be with little chance that location by itself even approaches the understanding necessary for us to grasp how such systems work (Batty, 2013). Flows of people and commodities represent material interactions and tend to be more visible than electronic flows that occupy the ether which makes them much less visible. As these varieties of flow proliferate in a global world, the complexity of cities becomes ever greater and the challenge to our understanding ever more daunting.

Historical antecedents

The first maps of cities were largely phrased in terms of locations. Their networks were very tightly coupled with their use of land with densities and city sizes limited by technologies of movement which before the industrial revolutions were based on walking or horse-riding. Villages tended to be no farther than 10 km apart and the biggest cities never reached more than a few hundred thousand persons but were much more compact in structure than today and at a much higher density. The invention of the internal combustion engine changed all this and very well-defined physical networks to take trains and automobiles had come to dominate the city by the early 20th century. This enabled a disconnect between location and transportation with populations able to exercise much more choice over their location and the ways in which they interacted and engaged with activities and social groups. The earliest maps can be intuitively guessed from stone age cave paintings but by 1500 BCE, maps were appearing on clay tablets in ancient Mesopotamia and we show one of these for the city of Nippur in Figure 4.1(a). These maps implicitly represent rudimentary networks although it was not until the Renaissance in Italy that speculations about networks in cities were made by scholars such as Leonardo da Vinci who was amongst the first to conceive of cities as analogous to the human body and its networks. Leonardo's maps however embedded networks into street blocks and vice versa, with his 1502 map of the city of Imola as good an example as one might find of urban form in the Medieval and Renaissance city (Figure 4.1(b)).

The idea of energy flowing through the city and binding its parts together gained massive momentum with the advent of the industrial revolution. Once machines for moving goods and people became widespread, a hierarchy of networks emerged for rail and then for road and in the 20th century, the airline network has reinforced the emergent global hierarchy of communications. The idea of abstracting the network began some 200 years ago. In empirical terms, Harness's map of traffic in the Pale of Dublin in 1837 shown in Figure 4.2(a)

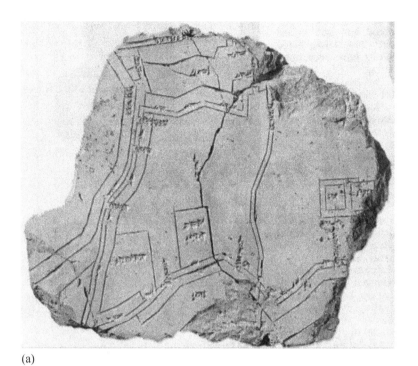

(a)

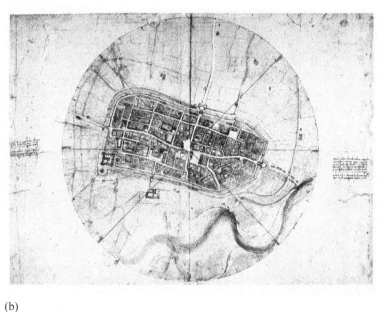

(b)

Figure 4.1 (a) A map of the city of Nippur on a clay tablet 13th century BCE; (b) Leonardo da Vinci's 1502 map of the Italian city of Imola.

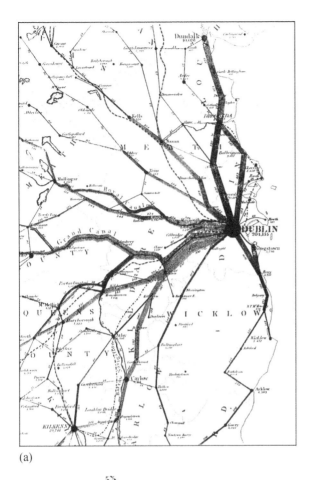

(a)

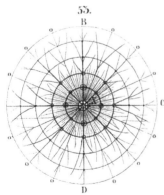

(b)

Figure 4.2 The earliest abstracted city networks.

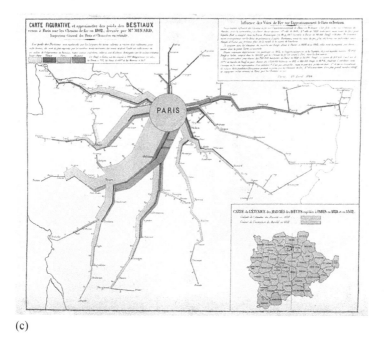

(c)

CURRENTS OF MIGRATION.

(d)

Figure 4.2 Continued.

abstracted flows to what are now called 'desire lines', while Kohl's idealisation of the network structure of a town produced in 1840 and illustrated in Figure 4.2(b) quite clearly defines the role of hierarchy in the dendritic – fractal – street network. Minard's maps produced in the 1850s assigned these kinds of flow to actual networks as in Figure 4.2(c), and then Ravenstein in 1888 abstracted these flows even more by defining average vectors of migration to illustrate dominant movement patterns and to simplify the necessary visualisations (Figure 4.2(d)).

Throughout the 19th and 20th centuries, networks delivering energy of various kinds dominated the form of the city with physical channels becoming dominant features in the urban landscape. Generally, these systems radiated from the traditional central cores of cities and at different scales as cities grew bigger, peripheral routes – ring roads and beltways – began to appear with new urban cores in peripheral locations growing in places where the accessibility of various locations was massively improved through the confluence of various transport hubs. The dominant form of the city moved during the 20th century from strongly monocentric to polycentric based on a combination of single towns growing into one another to form metropolitan agglomerations and new 'edge' cities appearing at points where their hinterland of population demand has reached the point where intense developments of retail and commercial activity could be easily sustained. To an extent, the development of cities by the late 20th century had begun to reveal a world in which most of us would be living in cities by the end of this century with the proportion passing the halfway mark in 2008. It is into this context that many new electronic networks that dramatically change the focus of location and interaction have emerged.

Cities, systems, and the biological analogy

The last century was largely dominated by the idea that the city could be treated as a machine. But as far back as Leonardo, there were glimmerings of metaphors and analogies between the city and the body in terms of the flow of blood, the nervous system, and many other space-filling organisms (Sennett, 1994). Victor Gruen's (1965) book *The Heart of Our Cities* impressed the idea that the city could be seen as a network of flows delivering energy to its parts. He went further in articulating this in terms of location saying "I can visualize a metro-politan organism in which cells, each one consisting of a nucleus and a proto-plasm, are combined into clusterisations to form specialised organs like towns". His analogy with the flow of blood has generated many animations from the flow of traffic over the diurnal cycle which are reminiscent of the pulsing of the heart but focused on distinct peaks and troughs in such activity which reflect the morning and evening peaks. We cannot show such animations here on the printed page but it is worth referring the reader to Reades' (2010) visualisation (https://vimeo.com/41760845) for it demonstrates that cities function more as biological systems than machines.

Flows are thus complementary to networks and although traditionally such flows have been hard to measure, as the world becomes ever more digital, such flows can be measured routinely often in real time as in the 'blood flow' maps of traffic noted above. To an extent, networks as physical infrastructures are easier to measure and only now is it possible to measure physical traffic that uses such networks in any complete way. Really complex systems built on networks with many nodes encapsulate flows that require visualisations involving assignments of the kind first pictured by Harness and Minard shown in Figures 4.2(a) and 4.2(c). But better pictures of the functional structure of locations require vector flows of the kind first implied by Ravenstein in Figure 4.2(d). In Figure 4.3 we show such flows based on the journey to work between small census units at two scales – for England and Wales where the hierarchy of towns is quite clear and for metropolitan London and the south east where the monocentric bias of the city is very clearly evident. The vectors here are based on movements from home to work and are scaled proportionality to the average flow from each node in the network to all others. The direction is an average of all the directions from the place in question.

The idea that form is composed of flows is as old as science itself. Plato is credited with saying that: "All is flux, nothing stays still" while as we have already noted, Leonardo da Vinci speculated that landscapes mirrored the fluid flows in the structure of the human body, his paintings often reflecting the pattern of water and its turbulence in the landscape. Contemporary landscapes in populated places reflect not only physical flows but also human, and a particularly intriguing perspective is the one that seeks to integrate patterns in form that are woven together by human and physical movements. These ideas are not new. Nearly a century ago, Benton MacKaye defined regional landscapes as being a synthesis of flows originating from geological and climatic changes through which agricultural patterns had evolved, thence being influenced by man-made structures. This viewpoint he expressed in his book *The New Exploration* (1928) where he proceeded to define how the old evolved into a new urban landscape. He articulated this approach using a model of flow which we will extend and apply in terms of our discussion here. This is strangely prescient to our current concerns for capturing and simulating what is happening in cities using many of the new digital tools that now allow us to articulate and visualise complexity in ways that could only be imagined in the bygone age.

MacKaye's model of a developed urban landscape assumes a bounded hinterland or basin which is drained physically in terms of what he called its indigenous structure. The flows that characterised this landscape were of everything from water to people, all usually focused on some sink point, often the centre of a market – the CBD – where physical flows discharge. This he called the *inflow*. In almost symmetrical but opposite fashion, he defined the *outflow* as the movement of peoples and materials out from the market to the hinterland, arguing that these two reversible sets of flows, when balanced, defined a sustainable landscape: a pattern of circular flows mirroring production and consumption. He then argued that this sustainability was in fact being destroyed in contemporary urban systems by a *backflow* which results when too much activity is attracted to the sink – when cities, for example, become so large that their economies of agglomeration

(a)

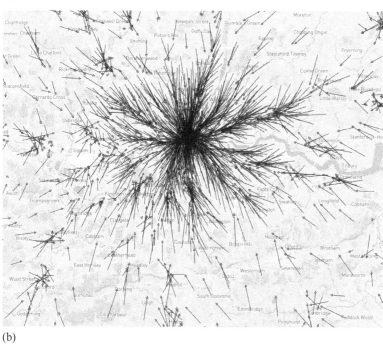

(b)

Figure 4.3 Predominant vector flows from home to work: (a) England and Wales; (b) Metropolitan London.

disappear and diseconomies of scale set in. In fact, in the evolution of such a landscape, he talks of a *reflow* that is a second wave of inflow but in essence, his model is one which treats any landscape as a complex co-evolution and convolution of these flow patterns. As our concern with location per se has lessened and as networks have become the key organising concept on which urban form is built, outflows and inflows, backflows and reflows are rapidly establishing a new vocabulary around which to discuss contemporary spatial organisation.

We picture MacKaye's outflows for Boston in Figure 4.4(a) which was based on the emergent sprawl of the expanding metropolis. There are many such pictures which mirror the centralising and decentralising forces and fluxes in the city but nowhere are they as clear as in the detailed digital traces that can now be routinely archived and measured from a variety of passive and active digital devices. In Figure 4.4(b) we show streams of geotagged photographs from Flickr captured by Fischer (2016) over a five-year period which provide a detailed digital trace of how people have perceived the visual structure of the city though their photographs.

Although telecommunication networks have been significant in cities for nearly a century, there are a surprisingly limited number of examples of such networks which have been measured and visualised. With the advent of email which became significant in the late 1980s, first in academic and scientific environments, and the web from the mid 1990s on, there is now a plethora of digital networks underpinning the form of cities and regions but still a very limited number of measurements or visualisations. Fischer's Flickr feeds and his visualisation of tweets are typical examples but invariably these visualisations are locations not interactions. It is extremely hard to extract network data from social media data for interactions from social networks must be inferred while most such data is not geotagged in any case. Data from mobile phone calls does generate network flow data although the networks tend to be invisible with transmissions through the ether while financial flows in terms of online marketing and sales, flows of capital, and so on are exceptionally hard to observe. Thus there are few examples of such visualisations and this reveals a major problem in understanding how the physical and informational worlds underpinning the functioning of cities actually work. This problem is getting ever more severe as more and more information technologies are coming to dominate the way we live in cities, and this is part of the growing complexity of urban form and function which provide some radically new challenges to our understanding of the contemporary and future city. The visualisations that do exist of such electronic traces do not reveal much that is different from our view of cities as physical networks and flows (for example, see Lenormand et al., 2015). But as yet, so little has been observed and so much of the physical stock of cities is long lived and inert compared to the volatility of electronic and informational flows, that we do not have any sense of whether or not cities will blow themselves apart as this century progresses or become denser and more clustered due to the impact of new information technologies.

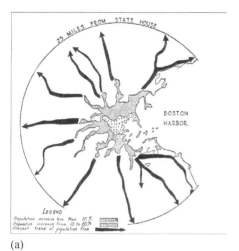

(a)

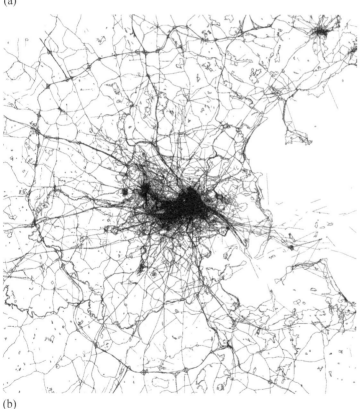

(b)

Figure 4.4 Force and flux in the modern metropolis: (a) MacKaye's image of outflows of population in Boston in the 1920s; (b) Fischer's geotagged photographs from Flickr connected from adjacent streaming.

Complexity and information in cities

The notion that cities evolve rather than are manufactured, growing from the bottom up rather than being planned from the top down, is a necessary abstraction that serves to emphasise that the organic analogy is more appropriate than the machine analogy. As we have implied, the idea of cities being ordered in a strict hierarchy with a distinct controller – the planning system – was the basis on which our understanding was based over half a century ago. This has given way to almost the exact opposite with evolution becoming the key construct in the way cities develop, mirroring and impressing the messages of old such as that due to Patrick Geddes (1915), Jane Jacobs (1961) and Christopher Alexander (1965) amongst many others (Batty & Marshall, 2016).

A consequence of complexity thinking is that cities get ever more complex as they grow. This is beyond complicatedness in that cities change qualitatively as they get larger and as their form adapts to embrace more and more human and physical interactions. The increasing globalisation of cities, the emergence and elaboration of many new kinds of digital interaction, and the growth of artificial intelligences alongside natural and human structure is leading to ever greater complexity, often at a rate that outstrips our understanding of what is happening to urban form and function. It is worth giving this theme a little more coherence in terms of interaction patterns and locations and to this end we will introduce albeit very briefly the standard measure of information that was defined by Shannon (1948) some 70 years ago.

Let us divide a city into places or locations that we define by the indices i and j. There are n such places and a reasonable assumption is that as this number of places grows – which is a synonym for city or population size – the complexity of the city also grows. So complexity or information $I(n)$ is proportional to size n. The simplest measure of complexity which is a starting point – but as we will see is not the best measure – is to assume that the probability of occupying or locating in a place i is p_i. The information or complexity of the city is thus the weighted sum of the logs of these probabilities, that is $I(n) = -\sum_i p_i \log_e p_i$. This is Shannon's famous formula: when everyone lives in one place and the probability of occupying that place is 1 and the probability of occupying every other place is 0, then the information or complexity is at a minimum where $I(n) = 0$. When there is an equal probability of occupying a place and no one place is preferred to any other, then $p_i = \dfrac{1}{n}$ and it is easy to show that the information is at a maximum, that is $I(n) = \log_e n$.

Now what all this means is as follows. When everyone lives in one place, then one might envisage everyone living at a point where the density of population is at a maximum and the density everywhere else is zero. This implies a very strong and well-defined structure to the city with no flexibility and thus this is a simple but almost impossible order to envisage. It is like everyone living in Frank Lloyd Wright's mile-high skyscraper – the Illinois – that he proposed and sketched in 1957. It is in fact still a physical impossibility. However, if everyone lives where they like and there is no preference for any location over any other, then the city is spread at even density over the landscape of *n* locations. The information or complexity is thus said to be at a maximum. Of course in this chapter, we have argued that locations must defer to interactions but this simplest of measures does reveal that as *n* gets bigger – as the city grows, the complexity or information imparted gets greater. These ideas are not that new. Richard Meier (1962) argued very much along the same lines in the early computer age in his book *A Communications Theory of Urban Growth.*

We can now generalise our measure to deal with patterns of interaction. Now let us assume that there is a probability p_{ij} of locating in any one place *i* and interacting with another place *j*. If all of these probabilities were zero except one which is the single place where everyone interacted with one another (in the mile-high tower, for example), then the information or complexity would be zero. Shannon's formula now becomes $I(n) = -\sum_{ij} p_{ij} \log_e p_{ij}$ which is equal to zero when $p_{ii} = 1$, $p_{ij} = 0$ where $j \neq i$. Now let us assume a situation where location no longer matters and everyone interacts with one another with the same probability between any two places in the system, then the probabilities are all the same, that is $p_{ij} = \dfrac{1}{n^2}$ and the information or complexity is at a maximum $I(n) = 2\log_e n$. The same considerations apply as in the one-dimensional case: as *n* gets bigger, complexity grows but at a decreasing rate. What might enhance this argument, and we will explore this in a moment, is the fact that new technologies are being introduced as additional network layers of complexity as cities grow and as humankind invents more and different ways of communications, and this gives added impetus to the argument.

In some respects, we might think of the preindustrial city as mirroring the simplest possible arrangement – everyone living and interacting with each other in the same place. In contrast, the post-industrial city is one where everyone interacts with everyone else in different places. A world where the 'death of distance' has taken place and where spatial interaction is frictionless. This kind of global society that our cities are fast embracing would appear to be nearer to what we see now. The industrial city is somewhere between, in a world where distance does matter, and in a world where everyone interacts with some core location – the CBD. We can actually measure actual physical urban forms and movement patterns in this way. Our two extremes bounded by $0 \leq I(n) \leq 2\log n$ define the limits but if we say assume that $p_{ij} = Kd_{ij}^{-2}$ where *K* is some normalising constant, then it is easy to show that the complexity of this typical city system of the industrial age has a complexity somewhere between the two limits. In fact we have computed this for the greater London area where we have divided the city into n = 633 zones noting that the upper level of complexity is $I(n) = 2\log_e 633 \cong 12.9$. The actual measured complexity from the simple model is $I(n) \cong 5.62$ and this is a good deal smaller than the upper bound, illustrating that things would have to spread out much more for London to become truly globalised where distance no longer mattered. In fact, London is a strongly monocentric city. Somewhere like Phoenix would be closer to its upper bound. However, to give this argument greater realism, we need to enhance our measure of complexity with a much richer discussion of different varieties of networks, ethereal as well as physical.

Cities as multiple networks carrying a diversity of flows

In network engineering, multiplexing is the art of combining several different communications media into single channels or at least channels that serve to contain two or more different varieties of flow. In fact, from the earliest settlements of any kind, physical tracks and trails have been used for more than a single purpose. Walking and riding on horseback while using other augmented animals for travel are basic and once the industrial revolution began, all kinds of devices based on the internal combustion engine came to occupy the same road space. In fact, railways were always designed around special purpose tracks as were trams but on the rail network, different types of train used the same track while roadways came to be increasingly divided and reserved for special movements, especially for longer distance travel. The last half century has seen the emergence of flexible spaces within cities where different kinds of movement use different kinds of space at different times. Programming use with respect to local conditions has also become popular, as in congestion or cordon charging at different times of the day.

It is however the emergence of largely invisible electronic networks that represents the greatest challenge. The telegraph was the first all-purpose network but thence came the telephone, radio, and television. But all these networks were passive in that users could mainly receive but only in special circumstances could they use such media actively in a two-way sense. The telephone perhaps is an exception but prior to the digital computer there was little or no interactivity where information could be up- and down-loaded and then altered on-the-fly. The invention of new forms of networking such as the Ethernet and then the Internet changed all this and for the last 20 or more years, the world has been increasingly networked using a general purpose technology that enables vastly diverse flows of information to be transmitted for multiple purposes.

It is quite clear that we use different networks in a coordinated way to progress many tasks from work to entertainment. The study of cascades that ripple or rush through such networks is in its infancy but there is no doubt that different networks are activated purposively reflecting a mixture of processes that pertain to the physical movements of energy and the ethereal movement of information. How these link to one another is extremely problematic for we have little sense of how these kinds of multiplexed flows can be measured and visualised. How these are represented and embedded in space and time pose difficulties as well. What information we have is largely derived from disasters and disruptions of various shapes and sizes especially in terms of disruptions to electrical supply systems (Buldyrev, Parshani, Paul, Stanley, & Havlin, 2010). We are but at the beginning of how to map and observe the operation of these many physical and electrical networks that define the city.

To conclude, then cities can no longer be explained in terms of locational patterns. To the extent they have in the past, this has always been an oversimplification of how cities evolve and form. Traffic of any kind is a function of land use as Mitchell and Rapkin (1954) argued just prior to the development of the first transportation models. Physical channels – road and rail and related fixed track – together with wired electrical systems taking email, web, etc. dominate the urban landscape. Combined with specialist data from point of sales and such like with sensors embedded in the terrain and in the built environment are providing a constant stream of data all of which is hard to integrate. On top of this, many electronic transactions are now based on Wi-Fi systems with the picture of who communicates what and in which way becoming ever more confused. The imperative is for a concerted effort to provide new ways of integrating all this diversity and this is rapidly becoming a major issue for a future science of the smart city (Batty, 2013).

References

Alexander, C. (1965). A city is not a tree. *Architectural Forum, 122*(1) (April), 58–62 (Part I), and *Architectural Forum, 122*(2) (May), 58–62 (Part II).

Batty, M. (2013). *The new science of cities*. Cambridge, MA: MIT Press.

Batty, M., & Marshall, S. (2016). Thinking organic, acting civic: The paradox of planning for *Cities in Evolution*. *Landscape and Urban Planning*. Retrieved June 28, 2017, from http://dx.doi.org/10.1016/j.landurbplan.2016.06.002.

Buldyrev, S. V., Parshani, R., Paul, G., Stanley, H. E., & Havlin, S. (2010). Catastrophic cascade of failures in interdependent networks. *Nature, 464*(7291), 1025–1028.

Fischer, E. (2016). *The geotaggers' world atlas*. Retrieved June 28, 2017, from www. flickr.com/photos/walkingsf/sets/72157623971287575/.

Geddes, P. (1915). *The evolution of cities*. London: Williams and Norgate.

Gruen, V. (1965). *The heart of our cities: The urban crisis: Diagnosis and cure*. London: Thames and Hudson.

Jacobs, J. (1961). *The death and life of great American cities*. New York: Random House.

Lenormand, M., Louail, T., Cantú, O. G., Picornell, M., Herranz, R., Arias, J. M., ... & Ramasco, J. J. (2015). Influence of sociodemographic characteristics on human mobility. *Scientific Reports, 5*(10075).

MacKaye, B. (1928). *The new exploration*. New York: Harcourt and Brace.

Meier, R. L. (1962). *A communications theory of urban growth*. Joint Center for Urban Studies of the Massachusetts Institute of Technology and Harvard University. Cambridge, MA: MIT Press.

Mitchell, R. B., & Rapkin, C. (1954). *Urban traffic: A function of land use*. New York: Columbia University Press.

Reades, J. (2010). *Pulse of the city*. Retrieved June 28, 2017, from https://vimeo. com/41760845.

Sennett, R. (1994). *Flesh and stone: The body and the city in western civilization*. London: Faber and Faber.

Shannon, C. (1948). A mathematical theory of communication. *Bell System Technical Journal, 27*(July and October), 379–423, 623–656.

5 Urban-rural relations in the post-urban world

Hans Westlund

I'll begin with the following hypothesis: Society has been completely urbanized. This hypothesis implies a definition: An *urban society* is a society that results from a process of complete urbanization. This urbanization is virtual today, but will become real in the future.

(Lefebvre, 2003, p. 1)

[T]he city region is not just an expression of globalization but represents a more fundamental change in the urbanization process, arising from the regionalization of the modern metropolis and involving a shift from the typically monocentric dualism of dense city and sprawling low-density suburbanization to a polycentric network of urban agglomerations where relatively high densities are found throughout the urbanized region.

(Soja, 2011, p. 684)

[A]s property size increases in a built environment, so does the distance between various land uses, and thereby the amount of movement required for the same amount of exchange and interaction. To fulfil the increased need for movement between places, the domains dedicated to transportation are expanded, in length and breadth, creating even greater distances between land uses.

(Hägerstrand & Clark, 1998, p. 25)

The first quote above is the first sentences in Henri Lefebvre's book *The Urban Revolution*, published in French in 1970 but not until 2003 in English. In the introductory chapter he summarized the results of this complete urbanization:

[A]gricultural production has lost all its autonomy in the major industrialized nations and as part of a global economy. It is no longer the principal sector of the economy, nor even a sector characterized by any distinctive features (aside from underdevelopment).... as a result, the traditional unit typical of peasant life, namely the village, has been transformed. Absorbed or obliterated by larger units, it has become an integral part of industrial production and consumption.... In this sense, a vacation home, a highway, a supermarket in the countryside are all part of the urban fabric. Of varying density, thickness, and activity the only regions untouched by it are those that are stagnant or dying, those that are given over to "nature" ... Small and midsize cities became dependencies, partial colonies of the metropolis. In this way my hypothesis serves both as a point of arrival for existing knowledge and a point of departure for a new study and new projects: complete urbanization. The hypothesis is anticipatory. It prolongs the fundamental tendency of the present.

(Lefebvre, 2003, p. 3f)

As Lefevbre's book was not published in English until 2003, his "anticipative" statements were for a long time only known in the French-speaking world. During the counterurbanization of the 1970s (see, e.g., Beale, 1975; Champion, 1992), his claims were also provoking and contentious. However, during the scant half-century since Lefevbre published his book, development itself has proved that he indeed was on the right track, both theoretically and empirically. Society has become "completely urbanized." From the year 2008 more than 50% of the world's population has been living in cities (The World Bank, 2016). Currently there are about 500 cities with over one million inhabitants in the world and it is estimated that in the year 2030 the number will be 663 (The Globalist, 2015).

The second quote above is from Edward Soja. Soja (2000) discussed the transformation of cities and suburbs in terms of "postmetropolis" regions, mainly based on experiences of the transformation of Greater Los Angeles. One of the features of the postmetropolis regions are, according to Soja, a globalization of the urban population, resulting both in "the most culturally and economically heterogeneous cities the world has ever known" (Soja, 2011, p. 683) and in increased social and political polarization. However, this increased heterogeneity is paralleled with a "homogenization of built environments, visual landscapes, and popular tastes and fashions" (Soja, 2011, p. 683). "Suburbia and suburban ways of life are changing, becoming more dense and heterogeneous [in demographic and economic terms], more like what the urban used to be" (Soja, 2011, p. 684). The result is the transformation of big cities from dense centers with sprawling low-density suburbs, to polycentric city regions with relatively high density all over.

The third quote above is a remark by Thorsten Hägerstrand and Eric Clark. Their observation reflects another feature of global urbanization, namely the transformation of dense cities to considerably sparser city regions that include not only urban activities and land use but also former rural activities and land use that have been integrated in "the urban fabric." The transformation of cities to city regions is a process in which market and planning have gone hand in hand. Markets of labor, housing, and daily consumption (including leisure) have been spatially extended by the population increase caused by urbanization, but spatial extension without extended transportation infrastructure soon comes to a halt. Planning and construction of infrastructure for trams, railroads, subways, cars, buses, and trucks made the forming of functional city regions possible – and the extended transportation infrastructure has also made non-planned spatial extension of the city regions, like urban sprawl, possible.

The three quotations might seem almost incompatible, but it is more reasonable to say that they underscore different aspects of the urban transformation to a post-urban world. Lefebvre discussed the urbanization of society at large in economic, social, and cultural terms and how also rural areas are integrated in this process, but he wrote his book before the age of globalization and he left the aspects of density outside his analysis. Soja emphasizes the transformation of the city-suburb dichotomy to polycentric city regions with much more equalized population density than in the previous stage. Hägerstrand's and Clark's remark about the increased need for movement between places concerned the density issue at another spatial level. However, it is also strongly connected to the role of transportation infrastructure for the "region enlargement" outside the city-suburban fringe that takes place as a result of improved transportation supply.

The notion of a post-urban world leads not only to a wide range of issues on the future of integrated city regions and their internal and external networks. The fact that neither the urban nor the rural is what it was, also leads to questions on the future of urban-rural relations. This chapter starts with an overview of how urban-rural relations have been interpreted in spatial theories from the pre-industrial era and onwards. It thereafter discusses urban-rural relations in the knowledge economy and the dissolution of the urban-rural dichotomy in the post-urban world. Finally, possible development strategies for the peripheral countryside to avoid turning back "over to nature" are discussed.

From concentric rings to sprawling city-networks

The urban-rural dichotomy has existed ever since the origin of cities, i.e., when the agricultural surplus was large enough to feed agglomerations of non-peasants. In the pre-industrial economy, cities remained small (with a few exceptions) and agriculture's productivity low. When von Thünen (1826) presented his theory on the isolated state, around which the variations in land use could be described in the form of concentric rings, it meant the foundation for spatial economic theory. The city and its hinterland existed in a harmonic, mutual relationship, where the countryside produced for the city and land use was determined by the yield of the land, the products' prices, and the costs for production and transportation to the city. The theory described the major spatial relation of the pre-industrial economy, i.e., the hinterland's agricultural production (and production's location) for the market in the city.

The agricultural and industrial revolutions were the signals to a wave of urbanization that changed urban-rural relations considerably. The growing cities demanded increasingly more foodstuff, building materials and firewood from their hinterlands and in addition they demanded raw material for their industries. All this meant that the development of cities and their hinterlands went hand in hand. Christaller's (1933) central-place theory extended von Thünen's theory from a single center and its hinterland to a multitude of central-places at hierarchical levels. Central-place theory also included the service sector that had developed within the manufacturing-industrial economy – but manufacturing itself was left outside central-place theory. Instead, the location theory of manu-facturing industry developed along another strand of thought in which the contri-butions of Hoover (1948), Launhardt (1885), Lösch (1940), Palander (1935), and Weber (1909) were important landmarks. A common feature among these works was the focus on the spot of production and the costs of inputs, production, and transportation at that spot. The hinterland was no longer a fixed area, but varied with the type of production. Another important difference from central-place theory was that the location theories of manufacturing also laid an emphasis on the market outside the center of production. This was a recognition that the centers of production, the cities, not only interacted with places of higher or lower order in the strict hierarchy, but with the rest of the world. Still, these loca-tion theories were based on the traditional industrial manufacturing with exploitation of raw materials, transportation of them to the production site, the processing of them to semi-factures or final products, and the transportation to their markets.

The knowledge economy has brought tremendous changes to this relationship. Agriculture and exploitation of raw materials have changed from labor intense to capital intense activities which has meant that the demand for labor in these rural sectors has decreased to a small fraction of what it was. Simultaneously, the trans-formation of the cities' economies to knowledge economies means that the input from the rural hinterlands stands for an ever decreasing share of cities' inflows, and that the share of cities' production that finds its markets in the hinterlands steadily is decreasing. The emergence of the knowledge economy has therefore brought new theories. It is no longer the single industry that is in focus, but the agglomerations of production and consumption – cities – and the interaction between them. Within the broad field of spatial sciences, various approaches on city-systems (Pred, 1977), world cities (Friedmann & Wolff, 1982), global cities (Castells, 1996; Sassen, 1991), city-networks (Taylor, Catalano, & Walker, 2002), global city region (Scott, 2001a, 2001b), and global mega-city region (Hall & Pain, 2006) have been launched by leading scholars of different disciplines. Today, these approaches and their implications are more or less taken for granted, but, as pointed out by Taylor and Derudder (2015), they reflect a very different world than the paradigm that was dominating half a century ago, the central-place theory. The "city-networks" theories have replaced central-place theory as the dominating models; as a consequence of that relations and exchange of the city-networks have become so much more important than the relations and exchange between a city and its rural surroundings. This circumstance has brought this "urban revolution" in the spatial sciences.

The main theoretical approaches for spatial interaction in the pre-industrial, the industrial, and the knowledge economy were briefly summarized above. What are the causes behind this transformation from predominating central-place–hinterland relations to the city-networks of today? A general explanation might be *the transition from regional and national pre-industrial and manufacturing-industrial economies to a global knowledge economy* (Westlund, 2006). The generally small cities of the pre-industrial world were in most cases totally dependent on their hinterlands for food, building material, and firewood. The few larger cities were those who had developed networks with the rest of the world – by colonization, conquests, and trade, but still their hinterlands were highly important for them. Industrialization meant growth of many existing cities as well as emergence of many new ones. The classic industrialization was based on exploitation of natural resources. They could be transported on water or by the new means of transportation, the railroad, but there were often obvious cost-minimizing reasons to exploit them on site in the home region and then transport the finished products to their markets. In this way, the vast majority of cities in both the pre-industrial era and during the manufacturing-industrial period were based on the dominating production factors of the periods, which were local or regional natural resources.

The knowledge economy is in many ways different from its predecessors. One of the most important differences is that human capital, i.e., people with knowledge and skills, has replaced raw materials and physical capital as the main production and location factor. This has far-reaching consequences. Natural resources and raw materials are no longer driving forces for regional development, as they can be exploited by "fly-in-fly-out" workforce. The most important location factor for the knowledge economy's enterprises is instead trained work-force – which usually is found in large cities and university towns. Large, diversified labor markets become a key location factor for both businesses and labor, while also other attractive features as e.g. amenities are increasing in importance in the competition between cities.

Another key difference between the knowledge economy and the manufac-turing economy is the big cities' relationships to smaller cities and rural areas. The manufacturing economy built to a large extent on regional raw materials, which created a certain balance between urban and rural areas. The development of peripheral rural areas during the manufacturing economy can be considered supporting Innis' (1930) and North's (1955) staple-base theory. Exogenous demand for natural resources, energy, and agricultural products brought incomes for consumption and investment to the centers of exploitation – but changes in the capital/labor ratio or/and diminishing demand subsequently turned expansion to retrogression.

The knowledge economy has created very different relationships between city and countryside. The booming big cities have been transformed into city regions in which neighboring smaller cities, towns, and pure countryside have been integrated and become a part of the functional region, for which the possibilities of commuting has become a decisive factor for the size of the region. Outside the big cities are mainly large areas of countryside and smaller cities and towns that decrease in population. As a rule, these large areas lack sufficient concentra-tions of the now most important production factor, namely human capital, which means that labor markets remain small and that the knowledge economy has dif-ficulties to grow there.

The emergence of metropolitan regions where small towns as well as rural areas are included, while other, more peripheral rural areas and smaller cities ends "outside" means that the traditional urban-rural dichotomy has disappeared. The cities that grow are decreasingly functioning as the centers for their rural areas they once were, but increasingly as centers of multi-functional regions and nodes in border-crossing city-networks. Cities, towns, and rural areas that fall outside the expansive regions have in a relative sense less and less to offer the city regions and their global networks. If they cannot create new exchanges with these city regions, based on what the expanding regions are demanding, they end up in a downward spiral.

It should of course be pointed out that the rural surroundings of the city regions still are of importance for the cities. Many people work in the city but live in the countryside. This means that the relations between the city and the city-close countryside in certain aspects even have been strengthened and that the city-close countryside has become an integrated part of the city region. However, cities' (positive) influence on their surrounding regions decreases with distance. The potential for living in the countryside and working in the city depends on commuting time. Swedish studies (Johansson, Klaesson, & Olsson, 2002) have shown that the share of commuters decreases rapidly after one hour's commuting time. Even though the acceptable commuting time varies between countries and regions due to traditions and social conditions, the general pattern that commuting is decreasing with distance is undisputable.

It could also be argued that cities need agricultural products and building material, and that city dwellers relax happy in their summer houses in the countryside – but these once strong city-hinterland linkages are now urban-rural relations of a much wider context, far beyond what was the former hinterland. Dairy products, bricks, and construction timber are today subjects of a trade which is much more extended than intraregional. Hinterland firewood for heating the city houses during winter was once the single main commodity of many cities' inflows, but is now totally replaced by other, non-hinterland, energy resources. Rural summer houses in cities' rural environments are still important nodes for the extension of urban influence and demand to the surrounding region, but with increasing incomes, proximity has become less important for the leisure house market, which has become international and obtained a network character.

To sum up, the transformation from an agricultural, over a manufacturing-industrial, to a knowledge economy has meant dramatic changes of urban-rural relations. This is reflected both in the "real" economy and in the spatial-economic theories. With the "complete urbanization" cities have become less and less dependent on their former hinterlands and more and more dependent on their links to other cities. We have come to a point where it is necessary to ask the question: Is the traditional urban-rural dichotomy applicable at all on the relations between the current city regions, and the areas outside them? This issue will be discussed in the next section.

The dissolution of the urban-rural dichotomy in the post-urban world

The above described development can be summarized in three points:

- Cities have developed from small, isolated islands in seas of countryside to city regions being nodes of global city-networks. Their interactions with the hinterlands outside the city region have gradually decreased in importance and are with "complete urbanization" becoming almost negligible.
- These conversions are strongly related to the prevailing type of economy of each period. During the agricultural period, cities were heavily dependent on foodstuff from their hinterlands. In the industrial economy cities were still strongly dependent on foodstuff and raw material from the hinterlands but increasingly also on markets and inputs from other cities. In the current knowledge economy, the dependency on hinterlands' foodstuff and raw material is small while the dependency of exchange with other city regions has multiplied.
- This transformation of urban-rural relations is reflected in the predominating theoretical spatial-economic paradigms of each period.

Figure 5.1 depicts cities' major economic linkages during the three economic periods. Figure 5.1a shows the linkages between the market in the isolated city in the pre-industrial period and the agricultural hinterland's various belts of production, marked by rings. Figure 5.1b illustrates on the one hand that cities were larger during the industrial period than previously. The industrial and agricultural revolutions had changed urban-rural relations dramatically. Increased agricultural productivity meant that the countryside could feed much larger urban populations. The industrial production in the growing cities became the other side of this new relationship, with an urban-rural exchange at multiple levels compared with the pre-industrial epoch. On the other hand, Figure 5.1b illustrates cities' linkages to both their hinterlands and to other cities that now act both as markets for cities' production as well as sources of input for this production. Figure 5.1c marks that the predominating relationships of cities in the knowledge economy are those between cities, while the relations to the former hinterlands have withered down to negligibility. This is an aspect of the complete urbanization that Lefebvre anticipated. The urban-rural dichotomy has been dissolved. However, if the urban-rural dichotomy, expressed in the form of city and hinterland, has ceased to exist, how is this claim compatible with the examples given in the second section of rural-urban commuting, rural summer houses, and rural leisure activities? The answer is that the former rural hinterlands, with the "complete urbanization" and the predominance of city-networks, have ceased to exist as the prime provider of cities' foodstuff and raw material, and with this they have ceased to exist as traditional hinterlands. Instead, the rural areas that surround cities have developed into two completely different types of areas: those that have become "part of the urban fabric" and "those that are stagnant or dying, those that are given over to 'nature'" (Lefebvre , 2003, p. 3).

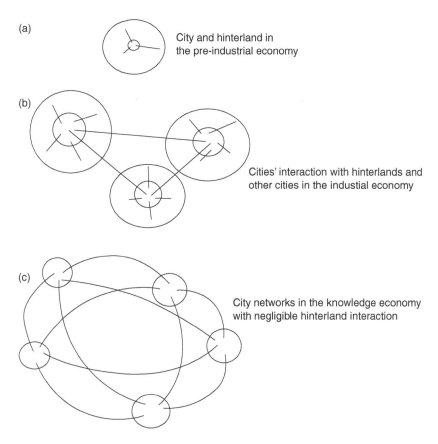

(a) City and hinterland in the pre-industrial economy

(b) Cities' interaction with hinterlands and other cities in the industial economy

(c) City networks in the knowledge economy with negligible hinterland interaction

Figure 5.1 Cities' major spatial-economic linkages in: (a) the preindustrial economy; (b) the industrial economy; (c) the knowledge economy.

The first type of rural area, the city-close countryside, has become a part of the city regions through region enlargement. It is completely urbanized in all aspects but density of housing and population (although this peri-urban country-side is more densely populated than the rural periphery). Otherwise, the inhabit-ants have urban occupations, values, norms and culture, consumption patterns and lifestyles. This transformation of the city-close countryside is particularly in Great Britain referred to as "gentrification," based on the fact that a conspicuous group of the inhabitants are out-migrated upper middleclass people enjoying a combined urban-rural lifestyle (see e.g. Phillips, 1993). However, it is not only former rural areas that are objects of this transformation. Also "small and midsize cities became dependencies, partial colonies of the metropolis" (Lefeb-vre, 2003, p. 3). Thus, these city-close parts of the former hinterlands become integrated in the expanding city regions. This development not only transforms parts of the former rural hinterlands to component parts of the urban system – it also transforms the big cities to city regions with a multitude of densities and activities, among them also certain forms of agriculture that becomes an "urban agriculture."

For the other type of rural areas, beyond commuting distance to the growing city regions' labor markets, the development potential is significantly lower. Are they, in Lefebvre's words, slowly being "given over to 'nature'"? The next section discusses possible strategies for the rural peripheries in the post-urban world.

Possible strategies for the rural peripheries

The basic perspective is that cities, towns, and rural areas that are located outside the positive influence of the city regions lack any potential for endogenous growth and development and that only exogenous demand for their products or resources can stimulate their economies to grow (Westlund & Kobayashi, 2013). Exogenous demand for foodstuff, raw material, and energy made many of these areas flourish during the industrial epoch, but ever increasing capital intensity in production has reduced the need for labor in these sectors to a small fraction of what it was. Still, exploitation of ore, oil shale, and other minerals makes certain peripheral areas thrive – as long as the deposits are profitable to exploit – even if increasing parts of the labor force are fly-in fly-out labor.

The growth of the tourism industry has brought attention to the concept of amenities. Amenities can be defined as qualities of a place or a region that make it attractive for living and/or working in (Green, Deller, & Marcouiller, 2005; Power, 1988). From the definition it follows that amenities are not only attractive for visitors, but also for in-movers and permanent residents in an area. Even if exploitation of natural resources still is of importance in a number of rural areas, there has been a shift in rural economies from resource extraction to use of amenities and there are examples in the US that counties with a high amount of natural amenities have experienced high employment growth in a broad range of service sectors (Green et al., 2005; Shumway & Otterstrom, 2001). In an international research overview, Naldi, Nilsson, Westlund, and Wixe (2015a) draw the conclusion that rural areas that are endowed with natural amenities seem to have a better growth potential compared to other areas. A Swedish study (Naldi, Nilsson, Westlund, & Wixe, 2015b) showed that external local conditions and local amenity supply are important factors in determining the rate of new firm formation. A comparison of urban and rural neighborhoods showed that the supply of nature- and culture-based amenities were relatively more important in explaining new firm formation in rural regions, compared to urban regions.

However, even if certain rural areas have natural and cultural amenities that can make them attractive for tourism or as residential areas, amenities per se are not enough. It must be possible for tourists to get to the amenity-rich areas at reasonable costs and it must be possible for residents in these areas to commute to work in cities. Business life in amenity-rich areas must have access to the urban markets through good transportation infrastructure and broadband connections. Without infrastructure for communication and transportation rural development will be impossible.

Several studies have shown that social networks and other aspects of social capital are of significance for growth in rural communities. Kilkenny, Nalbarte, and Besser (1999) showed the importance of reciprocated community support for the growth of small businesses in small towns of Iowa, USA. Eliasson, Westlund, Fölster, Westlund, and Kobayashi (2013) found a positive relationship between business owners' opinion on the quality of the local business-related social capital and economic growth in the municipalities of Sweden, and that the importance of social capital decreased with municipality size. However, there are also studies that indicate that local collaboration is not enough to achieve rural development. In a study of Swedish, small food producing firms, Naldi, Nilsson, Westlund, and Wixe (2017) showed the importance of extra-local and extra-regional connections for rural firms' innovation. This indicates that rural firms can compensate for lower accessibility by building links to non-local and non-regional actors and markets.

Concluding remarks

The emergence of the post-urban world has meant a fundamental change in urban-rural relations. The city-close countryside has become integrated in the city regions while the peripheral countryside is, with certain exceptions, less and less needed by the city regions. Just like developed countries have their largest exchange with each other rather than with developing countries, the cities that have expanded to become city regions have the largest exchange with each other rather than with their former outer hinterlands. Distance-bridging networks have replaced linear distance as the main principle for spatial interaction. For the survival of peripheral rural areas this is indeed a challenge.

References

Beale, C. L. (1975). *The revival of population growth in nonmetropolitan America*. Economic Research Service, publication 605, US Department of Agriculture, Washington, DC.

Castells, M. (1996). *The rise of the network society: The information age: Economy, society, and culture* (Vol. 1). New York: John Wiley & Sons.

Champion, A. G. (1992). Urban and regional demographic trends in the developed world. *Urban Studies, 29*(3–4), 461–482.

Christaller, W. (1933). *Die zentralen Orte in Süddeutschland: Eine ökonomisch-geographische Untersuchung über die Gesetzmässigkeit der Verbreitung und Entwicklung der Siedlungen mit städtischen Funktionen*. Jena: Gustav Fischer

Eliasson, K., Westlund, H., Fölster, S., Westlund, H., & Kobayashi, K. (2013). Does social capital contribute to regional economic growth? Swedish experiences. In H. Westlund & K. Kobayashi (Eds.), *Social capital and rural development in the knowledge society* (pp. 113–126). Cheltenham, UK: Edward Elgar.

Friedmann, J., & Wolff, G. (1982). World city formation: An agenda for research and action. *International Journal of Urban and Regional Research, 6*(3), 309–344.

Green, P. G., Deller, S. C., & Marcouiller, D. W. (2005). Introduction. In P. G. Green, S. C. Deller, & D. W. Marcouiller (Eds.), *Amenities and rural development: Theory, methods and public policy* (pp. 1–5). Cheltenham, UK and Northampton, MA: Edward Elgar.

Hägerstrand, T., & Clark, E. (1998). On the political geography of transportation and land use policy coordination. Transport and Land-use Policies: Resistance and Hopes for Coordination. *COST, 332,* 19–31.

Hall, P., & Pain, K. (2006). *The polycentric metropolis*. London: Earthscan.

Hoover, E. M. (1948). *The location of economic activity*. New York: McGraw Hill.

Innis, H. A. (1930). *The fur trade in Canada: An introduction to Canadian economic history*. Toronto: University of Toronto Press.

Johansson, B., Klaesson, J., & Olsson, M. (2002). On the non-linearity of the willingness to commute. Retrieved June 29, 2017, from www-sre.wu.ac.at/ersa/ersaconfs/ersa02/cd-rom/papers/476.pdf.

Kilkenny, M., Nalbarte, L., & Besser, T. (1999). Reciprocated community support and small town-small business success. *Entrepreneurship & Regional Development, 11*(3), 231–246.

Launhardt, W. (1885). *Mathematische begründung der volkswirtschaftslehre*. Leipzig: BG Teubner. English translation: *Mathematical principles of economics* (1993).

Lefebvre, H. (2003). *The urban revolution*. Minneapolis: University of Minnesota Press. (French original first published 1970).

Lösch, A. (1940). *Die räumliche Ordnung der Wirtschaft: Eine Untersuchung über Standort, Wirtschaftsgebiete und internationalen Handel*. Jena: G. Fischer.

Naldi, L., Nilsson, P., Westlund, H., & Wixe, S. (2015a). What is smart rural development? *Journal of Rural Studies, 40,* 90–101.

Naldi, L., Nilsson, P., Westlund, H., & Wixe, S. (2015b). What makes certain rural areas more attractive than others for new firms? The role of place based-amenities. Paper presented at the 18th Uddevalla Symposium, June 11–13, 2015, Sonderborg, Denmark.

Naldi, L., Nilsson, P., Westlund, H., & Wixe, S. (2017). Disentangling innovation in small food firms: The role of external knowledge, support, and collaboration. *CESIS WP Series No. 446*. Retrieved July 6, 2017, from https://static.sys.kth.se/itm/wp/cesis/cesiswp446.pdf.

North, D. C. (1955). Location theory and regional economic growth. *Journal of Political Economy, 63*(3), 243–258.

Palander, T. (1935). *Beiträge zur standortstheorie* (Doctoral dissertation, Almqvist & Wiksell).

Phillips, M. (1993). Rural gentrification and the processes of class colonisation. *Journal of Rural Studies, 9*(2), 123–140.

Power, T. M. (1988). *The economic pursuit of quality*. Armonk, NY: M.E. Sharpe.

Pred, A. (1977). *City-systems in advanced economies: Past growth, present processes, and future development options*. New York: Halsted Press.

Sassen, S. (1991). *The global city. New York, London, Tokyo*. Princeton, NJ: Princeton University Press.

Scott, A. J. (Ed.). (2001a). *Global city regions: Trends, theory, policy*. Oxford: Oxford University Press.

Shumway, J. M., & Otterstrom, S. M. (2001). Spatial patterns of migration and income change in the Mountain West: The dominance of service-based, amenity-rich counties. *Professional Geographer, 53,* 492–502.

Scott, A. J. (2001b). Globalization and the rise of city regions. *European Planning Studies, 9*(7), 813–826.

Soja, E. W. (2000). *Postmetropolis: Critical studies of cities and regions.* Oxford: Blackwell.

Soja, E. (2011). Regional urbanization and the end of the metropolis era. In G. Bridge & S. Watson (Eds.), *The new Blackwell companion to the city* (pp. 679–689). Oxford: Blackwell.

Taylor, P. J., Catalano, G., & Walker, D. R. (2002). Exploratory analysis of the world city network. *Urban Studies, 39*(13), 2377–2394.

Taylor, P. J., & Derudder, B. (2015). *World city network: A global urban analysis* (2nd ed.). London: Routledge.

The Globalist. (2015). *Just the facts. World's million-people cities.* Retrieved June 29, 2017, from www.theglobalist.com/world-million-people-cities-china/.

The World Bank. (2016). *Urban population.* Retrieved June 29, 2017, from http://data.worldbank.org/indicator/SP.URB.TOTL.IN.ZS.

Thünen, J. H. von. (1826). Der isolierte Staat. *Beziehung auf Landwirtschaft und Nationalökonomie.* Hamburg: Perthes.

Weber, A. (1909). Über den Standort der Industrie. 1. Teil: Reine Theorie des Standorts. Tübingen. English translation: On the location of industries, 1929. *Theory of the location of industries.* Chicago: The University of Chicago Press.

Westlund, H. (2006). *Social capital in the knowledge economy: Theory and empirics.* Berlin, Heidelberg, New York: Springer.

Westlund, H., & Kobayashi, K. (2013). Social capital and sustainable urban-rural relationships in the global knowledge society. In H. Westlund & K. Kobayashi (Eds.), *Social capital and rural development in the knowledge society* (pp. 1–17). Cheltenham, UK: Edward Elgar.

6 Reflexive neoliberalism, urban design, and regeneration machines

Paul L. Knox

Global cities, particularly those in the West, are being quietly recast through coalitions and partnerships of real estate, finance, construction, and professional interests: 'regeneration machines' that draw on international capital and markets while engaging locally in tactical politics around land-use regulation, policy, and decision-making. These regeneration machines are a product of the reflexive neoliberalism of national and metropolitan governments and of the increasingly international dimension of inter-urban competition. Regeneration machines have replaced large tracts of metropolitan fabric and displaced their occupants. In the process the design professions – themselves implicated in regeneration machines – have been realigned, adopting new professional orthodoxies and abandoning old ones (Carmona, 2009; Madanipour, 2006).

Urban planning had already been emasculated by the first-wave neoliberalism of the 1980s. The postwar settlement that had seen the creation of welfare states, the ascendance of progressive city planning, and the appearance of everyday modernism in social housing estates amounted to a secular Reformation. It was overturned by a Counter-Reformation in the form of neoliberalism. As a result, planning practice became estranged from theory, divorced from any broad sense of the public interest and pragmatically tuned to economic and political constraints rather than being committed to change through progressive visions. The old reciprocity between society and state was denied: 'There is no such thing as society', declared Margaret Thatcher (1987, p. 10). It was everyone for themselves as the state's role switched from that of a regulator of markets and provider of welfare services to that of a facilitator of markets and agent of business. Communities and individuals would have to take responsibility for the conduct of their own lives. An early outcome of neoliberalism was the dismantling of national regulatory frameworks that had been designed to counter the consequences of uneven economic development. Instead, cities and regions were encouraged to compete more vigorously for private-sector investment. Other early initiatives of neoliberal policy included the deregulation of finance, cutbacks in redistributive welfare programmes, the sale of social housing, the privatization of public space, the introduction of curbs on the power and influence of labour unions and government agencies, and the privatization of transport systems and utility services (Sager, 2011).

Combined with the pressures of urban economic restructuring, this marked the beginning of the end of the golden era of city planning. The idea that cities could be successfully planned and managed along with the economy and society as a whole had become increasingly suspect among both politicians and the general public. The seed had been planted long before by Jane Jacobs: *The Death and Life of Great American Cities* (1961) played a significant role in tarnishing US social housing and urban renewal programmes. Urban form would henceforth follow market forces, and planners and urban designers would simply 'smooth' the rough spots. No longer able to afford grand schemes, cities turned to planning departments to assist in branding rather than in shaping real change. Stripped of their authoritative technocratic position and their comprehensive social mandate, planners were left to broker public-private partnerships and 'smart growth' strategies whose purpose and direction was almost always dominated by a private sector that had begun to boom, thanks to the 'new economy' that came to dominate Western countries in the 1980s.

In the decades that followed, neoliberalism was firmly established as the new orthodoxy, with successive governments reflexively developing policies that were grounded in assumptions about the efficiency of markets, the primacy of property ownership, and the responsibilities of individuals for their own welfare. The assault on the norms, values, and institutions of the postwar settlement was portrayed as a necessary precondition for securing a competitive advantage in the context of globalization. In lieu of progressive social programmes there emerged a discourse on the importance of resilience, in which the emphasis was on individual adaptability, self-reliance, and responsible decision-making (Coaffee, 2013; Hudson, 2010). The poor, along with vulnerable groups, economically depressed regions, and deprived neighbourhoods, were pathologized and blamed for their own failings. In the new orthodoxy, cities and local communities had to become responsible, resilient, and entrepreneurial.

While city planning professionals struggled to find a role in the everyone-for-themselves political economy of the 1980s and 1990s, architecture and urban design took on new roles. In the 'dream economy' (Jordan, 2007) of 'romantic capitalism' (Campbell, 1987) and supercharged, debt-fuelled consumerism, the design of the built environment became intimately involved with many aspects of metropolitan change. Ritzer (2005), following Baudrillard, Debord, and others, has pointed to the importance in contemporary material culture of spectacle, extravaganzas, simulation, theming, and sheer size. As Gospodini noted (2002), whereas in the past the quality of the built environment had been a by-product of economic development, it now came to be seen to be a prerequisite for it. A corollary of providing a good business climate, for many globalizing cities, was the promotion of urban design, iconic architecture, and trendy cultural quarters. Flagship projects, 'starchitecture', and monumentality in urban design were seen as necessary for cities that wanted to compete in a globalized post-industrial service economy (Knox, 2011). They also fit neatly with an embedded, reflexive neoliberalism: transforming the image of metropolitan centres while distracting from the reality of increased social polarization; and providing convenient precedents for granting exceptionality measures to planning and policy procedures (Cuthbert, 2005; Hackworth, 2007; MacLaren & Kelly, 2014).

The Sydney Opera House had provided an early example (1973) of the ability of a high-profile building of radical design to put a city on the global map. Shortly afterwards, the success of the Centre Georges Pompidou, built between 1971 and 1977 in the run-down Beaubourg area of Paris, created what Baudrillard, Krauss, and Michelson (1982) called a 'Beaubourg Effect'. Subsequently, cityscapes across much of the developed world began to be recast through urban megaprojects, flagship cultural sites, conference centres, big mixed-use developments, waterfront redevelopments, heritage sites, and major sports and entertainment complexes. Evans describes this as 'hard branding' and notes that without good urban design it can result in 'a form of Karaoke architecture where it is not important how well you can sing, but that you do it with verve and gusto' (2003, p. 417). As Julier (2005) notes, hard branding has resulted in the serial reproduction of signature buildings by 'name' architects as cities compete for global status through the erection of landmark towers. In the celebrity-oriented global culture that is now pervasive, about all it takes for 'signature' status is for a building to be the product of a cover-shot architect. When the building is also dramatic and/or radical in design, it can re-brand an entire city and elevate its perceived status within the global economy. This is, famously, what happened in Bilbao. The city was one of the first to develop a strategy of featuring signature structures as symbols of modernity and an affect of economic revitalization. It began with Frank Gehry's Guggenheim Museum, part of a riverside redevelopment scheme, the master plan for which was devised by César Pelli, Diana Balmori, and Eugenio Aguinaga. Other notable developments included a 35-storey office tower (César Pelli); the Euskalduna Juaregia conference centre and concert hall (Federico Soriano and Dolores Palacios); the Bilbao International Exhibition Centre (César Azcárate); a new metro system with striking fan-shaped entrances (Norman Foster); a new airport (Santiago Calatrava); a footbridge spanning Nervión River (also Calatrava); and the 'Gateway' project, a mixed-use quayside development containing luxury flats, cinemas, and restaurants (Arata Isozaki). The net effect was to trigger a 'Bilbao Effect' as other cities attempted to rebrand themselves and spark urban regeneration through the promotion of culture and design (Bell & Jayne, 2003). Every city, as Sharon Zukin put it (2010, p. 232), wanted a 'McGuggenheim'.

Corporations as well as municipalities took note, commodifying world-famous sites and ensembles of signature structures into corporate 'brandscapes' (Klingmann, 2007). Examples include Times Square in New York City and Potsdamer Platz in Berlin, both redeveloped through public-private partnerships in the early 1990s. Times Square, master-planned by Robert A. M. Stern, is now strongly linked to the identity of the Disney corporation, which has orchestrated a setting that draws – in an edited and sanitized way – on the history of the locality as a vibrant entertainment district. It is dominated by 'New York Land', a themed shopping area split among three properties owned by the Disney, Warner

Brothers, and Ford corporations. Potsdamer Platz, redeveloped to a plan by architect Renzo Piano, became strongly linked to the identities of Daimler and Sony (though Daimler subsequently sold its 19 buildings at the heart of Potsdamer Platz to the Swedish banking group SEB).

The most comprehensive exercise in metropolitan rebranding is surely that of Milan. Struggling with the combined effects of a banking industry that was losing ground to London and Frankfurt and the deindustrialization of its engineering and manufacturing industries, Milan has reinvented itself as a global capital of design (Knox, 2014). Underpinned by municipal policy and investment, the Milan metropolitan region shifted from manufacturing to product design and product development, taking advantage of the combination of the region's distinctive ecology of small firms, artisans, and workshops. The city also fostered its association with high-end prêt-à-porter menswear and womenswear, generating a workforce of more than 60,000. In order to achieve this, parts of the city and its infrastructure were redeveloped by coalitions of public authorities and private-sector developers. Most significant in this context was the construction of a new trade fair complex, the Fiera, with more than 475,000 square metres of exhibition space, designed by architect Massimiliano Fuksas at a cost of €750 million. In 2015 Milan hosted a World Exposition at the Fiera, an event that prompted a great deal of additional urban redevelopment as well as a new platform for city branding. Meanwhile, part of the city's old exhibition complex is being redeveloped into the 'CityLife' residential and business district, with proposed skyscrapers by starchitects Daniel Libeskind, Zaha Hadid, and Arata Isozaki. Other culture-led regeneration projects in the city include extensive facilities for the design faculties of the Politecnico di Milano in the former industrial district of Bovisa; the redevelopment of another derelict industrial district, Bicocca; around the campus of the new University of Milan-Bicocca; and the development of the industrial area adjacent to Garibaldi station as Città della Moda.

Spectacle and re-enchantment

Amid the aestheticization of everyday life of the 1980s and 1990s, architecture became unmoored from the canons of Modernist design. Postmodern architecture, well suited to the cultural sensibilities of neoliberalism, began to flourish. Whereas Modern architecture was attuned to the ascetic, future-oriented, universalistic, and utopian sensibilities of the postwar settlement, postmodern architecture played on the hedonistic, impulsive, and narcissistic sensibilities of increasingly materialistic societies. Postmodern design was a response to changing economic and social conditions, a facet of the 'society of the spectacle' in which the symbolic properties of places and material possessions took on unprecedented importance. But after some very visible and, mostly, unfortunate excursions into postmodernism, the predominant genre of new commercial architecture, speculative residential towers, and apartment buildings reverted to a techno-lux version of Modernism, its formerly clean lines embellished with balconies, terraces, sundecks, and various 'interesting' shapes with extensive use of glass, zinc sheeting, coloured concrete, and corrugated panels. Architecture critic Owen Hatherley (2010) described the effect as 'Pulp Modernism'.

Meanwhile, a distinctively reactionary and regressive design response emerged in the form of the so-called New Urbanism and suburban residential developments in neotraditional style. The packaged landscapes of 're-enchanted suburbia' (Knox, 2010) were perfectly suited to the shift in social, cultural, and political sensibilities that occurred with the rise of neoliberalism. Ironically, New Urbanism relies entirely on prescriptive codes and conventions, embedded in a series of trademarked regulatory documents: 'Regulating Plans', 'Urban Regulations', 'Architectural Regulations', 'Street Types', and 'Landscape Regulations'. In the deterministic reasoning of New Urbanism, design codes become behaviour codes and social exclusion masquerades as communality. David Harvey (2000), borrowing from Louis Marin's (1990) analysis of Disneyland, described the packaged landscapes of master-planned communities and the New Urbanism as paradigmatic 'degenerate utopias'. Like Disneyland, they are designed as harmonious and non-conflictual spaces, set aside from the real world. Like Disneyland, they incorporate spectacle and maintain security and exclusion through surveillance, walls, and gates; and, like Disneyland's Main Street, they deploy a sanitized and mythologized past in invoking identity and community. All of this is 'degenerate', in Harvey's view, because the oppositional force implicit in the progressive and utopian ideals embraced by the design professions has mutated, in the course of materialization, into a perpetuation of the fetish of commodity culture.

Regeneration machines

The neoliberal response to neighbourhoods at the other end of the socio-economic scale has been to upgrade the built environment and introduce middle-class residents or, better still, demolish whole sections and replace them with profitable housing. Gentrification, of course, has been the most pervasive process in this context: leading edge of neoliberal urbanism. While first- and second-wave gentrification was arguably driven by the intersection of economic, demographic, and cultural trends, facilitating gentrification clearly became a common urban strategy for city governments around the world. Catering to the emergent lifestyle and cultural choices of a mobile and expansive creative class, it was believed, would salvage the fortunes of struggling cities and declining inner-city districts (Florida, 2002). Then, as Neil Smith noted, a third wave of gentrification based on new-build projects 'evolved into a vehicle for transforming whole areas into new landscape complexes that pioneer a comprehensive class-inflected urban remake'. This was what brought regeneration machines into being:

> gentrification as urban strategy weaves global financial markets together with large- and medium-sized real-estate developers, local merchants, and property agents with brand-name retailers, all lubricated by city and local

governments for whom beneficent social outcomes are now assumed to derive from the market rather than from its regulation.

(Smith, 2002, p. 443; see also Davidson & Lees, 2010)

Low-income neighbourhoods that have proven resistant to gentrification – tracts of run-down social housing, in other words – have required a more explicit neoliberal policy based on the notion of promoting 'social mix' or 'social balance'. The terms derive from the idealistic beginnings of urban design and planning, championed by the likes of Ebenezer Howard, Clarence Perry, and Raymond Unwin. But the current use of the term is euphemistic rather than naïve. Social mix now means gentrifying social housing, replacing troublesome communities with a critical mass of better-off households in new or renovated housing. The US Federal Department of Housing and Urban Development's HOPE VI (Home Ownership and Opportunities for People Everywhere) pro-gramme is a good example (Hanlon, 2010). In the 25 years following the intro-duction of the policy in the early 1990s more than $6 billion was allocated to HOPE VI Revitalization grants. Most involved 'mixed-finance' partnerships between the public, private, and non-profit sectors. In terms of urban design, many were given a New Urbanist flavour. In this way, gentrification was rein-vented as 'urban regeneration' (Bridge, Butler, & Lees, 2012).

Early precedents like Hope VI soon gave rise to powerful regeneration machines involving governments working with private partners to facilitate property-led development across all sorts of devalued settings, from disused railway yards to run-down housing estates. Like the classic urban growth machines described by Logan and Molotch (1987), they involve coalitions and partnerships among government, finance, property, and construction interests that seek to encourage and secure investment in (re)development projects and engage in tactical politics around associated land-use regulation, housing and environmental policies, and decision-making. But, in addition to local actors and agents, contemporary regeneration machines also involve central government agencies, international capital, and international corporate interests. Today, fin-ancial, real estate, and design services for major metropolises are dominated by international suppliers capable of creating and shaping global cityscapes. Together they create both the demand for office buildings and supporting infra-structures (mixed-use retail, entertainment, restaurants, etc.) and organize their supply, thereby adding a global dimension to the web of actor interrelations in the local development process. This increasing interlinkage among finance, busi-ness, and professional design services at a global scale is explicitly evident at the Marché international des professionnels de l'immobilier (MIPIM) property fair held annually in Cannes, where the top real estate and architecture firms with global aspirations come together. Some regeneration machines are framed around the rhetoric of socially mixed housing while others are framed around technologically 'smart' infrastructure; and others still around the essentially neo-liberal concept of creating resilient cities. Few are articulated within a metropolitan-wide approach to strategic planning.

Regeneration machines involve a broad spectrum of actors and institutions, all embedded in time- and place-specific social relations. The specific actors will vary from one context to another and the relations among actors and institutions need to be understood in terms of their linkages within a specific local socio-political ecology and economic structure as well as the broader context of economic, social, and cultural change. These sets of relations represent 'structures of provision' (Ball & Harloe, 1992) in urban regeneration. They are locally embedded yet national and often transnational in character. Key local actors include banks and financiers, construction firms, engineering firms, planning and urban design consultants, realtors, local government agencies, elected officials, utility companies, technical subcontractors, planning and design consultants, chambers of commerce, and non-profit agencies. These all rely, however, on the mobilization of capital and expertise by central governments and national or international level investment companies, property development companies, real estate companies and engineering conglomerates like AECOM, Blackstone, Bechtel, CBRE, Savills, and Siemens. The range of actors and agencies involved in such projects means that the outcomes are typically mediated by way of a 'post-politics' that stifles conflict and dissent through carefully choreographed processes of technocratic management and orchestrated public participation (Swyngedouw, 2009) as well as relying on the 'silent complicity' that exists among architects, planners, and urban designers in relation to the agendas of the politically and economically powerful (Dovey, 2000; Gunder, 2010). This symbiotic relationship with capital is mobilized through (increasingly multidisciplinary) intra-firm and inter-firm networks of architecture, engineering, planning, and urban design firms, along with marketing, branding, and property consultants. Like everyone else, they are influenced by cultural and professional trends – 'travelling ideas' (Tait & Jensen, 2007) about design that are translated, through practice, into homogenizing trends in built form. The success of property-led redevelopment in Bilbao, Baltimore's Inner Harbor, London's Docklands, and La Défense in Paris has rapidly become the most seductive of all travelling ideas (Hubbard, 1996; Swyngedouw, Moulaert, & Rodriguez, 2002), resulting in the serial reproduction of 'designscapes': predictable ensembles of office buildings, retail space, condominium towers, cultural amenities, renovated spaces, landscaping, and street furniture (Julier, 2005). Thus we get, among others, London's South Bank, King's Cross, and Paddington Basin redevelopments, Atlantic Yards in Brooklyn, NY, Salford Docks, Espace Leopold and the EU District in Brussels, South Works, Chicago, the new financial district in the Dublin docklands, Potsdamer Platz and the science-university complex Adlershof in Berlin, the Kop van Zuid in Rotterdam, the River District in Portland, Oregon, the Euralille complex in Lille, Donau City in Vienna, Portsmouth's Gunwharf redevelopment, Hamburg's HafenCity, Birmingham's Brindleyplace, and Copenhagen's Ørestaden project.

London: making neoliberalism look nicer

London provides some of the clearest examples of regeneration machines, all products of the reflexive neoliberalism of national and metropolitan governance. The Conservative government had established a Private Finance Initiative in 1992 to deploy private sector capacity and public resources in order to deliver public sector infrastructure and services. It was expanded considerably by the New Labour government and rebranded as the Public Private Partnership (PPP) in 1997 as a vehicle for funding its commitment to tackle social exclusion and kick-starting an 'urban renaissance'. New Labour's approach was strongly influenced by the design determinism of architect Richard Rogers, whose close affiliations with the Labour Party had funded a book advocating the key role of urban design, public spaces, and density in envisaging A New London (Rogers & Fisher, 1992). In 1998 Rogers was appointed as head of an Urban Task Force charged with identifying the causes of urban decline and recommending practical solutions to bring people back into cities. The Task Force report (1999) was promptly followed by an Urban White Paper setting the agenda for the implementation of the anticipated urban renaissance (DETR, 1999). Implicit in both was an emphasis on cities as sites for consumption and living and the need to get the 'design and quality of the urban fabric right'. 'Successful urban regeneration', it was asserted, 'is design-led' (Urban Task Force, 1999, p. 49; see also Biddulph, 2011; Punter, 2009). A Commission for Architecture and the Built Environment (CABE) was established and charged with championing well-designed buildings, spaces, and places. CABE's first Chairman was Stuart Lipton, who was also CEO of the property developer Stanhope plc.

Social exclusion, meanwhile, was to be tackled by old-fashioned 'neighbourhood renewal'. Structural issues – wages, employment, housing affordability, and so on – were given relatively little attention. Echoing the rationale of the PPP, the Task Force asserted that 'One of the most efficient uses for public money in urban regeneration is to pave the way for investment of much larger sums by the private sector' (Urban Task Force, 1999, p. 23). Like New Labour's Social Exclusion Unit, the Task Force promoted the idea of mixed communities as a key objective of regeneration and as a solution to large (and troublesome) concentrations of the poor on council estates. Social mix duly became a priority criterion for public-private partnerships with any residential component, while 60% of any new housing was to be directed to 'brownfield' sites – that is, on land that had already gone through one or more cycles of development (Cochrane, 2003; Colomb, 2007; Holden & Iveson, 2003). Thus the parameters for regeneration machines were cast. The presumption that communities needed to be socially mixed or 'balanced' was reinforced by the Sustainable Communities Plan of 2003 (sustainable communities being defined rather myopically as 'places where people want to live – that promote opportunity and a better quality of life for all') and by the Mixed Community Initiative of 2005. Rhetorical prominence was given to the interdependence of civility, citizenship, good urban design (and, in particular, the imagery of 'urban villages'). Like Victorian reformers, New Labour wanted to create a new moral order around the presence of respectable and well-behaved middle-class residents.

In London, Ken Livingstone, the first mayor of the newly established Greater London Authority (GLA) promptly embraced a pro-growth, pro-business agenda. The immediate outcome was that tall buildings were to be entertained as part of the city's skyline. For someone branded 'Red Ken' by the Tory press, the role of developers' friend was unlikely and unexpected. It was in fact a pragmatic response to the opportunity to assert and consolidate London's status as a 'global city' and to secure significant levels of planning gain from developers: they could build as tall as they wanted in return for statutory contributions to affordable housing and urban design. Livingstone's administration included a small but influential Architecture and Urbanism Unit, with Richard Rogers as its Chief Advisor.

In spite of the worthy goals of the Architecture and Urbanism Unit and Rogers's Urban Task Force, the result in London was to encourage a feverish spate of regeneration and mixed-use projects: 'The Urban Task Force that he led, and the planning advice he gave to Ken Livingstone, [merely] entailed making neoliberalism look nicer' (Hatherley, 2012, p. 347). The cliquey CABE meanwhile proved to be no match for the uncompromising neoliberal political economy that had taken root and, like the Urban Task Force, it was largely cosmetic in its effects. It was quietly merged with the Design Council in 2011 by the Conservative/Liberal Democrat coalition government. Similarly, the GLA's Architecture and Urbanism Unit was able to realize few of its projects, largely because of the lack of any relevant statutory powers on the part of the GLA. In 2007 it was merged with London Development Agency's design team and the urban design team from Transport for London to become Design for London; and in 2012 it was succeeded within the GLA by a Mayor's Design Advisory Group, a unit with a similar lack of statutory powers.

Meanwhile, the reflexive neoliberalism implicit in this policy and planning framework effectively mobilized a powerful regeneration machine. Amid an increasingly acute shortage of housing across the metropolis, and with local authorities having been stripped of their capacity to deliver social housing, regeneration on brownfield sites, with higher-density, socially mixed housing as the product, was to be the solution. Derelict industrial sites and dilapidated social housing estates would provide the brownfield sites. Public-private partnerships would provide the fundamental mechanism, but would necessarily extend to a broad range of actors and agents (Future of London, 2015). A glimpse of the anatomy of London's contemporary regeneration machine is provided by the call for participation in the 2016 London Brownfield Summit ('Building Capacity, Partnerships and Solutions for Developers to Prosper') organized by Trueventus, a professional conference and training company. Their target market for the event included not only property developers and government agencies but also investors and investment managers, lawyers, architecture and design firms, surveyors, utility companies, facilities and construction companies, logistics companies, transport managers, environmental consultants, and executives from financial institutions. The brochure for the event lists a sample of organizations that were contacted in preparation for the summit agenda: TfL (Transport for London), Enfield Council, Cushman & Wakefield, Common Purpose, Savills, Square Bay, Secure Trust Bank, Grainger, MCR Property Group, Boyer, National Federation of Builders, London Borough of Newham, London Borough of Hackney, The Environmental Agency, Ballymore, NHBC (National House Building Council), Engineering Construction Board, University College London, National Grid, UK Land & Regeneration Ltd, DPA2, Wandsworth Council, Mayor for London, AECOM, GLA (Greater London Authority), Government of Malaysia, Urban Redevelopment Authority of Singapore, Imperial College London, Churchill Retirement Living, CBRE (Coldwell Banker Richard Ellis), SE Design Panel, Berkeley Capital, Malaysia Property Incorporated, Reapfield, Hutchinson Property, Inland Homes, Berkeley Homes, Circle Housing, Qube Homes, Ultrabox, BNP Paribas, Blackstone, Capital & Counties Properties, City of London, Art of the Office, Barton Willmore & Derwent.

The impact on the everyday modernism of London's social housing landscape of is already significant. Over the past decade more than 50 London social housing estates have undergone regeneration, directly affecting, in one way or another, more than 164,000 residents (London Assembly, 2015). The common pattern has been for developers to deliver an agreed number of homes, including a specified number of 'affordable' homes, cross-subsidizing them by constructing luxury apartments in towers and mid-rise blocks, usually in 'Pulp Modernism' styling. Although the overall number of homes on those estates increased significantly, there has been a net loss of some 8,000 social rented homes. And while socially rented housing in London typically runs at around 40% of local market rents, 'affordable' housing is now officially defined as up to 80% of the market rate (usually with less security of tenure).

At the time of writing than half of London's boroughs were in partnerships with the private sector that were aimed at regenerating social housing estates (Figure 6.1). Woodberry Down, one of London County Council's first postwar estates, with 2,500 homes in 57 blocks on just 26 hectares (64 acres) of land, provides a good example. Described as 'luxury flats' in the 1948 LCC (London County Council) press release announcing the opening of the first blocks, they were subsequently heralded as 'the estate of the future' by one national newspaper. The layout of the estate was based on Clarence Perry's neighbourhood unit concept, with schools, a community centre, public library and health clinic. The clinic was the very first to be built under the National Health Service and was publicized as the most advanced health centre in the world. Woodberry Down School, opened in 1955, was one of the first purpose-built comprehensive schools in the country. After a Structural Evaluation Report concluded that 31 out of the 57 blocks on the estate were beyond economic repair needed to meet the Decent Homes standard set by the central government in 2004, the estate was targeted for regeneration. Hackney Council duly partnered with Berkeley Homes. The regeneration of the estate (rebranded as 'Woodberry Park') is self-funded, with 2,700 private homes cross-subsidizing replacement affordable

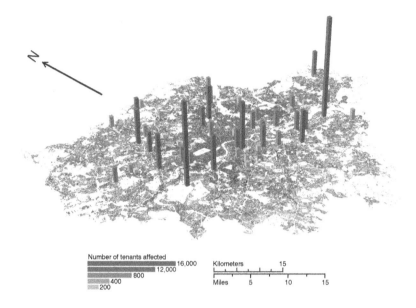

Figure 6.1 Social housing estates in Greater London undergoing regeneration, 2016.

housing while securing an agreed 21% profit for Berkeley. The number of units available for social renting will remain the same as in Woodberry Down but the tenure mix will shift from 67% social rented to 41%. The brochures for Woodberry Park are targeted in part toward overseas buyers and are full of smart models sipping champagne (The Economist, 2014). With offices in Singapore, Hong Kong, and Beijing, Berkeley sells many of its new homes off-plan to overseas investors who rent out them out in the open market for a combination of income and eventual capital gain.

Other cases of regenerated social housing have been successful to varying degrees, especially where 'soft regeneration' has combined the refurbishment of existing housing units with landscaping and improvements to security and estate management. Nevertheless, in many cases there is a net loss of affordable housing. Such losses often result from developers' ability to renegotiate partnership agreements about the amount of affordable social housing to be included in regeneration projects. Long-standing national planning legislation has required developers to provide between 35 and 50% of affordable housing in projects of more than 10 homes. Developers who claim their schemes are not commercially viable because of these obligations can submit a financial viability assessment explaining precisely why their profitability is threatened. The Heygate Estate, just south-east of the Elephant and Castle shopping centre in Southwark, provided an early example of what can go wrong. In the late 1990s the council stopped all but minimal maintenance of the 1,212 homes on the estate and began preparations for 'decanting' more than 3,000 residents prior to the regeneration of the estate. The council had to spend several million pounds on demolition and clearance before transferring ownership of the land to its private sector partner, Lend Lease. The initial agreement with Lend Lease was for 35% of the 2,535 new units on the new estate – now called Elephant Park – to be affordable housing, marketed with rents that are up to 80% of London's superheated market rate. This was renegotiated to 25% after submission of a financial viability assessment. The final tally of social rented units in Elephant Park will be 74 – just 3%. Former leaseholders do not have the right to return and some have had to accept below-market compensation for the flat they were encouraged to purchase under the Thatcher administration's 'right-to-buy' legislation.

The Heygate is not an isolated example. The nearby Aylesbury Estate has a similar history of displacement and lost capacity. Lewisham council, meanwhile, moved out all of the tenants of the 144 flats in Aragon Tower on its riverside Pepys Estate in order to sell it to Berkeley Homes, who required vacant possession. Berkeley refurbished the tower inside and out, added a new podium and five penthouse floors and turned it into a luxury gated development called 'Z apartments'. The remaining social housing tenants on the estate were either displaced or rehoused by the Hyde Housing Association that took over from the council. It is examples such as these that have led to regeneration being described in terms of 'social cleansing' and 'state-led gentrification' (Imrie & Lees, 2014; Lees, 2014); a process of 'enclosure' (Holloway, 2010m p. 29), of accumulation by dispossession. The displaced residents of regenerated districts not only lose their homes but also the 'commons' of place-based identity and distinctiveness that they have been part of (Blomley, 2008; Sevilla-Buitrago, 2015).

Accusations of social cleansing and state-led gentrification notwithstanding, the net effect of regeneration in London has been to fundamentally alter the system of housing provision. Local authorities no longer have the resources or authority to provide housing, while their successors, housing associations, have to rely on commercial loans and corporate bonds for construction or renovation. Like small and medium-sized firms in the private sector, they do not have the capacity to assemble large tracts of land or to remediate brownfield sites. It has left a few well-capitalized developers like Berkeley and Lend Lease to dominate housing provision in the metropolis. Meanwhile, the neoliberal agenda continues to evolve in ways that tend to favour the big developers. A wholesale transformation of the national urban planning system was completed in 2016 with the passage of the 2015–2016 Housing and Planning Bill with the result that proposals for new residential building on brownfield sites will be automatically granted planning permission. Office-to-residential conversions are to be encouraged by the introduction of a 'vacant building credit', which allows developers to convert empty buildings to housing without any of the requirements for affordable homes or amenity space that have hitherto been an accepted part of planning practice. The next target of neoliberal reform is likely to be London's Green

Belt. A key feature of Patrick Abercrombie's postwar planning strategy, the relevance of the Green Belt in the face of acute housing shortages is now being questioned (London First, 2015). Encouraged by the central government's 'localism agenda' (Turley & Wilson, 2012), some outer London boroughs have already become more generous in granting planning permission for development of Green Belt land. It is a trend that is likely to continue, and it is the big developers – who can afford to assemble substantial land banks – that will dominate the landscape. Their product will likely consist of the kind of packaged and branded landscapes that have proliferated around metropolitan areas in the United States: private master-planned subdivisions laid out with their own bicycle trails, 'town centres' and recreational facilities, dominated by single-family housing but containing a mixture of housing types that include condominium apartments and townhouses. Affordable and social rented housing: not so much.

References

Ball, M., & Harloe, M. (1992). Rhetorical barriers to understanding housing provision. *Housing Studies, 7*, 3–15.

Baudrillard, J., Krauss, R., & Michelson, A. (1982). The Beaubourg-effect: Implosion and deterrence. *October, 20*, 3–13.

Bell, D., & Jayne, M. (2003). 'Design-led' urban regeneration: A critical perspective. *Local Economy, 18*(2), 121–134.

Biddulph, M. (2011). Urban design, regeneration and the entrepreneurial city. *Progress in Planning, 76*(2), 63–103.

Blomley, N. (2008). Enclosure, common right and the property of the poor. *Social & Legal Studies, 17*(3), 311–331.

Bridge, G., Butler, T., & Lees, L. (Eds.). (2012). *Mixed communities: Gentrification by stealth?* Bristol: Policy Press.

Campbell, C. (1987). *The romantic ethic and the spirit of modern consumerism*. Oxford: Blackwell.

Carmona, M. (2009). Design coding and the creative, market and regulatory tyrannies of practice. *Urban Studies, 46*, 2643–2667.

Coaffee, J. (2013). Towards next-generation urban resilience in planning practice: From securitization to integrated place making. *Planning, Practice & Research, 28*, 323–339.

Cochrane, A. (2003). The new urban policy: Towards empowerment or incorporation? The practice of urban policy. In R. Imrie & M. Raco (Eds.), *Urban renaissance?: New labour, community and urban policy* (pp. 223–234). Bristol: Policy Press.

Colomb, C. (2007). Unpacking New Labour's 'Urban Renaissance' agenda: Towards a socially sustainable reurbanization of British cities? *Planning Practice and Research, 22*, 1–24.

Cuthbert, A. (2005). A debate from down-under: Spatial political economy and urban design. *Urban Design International, 10*, 223–234.

Davidson, M., & Lees, L. (2010). New-build gentrification: Its histories, trajectories, and critical geographies. *Population, Space and Place, 16*, 395–411.

DETR. (1999). *Towards an urban renaissance*. London: Department of the Environment, Transport and the Regions.

Dovey, K. (2000). The silent complicity of architecture. In J. Hillier & E. Rooksby (Eds.), *Habitus: A sense of place*. Aldershot: Ashgate.

The Economist. (2014, 16 August). *Berkeley Homes: Rise of the placemakers*. Retrieved 29 June 2017, from www.economist.com/news/britain/21612176-firm-has-transformed-property-development-london-rise-placemakers.

Evans, G. (2003). Hard-branding the cultural city: From Prado to Prada. *International Journal of Urban and Regional Research, 27*, 417–440.

Florida, R. (2002). *The rise of the creative class: And how it's transforming work, leisure and everyday life*. New York: Basic Books.

Future of London. (2015). *Estate renewal in the real world*, joint paper with New London Architecture and Urban Design London. http://futureoflondon.org.uk/publications/.

Gospodini, A. (2002). European cities in competition and the new 'uses' of urban design. *Journal of Urban Design, 7*, 59–73.

Gunder, M. (2010). Planning as the ideology of (neo-liberal) space. *Planning Theory, 9*, 298–314.

Hackworth, J. (2007). *The neoliberal city*. Ithaca, NY: Cornell University Press.

Hanlon, J. (2010). Success by design: HOPE VI, new urbanism, and the neoliberal transformation of public housing in the United States. *Environment and Planning A, 42*, 80–98.

Harvey, D. (2000). *Spaces of hope*. Berkeley, CA: University of California Press.

Hatherley, O. (2010). *A guide to the new ruins of Great Britain*. London: Verso.

Hatherley, O. (2012). *A new kind of bleak: Journeys through urban Britain*. London: Verso.

Holden, A., & Iveson, K. (2003). Designs on the urban: New Labour's urban renaissance and the spaces of citizenship. *City, 7*, 57–72.

Hudson, R. (2010). Resilient regions in an uncertain world: Wishful thinking or a practical reality? *Cambridge Journal of Regions, Economy and Society, 3*, 11–25.

Imrie, R., & Lees, L. (Eds.). (2014). *Sustainable London?* Bristol: Policy Press.

Jacobs, J. (1961). *The death and life of great American cities*. New York: Random House.

Jordan, P. W. (2007). The dream economy: Designing for success in the 21st century. *CoDesign, 3*, Supplement 1, 5–17.

Julier, G. (2005). Urban designscapes and the production of aesthetic consent. *Urban Studies, 42*, 869–887.

Holloway, J. (2010). *Crack capitalism*. London: Pluto.

Hubbard, P. (1996). Urban design and city regeneration: Social representations of entrepreneurial landscapes. *Urban Studies, 33*, 1441–1461.

Klingmann, A. (2007). *Brandscapes: Architecture in the experience economy*. Cambridge, MA: MIT Press.

Knox, P. L. (2010). *Cities and design*. London: Routledge.

Knox, P. L. (2011). Starchitects, starchitecture, and the symbolic capital of world cities. In B. Derudder, M. Hoyler, P. J. Taylor, & F. Witlox (Eds.), *International handbook of globalization and world cities* (pp. 469–483). London: Edward Elgar.

Knox, P. L. (Ed.). (2014). *Atlas of cities*. New York: Princeton University Press.

Lees, L. (2014). The urban injustices of New Labour's 'New Urban Renewal': The case of the Aylesbury Estate in London. *Antipode, 46*, 921–947.

Logan, J. R., & Molotch, H. (1987). *Urban fortunes: The political economy of place*. Berkeley, CA: University of California Press.

London Assembly. (2015). *Knock it down or do it up? The challenge of estate regeneration*. London: GLA.

London First. (2015). *The Green Belt: A place for Londoners?* London: London First. Retrieved 29 June 2017, from http://londonfirst.co.uk/wp-content/uploads/2015/02/Green-Belt-Report-February-2015.pdf.

MacLaren, A., & Kelly, S. (Eds.). (2014). *Neoliberal urban policy and the transformation of the city: Reshaping Dublin.* London: Palgrave Macmillan.

Madanipour, A. (2006). Roles and challenges of urban design. *Journal of Urban Design, 11*, 173–193.

Marin, L. (1990). *Utopics: The semiological play of textual spaces.* Amherst, NY: Prometheus.

Punter, J. (Ed.). (2009). *Urban design and the British urban renaissance.* London: Routledge.

Ritzer, G. (2005) *Enchanting a disenchanted world: Continuity and change in the cathedrals of consumption* (2nd ed.). Thousand Oaks, CA: Pine Forge Press.

Rogers, R., & Fisher, M. (1992). *A new London.* London: Penguin Books.

Sager, T. (2011). Neo-liberal urban planning policies: A literature survey 1990–2010. *Progress in Planning, 76*, 147–199.

Sevilla-Buitrago, A. (2015). Capitalist formations of enclosure: Space and the extinction of the commons. *Antipode, 47*, 999–1020.

Smith, N. (2002). New globalism, new urbanism: Gentrification as global urban strategy. *Antipode, 34*, 427–450.

Swyngedouw, E. (2009). The antinomies of the postpolitical city: In search of a democratic politics of environmental production. *International Journal of Urban and Regional Research, 33*, 601–620.

Swyngedouw, E., Moulaert, F., & Rodriguez, A. (2002). Neoliberal urbanization in Europe: Large-scale urban development projects and the new urban policy. *Antipode, 34*, 542–577.

Tait, M., & Jensen, O. B. (2007). Travelling ideas, power and place: The cases of urban villages and business improvement districts. *International Planning Studies, 12*(2), 107–128.

Thatcher, M. (1987, 31 October). Interview. *Woman's Own*, 10.

Turley, A., & Wilson, J. (2012). Localism in London. *The implications for planning and regeneration in the capital.* London: Future of London. http://futureoflondon.org.uk/publications/.

Urban Task Force [Britain, G., & Rogers, R. G.]. (1999). *Towards an urban renaissance.* London: Spon.

Zukin, S. (2010). *Naked city: The death and life of authentic urban places.* New York: Oxford University Press.

7 The open city

Richard Sennett

The closed system and the Brittle City

The cities everyone wants to live in should be clean and safe, possess efficient public services, be supported by a dynamic economy, provide cultural stimulation, and also do their best to heal society's divisions of race, class, and ethnicity. These are not the cities we live in.

Cities fail on all these counts due to government policy, irreparable social ills, and economic forces beyond local control. The city is not its own master. Still, something has gone wrong, radically wrong, in our conception of what a city itself should be. We need to imagine just what a clean, safe, efficient, dynamic, stimulating, just city would look like concretely – we need those images to confront critically our masters with what they should be doing – and just this critical imagination of the city is weak.

This weakness is a particularly modern problem: the art of designing cities declined drastically in the middle of the 20th century. In saying this, I am propounding a paradox, for today's planner has an arsenal of technological tools – from lighting to bridging and tunneling to materials for buildings – which urbanists even a hundred years ago could not begin to imagine: we have more resources to use than in the past, but resources we don't use very creatively.

This paradox can be traced to one big fault, the over-determination both of the city's visual forms and its social functions. The technologies which make possible experiment have been subordinated to a regime of power which wants order and control. Urbanists, globally, anticipated the "control freakery" of current planning law by a good half century; in the grip of rigid images, precise delineations, the urban imagination lost vitality. In particular what's missing in modern urbanism is a sense of time – not time looking backward nostalgically but forward-looking time, the city understood as process, its imagery changing through use, an urban imagination images formed by anticipation, friendly to surprise.

A portent of the freezing of the imagination of cities appeared in Le Corbusier's "Plan Voisin" in the mid-1920s for Paris. The architect conceived of replacing a large swath of the historic center of Paris with uniform, X shaped buildings; public life on the ground plane of the street would be eliminated; the use of all buildings would be coordinated by a single master plan. Not only is Corbusier's architecture a kind of industrial manufacture of buildings. He has tried in the "Plan Voisin" to destroy just those social elements of the city which produce change in time, by eliminating unregulated life on the ground plane; people live and work, in isolation, higher up.

This dystopia became reality in various ways. The Plan's building-type shaped public housing from Chicago to Moscow, housing estates which came to resemble warehouses for the poor. Corbusier's intended destruction of vibrant street life was realized in suburban growth for the middle classes, with the replacement of high streets by monofunction shopping malls, by gated communities, by schools and hospitals built as isolated campuses. The proliferation of zoning regulations in the 20th century is unprecedented in the history of urban design, and this proliferation of rules and bureaucratic regulations has disabled local innovation and growth, frozen the city in time.

The result of over-determination is what could be called the Brittle City. Modern urban environments decay much more quickly than urban fabric inherited from the past. As uses change, buildings are now destroyed rather than adapted; indeed, the over-specification of form and function makes the modern urban environment peculiarly susceptible to decay. The average life-span of new public housing in Britain is now 40 years; the average life-span of new skyscrapers in New York is 35 years.

It might seem that the Brittle City would in fact stimulate urban growth, the new now more rapidly sweeping away the old, but again the facts argue against this view. In the United States, people flee decaying suburbs rather than reinvest in them; in Britain and on the Continent, as in America, "renewing" the inner city most often means displacing the people who have lived there before. "Growth" in an urban environment is a more complicated phenomenon than simple replacement of what existed before; growth requires a dialogue between past and present, it is a matter of evolution rather than erasure.

This principle is as true socially as it is architecturally. The bonds of community cannot be conjured up in an instant, with a stroke of the planner's pen; they too require time to develop. Today's ways of building cities – segregating functions, homogenizing population, pre-empting through zoning and regulation the meaning of place – fail to provide communities the time in space needed for growth.

The Brittle City is a symptom. It represents a view of society itself as a closed system. The closed system is a conception which dogged state socialism throughout the 20th century as much as it shaped bureaucratic capitalism. This view of society has two essential attributes: equilibrium and integration.

The closed system ruled by equilibrium derives from a pre-Keynesian idea of how markets work. It supposes something like a bottom line in which income and expenses balance. In state planning, information feedback loops and internal markets are meant to insure that programs do not "over-commit," do not "suck resources into a black hole" – such is the language of recent reforms of the health service, familiar again to urban planners in the ways infrastructure resources for transport get allocated. The limits on doing any one thing really well are set by the fear of neglecting other tasks. In a closed system, a little bit of everything happens all at once.

Second, a closed system is meant to be integrate. Ideally, every part of the system has a place in an overall design; the consequence of that ideal is to reject, to vomit out, experiences which are stick out because they are contestatory or disorienting; things that "don't fit" are diminished in value. The emphasis on integration puts an obvious bar on experiment; as the inventor of the computer icon, John Seely Brown, once remarked, every technological advance poses at the moment of its birth a threat of disruption and dysfunction to a larger system. The same threatening exceptions occur in the urban environment, threats which modern city planning has tried to forestall by accumulating a mountain of rules defining historical, architectural, economic, and social context – "context" being a polite but potent word in repressing anything that doesn't fit in, context insuring that nothing sticks out, offends, or challenges.

As I say, the sins of equilibrium and integration bedevil coherence, planners of education or planners as much as planners of cities, planning sins which crossed the line between state capitalism or state socialism. The closed system betrays the 20th century bureaucrat's horror of disorder.

The social contrast to the closed system is not the free market, nor is the alternative to the Brittle City a place ruled by developers. That opposition is in fact not what it seems. The cunning of neoliberalism in general, and of Thatcherism in particular, was to speak the language of freedom whilst manipulating closed bureaucratic systems for private gain by an elite. Equally, in my experience as a planner, those developers in London, as in New York, who complain most loudly about zoning restrictions are all too adept in using these rules at the expense of communities.

The contrast to the closed system lies in a different kind of social system, not in brute private enterprise, a social system which is open rather than closed.

The characteristics of such an open system and its realization in an open city are what I wish to explore with you tonight.

The open system

The idea of an open city is not my own: credit for it belongs to the great urbanist Jane Jacobs in the course of arguing against the urban vision of Le Corbusier. She tried to understand what results when places become both dense and diverse, as in packed streets or squares, their functions both public and private; out of such conditions comes the unexpected encounter, the chance discovery, the innovation. Hers is a view reflected in the bon mot of William Empson that "the arts result from over-crowding."

Jacobs sought to definite particular strategies for urban development, once a city is freed of the constraints of either equilibrium or integration. These include encouraging quirky, jerry-built adaptations or additions to existing buildings; encouraging uses of public spaces which don't fit neatly together, such as putting an AIDS hospice square in the middle of a shopping street. In her view, big capitalism and powerful developers tend to favor homogeneity: determinate, predictable, and balanced in form; the role of the radical planner therefore to champion dissonance. In her famous declaration, "if density and diversity give life, the life they breed is disorderly." The open city feels like Naples, the closed city feels like Frankfurt.

For a long time, I dwelt in my own work happily in Jacobs' shadow – both her enmity to the closed system (though the formal concept is mine not hers) and her advocacy of complexity, diversity, and dissonance. Recently, in re-reading her work, I've detected glints of something lurking beneath this stark contrast.

If Jane Jacobs is the urban anarchist she is often said to be, then she is an anarchist of a peculiar sort, her spiritual ties closer to Edmund Burke than to Emma Goldmann. She believes that in an open city, as in the natural world, social and visual forms mutate through chance variation; people can best absorb, participate, and adapt to change if it happens step-by-lived-step. This is evolutionary urban time, the slow time needed for an urban culture to take root, then to foster, then to absorb chance and change. It is why Naples, Cairo, or New York's lower East Side, though resource-poor, still "work" in the sense people care deeply about where they live. People live into these place, like nesting. Time breeds that attachment to place.

In my own thinking, I've wondered what kinds of visual forms might promote this experience of time. Can these attachments be designed by architects? Which designs might abet social relationships which endure just because they can evolve and mutate? The visual structuring of evolutionary time is a systemic property of the open city. To make statement this more concrete, I'd like to describe three systematic elements of an open city: (1) passage territories; (2) incomplete form; (3) development narratives.

1 Passage territories

I'd like to describe in some detail the experience of passing through different territories of the city, both because that act of passage is how we know the city as a whole, and also because planners and architects have such difficulties designing the experience of passage from place to place. I'll start with walls, which seem to be structures inhibiting passage, and then explore some of the ways edges of urban territory function like walls.

a Walls

The wall would seem an unlikely choice; it is an urban construction which literally closes in a city. Until the invention of artillery, people sheltered behind walls when attacked; the gates in walls also served to regulate commerce coming into cities, often being the place in which taxes were collected. Massive medieval walls such as those surviving in Aix-en-Provence or in Rome furnish a perhaps misleading general picture; ancient Greek walls were lower and thinner. But we also mis-imagine how those medieval walls in themselves functioned.

Though they shut closed, they also served as sites for unregulated development in the city; houses were built on both sides of medieval town walls; informal markets selling black-market or untaxed goods sprung up nestled against them; the zone of the wall was where heretics, foreign exiles, and other misfits tended to gravitate, again far from the controls of the center. They were spaces which would have attracted the anarchic Jane Jacobs.

But they were also sites which might have suited her organic temperament. These walls functioned much like cell membranes, both porous and resistant. That dual function of the membrane is, I believe, an important principle for visualizing more modern living urban forms. Whenever we construct a barrier, we have equally to make the barrier porous; the distinction between inside and outside has to be breachable, if not ambiguous.

The usual contemporary use of plate glass for walls doesn't do this; true, on the ground plane you see what's inside the building, but you can't touch, smell, or hear anything within; the plates are usually rigidly fixed so that there is only one, regulated, entrance within. The result is that nothing much develops on either side of these transparent walls; as in Mies van der Rohe's Seagram Building in New York or Norman Foster's new London City Hall, you have dead space on both sides of the wall; life in the building does accumulate here. By contrast, the 19th century architect Louis Sullivan used much more primitive forms of plate glass more flexibly, as invitations to gather, to enter a building or to dwell at its edge; his plate glass panels function as porous walls. This contrast in plate glass design brings out one current failure of imagination in using a modern material so that it has a sociable effect.

The idea of a cellular wall, which is both resistant and porous, can be extended from single buildings to the zones at which meet the different communities of a city.

b Borders

Ecologists like Steven Gould draw our attention to an important distinction in the natural world, that between boundaries and borders. The boundary is an edge where things end; the border is an edge where different groups interact. In natural ecologies, borders are the places where organisms become more interactive, due to the meeting of different species or physical conditions. For instance, where the shoreline of a lake meets solid land is an active zone of exchange; here is where organisms find and feed off other organisms. The same is true of temperature layers within a lake: where layer meets layer defines the zone of the most intense biological activity. Not surprisingly, it is also at the borderline where the work of natural selection is the most intense. Whereas the boundary is a guarded territory, as established by prides of lions or packs of wolves. The boundary establishes closure, whereas the border functions more like a medieval wall. The border is a liminal space.

In the realm of human culture, territories consist similarly of boundaries and borders – in cities, most simply, there is a contrast between gated communities and complex, open streets. But the distinction cuts deeper in urban planning.

When we imagine where the life of a community is to be found, we usually look for it in the center of a community; when we want to strengthen community life, we try to intensify life at the center. The edge condition is seen to be more inert, and indeed modern planning practices, such as sealing the edges of communities with highways, create rigid boundaries, lacking any porosity. But neglect of the edge condition – boundary-thinking, if you like – means that exchange between different racial, ethnic, or class communities is diminished. By privileging the center we can thus weaken the complex interactions necessary to join up the different human groups the city contains.

Let me give as an example a failure of my own in my planning practice. Some years ago I was involved in plans for creating a market to serve the Hispanic community of Spanish Harlem in New York. This community, one of the poorest in the city, lies above 96th Street on Manhattan's upper east side. Just below 96th Street, in an abrupt shift, lies one of the richest communities in the world, running from 96th down to 59th Street, comparable to Mayfair in London or the 7th Arrondissement in Paris. 96th Street itself could function either as a boundary or a border. We planners chose to locate La Marqueta in the center of Spanish Harlem 20 blocks away, in the very center of the community, and to regard 96th Street as a dead edge, where nothing much happens. We chose wrongly. Had we located the market on that street, we might have encouraged activity which brought the rich and the poor into some daily commercial contact. Wiser planners have since learned from our mistake, and on the West Side of Manhattan sought to locate new community resources at the edges between communities, in order, as it were, to open the gates between different racial and economic communities. Our imagination of the importance of the center proved isolating, their understanding of the value of the edge and border has proved integrating.

I don't mean to paint a Panglossian picture of such ventures in planning: opening up borders means people of different strengths are exposed to competition. Borders can serve as tense rather than friendly sites of exchange – evoking some of the predatory quality of border conditions in natural ecologies. But taking that risk, which planners are now doing under more explosive conditions in Beirut and in Nicosia, is the only way, I believe, in which we create conditions for a socially sustained collective life in cities; ultimately isolation is not a true guarantor of civil order.

The porous wall and the edge as border create essential physical elements for an open system in cities. Both porous walls and borders create liminal space; that is, space at the limits of control, limits which permit the appearance of things, acts, and persons unforeseen, yet focused and sited. The biological psychologist Lionel Festinger once characterized such liminal spaces as defining the importance of "peripheral vision"; sociologically and urbanistically, these sites operate differently than those places which concentrate differences in a center; on the horizon, at the periphery, at the border, differences stand out since one is aware one is crossing out of one territory into another.

2 Incomplete form

This discussion of walls and borders leads logically to a second systematic characteristic of the open city: incomplete form. Incompleteness may seem the enemy of structure, but this is not the case. The designer needs to create physical forms of a particular sort, "incomplete" in a special way.

When we design a street, for instance, so that buildings are set back from a street wall, the space left open in front is not truly public space; instead the building has been withdrawn from the street. We know the practical consequences; people walking on a street tend to avoid these recessed spaces. It's better planning if the building is brought forward, into the context of other buildings; though the building will become part of the urban fabric, some of its volumetric elements will now be incompletely disclosed. There is incompleteness in the perception of what the object is.

Incompleteness of form extends to the very context of buildings themselves. In classical Rome, Hadrian's Pantheon co-existed with the less distinguished buildings which surrounded it in the urban fabric, though Hadrian's architects conceived the Pantheon as a self-referential object. We find the same co-existence in many other architectural monuments: St. Paul's in London, Rockefeller Center in New York, the Maison Arabe in Paris – all great works of architecture which stimulate building around themselves. It's the fact of that stimulation, rather than the fact the buildings are of lesser quality, which counts in urban terms: the existence of one building is sited in such a way that it encourages the growth of other buildings around it. And now the buildings acquire their specifically urban value by their relationship to each other; they become in time incomplete forms if considered alone, in themselves.

Incomplete form is most of all a kind of creative credo. In the plastic arts it is conveyed in sculpture purposely left unfinished; in poetry it is conveyed in, to use Wallace Steven's phrase, the "engineering of the fragment." The architect Peter Eisenman has sought to evoke something of the same credo in the term "light architecture," meaning an architecture planned so that it can be added to, or more importantly, revised internally in the course of time as the needs of habitation change.

This credo opposes the simple idea of replacement of form which characterizes the Brittle City, but it is a demanding opposition. When we try to convert office blocks to residential use, for instance.

3 Narratives of development

Our work aims first of all to shape the narratives of urban development. By that, we mean that we focus on the stages in which a particular project unfolds. Specifically, we try to understand what elements should happen first, what then are the consequences of this initial move. Rather than a lock-step march toward achieving a single end, we look at the different and conflicting possibilities which each stage of the design process should open up; keeping these possibilities intact, leaving conflict elements in play, opens up the design system.

We claim no originality for this approach. If a novelist were to announce at the beginning of a story, here's what will happen, what the characters will become, and what the story means, we would immediately close the book. All good narrative has the property of exploring the unforeseen, of discovery; the novelist's art is to shape the process of that exploration. The urban designer's art is akin.

In sum, we can define an open system as one in which growth admits conflict and dissonance. This definition is at the heart of Darwin's understanding of evolution; rather than the survival of the fittest (or the most beautiful), he emphasized the process of growth as a continual struggle between equilibrium and disequilibrium; an environment rigid in form, static in program, is doomed in time; bio-diversity instead gives the natural world the resources to provision change.

That ecological vision makes equal sense of human settlements, but it is not the vision which guided 20th century state planning. Neither of state capitalism or state socialism embraced growth in the sense Darwin understood it in the natural world, in environments which permitted interaction amongst organisms with different functions, endowed with different powers.

I'd like to conclude this not with a statement of regret over the decline of planning, but by making a connection between the systematics of the open city to the politics we all espouse, the politics of democracy. In what sense could the spaces I've described contribute to the practice of democracy?

Democratic space

When the city operates as an open system – incorporating principles of porosity of territory, narrative indeterminacy, and incomplete form – it becomes democratic not in a legal sense, but as physical experience.

In the past, thinking about democracy focused on issues of formal governance; today, it focuses on citizenship and issues of participation. Participation is an issue which has everything to do with the physical city and its design. For example, in the ancient polis, the Athenians put the semi-circular theater to political use; this architectural form provided good acoustics and a clear view and of speakers in debates, more, it made possible the perception of other people's responses during debates.

In modern times, we have no similar model of democratic space – certainly no clear imagination of an urban democratic space. John Locke defined democracy in terms of a body of laws which could be practiced anywhere. Democracy in the eyes of Thomas Jefferson was inimical to life in cities; he thought the spaces it required could be no larger than a village. His view has persisted. Throughout the 19th and 20th centuries, champions of democratic practices have identified them with small, local communities, face-to-face relationships.

Today's city is big, filled with migrants and ethnic diversities, a city in which people belong to many different kinds of community at the same time – through their work, families, consumption habits, and leisure pursuits. For cities like

London and New York becoming global in scale, the problem of citizen participation is how people can feel connected to others whom, necessarily, they cannot know. Democratic space means creating a forum for these strangers to interact.

In London, a good example of how this can occur is the creation of a corridor connection between St. Paul's Cathedral and the Tate Modern Gallery, spanned by the new Millennium Bridge. Though highly defined, the corridor is not a closed form; along both the north bank of the Thames it is generating regeneration of lateral buildings unrelated to its own purposes and design. And almost immediately upon opening, within its confines this corridor has stimulated informal mixings and connections among people walking the span, prompted an ease among strangers which is the foundation for a truly modern sense of "us." This is democratic space.

The problem of participation cities face today is how to create, in less ceremonial spaces, some of the same sense of relatedness among strangers. It is a problem in the design of public spaces in hospitals, in the making of urban schools, in big office complexes, in the renewal of high streets, and most particularly in the places where the work of government gets done. How can such places be opened up? How can the divide between inside and outside be bridged? How can design generate new growth? How can visual form invite engagement and identification?

In principle good urban design can answer these questions.

Part II
Urbanization, knowledge economies, and social structuration

8 Brawn to brain

Rustbelt, Southern, and Southeastern Sunbelt metropolitan cities

Jessie P. H. Poon and Wei Yin

Introduction

Cities in the Northeast of the United States (US) have been in the news lately. Media reports such as the Yahoo! documentary on "Cities rising: rebuilding America" are providing new narratives of urban decline and turnaround in the region. The story of Rustbelt cities in the Northeast is well-known: historically, they were centers of growth and prosperity, heavyweights in the nation's industrial output, and gravities of innovation and skill. American industrial revolution began here, in cities such as Detroit, Buffalo, Chicago, Cleveland, and Pittsburgh, scattered along prominent waterways and surrounded by rich agricultural hinterlands. Building networks of transportation across the country, cities in the Northeast traded with other regions, revolutionarized steel and automobile technology, and welcomed immigrants from Europe. In the 20 years between 1900 and 1920, urban population in the region exploded and gross domestic product increased from $423 to $688 million (Bowen & Kinahan, 2014).

Fifty years later, urban growth reversed as young, often talented, people left cities in the Northeast and headed to Austin, Raleigh, Seattle, Portland, Los Angeles, and San Francisco for higher wages. The "once-mighty cities" (Beauregard, 2003) of the Northeast began to experience slippage in national rankings. Of the 15 most dynamic cities ranked by the wealth management magazine *Worth*, only one Rustbelt city (that is, Pittsburgh) made the list.[1] Except for New York City, the rest are in Southern regions popularly characterized as the Sunbelt. A sense of economic and political lagging began to set in as population loss was paralleled by urban deterioration (both in terms of infrastructure and property values) earning cities here the label of Rustbelt cities and more recently "shrinking cities" (Mallach, 2015). In turn, modernist scholars, preoccupied with urban growth, turned their attention to more successful landscapes of growth, namely the warmer Sunbelt cities of the South (Beauregard, 2003). Since then, much of the work on cities has focused on the latter's attractiveness for the skilled linking modern urban vibrancy and resilience to the creative and innovative energies and interactions of mobile educated individuals (Florida, 2002; Glaeser, Ponzetto, & Tobio, 2014).

The doom-and-gloom picture of post-war Rustbelt cities however is being revised (Bowen, 2014; Neumann, 2016). In 2014, half of Forbes' 20 most affordable cities may be found in the region. Leading the list is Buffalo (New York) followed by Cincinnati and Dayton in Ohio. Like other American cities, decline is visible in the central cities while previous industrial behemoths have turned into derelict factories and mills. But many suburbs have also witnessed growth or stability hosting schools of reasonable quality. The confluence of real estate affordability and good schools has attracted talented individuals to stay or relocate to other metropolitan cities within the region, and encouraged new skilled immigrants to settle here. This chapter documents the role of human capital in Rustbelt cities' resurgence. Employing a comparative analysis with Sunbelt cities, the chapter points to a variegated landscape where certain old industrial cities have managed to build or retain a stock of human capital despite profound shifts in the geography of production.

Rustbelt and Sunbelt urban dynamics

Theorization of cities has long sought to answer the question of why people and firms concentrate geographically. Storper and Scott (2009, 2016) maintain that explanations of urban growth must focus on production logics. Historically, industrial cities developed in response to manufacturing processes and their organizational modes. They place such logics squarely on the dynamics of agglomeration, specifically those related to localized economies and successful specialization. Such an argument may be traced to the work of Jacobs (1969, p. 262) who saw a city as a place that "consistently generates its economic growth from its own local economy." Once the antecedents of specialization are initiated,[2] firms cluster in cities because of advantages of information exchange and spillover. Tacit knowledge is subjected to friction of distance: both competitors and customers are a valuable source of information, and being close enables firms to adapt and improve their process and product innovation. Since knowledge is embodied in people, their concentration in cities renders the latter a driver of urban growth (Lucas, 1988). Information spillovers improve local governments while firms are able to internalize localized knowledge externalities leading to better allocation of resources. Black and Henderson's (1999) theoretical model for instance shows that growth in city sizes and growth in number of cities from 1900 to 1950 went hand in hand with the rise of average human capital. Over the period, national urbanization level rose from 40 to 60% while the number of 17-year-olds who completed high school increased from 6.3 to 57.4%. Growth of individual city size occurred at a rate that is proportional to the human capital accumulation rate.

From Storper and Scott's view, once firm efficiency develops from proximate production and social relations, this unravels the process of agglomeration that in turn triggers the complex coordination of resources and information in space. As rising firm output and urban economic development mutually reinforce one another, urban expansion is path-dependent because it is locked into a set of industrial and institutional conditions. Black and Henderson's (1999) work suggests that production specialization is responsible for such lock-in which in turn may explain why cities that specialize in finance and business are larger than those that specialize in manufacturing. In the context of the Northeast, industrialization in the early 20th century drew heavily on the Fordist mode of mass production. Locational dynamics associated with such production and organizational mode created the steel and automobile cities of Pittsburgh, Buffalo, Cleveland, Toledo, Detroit, Gary, and Flint. However, Storper and Scott (2009) reject human capital as an independent variable of urban growth. They argue that workers are more likely to follow work and not the other way round. For them, industrial cities began as sites of employment. One major reason for this view rests in their criticisms of studies surrounding skilled (Glaeser & Maré, 2001; Glaeser & Resseger, 2010) and creative workers (Florida, 2002), a point we will return to in later paragraphs.

The literature on skilled and creative workers has tended to highlight successful cities in the Sunbelt: of Florida's (2005) top 15 Milken tech-pole city rankings, only two Rustbelt cities, namely Chicago and Philadelphia, made the list. Yet some cities in the Rustbelt have witnessed a surge in innovation in recent years (van Agtmael and Bakker, 2016). Meanwhile, studies have shown that population decline in the Rustbelt peaked in the decade of the 1970s but many cities also gained or lost population at a decelerated rate by the 1990s (Simmons & Lang, 2006), an observation that this chapter will confirm for subsequent years as well. On the other hand, downplaying the role of contemporary human capital by Storper and Scott requires greater scrutiny.

Eighteenth century industrial revolution did not seem to require many college graduates. The average worker could make a reasonable living working in factories without a formal education. Technology level in the textile industry was not high and did not require much human capital. This is well-documented by Mokyr (2000, 2005) in his study of technology during the industrial revolution. Mokyr suggests that there was little need for human capital during the 18th century because knowledge production was largely unsystematic and uncodified. Knowledge was closely guarded by a group of elites and its access and diffusion was poor. Additionally, the scientific knowledge base remained relatively small resulting in many dead ends for industrial application. It was not until the scientific method became widely accepted as a community practice in the latter half of the 19th century that scientific knowledge came to be associated with economic and industrial growth. Once technology was linked to material progress, and entrepreneurs were able to identify what Mokyr calls "useful knowledge," they became adept in applying the knowledge for industrial applications. Moreover this period coincided with a time of institutional-building particularly the expansion of universities. Human capital came to assume a more central role in urban growth as institutions expanded, and as scientific knowledge was more intimately related to industrial development.

Squicciarini and Voigtander (2015) have challenged the view that human capital may have played little role in early industrialization and, for the purpose of this chapter, the implication that this holds in explaining the genesis of industrial cities. Their study of French cities indicates that a very small group of knowledge elites helped propel innovation during the industrial revolution. The authors conclude that while early industrialization by far and large did not need a high level of average human capital, nonetheless, this small group of knowledge individuals plays an important role in innovation. Indeed Mokyr makes the point that in the years following the scientific revolution – a revolution that contributed to the rise of Fordist manufacturing – economic growth became more technologically driven compared to the earlier period when growth was a function of commercial success.

Taken together, the jury is still out regarding the role that human capital had played as American Rustbelt cities were forming though Simon and Nardinelli's study (2002) of cities before 1900 seems to support the marginal role of human capital. They attribute this to the dominance of automobile production. Once the industry stabilized in 1940, however, human capital became much more important, a point that appears to support Mokyr (2005) and Ceh and Gatrell (2006). In their analysis of the geography of research and development (R&D) activities, Ceh and Gatrell suggest that patterns of R&D concentration in the Northeast, at least before 1970, were associated with Fordist manufacturing innovation. Interestingly, Simon and Nardinelli (2002) report that many of the 20 most skilled cities in 1900 may be found in the Rustbelt while most of the least skilled cities were in the Sunbelt although the pattern was reversed by 1960. That the skill factor is relevant has been discussed by Morris (2012) who documents the role of early innovators such as brothers-in-law Proctor and Gamble in creating the country's first chemical plant in Cincinnati. This same city is also responsible for the meat packing "disassembly" line that subsequently inspired Henry Ford to build his T-model automobile factory (Morris, 2012). The period of Fordist manufacturing thus saw Rustbelt cities becoming places for bringing people together to organize complex division of labor. As Morris notes, American Fordist manufacturing was machine-oriented and emphasized scale and speed. This required feats of coordination and organization that came to be a distinctive feature of manufacturing in Fordist cities.

Fordist manufacturing had a remarkable effect on the growth of population size. Cities here more than doubled their populations between 1900 and 1920 from 76 to 106 million (Bowen & Kinahan, 2014). All this however came to a halt in the 1950s as they entered into a period of crisis marked by global competition and new technological changes (Warf & Holly, 1997). The steel industry for example made no investment by the 1970s turning to finance and real estate for growth instead (Goldstein, 2009). Goldstein shows that decision-making in the industry became more financialized focusing on stock returns while innovation was stalled by widespread downsizing. Deindustrialization began in earnest at this point. At its peak, population loss averaged 30% over the decade of the 1970s. Binelli's (2012) vivid account of quintessential Rustbelt city Detroit portrays a city of industrial ruination where population had fallen from its peak of nearly 2 million to just over 700,000 in 2010 accompanied by a cityscape of abandoned factories and buildings. Before deindustrialization, cities in the region had earned a positive image. They were important nodes in the industrial heartland that had successfully tamed the wild frontier (High, 2003). As images of decline began to set in, and in particular, as cities in the Sunbelt began to ascend and challenge the Rustbelt's economic prominence, the latter cities acquired a stigma of urban decline projecting images of decay, blizzard, and blight.

On the other hand, Sunbelt cities' dominance is set against the technological upsurge of the middle 20th century, particularly the rise of the digital and information economy. Indeed Sunbelt cities are often contrasted with Rustbelt cities as "high-wage, high-skill, housing scarce" and "lower-wage, lower-skill, housing abundant" cities (Storper, 2010, p. 2030). This follows in part from a number of works on Southern cities, particularly cities in California, that were set apart from their Rustbelt counterparts in terms of new industrial sectors, flexible production, and highly mobile technology workers (Saxenian, 2006; Scott, 1992; Storper & Scott, 2009). Sunbelt cities were said to be unshackled by labor unions as well as sunset technologies and organization. They were forward-looking brimming with innovation and their vibrancy stems from a "rupture with the past" (Storper, 2010, p. 2044). In particular, human capital occupies a more prominent role in the making of Sunbelt cities. Silicon Valley became a major growth pole for the Southwest, driven by the microelectronic revolution and more recently, digital and social technologies. The new economy was and still is rooted in openness – 52.4% of startups in the Silicon Valley may be traced to at least one immigrant founder compared to 38.8% for California (Wadhwa, 2012). Skilled immigrants from China, Taiwan, and India formed a significant share of the startups. Wadhwa shows that Indian scientists and engineers in particular grew by 64% between 1995 and 2005. He reports similar immigrant growth statistics in other Sunbelt areas. Not surprising, San-Jose, Austin, Raleigh-Durham, and San Francisco became the new technological poles just as deindustrialization took off in the Northeast (see Acs, 2002 for a spatial analysis of urban technological poles).

Openness is expressed in another set of literature that proffers a relationship between skill/creativity and urban development (Florida, 2002; Florida, Mellander, & Stolarick, 2008; Glaeser; 2010). This literature highlights the role of urban amenities, consumption, and tolerance in specialized labor pooling, the latter of which extends from Lucas' (1988) infamous observation that talented people prefer to be around other talented people in cities. Many of the benefits of human capital externalities have been studied in the context of wages but Moretti (2004) notes that there are also social returns such as lower crime. Moreover, Bublitz et al. (2015) find that entrepreneurs with low-skill balance benefit significantly from location in cities because the agglomeration of skills or thick labor markets compensate for their lack of specific skill sets. Cities also generate human capital externalities through product variety (Glaeser et al., 2014). Hence while industrial specialization may have driven the early growth of industrial cities, like Lucas, Glaeser and his colleagues point out that the skilled find it more productive to be around one another in the present context. Not surprising, a trend of urban sorting has emerged with certain cognitive skills concentrating in large cities and less technical skills in smaller cities (Scott, 2010). Whatever the debate on the role of human capital on urban growth, there is little doubt that knowledge sectors increasingly drive innovation. Firms that value innovation will continue to locate in places where the skilled is readily available.

Taken together, Rustbelt-Sunbelt divergence of the 1970s took place at a time when cities in the South and Southeast embarked on urban development programs, expanded interstate highways, and fomented a favorable business climate that included the right to work. Local officials courted investment leaving the Rustbelt promising little government interference (Bernard & Rice, 1983). While there is little doubt that there was significant migration of the talented to Sunbelt cities, Rustbelt cities also continued to retain some level of human capital. As we attempt to demonstrate in the next section, human capital level is presently comparable to cities in the Sunbelt South and Southeast. While the Southwest also benefited from the relocation of the skilled and defense manufacturing away from the Rustbelt, it has been examined in another paper and will not be studied here (Poon & Yin, 2014).

Spatial urban patterns of human capital

To examine the geography of human capital, we draw on PUMS data from the US Census from 1980 to 2010. The statistics on human capital (defined as individuals with a college degree and above) were compiled for metropolitan areas which we will refer to as "cities" in this chapter. Table 8.1 presents the growth of population over the 30 years. As expected, most Rustbelt cities grew very slowly and nearly one-third of the 48 cities experienced negative rates including Buffalo, Detroit, Pittsburgh, and Toledo. Flint and Lima topped the list with negative growth rates of over 30%. In contrast, virtually all cities in the South and Southeast saw positive growth rates led by Austin, Dallas, Houston, Orlando, and Atlanta. Only three cities, Alexandria, New Orleans, and Anniston experienced negative growth. The figures are consistent with the relatively well-narrated story of depopulation and urban growth between the three regions. However, it is also clear that population decline is not pervasive throughout the Great Lakes. Baltimore, Chicago, Bloomington, Rochester, Syracuse, Lafayette, and Grand Rapids all gained population at a rate that is comparable to certain Sunbelt cities. Except for Austin, Southeastern cities on the whole had stronger growth than cities in the South: 35% of Southeastern cities experienced growth rates of over 100% compared to 16% of Southern cities. Some of that growth is driven by the influx of retirees, for example the city of Sarasota, but much of it also captures industrial shift and expansion in the Sunbelt.

Next we examine the spatial distribution of the skilled. We distinguished between skilled natives and skilled immigrants or foreign-born. While skilled natives form the larger share of human capital, skilled immigrants are increasingly contributing to the growth of urban economies as well. One notable example is Baltimore as the city's mayor openly courts immigrants to raise the

Table 8.1 Population growth of Rustbelt and Southern/Southeastern Sunbelt cities, 1980–2010

Rustbelt cities	Growth (%)	Southern cities	Growth (%)	Southeastern cities	Growth (%)
Flint, MI	−53.8	Alexandria, LA	−2.6	Albany, GA	10.0
Lima, OH	−30.2	New Orleans, LA	−2.3	Columbus, GA	11.1
Davenport, IA-Rock Island-Moline, IL	−17.1	Anniston, AL	−1.5	Charleston, SC	22.9
Decatur, IL	−15.4	Gadsden, AL	1.5	Chattanooga, TN	24.7
Toledo, OH	−14.8	Beaumont-Port Arthur-Orange, TX	3.9	Fayetteville, NC	28.3
Benton Harbor, MI	−10.0	Corpus Christi, TX	7.2	Savannah, GA	31.8
		Monroe, LA	9.0	Athens, GA	36.1
Buffalo-Niagara Falls, NY	−8.5	Shreveport, LA	9.6	Greenville-Spartanburg-Anderson, SC	48.2
Muncie, IN	−8.1	Birmingham, AL	9.7	Pensacola, FL	54.7
Dayton-Springfield, OH	−7.6	Wichita Falls, TX	10.0	Jacksonville, NC	57.9
Mansfield, OH	−5.3	Abilene, TX	18.4	Columbia, SC	59.1
Kokomo, IN	−2.7	Longview-Marshall, TX	22.78	Gainesville, FL	63.1
Pittsburgh, PA	−2.3	Lubbock, TX	33.2	Miami-Hialeah, FL	64.4
Detroit, MI	−0.5	Montgomery, AL	33.6	Fort Walton Beach, FL	64.8
Erie, PA	0.3	Huntsville, AL	35.4	Fort Lauderdale-Hollywood-Pompano Beach, FL	72.2
Youngstown-Warren, OH	4.5	Waco, TX	36.7	Augusta-Aiken, GA-SC	75.5
Akron, OH	5.8	Memphis, TN	40.6	Tampa-St. Petersburg-Clearwater, FL	77.6
Canton, OH	6.7	Amarillo, TX	40.6	Lakeland-Winterhaven, FL	88.5
Peoria, IL	8.1	Tuscaloosa, AL	40.7	Daytona Beach, FL	91.0
Kankakee, IL	9.4	Baton Rouge, LA	47.1	Jacksonville, FL	91.8
South Bend-Mishawaka, IN	9.8	Galveston, TX	49.1	Melbourne-Titusville-Cocoa-Palm Bay, FL	99.1
Lansing-E. Lansing, MI	9.8	Mobile, AL	62.6	Tallahassee, FL	115.7
Scranton-Wilkes-Barre, PA	10.8	Tyler, TX	63.9	West Palm Beach-Boca Raton-Delray Beach, FL	130.3
Milwaukee, WI	10.9	El Paso, TX	66.7	Macon-Warner Robins, GA	139.9
Saginaw-Bay City-Midland, MI	11.8	Lake Charles, LA	71.2	Charlotte-Gastonia-Rock Hill, NC-SC	161.1
Philadelphia, PA/NJ	12.7	Kileen-Temple, TX	78.1	Ocala, FL	170.4
Albany-Schenectady-Troy, NY	13.2	Lafayette, LA	87.5	Atlanta, GA	176.3
Racine, WI	14.2	Jackson, MS	91.0	Wilmington, NC	195.7
Cleveland, OH	14.6	Brownsville-Harlingen-San Benito, TX	91.8	Fort Myers-Cape Coral, FL	199.6
Janesville-Beloit, WI	15.3	San Antonio, TX	98.1	Orlando, FL	206.2
Utica-Rome, NY	17.7	Houston, TX	105.1	Sarasota, FL	247.9
Chicago, IL	17.7	Biloxi-Gulfport, MS	106.5	Raleigh-Durham, NC	251.5
Johnstown, PA	20.2	Dallas-Fort Worth, TX	110.1		
St. Louis, MO	21.8	Odessa, TX	134.3		
Cincinnati-Hamilton, OH/KY/IN	22.7	McAllen-Edinburg-Pharr-Mission, TX	174.4		

continued

Table 8.1 Continued

Rustbelt cities	Growth (%)	Southern cities	Growth (%)	Southeastern cities	Growth (%)
Baltimore, MD	22.8	Austin, TX	200.8		
Syracuse, NY	28.7				
Reading, PA	31.5				
Kenosha, WI	35.6				
Rockford, IL	39.8				
Allentown-Bethlehem-Easton, PA/NJ	42.4				
Hamilton-Middleton, OH	42.7				
Bloomington-Normal, IL	43.0				
Rochester, NY	49.4				
Evansville, IN/KY	58.9				
Fort Wayne, IN	65.3				
Lafayette-W. Lafayette, IN	67.6				
Grand Rapids, MI	73.3				

Source: American Community Survey, US Census.

city's entrepreneurial level (Scola, 2016).[3] Hunt and Gauthier-Loiselle (2010) found that immigrants, particularly those from Asia, are over-represented in science and engineering and they patent at twice the rate of natives. This source of human capital has become increasingly relevant for urban resurgence in the Rustbelt. Like Hunt, we define an immigrant as a person who is born outside the US.

The shares of skilled natives and immigrants by city types are reported in Tables 8.2 through 8.4 depending on the population size. Large (L) cities have a population of over one million, medium-sized (M) cities are between half and one million, and small (S) cities host less than half a million people. Except for a few cities, the share of skilled natives is strikingly similar among cities of the three regions averaging between 15% and 17% in 1980. During this time, only five cities or fewer in each region had shares of at least 20%. Two cities, Gainesville and Tallahassee, had the highest share of 30–31%. The foreign-born skilled is much lower with many cities hosting less than 3%. Miami is clearly an outlier with a share of 7.3%. Despite their low shares, the figures are nonetheless significant when all immigrants are taken into account. Between one-third to half of immigrants in cities like Cincinnati, Lansing-East Lansing, Hamilton, Bloomington, and Lafayette are skilled. Similar levels of the skilled may be found in the South (e.g., Memphis, Austin, Birmingham, Baton-Rouge, Tuscaloosa, Jackson) and the Southeast (Atlanta, Raleigh-Durham, Chattanooga, Gainesville, Tallahassee). However, the highest shares tend to be associated with university towns. Moreover, large cities are more likely to see a higher share of skilled immigrants.

By 2010, shares of the skilled have risen for most cities in the Rustbelt. Both skilled natives and the foreign-born rose in virtually all of the cities except for Flint and Mansfield which had marginal decreases. The picture for the Sunbelt is a bit more mixed. Miami and Tallahassee in the Southeast saw a fall in skilled natives but this was offset by an increase in skilled immigrants, allowing both cities to stabilize their human capital level. Similarly, several cities in the South experienced a decline in the share of skilled natives. But increase in the share of skilled immigrants helped compensate for the decline. This means that overall the human capital level remained relatively similar to the 1980 level compared to Rustbelt cities where human capital rose for the majority of cities. It is fair however to say that some of the Rustbelt increase was the result of a relatively low base among smaller cities in 1980. But this low base was not confined to the region as it may also be found among smaller Southern cities. Overall however human capital level has not lagged behind that of their Southern counterparts. Rustbelt cities' average share of the skilled was 23.4% in 2010 compared to 15.9% in 1980. The respective shares for Southern and Southeast cities are 20.5 versus 17.1% and 25.2 versus 18.6% respectively. The 30 years thus saw turnaround for some cities in the Rustbelt. Overall, Tables 8.2 through 8.4 show that the educated foreign-born played some role in the Rustbelt turnaround while it enhanced talent level in the Southeast and stabilized human capital in the South.

To shed further light on the role of the foreign born, we calculate the skill ratio expressing the ratio of the number of college or higher foreign-born to the number of foreign-born without a high school education (see also Grieco et al., 2012). The results are presented in Tables 8.5 through 8.7. Table 8.5 shows that Rustbelt cities were generally characterized by low ratios in 1980. Only three cities, Lansing-East Lansing, Bloomington, and Hamilton, achieved ratios that were greater than one. Cincinnati and Buffalo just about made the 1.0 mark but largely from rounding up. By 2010, however, the pattern had changed dramatically. Only 10 cities – all small cities – were still below one. The ratios of two cities, Pittsburgh and Albany, had risen to over 3.0. For about 80% of the cities, skill ratios shifted from low to high. In the case of the Southern Sunbelt, one-fifth already had relatively high skill ratios of over one in 1980. While the number of high skill ratio cities rose in 2010, approximately half of the cities continued to be characterized by low skill ratios. Moreover compared to the Rustbelt, low skill ratios may be found in all city types from small to large. Likewise, a number of cities in the Southeast were characterized by high skill ratios in 1980 including Tallahassee (3.2), Athens (3.0), Gainesville (2.5), and Raleigh-Durham (2.0). Only four small to medium-sized cities had low skill ratios in 2010. Unlike their Southern counterparts, the skill ratio increased for many large cities such as Jacksonville and Orlando. But Atlanta, Raleigh-Durham, and Tallahassee saw a marginal decrease although they are still well above 1.0.

In a sense, the skill ratios of Rustbelt cities resemble those of their Southeastern counterparts driven by the in-migration of educated foreign born. But cities also attract unskilled immigrants. As Sassens (2012) and Scott (2010) point out, large cities are not only home to high-level managers and skilled professionals. They also attract service workers, janitors, nannies, and other low-wage workers. In other words, large cities attract both high-skilled and low-skilled immigrants. The tables suggest that such a phenomenon is not confined

Table 8.2 Distribution of the skilled in Rustbelt cities

City	Type	1980			2010		
		Skilled immigrants (%)	Skilled natives (%)	Skilled immigrant share of total immigrants (%)	Skilled immigrants (%)	Skilled natives (%)	Skilled immigrant share of total immigrants (%)
Baltimore, MD	L	1.1	16.4	27.5	4.5	25.0	43.4
Buffalo–Niagara Falls, NY	L	1.1	16.5	19.7	2.2	27.2	33.1
Detroit, MI	L	1.3	14.6	19.1	3.3	21.7	36.6
Pittsburgh, PA	L	0.7	15.7	19.3	1.8	27.2	49.7
Milwaukee, WI	L	0.9	17.4	20.7	2.3	24.8	32.7
Philadelphia, PA	L	1.2	16.4	21.4	3.8	24.3	37.1
Cleveland, OH	L	1.3	16.0	19.8	2.3	22.6	38.5
Chicago, IL	L	2.1	16.8	20.7	5.5	23.0	29.7
St. Louis, MO	L	0.7	16.3	27.2	2.0	25.1	38.2
Cincinnati, OH	L	0.7	16.7	30.8	2.0	24.7	41.6
Rochester, NY	L	1.7	21.2	21.8	2.7	28.8	34.3
Grand Rapids, MI	L	0.7	16.6	19.3	1.5	22.8	24.0
Akron, OH	M	0.9	16.3	24.2	1.6	24.5	41.0
Dayton–Springfield, OH	M	0.6	15.0	27.2	1.4	21.4	32.0
Toledo, OH/MI	M	0.6	15.0	22.9	1.6	21.0	36.8
Youngstown–Warren, OH-PA	M	0.5	11.8	11.7	0.7	17.5	26.2
Scranton–Wilkes-Barre, PA	M	0.4	13.0	14.3	1.2	21.7	27.4
Albany–Schenectady–Troy, NY	M	1.2	20.4	24.6	3.0	30.3	40.8
Syracuse, NY	M	1.1	18.5	21.4	2.0	26.0	34.7
Allentown–Bethlehem–Easton, PA/NJ	M	0.7	15.1	16.8	2.7	21.4	33.7
Benton Harbor, MI	S	1.0	13.4	25.4	2.1	20.3	36.9
Canton, OH	S	0.4	12.4	16.2	0.9	20.0	33.4
Davenport, IA-Rock Island-Moline, IL	S	0.5	15.9	17.0	1.2	25.9	22.3
Decatur, IL	S	0.4	14.4	23.8	0.6	19.4	25.6
Erie, PA	S	0.6	14.1	18.8	1.1	21.8	27.8
Flint, MI	S	0.6	12.2	20.5	0.3	13.1	15.8
Kankakee, IL	S	0.4	11.2	19.6	1.1	16.4	19.4
Kokomo, IN	S	0.3	10.4	18.4	0.3	18.9	13.5
Lansing-E. Lansing, MI	S	1.3	22.4	35.7	2.5	24.1	34.0
Lima, OH	S	0.2	9.5	16.0	0.4	18.4	21.9
Mansfield, OH	S	0.4	10.6	16.3	0.3	16.6	14.3

Muncie, IN	S	0.4	15.5	34.1	0.5	20.0	16.8
Peoria, IL	S	0.5	14.8	22.4	1.3	23.5	39.6
Sharon, PA	S	0.2	12.5	9.8	0.5	19.4	27.2
South Bend-Mishawaka, IN	S	0.6	15.8	18.3	2.3	21.3	39.4
Saginaw-Bay City-Midland, MI	S	0.5	11.0	19.4	1.0	21.8	39.1
Racine, WI	S	0.6	14.2	15.2	1.4	20.7	21.5
Janesville-Beloit, WI	S	0.3	12.9	16.1	0.4	20.0	8.5
Utica-Rome, NY	S	0.6	15.8	13.5	1.9	22.6	28.0
Johnstown, PA	S	0.2	10.0	9.1	0.5	19.0	34.6
Reading, PA	S	0.4	12.4	13.7	1.6	18.4	20.9
Kenosha, WI	S	0.7	12.2	13.6	2.0	18.8	30.6
Rockford, IL	S	0.7	14.5	16.6	1.8	18.2	20.7
Hamilton-Middleton, OH	S	0.5	15.5	35.0	2.2	20.3	39.4
Bloomington-Normal, IL	S	1.0	26.1	50.4	2.7	29.2	47.6
Elkhart-Goshen, IN	S	0.6	11.7	23.4	1.6	13.4	16.5
Evansville, IN/KY	S	0.4	14.5	27.1	0.8	21.0	28.0
Fort Wayne, IN	S	0.7	16.0	25.5	1.1	20.3	24.8
Lafayette, IN	S	2.1	27.4	57.5	3.1	19.8	30.0

Source: American Community Survey, US Census.

Table 8.3 Distribution of the skilled in Southern Sunbelt cities

City	Type	1980			2010		
		Skilled immigrants (%)	Skilled natives (%)	Skilled immigrant share of total immigrants (%)	Skilled immigrants (%)	Skilled natives (%)	Skilled immigrant share of total immigrants (%)
New Orleans, LA	L	1.1	16.9	26.9	2.2	19.4	27.9
Memphis, TN/AR/MS	L	0.6	16.7	30.7	2.0	20.8	30.0
San Antonio, TX	L	1.1	15.6	12.6	3.3	18.7	22.4
Houston-Brazoria, TX	L	1.9	20.2	23.0	5.6	16.9	23.6
Dallas-Fort Worth, TX	L	1.1	20.4	22.2	4.5	20.6	24.0
Austin, TX	L	1.7	27.1	33.3	4.8	26.7	31.0
Birmingham, AL	M	0.4	17.5	30.7	1.6	25.8	29.9
Baton Rouge, LA	M	0.9	18.9	38.9	1.8	20.6	42.4
Mobile, AL	M	0.4	13.4	22.6	1.1	19.9	26.2
El Paso, TX	M	2.0	12.0	8.7	4.1	11.6	14.6
McAllen-Edinburg-Pharr-Mission, TX	M	0.9	9.4	4.5	3.7	8.6	12.6
Alexandria, LA	S	0.3	11.8	14.6	0.6	15.3	21.9
Anniston, AL	S	0.4	12.8	18.4	1.3	15.8	32.8
Gadsden, AL	S	0.1	12.2	13.0	0.1	15.2	5.2
Beaumont-Port Arthur-Orange, TX	S	0.5	14.5	20.5	1.2	14.2	19.0
Corpus Christi, TX	S	0.8	13.9	14.5	2.0	17.5	29.2
Monroe, LA	S	0.2	16.0	19.5	0.7	17.2	42.0
Shreveport, LA	S	0.3	15.0	15.1	0.9	18.3	27.7
Wichita Falls, TX	S	0.7	16.8	14.9	1.9	15.2	20.4
Abilene, TX	S	0.7	17.6	14.7	1.1	20.8	17.0
Longview-Marshall, TX	S	0.5	15.7	15.7	0.5	15.6	5.1
Lubbock, TX	S	1.0	21.2	30.6	1.9	20.8	29.2
Montgomery, AL	S	0.4	17.3	25.8	1.6	22.3	31.9
Huntsville, AL	S	0.9	16.1	30.8	2.6	27.1	38.7
Waco, TX	S	0.4	17.4	15.9	1.4	17.7	17.6
Amarillo, TX	S	0.6	18.6	17.0	1.8	19.5	17.7
Tuscaloosa, AL	S	0.5	18.9	39.8	1.2	19.6	31.3
Galveston-Texas City, TX	S	0.8	16.8	19.7	2.7	21.6	26.7
Tyler, TX	S	0.4	19.0	14.1	1.6	21.3	16.6
Lake Charles, LA	S	0.4	16.8	28.4	0.9	17.9	29.4
Killeen-Temple, LA	S	0.9	13.4	9.9	2.4	16.3	19.2
Lafayette, LA	S	1.1	18.7	35.2	1.0	17.9	20.4
Jackson, MS	S	0.5	23.5	40.0	1.2	23.5	44.0
Brownsville-Harlingen-San Benito, TX	S	1.2	9.3	5.7	3.0	9.4	11.5
Biloxi-Gulfport, MS	S	0.7	14.4	17.4	1.2	20.4	21.2
Odessa, TX	S	0.5	13.0	7.9	1.1	14.3	11.2

Table 8.4 Distribution of the skilled in Southeastern Sunbelt cities

City	Type	1980			2010		
		Skilled immigrants (%)	Skilled natives (%)	Skilled immigrant share of total immigrants (%)	Skilled immigrants (%)	Skilled natives (%)	Skilled immigrant share of total immigrants (%)
Miami-Hialeah, FL	L	7.3	12.8	19.8	14.7	10.2	27.4
Fort Lauderdale-Hollywood-Pompano Beach, FL	L	2.4	17.8	20.4	10.1	17.5	30.5
Tampa-St. Petersburg-Clearwater, FL	L	1.3	16.6	18.2	4.2	21.6	30.2
Jacksonville, FL	L	0.8	14.9	23.4	3.2	22.8	35.2
West Palm Beach-Boca Raton-Delray Beach, FL	L	2.1	19.7	20.6	6.8	22.8	27.6
Charlotte-Gastonia-Rock Hill, NC-SC	L	0.6	17.7	28.4	2.8	23.8	28.7
Atlanta, GA	L	1.1	21.6	36.7	4.8	23.1	32.4
Orlando, FL	L	1.3	17.5	22.4	5.5	21.2	32.8
Raleigh-Durham, NC	L	1.2	26.4	47.0	4.6	29.5	35.0
Charleston-N.Charleston, SC	M	0.7	15.7	22.2	2.0	27.1	27.5
Greenville-Spartanburg-Anderson, SC	M	0.5	14.3	27.0	1.8	21.6	25.3
Columbia, SC	M	1.0	21.4	28.7	2.2	26.2	35.0
Augusta-Aiken, GA-SC	M	0.6	14.3	17.3	1.8	21.6	29.7
Lakeland-Winterhaven, FL	M	0.7	13.2	18.9	2.4	16.2	20.9
Melbourne-Titusville-Cocoa-Palm Bay, FL	M	1.3	19.3	21.2	3.2	22.3	31.6
Fort Myers-Cape Coral, FL	M	1.1	15.7	20.3	3.6	20.5	21.9
Sarasota, FL	M	1.8	21.9	25.2	3.4	23.7	27.1
Albany, GA	S	0.3	13.0	15.6	0.5	15.3	17.1
Columbus, GA/AL	S	0.7	14.4	13.1	2.3	15.8	29.3
Chattanooga, TN/GA	S	0.5	14.9	31.5	1.0	20.6	23.5
Fayetteville, NC	S	0.8	13.2	12.8	2.8	19.8	28.2
Savannah, GA	S	0.6	14.9	23.7	2.3	22.7	31.9
Athens, GA	S	1.1	24.5	54.3	2.9	24.1	30.6
Pensacola, FL	S	0.7	15.3	23.0	2.3	22.2	34.2
Jacksonville, NC	S	0.5	8.9	12.0	1.0	14.1	15.6
Gainesville, FL	S	2.6	30.4	47.7	5.9	29.5	54.2
Fort Walton Beach, FL	S	0.9	15.6	12.4	2.3	23.5	24.2
Daytona Beach, FL	S	1.2	17.1	20.8	2.5	20.3	30.7
Tallahassee, FL	S	1.5	31.8	47.9	2.8	28.7	43.0
Macon-Warner Robins, GA	S	0.3	13.5	24.2	1.4	17.8	23.8
Ocala, FL	S	0.3	12.1	10.0	2.0	16.8	23.7
Wilmington, NC	S	0.4	16.7	23.2	1.5	31.6	30.8

Table 8.5 Skill ratios of Rustbelt cities

City	Type	1980	2010
Baltimore, MD	L	0.8	2.4
Chicago, IL	L	0.5	1.4
Cincinnati-Hamilton, OH/KY/IN	L	1.0	2.6
Cleveland, OH	L	0.5	2.4
Grand Rapids, MI	L	0.5	1.0
Milwaukee, WI	L	0.5	1.5
Philadelphia, PA/NJ	L	0.6	2.1
Rochester, NY	L	0.6	2.2
St. Louis, MO-IL	L	0.7	2.4
Buffalo-Niagara Falls, NY	L	0.5	1.7
Detroit, MI	L	0.5	1.8
Pittsburgh, PA	L	0.4	3.8
Albany-Schenectady-Troy, NY	M	0.6	3.1
Allentown-Bethlehem-Easton, PA/NJ	M	0.4	2.2
Scranton-Wilkes-Barre, PA	M	0.3	1.2
Syracuse, NY	M	0.6	1.8
Akron, OH	M	0.7	2.0
Dayton-Springfield, OH	M	0.9	1.3
Toledo, OH/MI	M	0.7	1.9
Youngstown-Warren, OH-PA	M	0.3	2.1
Bloomington-Normal, IL	S	4.2	2.6
Elkhart-Goshen, IN	S	0.7	0.6
Evansville, IN/KY	S	0.9	1.6
Fort Wayne, IN	S	0.8	0.8
Hamilton-Middleton, OH	S	1.5	3.3
Janesville-Beloit, WI	S	0.4	0.2
Johnstown, PA	S	0.1	1.8
Kenosha, WI	S	0.3	2.3
Lafayette-W. Lafayette, IN	S	3.5	1.3
Racine, WI	S	0.3	0.7
Reading, PA	S	0.3	0.8
Rockford, IL	S	0.4	1.0
Saginaw-Bay City-Midland, MI	S	0.5	4.9
Utica-Rome, NY	S	0.3	0.9
Benton Harbor, MI	S	0.7	1.3
Canton, OH	S	0.4	1.2
Davenport, IA-Rock Island-Moline, IL	S	0.4	0.9
Decatur, IL	S	0.6	3.0
Erie, PA	S	0.5	1.6
Flint, MI	S	0.6	1.0
Kankakee, IL	S	0.4	0.5
Kokomo, IN	S	0.5	0.5
Lansing-E. Lansing, MI	S	1.2	1.3
Lima, OH	S	0.4	1.2
Mansfield, OH	S	0.4	0.8
Muncie, IN	S	1.0	1.1
Peoria, IL	S	0.6	2.6
Sharon, PA	S	0.2	9.1
South Bend-Mishawaka, IN	S	0.4	3.0

Source: American Community Survey, US Census.

Table 8.6 Skill ratios of Southern Sunbelt cities

City	Type	1980	2010
Austin, TX	L	1.0	1.1
Dallas-Fort Worth, TX	L	0.5	0.9
Houston-Brazoria, TX	L	0.5	0.8
Memphis, TN/AR/MS	L	1.0	1.2
New Orleans, LA	L	0.8	1.3
San Antonio, TX	L	0.2	0.8
Baton Rouge, LA	M	1.4	2.5
Birmingham, AL	M	1.0	1.3
El Paso, TX	M	0.2	0.4
McAllen-Edinburg-Pharr-Mission, TX	M	0.1	0.3
Mobile, AL	M	0.8	1.1
Abilene, TX	S	0.3	0.5
Alexandria, LA	S	0.4	0.9
Amarillo, TX	S	0.3	0.5
Anniston, AL	S	0.5	1.2
Beaumont-Port Arthur-Orange, TX	S	0.5	0.6
Biloxi-Gulfport, MS	S	0.4	1.0
Brownsville-Harlingen-San Benito, TX	S	0.1	0.3
Corpus Christi, TX	S	0.3	1.5
Gadsden, AL	S	0.6	0.1
Galveston-Texas City, TX	S	0.5	1.1
Huntsville, AL	S	1.1	2.0
Jackson, MS	S	1.5	2.6
Kileen-Temple, TX	S	0.2	0.9
Lafayette, LA	S	1.5	0.8
Lake Charles, LA	S	1.5	2.2
Longview-Marshall, TX	S	0.3	0.1
Lubbock, TX	S	0.8	1.3
Monroe, LA	S	0.6	3.2
Montgomery, AL	S	0.9	1.5
Odessa, TX	S	0.1	0.2
Shreveport, LA	S	0.4	1.7
Tuscaloosa, AL	S	1.5	2.5
Tyler, TX	S	0.3	0.4
Waco, TX	S	0.3	0.6
Wichita Falls, TX	S	0.4	0.9

Source: American Community Survey, US Census.

to large cities either. It may explain why Southern cities such as Dallas, Houston, and El Paso have low skill ratios in 2010. These cities attract a relatively high level of unskilled immigrants, particularly unskilled Hispanics: between one-quarter to one-third Hispanic immigrants of all immigrants in these cities are unskilled.

Overall comparison of cities' human capital level indicates that Rustbelt cities have been able to attract or retain both educated natives and the foreign-born. Given recent literature's emphasis of skill in urban development, this opens up possible channels that may potentially contribute to urban revitalization in the region.

Table 8.7 Skill ratios of Southeastern Sunbelt cities

City	Type	1980	2010
Atlanta, GA	L	1.7	1.5
Charlotte-Gastonia-Rock Hill, NC-SC	L	1.0	1.2
Fort Lauderdale-Hollywood-Pompano Beach, FL	L	0.7	2.2
Jacksonville, FL	L	0.8	2.6
Miami-Hialeah, FL	L	0.5	1.5
Orlando, FL	L	0.8	2.4
Raleigh-Durham, NC	L	2.0	1.5
Tampa-St. Petersburg-Clearwater, FL	L	0.6	1.8
West Palm Beach-Boca Raton-Delray Beach, FL	L	0.7	1.4
Augusta-Aiken, GA-SC	M	0.5	1.6
Charleston-N.Charleston, SC	M	0.7	1.1
Columbia, SC	M	1.1	2.2
Fort Myers-Cape Coral, FL	M	0.7	0.9
Greenville-Spartanburg-Anderson, SC	M	0.8	1.0
Lakeland-Winterhaven, FL	M	0.6	0.7
Melbourne-Titusville-Cocoa-Palm Bay, FL	M	0.8	2.5
Sarasota, FL	M	1.0	1.5
Albany, GA	S	0.4	0.6
Athens, GA	S	3.0	1.3
Chattanooga, TN/GA	S	1.2	1.2
Columbus, GA/AL	S	0.5	1.7
Daytona Beach, FL	S	0.8	2.7
Fayetteville, NC	S	0.4	1.4
Fort Walton Beach, FL	S	0.3	1.9
Gainesville, FL	S	2.5	6.0
Jacksonville, NC	S	0.5	0.7
Macon-Warner Robins, GA	S	0.8	1.3
Ocala, FL	S	0.3	1.2
Pensacola, FL	S	0.8	3.1
Savannah, GA	S	0.8	1.9
Tallahassee, FL	S	3.2	2.9
Wilmington, NC	S	0.8	2.7

Source: American Community Survey, US Census.

Discussion and conclusion

Rustbelt cities have earned an image of urban decline since the 1970s. Consider the following description by Kotkin and Piiparinen (2014):

> For the most part, the cities of the Midwest – with the exception of Chicago and Minneapolis – have been consigned to the second and inferior class. Cleveland, Buffalo, Detroit or a host of smaller cities are rarely assessed, except as objects of pity whose only hope is to find a way, through new urbanist alchemy, to mimic the urban patterns of superstar cities like New York, San Francisco, Boston or Portland.

Beauregard (2003, p. 10) puts it more poignantly: "It was better to forget the city." Yet forgotten Rustbelt cities have continued to host a reasonable level of human capital. A recent *New York Times* report puts Buffalo, Baltimore, and Pittsburgh among the top three places in growth of college graduates aged 25–34 from 2000 to 2012 (Miller, 2014). Their growth rates are well above the top 51 metropolitan cities' average of 25%. Buffalo and Baltimore's growth of 34 and 32% respectively are higher than that of New York (25%), Boston (12%), and San Francisco (11%) although it is fair to say that the high growth reflects a smaller base in the earlier period. Nonetheless, such growth bodes well for the cities.

One explanation is that young people are drawn to urban living that is also affordable. Zimmerman and Beal (2002) have found that income inequality tends to be lower in cities dominated by manufacturing than those dominated by finance and advanced producer services. Access to housing also contributes to lower social inequality. Rustbelt cities may have shrunk or "rightsized" (Silverman, Patterson, Yu, & Ranahan, 2016), but the manufacturing sector here continues to be a source of demand for engineers and scientists (Kotkin, 2013). A good example is the rise of Akron and Albany as a "brainbelt" (van Agtmael and Bakker, 2016). Their emergence as a hub of brains reflects transformation from an industrial legacy that had depended on the domestic market to prosper in the past to the current outlook that is more internationally oriented. Akron's past specialized skills in manufacturing for instance has facilitated its transition to a center of new material production that draws on the cumulative benefits of knowledge over time. Likewise, cool watches and leather goods from Detroit's Shinola emerged out of skills that turned industrial goods to high-end luxury goods on the international market.

Overall, the analysis suggests that the human capital level is comparable to Southern and Southeastern Sunbelt cities. More specifically, the average human capital level is higher in the Rustbelt than the Southern Sunbelt in 2010. Growth of human capital is driven by the in-migration or retention of both college-educated natives and foreign-born. Notably as well, immigrants who have relocated to cities are more and more educated as the skill ratios demonstrate. Skill ratios of Rustbelt cities are comparable to their Southeastern counterparts today whereas this was not the case in 1980. This is not to say that Rustbelt cities' population will return to their highs of the past. However, there are signs that brain divergence between the Rustbelt and Sunbelt may be narrowing. Certain Sunbelt cities are already experiencing social distress that was once characteristic of Rustbelt cities as Hollander (2011) has shown. While Rustbelt turnaround is slow, at times spluttering, and cities like Flint have continued to see relative decline than turnaround, nonetheless its salience cannot be denied. Rightsizing cities in the Rustbelt may need to involve not just adjustment to a smaller population, but also how such adjustment can continue to maintain urban vitality through a smarter workforce.

Notes

1 See www.worth.com/destinations-2016, accessed July 2016.
2 One such antecedent could be historical accident as Krugman (1991) relates of the carpet industry at Dalton, Georgia.
3 Baltimore is located on the periphery of the Rustbelt and is included because it shares characteristics of Rustbelt cities.

References

Acs, Z. (2002). *Innovation and the growth of cities*. Cheltenham, UK: Edward Elgar.
Beauregard, R. (2003). *Voices of decline: The postwar fate of American cities*. New York: Routledge.
Bernard, R., & Rice, B. (1983). *Sunbelt cities: Politics and growth since World War II*. Austin: University of Texas Press.
Binelli, M. (2012). *Detroit City is the place to be*. New York: Metropolitan Books.
Black, D., & Henderson, V. (1999). A theory of urban growth. *Journal of Political Economy, 107*(2), 252–284.
Bowen, W. M. (2014). *The road through the Rust Belt: From preeminence to decline to prosperity*. Kalamazoo, MI: W.E. Upjohn Institute for Employment Research.
Bowen, W. M., & Kinahan, K. (2014). Midwestern urban and regional response to global economic transition. In W. M. Bowen, *The road through the Rust Belt* (pp. 7–36). Kalamazoo, MI: W.E. Upjohn Institute for Employment Research.
Bublitz, E., Fritsch, M., & Wyrwich, M. (2015). Balanced skills and the city. *Economic Geography, 91*(4), 475–508.
Ceh, B., & Gatrell, J. (2006). R&D production in the United States: Rethinking the Snowbelt-Sunbelt shift. *Social Science Journal, 43*(4), 529–551.
Florida, R. (2002). *The rise of the creative class*. New York: Basic Books.
Florida, R. (2005). *Cities and the creative class*. New York: Routledge.
Florida, R., Mellander, C., & Stolarick, K. (2008). Inside the black box of regional development: Human capital, the creative class and tolerance. *Journal of Economic Geography, 8*(5), 615–649.
Glaeser, E. (2010). *Triumph of the city*. New York: Penguin Press.
Glaeser, E. L., & Maré, D. C. (2001). Cities and skills. *Journal of Labor Economics, 19*(2), 316–342.
Glaeser, E., Ponzetto, G., & Tobio, K. (2014). Cities, skills and regional change. *Regional Studies, 48*(1), 7–43.
Glaeser, E.L., & Resseger, M. E. (2010). The complementarity between cities and skills. *Journal of Regional Science, 50*(1), 221–233.
Goldstein, D. (2009). Weirton revisited: Finance, the working class and rustbelt steel restructuring. *Review of Political Economics, 41*(3), 352–357.
Grieco, E., Acosta, Y., de la Cruz, T., Gambino, C., Gryn, T., Larsen, L., et al. (2012). *The foreign-born population in the United States 2010*. Washington, D.C.: Brookings Institution.
High, S. (2003). *Industrial sunset: The making of North America's Rust Belt, 1968–1984*. Toronto: University of Toronto Press.
Hollander, J. (2011). *Sunburnt cities: The great recession, depopulation and urban planning in the American Sunbelt*. New York: Routledge.
Hunt, J., & Gauthier-Loiselle, M. (2010). How much does immigration boost innovation? *American Economic Journal of Macroeconomics, 2*(2), 31–56.

Jacobs, J. (1969). *The economy of cities*. New York: Vintage Books.

Kotkin, J. (2013, August 30). Rust belt chic and the keys to reviving the Great Lakes. *Forbes*. Retrieved June 29, 2017, from www.forbes.com/sites/joelkotkin/2013/08/30/rust-belt-chic-and-the-keys-to-reviving-the-great-lakes/#31fe581e693f.

Kotkin, J., & Piiparinen, R. (2014, December 7). The rustbelt roars back from the dead. *The Daily Beast*. Retrieved June 29, 2017, from www.thedailybeast.com/the-rustbelt-roars-back-from-the-dead.

Krugman, P. (1991). *Geography and trade*. Cambridge, MA: MIT Press.

Lucas, R. J. (1988). On the mechanics of economic development. *Journal of Monetary Economics, 22*, 3–24.

Mallach, A. (2015). The uncoupling of the economic city. *Urban Affairs Review, 51*(4), 443–473.

Miller, C. C. (2014, October 10). Where young college graduates are choosing to live. *New York Times*. Retrieved June 29, 2017, from www.nytimes.com/2014/10/20/upshot/where-young-college-graduates-are-choosing-to-live.html.

Mokyr, J. (2000). *Knowledge, technology and economic growth during the industrial revolution*. Hague: Kluwert.

Mokyr, J. (2005). Long-term economic growth and the history of technology. In P. Aghion and S. Durlauf (Eds.), *Handbook of economic growth* (Vol. 1, pp. 1113–1180). Amsterdam: Elsevier.

Moretti, E. (2004). Human capital externalities in cities. In V. Henderson & J. F. Thisse (Eds.), *Handbook of regional and urban economics: Cities and geography* (Vol. 4). Amsterdam: Elsevier.

Morris, C. R. (2012). *The dawn of innovation*. New York: Public Affairs.

Neumann, T. (2016). *Remaking the Rustbelt*. Philadelphia: University of Pennsylvania Press.

Poon, J., & Yin, W. (2014). Human capital: A comparison of Rustbelt and Sunbelt. *Geography Compass, 8*(5), 287–299.

Sassens, S. (2012). *Cities in the world economy* (4th ed.). Thousand Oaks, CA: Sage.

Saxenian, A. (2006). *The new Argonauts: Regional advantage in a new global economy*. Cambridge, MA: Harvard University Press.

Scola, N. (2016). The rise of new Baltimoreans. In J. Gonzalez III & R. Kemp (Eds.), *Immigration and America's cities* (pp. 236–243). Jefferson, NC: McFarland & Company.

Scott, A. (1992). *Technopolis: Hi-technology industry and regional development in Southern California*. Berkeley and Los Angeles: University of California Press.

Scott, A. (2010). Space-time variations of human capital assets across US metropolitan areas, 1980–2000. *Economic Geography, 86*(3), 233–250.

Silverman, V., Patterson, K., Yu, L., & Ranahan, M. (2016). *Affordable housing in US shrinking cities*. Chicago: Policy Press.

Simmons, P., & Lang, R. (2006). The urban turnaround. In B. Katz & R. Lang (Eds.), *Redefining urban and suburban America* (pp. 51–62). Washington, D.C.: Brookings Institution.

Simon, C., & Nardinelli, C. (2002). Human capital and the rise of American cities, 1900–1990. *Regional Science and Urban Economics, 32*(1), 59–96.

Squicciarini, M., & Voigtander, N. (2015). Human capital and industrialization: Evidence from the age of Enlightenment. *Quarterly Journal of Economics, 130*(4), 1825–1883.

Storper, M. (2010). Why does a city grow? Specialization, human capital or institutions? *Urban Studies, 47*(10), 2027–2050.

Storper, M., & Scott, A. (2009). Rethinking human capital, creativity and urban growth. *Journal of Economic Geography, 9*(2), 147–167.

Storper, M., & Scott, A. J. (2016). Current debates in urban theory: A critical assessment. *Urban Studies, 53*(6), 1114–1136.

van Agtmael, A., & Bakker, F. (2016). *The smartest places on Earth*. New York: Public Affairs.

Wadhwa, V. (2012). *The immigrant exodus: Why America is losing the global race to capture entrepreneurial talent*. Philadelphia: Wharton Digital Publishing.

Warf, B., & Holly, B. (1997). The rise and fall and rise of Cleveland. *Annals of the American Academy of Political and Social Science, 551*(2), 208–221.

Zimmerman, F., & Beal, D. (2002). *Manufacturing works: The vital link between production and prosperity*. Chicago: Dearborn Financial Publishing.

9 The engagement gap

Social mobility and extracurricular participation among American youth[1]

Kaisa Snellman, Jennifer M. Silva,
Carl B. Frederick, and Robert D. Putnam

Public education was originally designed to be a great equalizer in American society, redistributing opportunities to children from less advantageous backgrounds and thus increasing social mobility. From the Common School movement of the 1840s to the GI Bill of the 1940s, reformers sought to level the playing field, enhance economic productivity, and strengthen democratic citizenship by making education available on a mass scale. Despite these hopeful beginnings, recent evidence suggests that schools may no longer be narrowing the gap between the "haves" and the "have-nots."

Over the past two generations, the difference in educational achievement between the children from poor families and that of children from wealthy families has grown substantially. Whether we look at standardized test scores, college admission, or college graduation, the achievement gaps between children from upper-middle-class families and children from working-class families are steadily increasing. Today, the income gap in test scores is 40% larger than it was three decades ago (Reardon, 2011). For high-income students, the college graduation rate increased by 18 percentage points over the past two decades; in contrast, the graduation rate of low-income students grew by only 4 percentage points (Bailey and Dynarski, 2011). Moreover, wealthy students make up an increasing share of the enrollment at the most selective and prestigious four-year institutions (Reardon, Baker, & Klasik, 2012), while low-income students with similar test scores and academic records are more likely to attend two-year colleges (Alon, 2009; Hoxby & Avery, 2012).

Discussions and debates about the state of education in America often focus on standardized test scores and "core competencies," but a great deal of evidence suggests that it is not only what happens inside the classroom that matters for children's outcomes. That is, participation in extracurricular activities (e.g., chess club, yearbook, soccer) have been shown to be no less important than test scores for predicting educational attainment and accumulated earnings 10 years later (Lleras, 2008). Simply put, participation in extracurricular activities is closely correlated with children's futures.

Activities, such as chess clubs, yearbook committees, and soccer teams, promote important noncognitive skills – in particular, teamwork, "grit," and leadership – that are associated with educational attainment and higher returns in the labor market (Borghans, Ter Weel, & Weinberg, 2014; Cunha, Heckman, & Schennach, 2010; Kuhn & Weinberger, 2005). Moreover, participation in activities has become an important proxy for qualities that are hard to measure, such as ambition and curiosity. Colleges seek to admit students who not only test well but who also exhibit a diversity of interests and willingness to learn new things. Being part of the synchronized swimming team and playing a friction harp reflect a diversity of interests and thus are rewarded by university admissions officers. Playing lacrosse or squash is indicative also of cultural capital, because it signals that a student will fit well at an elite institution (Rivera, 2012).

In theory, public schools provide equal opportunities for civic engagement and character building for all children in the form of extracurricular activities. In reality, participation in these voluntary activities varies widely across social class. Children from upper-middle-class families are much more likely to join school clubs and sports teams than their working-class peers (Beck & Jennings, 1982; Marsh, 1992; Marsh & Kleitman, 2002). It is troubling but hardly surprising that students from wealthy families are more likely than other students to participate in organized activities. However, it is alarming that this class gap in civic and social engagement has grown over the past two decades.

We raise this issue here because if a new initiative to monitor mobility were indeed undertaken, it should allow us to examine the role of extracurricular opportunities within the mobility process. To make the case that the role of extracurricular activities matters for mobility studies, we present new analyses of four national surveys of American high school students, analyses that will reveal a sharp increase in the class gap in extracurricular involvement. We find that since the 1970s, upper-middle-class high school seniors have become increasingly active in school clubs and sport teams. In contrast, participation among working-class students has veered in the opposite direction. In the 1990s, involvement in school clubs plummeted among working-class students and has continued to decrease ever since.

Examining the differences among high school students with respect to extra-curricular activities offers a glimpse of tomorrow's socioeconomic and civic landscape. Given that these factors predict important outcomes – including educational attainment and civic and political participation later in life – the consequence of the current gaps might be an even more polarized and unequal society than we have now, where children from upper-middle-class families become more socially and civically engaged while working-class children become more disconnected and disengaged (Silva, 2013; Wright, 2015). Furthermore, if class increasingly predicts participation in activities that in turn predict educational attainment and future income, in effect we may be witnessing a vicious cycle that shapes patterns of intergenerational mobility.

Extracurricular participation and life success

School clubs and sports teams have been a fundamental part of the American high school experience since public high schools were built across the nation

(Coleman, 1961). Extracurricular activities, including athletics and student government, were viewed as a way to promote character, build "soft" skills, and cultivate a sense of unity among students from different religious and socioeconomic backgrounds (O'Hanlon, 1980). While these goals appear to be threatened, at least with respect to social class (Beck & Jennings, 1982; Marsh, 1992), it remains true that extracurricular activities yield a wide array of benefits for participants.

The skills and social networks built through participation in organized activities have been shown to enhance educational achievement and promote well-being, healthy choices, and prosocial behavior (Eccles, Barber, Stone, & Hunt, 2003; Marsh & Kleitman, 2002). Participation in interscholastic athletics teaches perseverance and a strong work ethic while increasing the level of social capital available to student-athletes via coaches, teachers, and academically oriented peers. Team sports also teach students how they can work together to achieve a common goal. Student-athletes have higher test scores (Broh, 2002), lower dropout rates (McNeal, 1995), and higher rates of college enrollment and completion (Troutman & Dufur, 2007). Chess clubs, debate teams, school bands, and student councils similarly cultivate leadership skills, encourage initiative, and allow youths to develop emotional competencies and social skills.

The apparent effects of participation in organized activities extend well beyond high school. Involvement in high school extracurricular activities is associated not only with educational and occupational attainment but also with political and civic engagement in adulthood as well as mental and physical health much later in life (Hart, Donnelly, Youniss, & Atkins, 2007; McFarland & Thomas, 2006; Nie, Junn, & Stehlik-Barry, 1996; Putnam, 2000). The benefits of extracurricular participation are even stronger for students who assume a leadership role. Team captains and club leaders are more likely than other students to occupy managerial occupations as adults and to command a higher wage premium within managerial occupations (Kuhn & Weinberger, 2005). Participation in extracurricular activities, then, has implications for social mobility and adult success.

When studying the effects of extracurricular participation, concerns about potential endogeneity arise. For example, students who are more extroverted, ambitious, curious, or determined might be more likely than others to join clubs, while these same traits might also be rewarded later by the labor market. This problem has been well documented in the existing literature, and recent studies have addressed it to varying degrees using different econometric approaches and research designs. Notably, Stevenson (2010) found that increased sports participation due to Title IX[2] has a positive effect on female college attendance and labor force participation by using male participation rates as an instrumental variable. Similarly, Kosteas (2010) used information on siblings' clubs participation as an instrumental variable when studying the effects of participation on earnings. He finds that participation in both athletics and academic clubs has positive earnings effects comparable to more than half a year increase in years of education (see Barron, Ewing, & Waddell, 2000; Eide & Ronan, 2001 for other instrumental variable studies showing positive effects of sports participation).

Data

We appreciate that our claims about the importance of extracurricular activities for mobility have not been fully embraced by mobility scholars. If we want to make a persuasive case for monitoring these activities within any new mobility initiative, it is useful to present results that speak to the role of extracurricular activities in explaining changes in mobility.

We do so with data from the series of high school cohort studies conducted by the National Center for Education Statistics (NCES). The four cohorts that we use are (birth cohorts are given in brackets) the National Longitudinal Study of 1972 [1954], High School and Beyond [1964], the National Education Longitudinal Study of 1988 [1974], and the Education Longitudinal Study of 2002 [1986]. Each cohort study collects information from students, parents, and school administrators. These data include information on student attitudes and experiences in high school and on important downstream outcomes such as labor market experiences and postsecondary education enrollment and attainment.

The NCES surveys include information on several types of school-sponsored activities.

The general categories include service clubs (e.g., AFS, Key Club), student government, academic honor societies (e.g., National Honor Society), journalism clubs (e.g., school yearbook, newspaper, or literary magazine), music and drama clubs (e.g., school band, school play), academic clubs (e.g., for art, computer, engineering, foreign languages, science, math, psychology, etc.), hobby clubs (e.g., photography, chess, frisbee, etc.), and vocational clubs (e.g., Future Farmers of America, Future Teachers of America). In addition, the surveys ask about participation in various sports teams, including football and cheerleading.

We measure the class gaps by comparing extracurricular participation among the top and bottom quartiles of the socioeconomic status (SES) index for each cohort.[3] Our analytic sample is limited to non-Hispanic white high school seniors; this approach serves to emphasize that the gaps we find are driven by social class and not by race or ethnicity.[4] We further limit the sample to respondents with non-missing data on SES and extracurricular participation.[5] Participation estimates, social class gaps, and changes in those gaps over time are all estimated using sampling weights to account for the complex, clustered sampling designs.

Rising class disparities

National surveys show that class disparities in involvement with the school orchestra (or the French club or the soccer team) have steadily increased over the past three decades. Figure 9.1 shows the percentage of high school seniors who reported participating in at least one school sponsored, nonathletic extracurricular activity. The solid line shows the observed percentage among the students in each survey's highest SES quartile; the dashed line shows the trend for the students in the lowest SES quartile. The thin vertical lines show the 95% confidence intervals. All of the within-survey class gaps displayed in the figure are

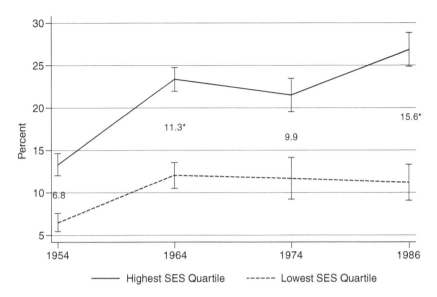

Figure 9.1 Participation in one or more extracurricular activities (excluding sports) in twelfth grade, by class and birth cohort.

Source: NCES Cohort Studies (NLS72, HS&B, NELS:88, ELS:2002).

Note
Non-Hispanic whites only.
* Indicates that gap is significantly different than previous survey.

statistically significant at the $p < 0.05$ level; class gaps that are statistically distinguishable (at the $p < 0.05$ level) from the class gap among the previous cohort are marked with an asterisk. For students born in the mid-1980s, participation among high-SES students trends steadily upward and plateaus at about 75%, whereas working-class participation increases between the first two cohorts but thereafter drops off to about 55%.

This general pattern of participation by social class holds when we focus on the nine individual types of extracurricular activities. There are two exceptions: student government, where upper-middle-class participation decreases while working-class participation is flat (but at a lower level); and vocational clubs, where working-class participation decreases steadily while upper-middle-class participation remains constant (at a lower level).

Class disparities have also increased in the context of participation in high school sports. Figure 9.2 shows the percentage of high school seniors who reported participating in at least one team or individual interscholastic sport. The participation rate of upper-middle-class youths increased from about 44% to almost 50% between the birth cohorts of 1964 and 1986. The participation rates of working-class youths were lower, yet they kept pace with upper-middle-class youths born between 1964 and 1974. The participation rate of working-class

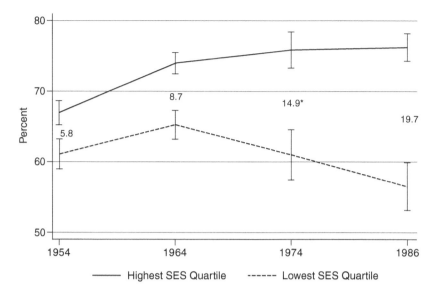

Figure 9.2 Participation in one or more sports in twelfth grade, by class and birth cohort.

Source: NCES Cohort Studies (NLS72, HS&B, NELS:88, ELS:2002).

Note
Non-Hispanic whites only.
* Indicates that gap is significantly different than previous survey.

youths born in 1986 dropped to the level of their counterparts born in 1964 – at just less than 25%.

Figure 9.3 shows the class gap for twelfth graders who report being team captains. Again, upper-middle-class youths show increasing participation over time. The proportion of upper-middle-class youths who are team captains almost doubles, from 13% among the birth cohort of 1954 to 25% for those born in 1986. The decreasing percentage of working-class team captains – from 12% to 11% between the cohorts of 1964–1986 – is less dramatic than in the cases of sports and club participation, but the class gap has nonetheless grown dramatically.

How to explain the growing gap

What explains these growing class gaps in extracurricular involvement? One part of the explanation lies in rising income inequality. The economic distance between the top and bottom rungs in the United States has been growing steadily since the 1970s, with high-income families pulling away from the median (Piketty & Saez, 2003; Western, Bloome, & Percheski, 2008). Simply stated, rising inequality means that wealthy families have more money to invest in their

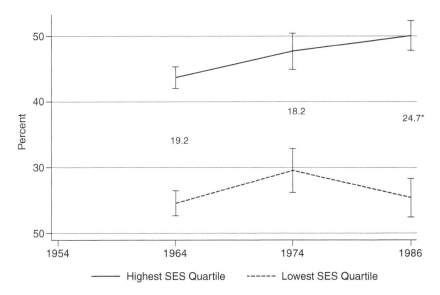

Figure 9.3 Percentage of twelfth graders who are team captains, by class and birth cohort.

Source: NCES Cohort Studies (NLS72, HS&B, NELS:88, ELS:2002).

Note
Non-Hispanic whites only.
* Indicates that gap is significantly different than previous survey.

children. Money helps families to pay for piano and ballet lessons, for science camps and traveling soccer teams, and for music instruments and sports equipment. In addition, not worrying about "making ends meet" every month allows parents to take time off from work to attend recitals and lacrosse games.

Not only do wealthy families have more money than before, they are also using it differently. Rich families now invest an increasing share of their income and time in providing learning experiences for their children. Consumer expenditure surveys show that, since the early 1970s, spending on child enrichment goods and services has increased to a far greater extent for families in the top income quintiles than for those in the bottom quintiles (Kaushal, Magnuson, & Waldfogel, 2011; Kornrich & Furstenberg, 2013). Despite the rise of consumer culture, parents have reduced their spending on toys, clothes, and games. Instead, much of the growth in spending has come from greater investments in books, tutoring, and lessons in sports and arts.

Moreover, college-educated parents who are wealthy invest relatively more time in reading to their children and in taking them to playgrounds, museums, and soccer practice (Ramey & Ramey, 2010; Sayer, Bianchi, & Robinson, 2004). Compared with less-educated parents, college-educated parents report spending about six more hours per week playing with their young children and engaging them in educational or organized activities (Ramey & Ramey, 2010).[6] Children of college-educated parents spend at least three more hours per week on organized activities than do children of less-educated parents (Mahoney, Harris, & Eccles, 2006). These seemingly small differences amount to large gaps. By age six, upper-middle-class children will have spent 1,300 more hours than working-class children in places other than their homes or day care, such as libraries, movie theaters, restaurants, and parks (Phillips, 2011).

Low-income parents, too, have increased the time and money they invest in the development of their children, but not to the same degree as wealthy parents have. Since 1975, the increase in time spent with children is twice as large for college-educated than for less-educated parents (Ramey & Ramey, 2010).

What is driving upper-middle-class parents to invest ever-greater amounts of time and money in extracurricular activities? Two factors account for this phenomenon: vast changes in the American economy's structure and an increasingly complex college landscape. In our contemporary, knowledge-based economy – which favors workers with college and advanced degrees – the four-year degree is a prerequisite for (though not a guarantee of) secure middle-class life (Kalleberg, 2009; Powell & Snellman, 2003). Meanwhile, blue-collar jobs now pay less and offer fewer benefits and less security than they did a generation ago. In the wake of falling blue-collar wages, demand for a college degree has soared; these trends have spurred competition in admissions, especially at the most selective four-year colleges and universities (Alon, 2009; Hoxby & Avery, 2012). The proliferation of college rankings (as published by U.S. News & World Report and others) has increased public awareness about the range and stratification of colleges. The University of Chicago accepted only 8.8% of its more than 30,300 applicants in 2013, while the Harvard and Stanford admission rates dipped below 6% (Abrams, 2013). The competition for elite college slots is now more intense than ever.

To make sure that their children stand a chance in the competition for college admission, upper-middle-class parents invest both time and money in building their children's "resumes" with the aim of making them look "measurably talented" and interesting to admissions committees (Ginsburg, 2007; Lareau, 2004; Stevens, 2009). Ramey and Ramey (2010) refer to this increasing investment in early childhood as the "rug rat race," whereby upper-middle-class parents are driven by the belief that early childhood experiences largely determine future educational and economic success. For working-class parents not in tune with the dynamic economy and college landscape, knowledge about cultivating their children can prove to be elusive.

Neighborhood segregation also affects the availability of and attitudes toward extracurricular activities for children. Extracurricular sports and clubs are largely social activities whose availability depends a great deal on others' engagement in them. Note also that little leagues, theater clubs, and local swim teams are public goods available only when communities choose (and can afford) to invest in the facilities that sustain them. This means that an increase in the income segregation across communities will amplify household-level differences in the expenditure on and participation in certain extracurricular activities. Income segregation has, indeed, increased in America concomitantly with the growth in income inequality. Since the 1970s, middle-income neighborhoods have been disappearing. More than a third of all families now live in either affluent or poor neighborhoods, twice as many as in 1970 (Reardon & Bischoff, 2011). Affluent and low-income families are now less likely to live near one another, which leads to increasing disparities in such public resources as parks, pools, libraries, services, and – in particular – schools.

It is widely recognized that where one goes to school matters a great deal for extracurricular participation. As a cost-cutting measure, many schools have reduced or even eliminated their sports programs, and such schools are the ones that low-income kids are more likely to attend. Thus, one part of the explanation is differences in extracurricular offerings. High schools with wealthy students offer twice the number of team sports as schools that serve mainly low-income students (Putnam, forthcoming).

As schools face pressure to tighten their belts, test scores and academic "core competencies" take priority over seemingly more frivolous activities such as sports and clubs. Schools across the economic spectrum have been pressured to reduce spending, but they have responded to that pressure in different ways. Poorer districts may simply cut back on their offerings, thus depriving students of chances to develop the soft skills that would prove so valuable in the future. In contrast, affluent districts have maintained or even expanded their extracurricular offerings by turning to private donations from parents and local community associations (Reich, 2005). Whereas wealthier parents can pool private donations to build a new running track or send the school band to Japan, less-affluent parents cannot make up for the loss of public funding for extracurricular activities. Data collected by the National Association of Independent Schools show that the median amount of annual giving raised per school increased 63% from $548,651 to $895,614 over the last decade (Anderson, 2012). In New York City, the median amount raised increased 268% during this period.

Even more importantly, in many school districts the introduction of "pay to play" programs has transformed school sports into a luxury that only wealthy families can afford. Conservative estimates set the cost of each activity at $600; this would be roughly $2,400 annually (or at least 15% of income) for a bottom quintile family with two kids doing two activities each. Indeed, when fees were introduced, one in three sports-playing kids from homes with annual income of $60,000 or less dropped out because of the increased cost, as compared to one in ten kids from families with incomes over $60,000 (Putnam, forthcoming). And even in districts offering waivers, the stigma of applying for a waiver may dissuade many parents from doing so. The increased prevalence of pay-to-play fees, combined with the disproportionate impact of these fees on bottom-earning families, appear to have contributed to widening the class gap in sports (and other pay-to-play activities).

Conclusion

Extracurricular activities have long been seen as a way to enrich the public sphere by helping raise young children to be leaders and citizens who participate in democratic governance, exhibit teamwork and grit, and bridge both social and economic divides. For this reason, investing in children's extracurricular activities was once a shared, public concern – important not only for the individual child's life chances but also for the nation's unity and prosperity. Yet shrinking social networks and cuts in public spending have since rendered investment in children's activities a private decision, the responsibility of parents alone (Silva, Snellman, & Frederick, 2014). The growing gap observed in extracurricular opportunities is another hallmark of the trend toward privatizing childhood: it is evident that concern for the well-being of children generally has shriveled to the point where such concern applies only to one's own offspring.

Extracurricular activities are often dismissed as being less vital than test scores and reading levels (or even as frivolous), but there is considerable research demonstrating the fundamental importance of such activities to children's life chances. Playing soccer or marching in the school band is not simply a fun activity; these activities teach valuable lessons in teamwork, communication, and perseverance – all of which pay off later in the workplace. For children from less advantaged backgrounds, the social connections and character traits gleaned from extracurricular activities may offer the key to upward mobility and a secure middle-class life. Furthermore, participation in such activities may plant the seeds of future political participation, setting children on a path toward social connectedness and civic involvement rather than isolation and disengagement (Putnam, Frederick, & Snellman 2012).

That class-based inequality in social and civic engagement has nearly quadrupled in three decades is startling and presents a challenge to the American ideal of equal opportunity. The growing class gaps in extracurricular activities are therefore an urgent social concern. Upper-middle-class children are being groomed – through private investment and cultivation – to thrive in the competitive, knowledge-based economy that they will inherit. Moreover, these children will enter adulthood as practiced citizens ready to participate in democracy and to collaborate with others. However, their working-class peers are missing out on these opportunities as public funding has dwindled and concern for their well-being has been relegated to the private sphere. These low-income students are losing the chance to develop grit and perseverance, work alongside others, build valuable connections with mentors, and learn how to lead. As a result, their ability to climb the economic ladder may be jeopardized. Living up to our national creed of equal opportunity requires closing the extracurricular gap as swiftly as possible.

It follows that any new initiative to monitor mobility should allow scholars to examine how extracurricular activities contribute to mobility and trends in mobility. More importantly, we should also consider how the growth in the "engagement gap" might be reversed. If we are concerned with enhancing social mobility, the increasing socioeconomic gap in extracurricular participation calls for urgent action from schools, parents, and policy-makers.

Acknowledgments

We thank David Grusky, Thomas Sander, and Timothy Van Zandt for their helpful feedback on the manuscript. We also acknowledge the contributions of Rebekah Crooks Horowitz, Josh Bolian, Matthew Wright, Evrim Altintas, and Chaeyoon Lim. Support for this research was generously provided by the Annie Casey Foundation, the Carnegie Corporation of New York, the Ford Foundation, the Bill and Melinda Gates Foundation, the W. K. Kellogg Foundation, the Markle Foundation, the Rockefeller Brothers Fund, and the Spencer Foundation. We also thank the INSEAD Alumni Fund (IAF) for its support of this project. The views expressed in this chapter do not necessarily represent those of any of the sponsoring organizations.

Notes

1 Kaisa Snellman, Jennifer M. Silva, Carl B. Frederick, Robert D. Putnam, "The Engagement Gap: Social Mobility and Extracurricular Participation among American Youth," published in *The ANNALS of the American Academy of Political and Social Science,* Sage Journals, Volume: 657, issue 1, pages, 194–207. Reproduced by kind permission from Robert Putnam and other authors and *The ANNALS of the American Academy of Political and Social Science Journal.*
2 Title IX of the Education Amendments Act of 1972 is a federal law that states: "No person in the United States shall, on the basis of sex, be excluded from participation in, be denied the benefits of, or be subjected to discrimination under any education program or activity receiving Federal financial assistance."
3 The SES index combines measures of income, parental education, and parental occupational status, although the precise calculation of the index varies slightly between the four cohorts. We find similar results using other markers of social class, such as family income or parental education (results not shown).
4 The same results hold when using the full sample that includes twelfth graders of all race-ethnicities and in models that control for race. We lack sufficient statistical power to do within-race-ethnicity analyses for black, Hispanic, or the residual race-ethnic category because of small sample sizes of race-ethnic minorities in the top SES quartile, an average of 268 per group per survey, especially in the earlier cohorts.
5 The growing gaps are robust to multivariate analyses that control for race-ethnicity (results not shown).
6 See Ramey and Ramey (2010, Figure 9.3).

References

Abrams, T. (2013, March 28). 7 of 8 Ivy League schools report lower acceptance rates. *New York Times.* Retrieved June 30, 2017, from https://india.blogs.nytimes.com/2013/03/28/7-of-8-ivy-league-schools-report-lower-acceptance-rates/.

Alon, S. (2009). The evolution of class inequality in higher education: Competition, exclusion, and adaptation. *American Sociological Review, 74*(5), 731–755.

Anderson, J. (2012, March 26). Private schools mine parents' data, and wallets. *New York Times*. Retrieved June 30, 2017, from www.nytimes.com/2012/03/27/nyregion/private-schools-mine-parents-data-and-wallets.html.

Bailey, M. J., & Dynarski, S. M. (2011). Inequality in postsecondary education. In G. J. Duncan & R. J. Murnane (Eds.), *Whither opportunity? Rising inequality, schools, and children's life chances* (pp. 117–132). New York and Chicago: Russell Sage Foundation and Spencer Foundation.

Barron, J. M., Ewing, B. T., & Waddell, G. R. (2000). The effects of high school athletic participation on education and labor market outcomes. *Review of Economics and Statistics, 82*(3), 409–421.

Beck, P. A., & Jennings, M. K. (1982). Pathways to participation. *American Political Science Review, 76*(01), 94–108.

Borghans, L., Ter Weel, B., & Weinberg, B. A. (2014). People skills and the labor-market outcomes of underrepresented groups. *ILR Review, 67*(2), 287–334.

Broh, B. A. (2002). Linking extracurricular programming to academic achievement: Who benefits and why? *Sociology of Education*, 69–95.

Coleman, J. S. (1961). *The adolescent society.* New York: The Free Press.

Cunha, F., Heckman, J. J., & Schennach, S. M. (2010). Estimating the technology of cognitive and noncognitive skill formation. *Econometrica, 78*(3), 883–931.

Eccles, J. S., Barber, B. L., Stone, M., & Hunt, J. (2003). Extracurricular activities and adolescent development. *Journal of Social Issues, 59*(4), 865–889.

Eide, E. R., & Ronan, N. (2001). Is participation in high school athletics an investment or a consumption good? Evidence from high school and beyond. *Economics of Education Review, 20*(5), 431–442.

Ginsburg, K. R. (2007). The importance of play in promoting healthy child development and maintaining strong parent-child bonds. *Pediatrics, 119*(1), 182–191.

Hart, D., Donnelly, T. M., Youniss, J., & Atkins, R. (2007). High school community service as a predictor of adult voting and volunteering. *American Educational Research Journal, 44*(1), 197–219.

Hoxby, C. M., & Avery, C. (2012). The missing "one-offs": The hidden supply of high-achieving, low-income students. *National Bureau of Economic Research Working Paper* 18586, Cambridge, MA.

Kalleberg, A. L. (2009). Precarious work, insecure workers: Employment relations in transition. *American Sociological Review, 74*(1), 1–22.

Kaushal, N., Magnuson, K., & Waldfogel, J. (2011). *How is family income related to investments in children's learning?* New York: Russell Sage Foundation.

Kornrich, S., & Furstenberg, F. (2013). Investing in children: Changes in parental spending on children, 1972–2007. *Demography, 50*(1), 1–23.

Kosteas, V. D. (2010). High school clubs participation and earnings. *Working Paper Series.* Social Science Research Network. Available from http://ssrn.com/abstract=1542360.

Kuhn, P., & Weinberger, C. (2005). Leadership skills and wages. *Journal of Labor Economics, 23*(3), 395–436.

Lareau, A. (2004). *Unequal childhoods: Class, race, and family life.* Oakland, CA: University of California Press.

Lleras, C. (2008). Do skills and behaviors in high school matter? The contribution of non-cognitive factors in explaining differences in educational attainment and earnings. *Social Science Research, 37*(3), 888–902.

Mahoney, J. L., Harris, A. L., & Eccles, J. S. (2006). Organized activity participation, positive youth development, and the overscheduling hypothesis. *Social Policy Report, 20*(4), 3–31.

Marsh, H. W. (1992). Extracurricular activities: Beneficial extension of the traditional curriculum or subversion of academic goals? *Journal of Educational Psychology, 84*(4), 553–562.

Marsh, H. W., & Kleitman, S. (2002). Extracurricular school activities: The good, the bad, and the nonlinear. *Harvard Educational Review, 72*(4), 464–515.

McFarland, D. A., & Thomas, R. J. (2006). Bowling young: How youth voluntary associations influence adult political participation. *American Sociological Review, 71*(3), 401–425.

McNeal, R. B., Jr. (1995). Extracurricular activities and high school dropouts. *Sociology of Education, 68*(1), 62–80.

Nie, N. H., Junn, J., & Stehlik-Barry, K. (1996). *Education and democratic citizenship in America.* Chicago: University of Chicago Press.

O'Hanlon, T. (1980). Interscholastic athletics, 1900–1940: Shaping citizens for unequal roles in the modern industrial state. *Educational Theory, 30*(2), 89–103.

Phillips, M. (2011). Parenting, time use, and disparities in academic outcomes. In G. J. Duncan & R. J. Murnane (Eds.), *Whither opportunity? Rising inequality, schools, and children's life chances* (pp. 207–228). New York and Chicago: Russell Sage Foundation and Spencer Foundation.

Piketty, T., & Saez, E. (2003). Income inequality in the United States, 1913. *Quarterly Journal of Economics, 118*(1), 1–39.

Powell, W. W., & Snellman, K. (2003). The knowledge economy. *Annual Review of Sociology, 30*, 199–220.

Putnam, R. D. (2000). *Bowling alone: The collapse and revival of American community.* New York: Simon & Schuster.

Putnam, R. D. (forthcoming). *Our kids: The American dream in crisis.* New York: Simon & Schuster.

Putnam, R. D., Frederick, C. F., & Snellman, K. (2012). *Growing class gaps in social connectedness among American youth.* Cambridge, MA: Harvard Kennedy School.

Ramey, G., & Ramey, V. A. (2010). The rug rat race. *Brookings Papers on Economic Activity, 41*, 129–176.

Reardon, S. F. (2011). The widening academic achievement gap between the rich and the poor: New evidence and possible explanations. In G. J. Duncan & R. J. Murnane (Eds.), *Whither opportunity? Rising inequality, schools, and children's life chances* (pp. 91–116). New York and Chicago: Russell Sage Foundation and Spencer Foundation.

Reardon, S. F., Baker, R., & Klasik, D. (2012). *Race, income, and enrolment patterns in highly selective colleges, 1982–2004.* Stanford, CA: Center for Education Policy Analysis, Stanford University.

Reardon, S. F., & Bischoff, K. (2011). Growth in the residential segregation of families by income, 1970–2009. *Technical report.* New York and Providence, RI: Russell Sage Foundation and American Communities Project of Brown University.

Reich, R. (2005). A failure of philanthropy: American charity shortchanges the poor, and public policy is partly to blame. *Stanford Social Innovation Review.* Available from www.ssireview.org/.

Rivera, L. A. (2012). Hiring as cultural matching: The case of elite professional service firms. *American Sociological Review, 77*(6), 999–1022.

Sayer, L. C., Bianchi, S. M., & Robinson, J. P. (2004). Are parents investing less in children? Trends in mothers' and fathers' time with children. *American Journal of Sociology, 110*(1), 1–43.

Silva, J. M. (2013). *Coming up short: Working-class adulthood in an age of uncertainty.* New York: Oxford University Press.

Silva, J. M., Snellman, K., & Frederick, C. B. (2014). The privatization of "savvy": Class reproduction in the era of college for all. *INSEAD Working Paper*, No. 2014/47/OBH. Available at SSRN: http://ssrn.com/abstract=2473462.

Stevens, M. L. (2009). *Creating a class: College admissions and the education of elites.* Cambridge, MA: Harvard University Press.

Stevenson, B. (2010). Beyond the classroom: Using Title IX to measure the return to high school sports. *The Review of Economics and Statistics, 92*(2), 284–301.

Troutman, K. P., & Dufur, M. J. (2007). From high school jocks to college grads: Assessing the long-term effects of high school sport participation on females' educational attainment. *Youth & Society, 38*(4), 443–462.

Western, B., Bloome, D., & Percheski, C. (2008). Inequality among American families with children, 1975 to 2005. *American Sociological Review, 73*(6), 903–920.

Wright, M. (2015). Economic inequality and the social capital gap in the United States across time and space. *Political Studies, 63*(3), 642–662.

10 The future of public spaces in the dawn of rapid urban growth

Shifting agendas and a new roadmap

Kyle Farrell and Tigran Haas

> We are faced today with a grave threat, not one solely based on the fact that we don't have answers to burning problems in society, but even more to the point that we don't possess a clear apprehension of what the main problems are and clear understanding of their real dimensions.
>
> (Žižek, 2012)

Introduction

As cities grow, the task of managing them becomes increasingly complex. The unprecedented speed and scale of urban growth in the global south is often cited as the largest obstacle to achieving sustainable urban development. This is because alongside the growth in the number of people living in cities, there is also the need to supply quality urban infrastructure and services such as housing, schools, policing, streets, and public spaces. If the supply of these assets does not keep pace with the growing urban population, then the effects of urban diseconomies set in – this manifests itself in the form of crime, congestion, decaying infrastructure, and the inefficient allocation of land, to name a few. With the urban population projected to grow from 4 to 5 billion people by 2030, and with the total built-up area of the world's cities projected to double in the same amount of time, there remains a high degree of uncertainty as to whether or not the cities of the future will be desirable sites of opportunity, or if they will manifest themselves in the form of urban wastelands. This threat is most prominent in the fast growing cities of the global south. Given that urban planning decisions have the ability to lock cities onto specific long term paths, the decisions (or lack thereof) of policymakers today mark a critical juncture for the future of our cities. With 2015 and 2016 having been host to multiple global development processes that have a significant influence on cities – Sustainable Development Goals (SDGs), the United Nations Conference on Climate Change (COP21), and the Third United Nations Conference on Housing and Sustainable Urban Development (Habitat III) – it appears to a certain extent, that the urbanization story has already been written. The imperative question that remains is, will these decisions set our cities on course for a sustainable urban future, or will they deliver the 'coup de grâce' that will lead to their spiraling demise?

This chapter examines the outcomes of the aforementioned global processes, reflecting on changes in the critical thinking underpinning cities and urban regions. Given that Habitat III is the most substantial process for the future of cities, particular attention has been directed towards this. The findings of which highlight a noticeable shift in emphasis from an approach to city-building focused on the quantitative supply of urban amenities, towards a growing trend that promotes livability and the importance of enhancing quality of life in cities. At the heart of this shift, is the growing recognition of a public space mandate that has been embedded in both the New Urban Agenda that arose out of the Habitat III process and Sustainable Development Goal 11: Sustainable Cities and Communities. Based on the findings of a four year research and policy project focused on public space, this chapter concludes by advancing a number of key principles for leveraging public space as a transformative element of city-building.

A mounting pressure...

The urban transformation that unfolded in Europe and North America more than a hundred years ago was driven mainly by rural push and urban pull factors. Breakthroughs in agricultural technology led to increased productivity, creating a surplus labor force in the countryside, or as Adna Weber aptly put it, "the divorce of men from the soil" (1899, p. 160). Simultaneously, an industrial revolution had been taking off in the English midlands and spreading elsewhere, attracting surplus labor from the countryside to economic agglomerations in the form of cities with the promise of employment and economic gain. Historically speaking, rural to urban migration was the dominant source of urban growth during this time; as demographic factors in the form of high mortality rates placed a natural ceiling on cities, safeguarding that they would not grow excessively in scale (Davis, 1965). Subsequently, these cities were appropriately labeled 'demographic sinks' (Fox & Goodfellow, 2016). Since then, breakthroughs in medical technology, public health, and improved sanitation resulted in changes in mortality and fertility patterns. A particularly large window between reductions in birth rates and death rates created a circumstance in which urban natural population increase has now replaced rural to urban migration as the dominant contributor to the growth of cities (Montgomery, Stren, Cohen, & Reed, 2004). The cumulative combination of these drivers has given rise to unique forms of rapid urban growth, placing substantial pressure on cities of the global south; alternatively earning them the label of 'mushrooming cities' (Jedwab, Christiansen, & Gidelsky, 2015). In many instances, this pressure has outstripped the capacity of local governments to respond to the needs of the city and to supply the necessary infrastructure needed to grow efficiently. Consequently, many of the over-congested megacities of the global south are plagued by features of unplanned urbanization. This is most commonly characterized by traffic congestion, infrastructure deficits, overwhelmed basic services, lack of adequate land and housing, and poor supply and maintenance of public spaces (Jedwab et al., 2015' Kumar & Kumar Rai, 2014). In 1950, there existed only six cities with a population greater than 5 million people, and out of those, all but one were located in developed countries; however, today, this amounts to 52 cities, of which 42 are located in developing countries (Cohen, 2004). In contrast to the incremental growth experienced in North America, Europe, and Oceania (and to a large extent in Latin America), the growth that is persistently unfolding in cities across Asia and Africa is of an unprecedented scale.

Figure 10.1 reflects urban population growth by all major regions of the world for the time period 1950–2050. Between 1950 and 2000, the urban population of Asia grew by more than one billion people, with this figure projected to nearly double between 2000 and 2050. Additionally, Africa's urban population grew by nearly 250 million people between 1950 and 2000, with projections of an additional billion people set to occur between 2000 and 2050. Today, urbanization is very much a product of the global south, requiring us to rethink the challenges cities face and how to best plan and manage their growth.

Alongside the growing trend of rapid urban growth set to continue in developing countries in the coming decades, local governments are tasked to come up with innovative approaches for municipal service delivery. If the required resources and planning foresight is not realized, negative externalities in cities are likely to triumph, overrunning the benefits that accrue from agglomeration and economies of scale (Fox & Goodfellow, 2016). Although the vast majority of countries today are celebrating the fact that we have entered an urban age, most countries – especially those located in developing regions – are significantly unprepared for the challenges that will accompany it. With more than 90% of urban population growth between now and 2050 occurring in Asia and

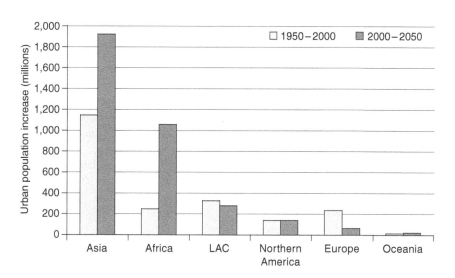

Figure 10.1 Urban population growth by major world region, 1950–2050.

Source: Fox & Goodfellow (2016), data originally from United Nations (2014).

Africa (United Nations, 2014), it is these cities that will be most affected by the decisions taken in the policy arenas of today. In an attempt to cope with such intensive growth and promote the principles of sustainable urban development, experts from around the world have joined forces under the auspices of Habitat III to establish a New Urban Agenda that aims to chart out how cities should be planned and managed over the next two decades.

The New Urban Agenda

The global urban agenda has undergone immense change over the past 40 years. During the 1970s, there was increasing recognition of the uncontrollable growth of cities around the world. In developing countries, the increasing pressure on cities led to high levels of unplanned urban growth, often manifesting itself in the form of informal settlements and decaying infrastructure (Bairoch, 1988). Cash-strapped local governments were unable to provide the necessary housing and basic services to accommodate the growth of cities and in many instances chose the route of forced eviction. At this time, there were hardly any international fora or collaborative dialogues to address such immense urban issues; as previous attention was focused towards rural development (Fox & Goodfellow, 2016). With growing concern over these experiences, it was decided that there would be significant value in shared cooperation, giving rise to the first United Nations Conference on Human Settlements (Habitat I). Attended by government representatives from around the world, the challenges of slums, poverty, and basic services were heavily discussed during Habitat I, leading to the adoption of the Vancouver Declaration on Human Settlements; which was primarily focused on the housing deficit and a lack of access to basic services. Merely 20 years later, economic, social, and environmental concerns persisted in both developed and developing countries. Member States from around the world reconvened in Istanbul in 1996 for the second United Nations Conference on Human Settlements (Habitat II). This gathering took the decision to reach beyond the fundamental issue of access to adequate shelter, broadening the urban development agenda to include issues related to governance, transportation, employment, and education. Given the success that followed the 1992 Earth Summit held in Rio de Janeiro, a sustainability mandate would come to serve as the backbone of the Istanbul Declaration on Human Settlements.

Today, many of the same challenges still persist. Informal settlements are on the rise, with more than 863 million people living in slums, 1 in 10 people live without access to safe water, and 1 in 3 lack access to a toilet (UN-Habitat, 2012). Growth in personal consumption has led to growing inequality, which has spatially manifested itself in the form of segregated neighborhoods, leading to profound volumes of urban sprawl. Today, most cities are experiencing lower densities and more dispersed patterns of urban growth (Angel, 2011); this has created competition between the public and private spheres and resulted in devastating effects to forests and wetlands. Coming out of Habitat III in Quito, Ecuador in 2016, it is difficult to predict what future cities will look like;

however, the adopted outcome document gives us some indication of the major concerns that need to be acknowledged and addressed. Figure 10.2 below showcases the substantive issues that have received the spotlight in the New Urban Agenda, and have been quantified based on the number of items in the agenda pertaining to each issue.

It is largely of no surprise to see that substantive issues related to the planning and design of cities, infrastructure and basic services, and housing rank near the top of the list; as these were all key concerns in which Habitat I was founded. Additionally, as Habitat II expanded its mandate, related issues such as ecology and resource management, jobs and livelihood, governance, and transportation and mobility found themselves central to the urban dialogue. That being said, the negotiations surrounding Habitat III have reflected quite a dramatic shift in mandate. Early discussions, issue papers, and preliminary drafts of the New Urban Agenda had demonstrated a growing awareness pertaining to improved quality of life through the enhancement of the social fabric of the city. This can be seen in the recognition of issues such as inclusive cities, safety, culture and heritage, and most interestingly, public space in the New Urban Agenda. Public space has received considerable attention in recent years, also having been highlighted in the Sustainable Development Goals. Target 11.7 calls for the provision of "universal access to safe, inclusive and accessible, green and public spaces, particularly for women and children, older persons and persons with disabilities." Such an inclusion marks a significant turning point in the dialogues surrounding urban development. Previously, the urban agendas had a tendency to emphasize quantitative approaches to planning cities, which focused predominantly on the supply of hard infrastructure. However, the New Urban Agenda and the Sustainable Development Goals appear to have broken this cycle,

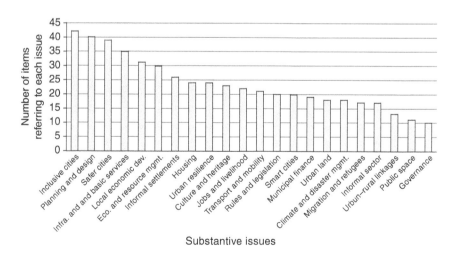

Figure 10.2 Frequency of substantive issues in the Habitat III New Urban Agenda, 2016.
Source: Diagram designed by authors.

emphasizing the addition of qualitative indicators for measuring progress and the issues of how to design cities that provide structure and empower people to create and control their own lives. Although public space can be viewed as a part of the hardware of cities, it very much characterizes elements of the software of cities as well – inclusivity, health, culture, the occasion for chance experiences, and a growing sense of pride and ownership.

The value of a public space agenda and beyond

As mentioned above, characteristics pertaining to the social fabric of the city have largely been overlooked in past agendas. This is because historically there has been a tendency to view cities as an assemblage of urban infrastructure (i.e., buildings, roads, and basic services). But this is only half the story. Studies have shown that cities that place a premium on immaterial values such as accessibility, health, safety, culture, and heritage have experienced significant urban transformations (UNESCO, 2016); take for example cities like Curitiba, Bogota, and Seoul. Additionally, it is those cities that commit to promoting quality of life and wellbeing that consistently rank among the most livable in the world – Vancouver, Zürich, and Melbourne, for example. The evidence seems to indicate that the most transformative and livable cities view themselves beyond physical assets and instead strive to become lively, vibrant, and dynamic places. At the center of such urban transformation and regeneration projects is the public realm. This is because public spaces – including streets, squares, parks, plazas, etc. – are complex, but also very simple multifunctional areas for human life. They have the ability to offer ecological diversity and appeal, economic exchange on multiple scales, and dynamic social interactions inclusive of cultural expression among a wide variety of people, religions, ethnicities, genders, and opinions. For planners and policymakers looking to enhance the social fabric of their cities, a public space agenda can be turned to as an effective strategy. Figure 10.3 highlights a range of benefits that result from active investment in quality public spaces: accessibility, local economy, social interaction, health and wellbeing, sense of community, and sense of comfort. A shift in focus towards a public space agenda incorporates a holistic, ecological approach to urban planning that correlates the smaller and more personal neighborhood scale with the metropolitan scale of the region. There, within a community led effort, principles of diversity, conservation, and human scale (Calthorpe, 2012) merge with the idea of economic, ecological, and social sustainability, where the benefits of public spaces become crucial for the community.

It is through the formation of 'community' that public spaces are most noted for (re)establishing social capital in cities. Traditionally, the main function of the community (or *gemeinschaft*) was to serve as a link between the people and society creating an arena of common interest; that way citizens could relate to their societies in both a geographic and non-geographic sense (Hoggett, 1997; Tönnies, 1988). This becomes a central concept of public space at every level of interaction and experience among people. At the backbone

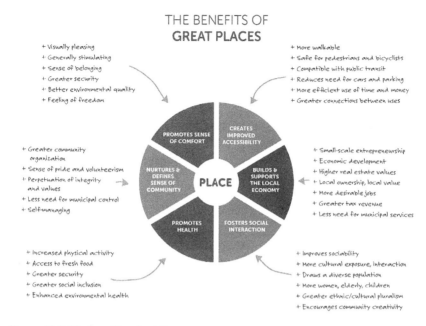

THE BENEFITS OF
GREAT PLACES

+ Visually pleasing
+ Generally stimulating
+ Sense of belonging
+ Greater security
+ Better environmental quality
+ Feeling of freedom

+ More walkable
+ Safe for pedestrians and bicyclists
+ Compatible with public transit
+ Reduces need for cars and parking
+ More efficient use of time and money
+ Greater connections between uses

+ Greater community organization
+ Sense of pride and volunteerism
+ Perpetuation of integrity and values
+ Less need for municipal control
+ Self-managing

+ Small-scale entrepreneurship
+ Economic development
+ Higher real estate values
+ Local ownership, local value
+ More desirable jobs
+ Greater tax revenue
+ Less need for municipal services

+ Increased physical activity
+ Access to fresh food
+ Greater security
+ Greater social inclusion
+ Enhanced environmental health

+ Improves sociability
+ More cultural exposure, interaction
+ Draws in diverse population
+ More women, elderly, children
+ Greater ethnic/cultural pluralism
+ Encourages community creativity

PROMOTES SENSE OF COMFORT · CREATES IMPROVED ACCESSIBILITY · NURTURES & DEFINES SENSE OF COMMUNITY · **PLACE** · BUILDS & SUPPORTS THE LOCAL ECONOMY · PROMOTES HEALTH · FOSTERS SOCIAL INTERACTION

Figure 10.3 The benefits of public spaces.
Source: Project for Public Spaces, 2016.

of 'community-building' is the notion of 'the third space.' This consists of the social surroundings separate from the 'first' and 'second places' – those of 'home' and 'work.' Such places are necessary for allowing diversity to flourish, and people to learn to live with and negotiate among each other. It is in these communal spaces that people generate a sense of pride, social cohesion, and civic identity. Oldenburg (1991) makes the case that third places are integral elements for establishing civil society, direct democracy, engagement, and the feeling of attachment and sense of place. Such spaces serve as arenas for equity, diversity, and justice. It is also in these places where marginalized groups can exercise their rights, voice their opinions, and stand up against injustice in a democratic forum; even if that means in some instances a temporary or permanent loss of order, control, and comfort.

Additionally, vibrant streets and inclusive public spaces become places of economic value and benefit – promoting income, investment, wealth creation, and providing employment (Andersson, 2016). The economic value of interconnected systems of quality public spaces manifests itself via direct attraction-marketing and business points in the form of bustling streets, active parks and squares, and other appealing forms of public space. These spaces attract, retain, and lock people of all kinds; especially if they are well maintained and of high aesthetic quality. Public spaces and good urban places provide numerous benefits to all forms of business, innovation, and entrepreneurship; spanning both formal and informal sectors. Furthermore, public spaces can be utilized as a novel approach to intensify the vitality of the city through urban renewal programs. This in turn has the ability to increase property values, which can then be captured in the form of taxes through innovative approaches to municipal finance, such as land value capture.

From an environmental perspective, public space plays an important role in reducing pollution in cities, increasing ecological diversity, and reducing energy consumption (Beatley, 2010). Research has shown that increased exposure to nature and green space has proven to offer additional health benefits, thus reducing the overall public expenditure on healthcare (Kaplan, 1995). Health benefits accrue due to increased access to clean air, reduction in noise pollution, reduced exposure to direct sunlight, and a decline in stress levels resulting from positive aesthetic appeal. Open space conservation and the creation of city parks and public spaces in general can thus be seen as investments that produce significant economic and health benefits for society (Wolf & Flora, 2010).

Threats to an emerging public space agenda

Where a clear and proactive public space agenda exists, public spaces have demonstrated an inherent ability to bring people together. However, when planned, designed, or managed poorly, they also have the ability to create or add to conflict between people and communities, and bring unattractive places of insecurity, loss, and fear. It is thus important to note that it is not just a matter of building public spaces to enhance the social fabric of cities, but also ensuring their quality in order to avoid generating cycles of urban decline. Although a well-planned public space agenda has the ability to redefine the image of a city, under conditions of rapid urban growth the public space agenda still faces many impending obstacles; most noticeable is a growing tendency towards increased privatization and homogenization (Kes-Erkul, 2014). Such obstacles threaten the effectiveness of public space as a means of enhancing quality of life in cities. According to De Magalhaes (2010) traditional functions of public spaces are frequently challenged by new approaches to and alternative forms of public space provision and management, from which several important new trends have emerged. These trends tend to concentrate on a shift towards profit-building, privatization, and strict planning approaches and measures. Alongside the growing privatization of public space, the changing patterns of urban growth begin to threaten the public space agenda. Today we see more and more privatization in the management of public space which also results in public space commodification and homogenization in cities of both the global north and the global south; this places social capital and publicness (the quality or state of public openness) under threat. The adverse effects of privatization, social exclusion, and increased control of space have drawn particular attention towards the concept of publicness in recent years (Németh & Schmidt, 2011). This is important, because it is the overall degree of publicness which tends to define the quality of public space and how effectively it can serve society.

A distinction between private and public is critical because it is exactly in the public realm that we find a prime drive toward more privatization, that is, residential desires for safety, security, stability, and relative social homogeneity; all of which influences the choices made on the provision of public space (Haas & Olsson, 2014; Low, 2006). That said, such choices have consequences for the people, whose sense of belonging to a specific area is based on their rights to universal access. The link between urban society, public space, and planning approaches becomes an important element in understanding the complexity of urban transformation in the public realm (Amin, 2008). The important nexus in this respect lies in the private and public domains and in what sense a public space can be defined as a public good (Haas & Olsson, 2014).

Public spaces have always been the arenas of conflict and potential struggle over claims to its control and over its accessibility to different groups in society. Public spaces are meant to characterize positive aspects of urban living – inclusivity, accessibility, the disregard of status, and serve as the domain of the common concern. However, too often, we are seeing private interests get in the way, leading to greater inequalities, growing signs of exclusivity and an overall erosion of 'the commons.' This raises questions as to who the city is meant to serve, and whether or not the public realm is really public (Sennett, 2013). Harvey (2008) warns of an increasing threat pertaining to the homogenization of public space in cities, to such an extent that they are no longer promoting a diversity of uses and people. The key issue is that the public realm needs to remain an open and democratic common good of transformative character and not one that is generic and stable.

Public space agendas must therefore ensure that processes are collaborative, inclusive of all actors, and strongly embedded in sustainable stewardship and a profound understanding of what urban commons and public goods really mean for the city. At the same time, to those in power, public space can be viewed as a threat, posing the risk of temporary or permanent loss of order. This is because public spaces serve as arenas for equity, diversity, and justice where marginalized groups are availed an opportunity to make themselves heard and even protest against injustice in a democratic forum (Parkinson, 2012). For the citizenry, public spaces can serve as the primary vehicle for change when other approaches prove to be ineffective. The 'January 25 Revolution' that unfolded in Tahrir Square, Cairo in 2011 speaks to the political dynamism surrounding a public space agenda (Figure 10.4). Thus, the struggle for the city and public space will always remain especially in light of the constant threats of neoliberal consumerist agendas.

Moving forward: a public space roadmap for livable cities

Over the past two decades, cities have gained relevance in all areas of environmental, social, cultural, and economic discourse. The most thriving and livable cities as well as sustainable ones in the future will be those that encapsulate the public realm and the people who utilize these places in a vibrant, connected, and

Figure 10.4 Protests in Tahrir Square, Cairo, Egypt.

dynamic way. Despite the numerous successful examples, the need for public spaces has not been given the attention that it deserves, especially in the cities of the global south. In general, public space is often overlooked and underestimated by policymakers, leaders, planners, architects, and real estate developers. That being said, the New Urban Agenda that arose out of Habitat III and the Sustainable Development Goal 11 will be the largest initiatives directed towards creating more livable cities; offering improved quality of life for their citizens. Although these global processes demonstrate the political will to leverage public space as a tool for making more sustainable and livable cities, the details of what such an agenda should look like have largely been neglected. The following overview provides some insight as to the necessary elements needed to generate a public space agenda capable of promoting livability and improved quality of life in cities. These represent the findings of a four year initiative titled 'The Future of Places' aimed at elevating the importance of a public space agenda in various global policy arenas (see Future of Places, 2015). Figure 10.5 below illustrates a selection of key findings from this study.

First, as an arena for public use and social interaction, public spaces are regularly developed, managed, and maintained by municipal governments, often creating a situation where other stakeholders are left out of the discussion. By adopting a people-centered approach to urban planning, local governments increase their potential to effectively establish a shared commitment, creating further opportunities for localized planning and maintenance of public space.

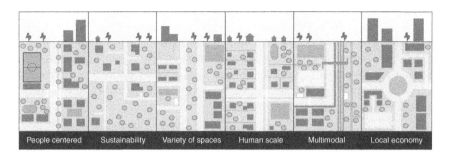

People centered | Sustainability | Variety of spaces | Human scale | Multimodal | Local economy

Figure 10.5 Selected key messages on public space from the Future of Places project.

Second, a public space agenda is strengthened by incorporating principles of social, economic, and environmental sustainability. Social sustainability requires security, equity, and justice; economic sustainability benefits from affordable capital and operating budgets; environmental sustainability addresses ecological and health issues. Additional attention to culture and heritage will help to ensure that public space is made unique through cultural and contextual elements that complement and enrich identity. Such an approach promotes a diversity of public space typologies.

Third, in many places around the world, there has been a reduction of urban public space, a lack of clear boundaries between the public and private spheres and diminished freedom of expression and movement. This is because the market alone does not always provide a diverse range of public and private spaces. Therefore, a more nuanced approach that provides a variety of open places, including semi-public and semi-private space, is needed. A diversity of public spaces helps to reinforce the idea that the city is there to serve a wide array of its citizens, and that it is not reserved for a select few.

Fourth, all public space needs to be of a human scale and respond to a variety of functions and patterns of use based on an understanding of human behavior, health, needs, sensibilities, and aspirations. In doing so, it should serve vulnerable members of the population, including elderly, disabled, youth, and low income groups, to ensure their physical, social, and political inclusion in the allocation and design of public spaces. Public space thus has a responsibility to be flexible and open enough to serve a variety of users and uses, ranging from informal to formal settlements.

Fifth, streets should serve as multimodal networks of social and economic exchange, forming the urban framework of interconnected public space. Walkability, social interaction, multimodal mobility, and accessibility should be supported by a fine grained block and street network lined with buildings providing amenities and services with a mix of uses and sizes. A holistic, evidence-based approach to the city is necessary with attention focused not only on the space itself, but its form, function, and connectivity.

Sixth, investing in public space can have powerful social, economic, cultural, and health benefits. If people are committed to their future in a specific place, they invest more time and capital in that place, which has a positive impact on the local economy and creates a virtuous cycle of economic growth. Public space stimulates the small scale, local, and informal economy, as well as generates tax revenue for municipal budgets. Innovative tools such as land value capture can help to ensure that investment in public space offers an economically sustainable approach to city-building.

Some conclusions

The common denominator that gives cities their decisive prowess is their ability to concentrate people; this is because the convenience of proximity benefits all, allowing the city to thrive by bringing people and ideas together. However, if gone unmanaged, cities can lose out to the 'demons of density,' paradoxically giving rise to negative consequences of urban concentration (Glaeser, 2011). The advent of rapid globalization and rapid urban growth has initiated a process of urban transformation, posing new challenges for planning and managing cities. As cities grow, the lack of infrastructure, open spaces, and public amenities begins to undermine the wellbeing of their inhabitants. Thus, as new cities and conurbations emerge globally, and older ones grow or decay in urban prosperity or urban blight, it is imperative that we be thoughtful in planning and designing their futures. The cities that will do best in the future will be those that capsulize the public realm and the people who utilize these places. This is because public spaces have the potential to systematically support a complex agenda of livability and sociability, economic prosperity, community cohesion, and overall sustainability for cities. The inclusion of public space in the New Urban Agenda and the Sustainable Development Goals is a welcome shift towards improving quality of life in cities. In doing so, it encourages urban planners and decision makers to shift away from the natural tendency of viewing the city as an assemblage of urban infrastructure, to instead focus on building integrated and holistic cities that deliver the experiences and interactions desired by their citizenry. However, success will not be achieved on its own. As elements of the New Urban Agenda are cemented into urban plans, strategies, and frameworks around the globe, it will take bold leadership from elected officials and the public to realize the true value of public space as a tool capable of defining the image of the city. Cities, both in the north and south, have fallen short in dealing with the most burning problems of our society and also recent critical transformations in the becoming: those of mass and hyper immigrations, financial crisis, breakdown of the traditional industries, globalization and more. They simply cannot fall short or fail on the public space agenda. Those cities currently experiencing rapid urban growth therefore need to be thoughtful in how they deal with public assets and amenities; those that do not plan ahead will find the public realm under serious threat. There is thus a need to encourage national and local governments to establish legislation, policies, norms, and best practices that enable a public space agenda to thrive, and thus promote a holistic and integrated approach to planning and designing cities (Andersson, 2016). Unlike other infrastructure, public spaces afford a human element to the city; offering an opportunity for residents to improve their health, prosperity, quality of life, and overall to enrich their social relations and cultural understanding. Although key decisions have already been taken in the policy arenas of 2015 and 2016, the future of cities is still in the hands of the stakeholders that comprise them. Any attempt to establish a public space agenda that does not place the citizens at the center of it will face severe constraints in their attempt to build livable cities.

References

Amin, A. (2008). Collective culture and urban public space. *City, 12*(1), 5–24.

Andersson, C. (2016). Public space and the New Urban Agenda. *The Journal of Public Space, 1*(1), 5–10.

Angel, S. (2011). Making room for a planet of cities. *Policy Focus Report*. Cambridge: Lincoln Institute of Land Policy.

Bairoch, P. (1988). *Cities and economic development: From the dawn of history to the present*. Chicago: University of Chicago Press.

Beatley, T. (2010). *Biophilic cities: Integrating nature into urban design and planning*. Washington, DC: Island Press.

Calthorpe, P. (2012). *Urbanism in the age of climate change*. Washington, DC: Island Press.

Cohen, B. (2004). Urban growth in developing countries: A review of current trends and a caution regarding existing forecasts. *World Development, 32*(1), 23–51.

Davis, K. (1965). The urbanization of the human population. *Scientific American, 213*(3), 40–53.

De Magalhaes, C. (2010). Public space and the contracting-out of publicness: A framework for analysis. *Journal of Urban Design, 15*(4), 559–574.

Fox, S., & Goodfellow, T. (2016). *Cities and development* (2nd ed.). New York: Routledge.

Future of Places (2015). *Key messages from the Future of Places conference series*. Ax:son Johnson Foundation: Stockholm.

Glaeser, E. (2011). *Triumph of the city: How our greatest invention makes us richer, smarter, greener, healthier and happier*. London: Pan Macmillan.

Haas, T., & Olsson, K. (2014). Transmutation and reinvention of public spaces through ideals of urban planning and design. *Space and Culture, 17*(1), 59–68.

Harvey, D. (2008). The right to the city. *New Left Review, 53*, 23–40.

Hoggett, P. (1997). *Contested communities: Experiences, struggles, policies*. Bristol: Policy Press.

Jedwab, R., Christiansen, L., & Gidelsky, M. (2015). Demography, urbanization and development: Rural push, urban pull and... urban push? *Policy Research Working Paper* 7333. Washington, DC: World Bank.

Kaplan, S. (1995). The restorative benefits of nature: Toward an integrative framework. *Journal of Environmental Psychology, 15*, 169–182.

Kes-Erkul, A. (2014). From privatized to constructed public space: Observations from Turkish cities. *American International Journal of Contemporary Research, 4*(7), 120–126.

Kumar, A., & Kumar Rai, A. (2014). Urbanization process, trend, pattern and its consequences in India. *Neo Graphia, 3*(4), 54–77.

Low, S. (2006). The erosion of public space and the public realm: Paranoia, surveillance and privatization in New York City. *City & Society, 18*(1), 43–49.

Montgomery, M., Stren, R., Cohen, B., & Reed, H. (2004). *Cities transformed: Demographic change and its implications in the developing world by the Panel on Urban Population Dynamics*. London: Earthscan, 75–107.

Németh, J., & Schmidt, S. (2011). The privatization of publicness: Modelling and measuring publicness. *Environment and Planning B: Planning and Design, 38*(1), 5–23.

Oldenburg, R. (1991). *The great good place: Cafes, coffee shops, community centers, beauty parlors, general stores, bars, hangouts, and how they get you through the day*. New York: Marlowe & Company.

Parkinson, R. (2012). *Democracy and public space: The physical sites of democratic performance*. New York: Oxford University Press.

Project for Public Spaces. (2016). *The benefits of great places*. Retrieved January 5, 2017, from www.pps.org/.

Sennett, R. (2013). Reflections on the public realm. In G. Bridge & S. Watson (Eds.), *The new Blackwell companion to the city* (Chapter 32, pp. 390–398). London: Wiley-Blackwell.

Tönnies, F. (1988). *Community and society* (Gemeinschaft und Gesellschaft). New Jersey: Transaction Publishers, Rutgers.

UNESCO. (2016). *Global report on culture for sustainable urban development*. Paris: UNESCO.

UN-Habitat. (2012). *State of the world cities 2012/2013: Prosperity of cities*. Nairobi: UN-Habitat.

United Nations. (2014). *World urbanization prospects*. ST/ESA/SER.A/366. New York: Department of Economic and Social Affairs.

Weber, A. (1899). *The growth of cities in the nineteenth century*. New York: The Macmillan Company.

Wolf, K., & Flora, K. (2010). Mental health and function: A literature review. In *Green Cities: Good Health*. College of the Environment, University of Washington.

Žižek, S. (2012, May 13). *Nedeljom u dva* (Hard talk). Hrvatska Radiotelevizija, HRT. Croatian Television.

11 Emerging Chinese cities

Implications for global urban studies[1]

Fulong Wu

Chinese cities are emerging in multiple senses: Physically, they are growing rapidly as a result of fast urbanization and the economic growth of the country. They have received millions of rural migrants. Theoretically speaking, they are emerging because of novel features and properties that cannot be easily described by existing urban theories mainly derived from Western countries. Traditionally the study of Chinese cities followed the category of third world cities. As argued by Dick and Rimmer (1998) in the context of Southeast Asian cities, however, this approach became less appropriate under globalization. Moreover, although Chinese cities share some features with third world cities in their underdeveloped economies and the challenges brought about by urbanization, socialist history since 1949 has created a distinctive political economy and urban spatial structure. On the other hand, the history of socialism did not bring Chinese cities closer to so-called postsocialist cities (Andrusz, Harloe, & Szelényi, 1996), because the economies of cities in Central and Eastern European countries are industrialized and urbanized, whereas China maintained an urbanization level below 20% before 1979 (Zhou & Ma, 2003). Chinese cities are emerging just like other cities in the Global South, despite significant differences between them. Because of their complexity and the emergent properties of that complexity, their future is not predefined by existing urban theory; future changes are full of uncertainties and thus can be transformed through active agencies and collective actions. The metaphor of using Chinese cities as a laboratory to observe contemporary urban changes across the planet means that we should be more flexible about the framework of research. The cities are lived experience, too. Research on Chinese cities could have important implications for global urban studies. In this case, the direction of travel in theories is from Shanghai to Los Angeles rather than the application of the Los Angeles School theories (Robinson, 2011).

This direction of travel means generating local knowledge for the development of global urban theories, or as "art of being global" (Roy & Ong, 2011). Focusing on Chinese cities, this chapter first reviews the political economic processes underlying urban transformation. A familiar paradigm is neoliberalism, initially developed in the West. In the regional context, another relevant perspective is the "developmental state" developed in East Asia. These two paradigms are quite contradictory regarding the role of the state. The case of Chinese cities reveals that these two seemingly contradictory processes might actually fit together well in the Chinese model of the world factory: the devolution of economic decision making to the urban scale and fiscal recentralization that consolidates the capacity of the state. Land development generates revenues for the local state and at the same time the system is maintained by retaining the power of the central state to appoint local officials. This means promotion on the basis of economic performance. By these specific local mechanisms, local competition states are created. Moreover, development is supported by other necessary institutions, namely, the commodification of housing and the establishment of locally managed land sales, leading to a local development regime that combines entrepreneurialism and the operation of state apparatus, forming a specific form of state entrepreneurialism. As a result, we see the paradoxical coexistence of competitive land bidding as a quite market-oriented behavior together with the prolonging of household registration (*hukou*) that represents state control. This dynamism of urbanization and growth creates diverse urban spatial forms: suburban "commodity housing" estates built into forms similar to North American gated communities and urban villages converted from former villages in periurban areas. These spatial presentations might be similar to gated communities or master-planned estates, informal settlements, and slums, but they have their own dynamics defined by local contexts. From these dynamics and diverse urban forms, the implications for global urban studies are considered in this chapter, with reference to the developed knowledge in the north, such as post-suburbia and gated communities (Blakely & Snyder, 1997) and social marginalization (Wacquant, 2008). Theoretically, the emergence of Chinese cities shows the value and limitation of using neoliberalism to understand emerging Asias.

Dynamism of Chinese urbanization

China's market transition started in rural areas. The participation of village cadres in township and village enterprises (TVEs) in the 1980s and early 1990s led to entrepreneurial governance. Oi (1995) described this close association between local state cadres and enterprises as local state corporatism. Wank (1996) used the term clientism to describe the relationship or *guanxi* between cadres and private business. Participation in the economy of private business brought both personal wealth to managers and taxation to the local government. Y. Q. Huang (2008) argued that these TVEs might be disguised as a collective economy but are actually privately controlled. This was not really corporatism, then, but privatization of rural collective economies. The concept of local state corporatism was invented in the context of rural China, where the power of the state was less developed compared with the cities. When Walder (1995) proposed the thesis of local government as industrial firms, his perspective was more structural or focused on the institutional dynamics of entrepreneurial governance. He emphasized the hardening of the budgets of local government through fiscal reform, which greatly incentivized the endeavors of local government to promote local economies. When real estate became an important sector in Chinese cities after the land and housing reform in the 1990s, Duckett (2001) found the participation of bureaucrats in real estate business, arguing, much like the local state corporatism developed for rural China, that entrepreneurialism had developed in urban China.

Extensive studies have been conducted on the impact of fiscal reform and rising localism. Economists suggest that China operated a de facto economic federalism (Qian & Weingast, 1997), which gave rise to the incentives of local economic growth. In 1994, however, the reformed tax system, known as a tax sharing system, hardened the boundary of local taxes, and strengthened the position of the central government in tax collection (Tsui & Wang, 2004). The income from land development and sales was given to the local government. Chinese urban studies reveal the transfer of power from the workplace to localities, or the so-called territorialization of land management (Hsing, 2006). Subsequently, local governments have participated directly in land and infrastructure development. Recent studies highlight the role of land development in Chinese urbanization and the sale of land to generate revenue. Land finance dominates the overall process and creates local entrepreneurialism (Chien, 2013; Wang, 2014; Zhu, 2004). Lin (2014) described land commodification leading to local development due to the rescaling and reshuffling of state power. This is used as "a strategy adopted by the Chinese municipal governments in their contestation of the scaling-up of fiscal power and scaling-down of developmental liabilities and responsibilities" (p. 1832). As a result of these studies, middle-range theories emerged to offer explanations more on the basis of institutional changes in China.

There are differences between local state corporatism and the thesis of the entrepreneurial city. The former sees involvement in market development as necessarily driven by direct personal benefits or engagement with business. The latter follows the theory of urban entrepreneurialism developed in the West and tends to see the change of governance in a more strategic way. There can be more strategic consideration, for example, in using the market to develop global cities (Chien, 2013). In geography and urban studies, although the notion of urban entrepreneurialism originated from a more structural interpretation of post-Fordist transformation (Harvey, 1989), Jessop and Sum (2000) proposed the concept of the entrepreneurial city and operationalized the concept by defining three aspects, namely pursuing entrepreneurial strategies, creating entrepreneurial discourses, and adopting entrepreneurial actions. Their prototype is Hong Kong, but their analogy to the Schumpeterian firm creates a theoretical tension: The city is a polity and in essence does not behave like a firm. Cochrane (2007) warned that

> there is also a danger that its mobilization in the analysis of "entrepreneurialism" in practice may either lead to an exaggeration of the significance of some aspects of the process or to a dismissal of the extent to which particular experiences meet the template.
>
> (p. 101)

For Shanghai, Wu (2003) adopted the same perspective but rather unintention-ally subverted the notion of the entrepreneurial city because the state had been at the center of reglobalizing Shanghai rather than the entrepreneurial city itself. The reason is that the strategy is less entrepreneurial and more structural and strategic, linking with the scale of the nation state that strived to revitalize the Yangtze River delta.

What triggered the transformation toward entrepreneurial governance? Chinese local governments are not allowed to borrow directly from the capital market and hence must resort to an indirect approach through land and infra-structure development. These investments are counted as fixed assets, which can be used to borrow capital from the banking system. Urban development is thus a value-added activity, raising land values. This has happened in an environment in which there has been a general trend of property value inflation. In other words, these properties are capital investments to retain value. Tao, Su, Liu, and Cao (2010) provide a more sophisticated explanation for entrepreneurial-like behavior and explain why local governments have tended to subsidize land and infrastructure for manufacturing investment since the mid-1990s. The local gov-ernments supplied cheaper land for industries, even at a cost below that of acqui-sition, because there was a positive spillover effect on land values in the cities. Industrial development raises the value of commercial and residential land. Real estate development driven by commercial and residential land development thus generates land profits, which belong entirely to local government. Overall eco-nomic development also raises sales tax, which is also a local tax. This explana-tion, although plausible, relies too much on the complex dynamics of the spillover effect. It nevertheless explains the race to the bottom in local develop-ment widely observed in Chinese cities (Chien, 2013; Yang & Wang, 2008).

Asymmetric political and fiscal concentration and decentralization of eco-nomic decision making (Chien & Gordon, 2008) are two major features. The central government uses economic performance indicators (especially gross domestic product [GDP] growth rate) to measure and promote local government officials. This has led to so-called GDPism, or a tournament of economic devel-opment according to economists. There has been a long tradition in economic explanation for decentralization, such as economic federalism or the "regionally decentralized authoritarian regime" (Xu, 2011, p. 1076). Local governments mobilize investment to fund infrastructure development. Development involves different economic sectors (cheaper land for industrial development while getting returns from real estate) and complex financial innovation (using the state-owned development corporation as the medium for local investment). The result is the need for a more aggressive and involved local state. In terms of the relation between globalization and Chinese urbanization, the national state has its own agenda in articulating globalization. The local state adopted a growth strategy to cope with the potential threat to its power faced with globalization and marketization. There has been a dialectical relation between the national state that is faced with a threat due to complexity and mobility unleashed by eco-nomic globalization, but at the same time the process has created an imperative to reinvent its regulatory capacity. Chinese urbanization thus does not follow the logic of global capital but rather the mentality of a developmental state, whose strategy is operationalized at the urban scale through market approaches. This can be seen in suburban development around Beijing, which is driven by state entrepreneurialism (Wu & Phelps, 2011), orchestrated by the development corporation of the Beijing Economic and Technological Development Zone (ETDZ) at Yizhuang. Rather than a spontaneous cluster of postsuburban businesses at an edge city location, the development of new towns in this case has been under close supervision and strategically planned for the municipality of Beijing to create a new growth pole along the Beijing–Tianjin development corridor.

Fiscal reform has enhanced the ability of the central state to extract revenue (Figure 11.1). The trajectory of the ratio shows a V shape, delineating different stages of Chinese economic reform. In the earlier stage, the percentage declined, characteristic of economic devolution and deregulation. The ratio declined from about 27% in 1979 to its lowest, 10%, in 1995. At that stage, local governments were more inclined to make tax concessions because the costs were borne by the central government. Since the establishment of the tax-sharing system, the ratio has been increasing, up to 20% in 2007 and 23% in 2012. This reflects the strengthened capacity for fiscal extraction through the operation of the current development regime.

Overall, the development regime was effective in surplus extraction as well as raising GDP. The income of urban households increased significantly but lagged behind GDP growth, with rural households lagging further behind (Figure 11.2). After the reform shifted into the cities, the income ratio of rural to urban

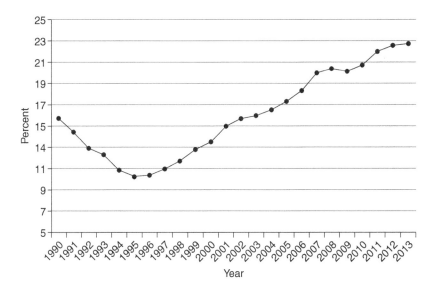

Figure 11.1 The ratio of national revenue income to gross domestic product in China, 1990–2013.

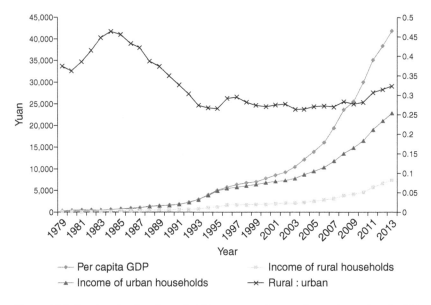

Figure 11.2 Rural and urban household incomes and gross domestic product in China, 1979–2013.

households declined from about 45% in 1984 to 27% in 2007, closing at 32% in 2013. This enlarged income gap between urban and rural households has been accompanied by an overall increase in social inequalities. Migrant workers have become the de facto working poor in the cities. Inequality between rural and urban areas is thus translated into inequalities between different social groups (local urban households vs. migrant workers) inside the cities. The outflow of younger workers from rural areas devastated the rural economy and society, creating social problems of family separation and instability, and leftbehind children in the countryside.

Social implications and marginalization

The preceding dynamics create social implications for Chinese cities. Development is increasingly driven by investment in fixed assets rather than consumption. Household consumption has been a decreasing share of GDP, with its contribution to GDP growth rate also declining in recent years. With the enhanced capacity of both the state and capital in surplus extraction, the return to the production factor of labor is declining. The proportion of wages in GDP declined from 51.5% in 2002 to 39.7% in 2007. The ratio of household consumption to GDP similarly declined, from 52% in 1981 to 35% in 2007 and 36% in 2013 (Figure 11.3). The problem of urban poverty emerged after market-oriented reform, although income levels in general have been increasing (see

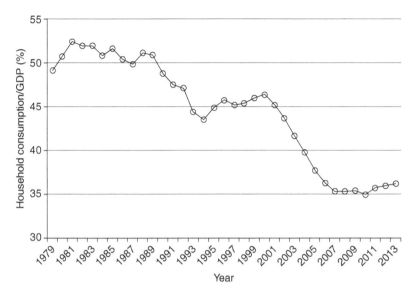

Figure 11.3 Household income and gross domestic product in China, 1979–2013.

earlier). The new poor have been created both as laid-off workers and as the working poor of rural migrants (Solinger, 2006; Wu, 2004).

The issue of urban poverty in China is different from advanced marginality, however, in that it is not a case of "outcast ghettos" inhabited by those excluded from the post-Fordist economy (Marcuse, 1997; Wacquant, 2008). The urban poor have links with the emerging economy of global production, as can be seen from informal workshops and rural migrants as the workforce for these manufacturing industries. They might live in factory-run dormitories (Yang, 2013) where maintenance is quite strict and disciplined or in urban villages that generate private rental income for local farmers. These villages are living places, small markets, and even small workshops (e.g., the clothing market in Guangzhou) that play a role in global production circulation and networks. To understand this Chinese form of marginalization, it is pertinent to understand local institutions and the historical definition of citizenship. Under state socialism, social welfare provision was associated with workplace affiliation, effectively distinguishing insiders and outsiders in the system. Moreover, rural areas were outside the state realm. These fragmented structures have had different implications for different social groups in the aftermath of market reform.

The rural migrants who were outside the state realm have had to rely on the market provision of social services. In terms of housing, they mostly stay in rental housing in urban villages or factory dormitories (Wu, 2008). As for the employees of state-owned enterprises, after being laid off, they were transferred from their workplaces to local governments. The system of minimum income support covers those below the minimum income line, but the majority of workers now receive services in commoditized form – as seen in the process of privatization and commodification of health care, education, and housing. The process of marginalization, therefore, is not just a result of economic restructuring and globalization but also a result of the interaction of these macroeconomic processes with local institutions. Urban development and redevelopment under market transition has been a process of expansion and clarification of property rights, but the process has had different impacts on social groups, depending on their status in locally defined institutions. The result is to constrain claims based on citizenship, replacing these with a more local form of provision.

Diverse spatial forms

As can be seen in Chinese urban studies, diverse spatial forms have been generated in the process of market transition (Logan, 2008). Housing inequalities and spatial segregation have emerged (Liu, He, & Wu, 2012). Migrant settlements are distributed in the periurban areas (Wu, 2008). Chinese cities have seen the creation of complex and contrasting urban landscapes. There are formal and master planned residential enclaves (He, 2013; Pow, 2009; Zhang, 2010) and informal settlements developed from rural villages (Tian, 2008; Wu, Zhang, & Webster, 2013). The city proper is developed in a more orderly way, in the form of skyscrapers and high-rise residential buildings. The order of urban areas is created by the legacy of strong state control, especially through state workunits. Land development is more informal in periurban areas, however. As much as one third of new development is in the category of so-called limited property rights (Deng, 2009), where farmers developed housing for sale in the housing market without full endorsement of the state in terms of land uses and land development rights, which have to be obtained through competitive bidding in urban land markets.

In southern China, Shantou has seen the appearance of densely mixed rural and urban land uses, resulting from globally driven industrialization (Figure 11.4). The development of industrial land is mixed with preexisting rural villages, creating severe spatial fragmentation. A novel type of spatial form has been created, known as three in one (*san he yi*), combining workshop, warehouse, and residence. It creates a convenient place for rural workers to live on site but at the same time creates serious public health and environmental problems. Tranquil rural areas were converted to sites for world factories, but some areas developed into haphazard and polluting family-based workshops, for example, disassembling waste electronic products and extracting their metals. In some larger workshops, factory-run workers' dormitories provide effective accommodation for the influx of workers from rural areas, but at the same time they are subject to the regimes of factory management and dominant overseers. This form of residence dismantled the potential social networks existing among fellow migrants from the same origin of place (Ma & Xiang, 1998) and imposed the disciplinary power of capital (Yang, 2013).

Figure 11.4 Rural and urban land use mix in Southern China: Shantou city.

The most widespread form is urban villages, developed through farmers' self-building and the extension of rural villages now encroached on by the city (Tian, 2008). Chinese urban informality is derived from urban–rural dualism, in which urban and rural land have been subject to different land systems. Urban land is state-owned, whereas rural land is collectively owned by farmers (Hsing, 2010; Xu, Yeh, & Wu, 2009). In urban areas, a significant proportion was under individual workplaces or "socialist land masters" (Hsing, 2006, 2010). In rural areas, though, collective ownership meant that the power of dealing with land development was ambiguous (Zhu, 2004). Urban villages can be regarded as Chinese informal settlements (Wang, Wang, & Wu, 2009). The traditional lax land management and planning control in the countryside is another source of informality (Wu et al., 2013). Service provision in these rural villages is not funded through public finance (Po, 2012; Wu et al., 2013). Provision is thus not a welfare delivery but rather a benefit managed by rural collectives. This mode of service delivery reduces the fiscal burden on the municipal government, which virtually ignores the issue of accommodation for rural migrants. Their housing needs are exclusively met by private rentals in the housing market, and they remain spatially segregated from other urban areas (Wu, 2008).

In contrast to informal development, commodity housing estates present a strong spatial order (He, 2013; Wu, 2005). They are in essence master-planned communities, a term used in Australia to describe new development through packaged design (McGuirk & Dowling, 2009). In that context, the type of residence is associated with neoliberal urbanism. The perspective has been applied in the study of Chinese suburban residential areas (Shen & Wu, 2012). It has been shown, however, that gated communities demonstrate a strong characteristic of collectivism inherited from Chinese tradition (Huang, 2006). In China, they also represent the rising aspiration of middle-class life to style and privacy (Pow, 2009; Wu, 2010a; Zhang, 2010). These gated communities are often within a larger development zone that is under the management of more entrepreneurial governance. The development is often zoned into industrial and residential uses, using modern planning principles. Figure 11.5 shows the pattern of land uses in Beijing ETDZ in Yizhuang, recently scaled up into a new town. The development has been driven by the forces of both market and state.

The contrast between formal and informal housing is quite similar to what has been observed between more orderly European living quarters and organic and mixed indigenous areas in third world cities (Dick & Rimmer, 1998). In the Chinese case, though, they are within the same development regime. Table 11.1 compares formal and informal development in Chinese cities. They are significantly different in terms of spatial forms and features. The state is absent in social provision in informal developments, whereas state entrepreneurialism under development corporations dominates in formal development. For formal development, land finance is part and parcel of urban expansion, but informal development is mainly for rental income and used as a tactic of rural farmers in periurban areas to divert land income from the state through their own supply of rental housing or even illegal sales. Accordingly, there are different governance

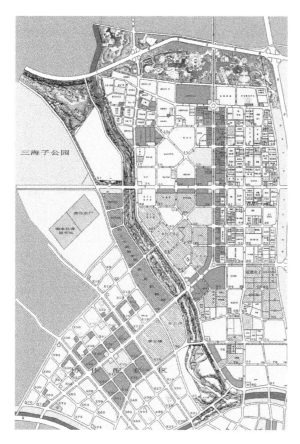

Figure 11.5 The planning layout of the Beijing economic and technological zone.

Table 11.1 Comparison of formal and informal development in Chinese cities

	Formal development	Informal development
Spatial forms	Commodity housing estates	Urban villages
Spatial features	Overly designed and packaged	Irregular uses and spontaneous changes
The role of the state	State entrepreneurialism	Absence in social provision
Capital accumulation	Land-driven development Land finance	Rural migrants' accommodation Rental income for property owners
Governance	Homeowners' associations Property management companies	Villagers' committees Village collectives Private owners

modes. Formal development has seen growing awareness of property rights and the formation of homeowners' associations. Informal village development is still under village governance and the reformulated market form of villager stock-holding companies.

Discussion

Table 11.2 shows the understanding of Chinese cities in terms of processes and spatial forms in comparison with global urban studies. First, Chinese urbanization contributes to Western urban research about neoliberalism in general and urban entrepreneurialism in particular. In contrast to an ideology of free market dominance, Chinese local development shows a hybrid form, combining the features of the developmental state with instruments created in the market. Pragmatism is adopted to legitimize the state as a key driver for economic growth. The institutions of land, fiscal policy, and cadre promotion laid down the foundation on which the local state has been incentivized and transformed. Given a very different historical context, it is a surprise to see that Chinese cities demonstrate features remarkably similar to the local competition state but with varying degrees of state persistence. These are noted as neoliberalism with Chinese characteristics (Harvey, 2005), localized neoliberalization processes (He & Wu, 2009), and state neoliberalism (Chu & So, 2012). Despite complaining about the use of neoliberalism (Ong, 2007), Chinese urban studies provide a wide middle range of explanations for the dynamism of entrepreneurial-like government behavior, which include the system of cadre promotion, GDP growth mentality, property rights ambiguity,

Table 11.2 Comparison of prevailing concepts about the process of urban development and spatial forms and the Chinese cases

	Prevailing concepts	*The Chinese cities*
Neoliberalism	Ideology Dominance of the market	Pragmatism State legitimacy Hybrid governance
Marginalization	Economic restructuring State retreat Outcasts	State dominance Restraining the citizenship claims

Informality/informal
  settlements
	"Zones of exception"
	Absence of property rights
		Urban rural dualism
		  Complex and void of land
		  management

Gated communities	Consumer and lifestyle
	  choice
	Private governance
	Concern for security
		Imaginary lifestyles of
		  suburbia
		Place-branding

Edge cities/postsuburbia	Postindustrial, flexible spaces	Land-driven development Land finance Place creation

fiscal policy and incentives, and land-based finance. These highlight the various institutional foundations that generate the new process of urban development in China.

Second, marginalization is associated with economic restructuring, globalization, and changing redistributive policies. But Chinese cities show that the process of marginalization does not mean separation from new production processes but rather, as a result of state dominance, the withholding of some citizenship claims. In contrast to the thesis of state retreat and social exclusion, Chinese cities see more state monopolization in resource generation and control and the effects of constraints on citizenship. The delivery of social welfare has been transferred to the local government and through the market as paid services (e.g., for rural migrants to send their children to migrant schools run by companies).

Third, regarding spatial forms, globalization has created immense impacts on Chinese cities. As seen in Southeast Asian cities (Ginsburg, Koppel, & McGee, 1991), the spatial form is a mixed pattern of urban and rural land uses described as *desakota*, a term coined in Indonesia for urban and rural mixes. The concept was applied to the Chinese context by McGee, Lin, Marton, Wang, & Wu (2007). Informality is described as zones of exception (Roy, 2011), applied both to upper market development and to slums. In the former, mafia developers in India (Weinstein, 2008) create informality through corruption and bribes as well as their historical influence. Slums are seen as the absence of property rights or ambiguous property rights. The difficulty of enforcing property rights leads to squatter areas. In the Chinese case, informality resulted from the legacy of urban–rural dualism as well as land management complexity. Whereas the *desakota* model suggests the morphological feature of mixing, the case of Chinese villages shows how development is indeed linked to globalization processes while depending also on unique local land and political institutions.

Fourth, gated communities are seen as the outcome of consumer clubs (Webster, Glasze, & Frantz, 2002) and private governance, lifestyle choice, and concern for security (Blakely & Snyder, 1997). In the Chinese case, though, the development of gated communities is promoted by developers as a place-branding tactic to enhance the attractiveness of underdeveloped suburbs (Wu, 2010a). The local government endorses this practice because it helps promote land development, bringing the local government land income. The state is heavily involved in capital mobilization to fund key infrastructure enabling the suburban development of gated communities (Shen & Wu, 2012; Wu, 2015). In this case we see state-led Imagineering rather than absence of the state.

Finally, associated with suburban gated communities is the concept of edge cities and postsuburbia, a notion used to describe economic structural changes, the move toward a postindustrial economy, and a flexible space of businesses. In the Chinese case, though, land-driven development has been a key reason for suburban development, with local government, together with planning professionals, playing an important role in place creation.

Conclusion

Emerging Chinese cities provide a laboratory to observe planetary urbanization (Brenner, 2013). These cities do not represent the model of emerging urbanism but contain some constellated elements of this process. Urban-based accumulation permeates the whole planet, drawing the spaces outside global capitalism into its orbit. Nevertheless, diverse spatial forms persist. The new world-scale development process interacts with historical and existing local structures, which reinforce and reinvent themselves into new market-compatible forms. During the process of remodeling, new properties and features are created. It is in this sense that both the cities themselves and their properties are emergent: neither predefined nor predictable, they reflect contingent social interactions, and open possibilities for more sustainable and just forms.

The notion of emergence has a sense of complexity. It is not a result of the global process that dominates the locality. Emerging Chinese cities show that local institutions are an indispensable part of urban transformation. For example, *hukou* and state ownership of land have been given a new meaning in the process of market development. Their lasting effects create a new space of informality in Chinese urban villages where rural migrants, subject to *hukou*, become tenants of private and informal housing. The growth of cities relies highly on the mechanism of the state land monopoly. The state strives to control land and eliminate informality through urban renewal. Rather than being eliminated, however, informality is reinforced, reemerging with its peculiar mode of development as more rural villages are converted into private rentals through self-development (Wu et al., 2013). The renewal process itself must make exceptions for developers to give them viable real estate projects. This is seen in southern China, where intensity and plot ratio have to exceed the city plans or the government has to put aside development controls. The peculiar state dominance in land supply lays down the foundation of this mode of development, known as land-based finance. These are specific geographical processes and spatial forms in China that, together with other examples from other Asian cities and the cities of the Global South, require us to rethink the Western urban theory (Roy, 2009). As shown in this chapter, land-driven urban development and urban village expansion both reveal a wide process of neoliberalization and associated informality.

This chapter examines emerging Chinese cities as an example of emerging Asia. Chinese cities no doubt demonstrate some special features, but they are not entirely unique. The development of Chinese cities is promoted and intervened by the developmental state, as seen in other East Asian countries. The emergence of Chinese cities is an outcome of not just the developmental state at the central level and its national development strategies but also the entrepreneurial local state that taps into the market resources to act for its own political and fiscal objectives. In this sense, the Chinese state challenges the dichotomy of the developmental state of authoritarianism and the entrepreneurial state of neoliberalism. Rather, these contradictory characteristics are combined into the emerging property of the Chinese state in the new phase of planning for growth

(Wu, 2015), in which growth has been pursued to legitimize state dominance. Second, emerging Chinese cities departed from its tradition of the socialist planned economy and demonstrated widespread informality and irregularity in governance, as typically shown in South and Southeast Asian countries (Roy, 2011). The introduction of market mechanisms and relaxation of state control mean inevitable creation of unruly spaces. But what is more, as shown in emerging Chinese cities, is that this informality is not simply a result of state incompetence and weak governance. Rather, the informality is a deliberate strategy, not only giving much discretion to developers through exception of governance, for example, in city planning (Wu, 2015) but also being a practical solution of labor reproduction, as seen in self-building in urban villages.

These Chinese studies contribute to the understanding of concrete institutional mechanisms, which are not derivative from but are an integral part of transformation. The changes are both relational (flow and networks) and scalar (decentralization and territorialization). Concrete institutional mechanisms trigger the entrepreneurial-like behavior of the local state, which becomes a market agent. Chinese cities thus prompt us to treat the property of emergence seriously. Rather than caricaturing the Chinese state as an authoritarian regime, the emergence perspective allows us to comprehend how contradictory approaches could be adopted simultaneously: an absence of housing provision to rural migrants as a neoliberal retreat from social provision, aggressive land acquisition by the state-backed development corporations, and place promotion and branding through entrepreneurial strategy, discourse, and action (Jessop & Sum, 2000). These are combined to create a version of state entrepreneurialism, as seen in the development of the Beijing ETDZ at Yizhuang: an edge city location (Garreau, 1991) that is more a postsuburbia outcome of state entrepreneurialism (Wu & Phelps, 2011). Similarly, Zhangjiang High-Tech Park at Pudong in Shanghai is more than a cluster of urban agglomeration but is driven by state promotion of indigenous innovation capacities (Zhang & Wu, 2012) and the formation of a regional innovation system under state guidance (Zhang, 2015). Without seeing the deeply embedded institutions, there is a temptation to interpret these as yet another edge city or multinational research and development cluster.

As seen in emerging Chinese cities, market transition is not an ideology but a governance technique (Wu, 2010b). The introduction of market mechanisms and market operational instruments (including commodification and techniques) has intrinsically changed the nature of the developmental state at the national scale. It is thus equally tempting to see emerging Chinese cities as derivative of the entrepreneurial city. As Cochrane (2007) appropriately complained, however, the city is not a firm but a polity and thus subject to political forces. Chinese cities provide a chance to expand the geography of theories (Roy, 2009) and, together with other cities in the global south, contribute to global urban studies.

172   *F. Wu*

Note

1 Fulong Wu, "Emerging Chinese Cities: Implications for Global Urban Studies," published in the journal *The Professional Geographer*, Taylor & Francis, Volume 68, 2016 – Issue 2, pages 338–348. Reproduced by kind permission from Fulong Wu and *The Professional Geographer* journal.

References

Andrusz, G., Harloe, M., & Szelényi, I. (Eds.). (1996). *Cities after socialism: Urban and regional change and conflict in postsocialist societies.* Oxford, UK: Blackwell.
Blakely, E. J., & Snyder, M. G. (1997). *Fortress America: Gated communities in the United States.* Washington, DC: Brookings Institution Press.
Brenner, N. (2013). Theses on urbanization. *Public Culture, 25*(1), 85–114.
Chien, S. S. (2013). New local state power through administrative restructuring: A case study of post-Mao China county-level urban entrepreneurialism in Kunshan. *Geoforum, 46,* 103–112.
Chien, S. S., & Gordon, I. (2008). Territorial competition in China and the west. *Regional Studies, 42*(1), 31–49.
Chu, Y.-W., & So, A. Y. (2012). *The transition from neoliberalism to state neoliberalism in China at the turn of the twenty-first century.* Basingstoke, UK: Palgrave Macmillan.
Cochrane, A. (2007). *Understanding urban policy: A critical approach.* Oxford, UK: Blackwell.
Deng, F. (2009). Housing of limited property rights: A paradox inside and outside Chinese cities. *Housing Studies, 24*(6), 825–841.
Dick, H. W., & Rimmer, P. J. (1998). Beyond the third world city: The new urban geography of South-east Asia. *Urban Studies, 35*(12), 2303–2321.
Duckett, J. (2001). Bureaucrats in business, Chinese-style: The lessons of market reform and state entrepreneurialism in the People's Republic of China. *World Development, 29*(1), 23–37.
Garreau, J. (1991). *Edge city: Life on the new frontier.* New York: Doubleday.
Ginsburg, N., Koppel, B., & McGee, T. G. (Eds.). (1991). *The extended metropolis: Settlement in transition in Asia.* Honolulu: University of Hawaii Press.
Harvey, D. (1989). From managerialism to entrepreneurialism: The transformation in urban governance in late capitalism. *Geografiska Annaler, 71B*(1), 3–18.
Harvey, D. (2005). *A brief history of neoliberalism.* Oxford, UK: Oxford University Press.
He, S. J. (2013). Evolving enclave urbanism in China and its socio-spatial implications: The case of Guangzhou. *Social & Cultural Geography, 14*(3), 243–275.
He, S., & Wu, F. (2009). China's emerging neoliberal urbanism: Perspectives from urban redevelopment. *Antipode, 41*(2), 282–304.
Hsing, Y.-T. (2006). Land and territorial politics in urban China. *China Quarterly, 187,* 1–18.
Hsing, Y.-T. (2010). *The great urban transformation: Politics of land and property in China.* Oxford, UK: Oxford University Press.
Huang, Y. S. (2006). Collectivism, political control, and gating in Chinese cities. *Urban Geography, 27*(6), 507–525.
Huang, Y. Q. (2008). *Capitalism with Chinese characteristics: Entrepreneurship and the state.* Cambridge, UK: Cambridge University Press.

Jessop, B., & Sum, N. L. (2000). An entrepreneurial city in action: Hong Kong's emerging strategies in and for (inter)urban competition. *Urban Studies, 37*(12), 2287–2313.

Lin, G. C. S. (2014). China's landed urbanization: Neoliberalizing politics, land commodification, and municipal finance in the growth of metropolises. *Environment and Planning, A 46*, 1814–1835.

Liu, Y., He, S., & Wu, F. (2012). Housing differentiation under market transition in Nanjing, China. *The Professional Geographer, 64*(4), 554–571.

Logan, J. (Ed.). (2008). *Urban China in transition*. Oxford, UK: Blackwell.

Ma, L. J. C., & Xiang, B. (1998). Native place, migration and the emergence of peasant enclaves in Beijing. *The China Quarterly, 155*, 546–581.

Marcuse, P. (1997). The enclave, the citadel, and the ghetto: What has changed in the post-Fordist U.S. city. *Urban Affairs Review, 33*(2), 228–264.

McGee, T. G., Lin, G. C. S., Marton, A. M., Wang, M. Y. L., & Wu, J. (2007). *China's urban space: Development under market transition*. London and New York: Routledge.

McGuirk, P., & Dowling, R. (2009). Neoliberal privatisation? Remapping the public and the private in Sydney's masterplanned residential estates. *Political Geography, 28*(3), 174–185.

Oi, J. C. (1995). The role of the local state in China's transitional economy. *China Quarterly, 144*, 1132–1149.

Ong, A. (2007). Neoliberalism as a mobile technology. *Transactions of the Institute of British Geographers, 32*(1), 3–8.

Po, L. (2012). Asymmetrical integration: Public finance deprivation in China's urbanized villages. *Environment and Planning, A 44*(12), 2834–2851.

Pow, C.-P. (2009). *Gated communities in China: Class, privilege and the moral politics of the good life*. London and New York: Routledge.

Qian, Y., & Weingast, B. R. (1997). Federalism as a commitment to preserving market incentives. *Journal of Economic Perspectives, 11*(4), 83–92.

Robinson, J. (2011). The travels of urban neoliberalism: Taking stock of the internationalization of urban theory. *Urban Geography, 32*(8), 1087–1109.

Roy, A. (2009). The 21st-century metropolis: New geographies of theory. *Regional Studies, 43*(6), 819–830.

Roy, A. (2011). Slumdog cities: Rethinking subaltern urbanism. *International Journal of Urban and Regional Research, 35*(2), 223–238.

Roy, A., & Ong, A. (Eds.). (2011). *Worlding cities: Asian experiments and the art of being global*. Oxford, UK: Wiley-Blackwell.

Shen, J., & Wu, F. L. (2012). The development of masterplanned communities in Chinese suburbs: A case study of Shanghai's Thames Town. *Urban Geography, 33*(2), 183–203.

Solinger, D. J. (2006). The creation of a new underclass in China and its implications. *Environment and Urbanization, 18*(1), 177–193.

Tao, R., Su, F. B., Liu, M. X., & Cao, G. Z. (2010). Landleasing and local public finance in China's regional development: Evidence from prefecture-level cities. *Urban Studies, 47*(10), 2217–2236.

Tian, L. (2008). The Chengzhongcun landmarket in China: Boon or bane? A perspective on property rights. *International Journal of Urban and Regional Research, 32*(2), 282–304.

Tsui, K., & Wang, Y. (2004). Between separate stoves and a single menu: Fiscal decentralization in China. *The China Quarterly, 177*, 71–90.

Wacquant, L. (2008). *Urban outcasts: A comparative sociology of advanced marginality.* Cambridge, UK: Polity.

Walder, A. (1995). Local governments as industrial firms: An organizational analysis of China's transitional economy. *American Journal of Sociology, 101*(2), 263–301.

Wang, L. (2014). Forging growth by governing the market in reform-era urban China. *Cities, 41*, 187–193.

Wang, Y. P., Wang, Y., & Wu, J. (2009). Urbanization and informal development in China: Urban villages in Shenzhen. *International Journal of Urban and Regional Research, 33*(4), 957–973.

Wank, D. L. (1996). The institutional process of market clientelism: Guanxi and private business in a South China city. *The China Quarterly, 147*, 820–838.

Webster, C., Glasze, G., & Frantz, K. (2002). The global spread of gated communities. *Environment and Planning, B 29*(3), 315–320.

Weinstein, L. (2008). Mumbai's development mafias: Globalization, organized crime and land development. *International Journal of Urban and Regional Research, 32*(1), 22–39.

Wu, F. (2003). The (post-) socialist entrepreneurial city as a state project: Shanghai's reglobalisation in question. *Urban Studies, 40*(9), 1673–1698.

Wu, F. (2004). Urban poverty and marginalization under market transition: The case of Chinese cities. *International Journal of Urban and Regional Research, 28*(2), 401–423.

Wu, F. (2005). Rediscovering the "gate" under market transition: From work-unit compounds to commodity housing enclaves. *Housing Studies, 20*(2), 235–254.

Wu, F. (2010a). Gated and packaged suburbia: Packaging and branding Chinese suburban residential development. *Cities, 27*(5), 385–396.

Wu, F. (2010b). How neoliberal is China's reform? The origins of change during transition. *Eurasian Geography and Economics, 51*(5), 619–631.

Wu, F. (2015). *Planning for growth: Urban and regional planning in China.* London and New York: Routledge.

Wu, F., & Phelps, N. A. (2011). (Post)suburban development and state entrepreneurialism in Beijing's outer suburbs. *Environment and Planning, A 43*(2), 410–430.

Wu, F., Zhang, F. Z., & Webster, C. (2013). Informality and the development and demolition of urban villages in the Chinese peri-urban area. *Urban Studies, 50*(10), 1919–1934.

Wu, W. (2008). Migrant settlement and spatial distribution in metropolitan Shanghai. *The Professional Geographer, 60*(1), 101–120.

Xu, C. (2011). The fundamental institutions of China's reform and development. *Journal of Economic Literature, 49*(4), 1076–1151.

Xu, J., Yeh, A., & Wu, F. L. (2009). Land commodification: New land development and politics in China since the late 1990s. *International Journal of Urban and Regional Research, 33*(4), 890–913.

Yang, D. Y. R., & Wang, H. K. (2008). Dilemmas of local governance under the development zone fever in China: A case study of the Suzhou region. *Urban Studies, 45*(5–6), 1037–1054.

Yang, Y.-R. D. (2013). A tale of Foxconn city: Urban village, migrant workers and alienated urbanism. In F. Wu, F. Zhang, & C. Webster (Eds.), *Rural migrants in urban China: Enclaves and transient urbanism* (pp. 147–163). London and New York: Routledge.

Zhang, F. Z. (2015). Building biotech in Shanghai: A perspective of regional innovation system. *European Planning Studies, 23*(10), 2062–2078.

Zhang, F. Z., & Wu, F. L. (2012). Fostering "indigenous innovation capacities": The development of biotechnology in Shanghai's Zhangjiang High-Tech Park. *Urban Geography, 33*(5), 728–755.

Zhang, L. (2010). *In search of paradise: Middle-class living in a Chinese metropolis.* Ithaca, NY: Cornell University Press.

Zhou, Y., & Ma, L. J. C. (2003). China's urbanization levels: Reconstructing a baseline from the fifth population census. *The China Quarterly, 173*, 176–196.

Zhu, J. (2004). Local development state and order in China's urban development during transition. *International Journal of Urban and Regional Research, 28*, 424–447.

12 Urban Facebooks as digital planning and marketing tools in the 'New Urban World'

Karima Kourtit and Peter Nijkamp

The rise of the 'New Urban World'

The geography of our planet in the 21st century is characterized by a new meg-atrend of rapid world-wide urbanization. Kourtit (2015) has described this emerging trend as follows:

> In the 'century of cities', our planet is gradually moving towards a 'New Urban World': more and more people are moving towards cities or urban agglomerations, so that urban areas have become the 'new home of humankind'. The 'New Urban World' is a recent phenomenon in the rich history of cities. At present, not only does more than 50 per cent of the world's population live in cities, but also urbanisation is still persistently and rapidly increasing, in particular in the developing world. Con-sequently, modern cities tend to become magnets of economic, cultural, political and technological power. This phenomenon is often referred to as the 'New Urban World' or sometimes also as the 'post-urban world' (see Westlund 2014). This 'New Urban World' marks a new stage in the urban landscape of our planet that is characterised by a rapid and structural transformation of settlement patterns of people, firms, and activities into urbanised patterns of living and working as the new dominant locational map of our world.
>
> (p. 8)

In the same vein, she argues:

> The agglomeration advantages of the 'New Urban World' originate from economies of density, proximity, accessibility and connectivity. In other words, urbanized areas are able to generate increasing returns to scale, and, hence, are generating self-propelling growth. Urban agglomerations will most likely also become the socio-economic powerhouses of the future and exhibit a fast dynamics in the decades to come. Cities are certainly not crafted in stone, but are a 'process', always 'on the move', in order to create favourable conditions for economic agents. The 'New Urban World' tends

to turn into a complex and critical evolutionary system for spatial development in the future.

(p. 8)

Worldwide, urban areas are most likely to become the new engines of economic development of regions and countries. Clearly, over a longer period, they tend to exhibit a product life-cycle pattern, characterised by ups and downs and by expansion and contraction. Such fluctuating patterns may be caused by external shocks (e.g. a large migration influx, an earthquake, an energy boom) or by endogenous dynamics (e.g. decay in infrastructure capital, deterioration of the quality of the housing stock). The governance of the complex dynamics of urban agglomerations raises various intriguing questions, such as: Should cities in a post-urban age be maintained at all cost, and do we have appropriate strategic information and data to govern long-run urban dynamics?

The above questions have now become important again as currently cities show a tendency towards two extreme developmental directions, namely accelerated growth (e.g. in many emerging and developing economies) versus urban decay or shrinking (e.g. in older industrial areas) (see, e.g., Cheshire & Gordon, 2006; Nijkamp, Kourtit, & Westlund, 2016). Such developments prompt the question whether our analysis methods are geared towards the achievement of long-run urban sustainability? In all cases, it is a valid and relevant question whether the analytical apparatus available in urban planning methods is fit-for-purpose in the light of the above-mentioned dynamics in and between urban areas.

Over recent decades, the concept of sustainable urban development has turned into a widely accepted policy objective for urban agglomerations all over the world. Clearly, this policy objective has multiple dimensions, as it may range from coping with emerging issues (such as environmental decay or social tension) to anticipating future threats (such as sea level rise or mass migration). In a recent study (see Insight, 2014), the following systematic classification of challenges for the sustainable development of urban agglomerations was presented:

- *Social-demographic change*
  This megatrend comprises, inter alia, threats caused by demographic decline, ageing of population, migration of the active population and skilled workers, socio-economic polarisation, social segregation, socio-spatial segregation, and lack of affordable housing.
- *Depletion of natural resources and environmental impact*
  This challenge refers to the ecology of cities, where it concerns energy consumption and contribution to the greenhouse effect, energy-free buildings, fuel dependence, poor air quality and noise pollution, and the degradation of space in the human environment.
- *Economic decline and development and competiveness under pressure*
  This third threat to sustainable development of urban systems includes in particular the following components: low productivity, unemployment, and declining revenues and demand in cities.

- *Urban sprawl*

  Urban sprawl is often seen as a main impediment to balanced urban development, and leads to a series of challenges, such as socio-spatial segregation
  and social polarisation, land occupation and environmental degradation, and
  economic losses and inefficiencies in services delivery.

It goes without saying that many more challenges can be distinguished, such as
transportation accessibility in large cities (see, e.g., Preston & Rajé, 2007) or
human health in urban agglomerations (see, e.g., Ishikawa, Kourtit, & Nijkamp,
2015). But irrespective of the list of threats or challenges, it is evident that
modern cities – as magnets for sustainable development – are not in the first
place to be regarded as 'problem cases', but offer promising opportunities for
balanced urban, regional, or national development.

Urban agglomerations have become dynamic engines for wealth creation and
global competiveness. Such urban areas need to be responsive and resilient, by
taking into consideration the justified motives, needs, values, and arguments of
their inhabitants, tourists, businesses, etc. In this context, modern interactive
tools for information and data exchange and possible conflicting perspectives
between different actors may become extremely relevant for the continuing
process of efficient sustainable urban development (see also Koglin, 2009). This
chapter aims to highlight the strategic importance of modern digital information
and data tools (e.g., Facebooks) and operational management systems to address
the challenges of complex urban systems for building a sustainable urban future.
The chapter is organised as follows. We start by explaining the great potential of
sophisticated digital information tools for a balanced future-oriented urban
policy. Next, there follows a series of empirical illustrations in order to highlight
the great power of such modern policy tools.

City marketing in competitive urban systems

The life cycle of the rise and decay of cities raises important policy issues with
regard to long-term urban strategies. What are the critical determinants of urban
attractiveness for various kinds of users? Urban attractiveness is, therefore, a key
ingredient in modern urban strategic planning and marketing strategies. It has
become fashionable to rank cities according to their economic, cultural, or technological performance (see, e.g., Kourtit, Nijkamp, & Suzuki, 2013). City competition has become a new trend in the globalising world: cities are no longer islands
of isolation, but key players in an open international urban system. And hence,
the question emerges: which is the best? Or, which is the world-class city? This is
not only a question born out of curiosity; the performance of cities impacts their
attractiveness, e.g. for international business or FDI. Consequently, we observe a
rising need for city (or place) marketing or branding (see, e.g., Braun, Kavaratzis,
& Zenker, 2013; Ham, 2008; Hospers, 2004; Kavaratzis & Ashworth, 2008;
Moilanen & Rainisto 2009; Paddinson, 1993; Smyth, 1994), oriented towards
promoting the city's (global) competitive advantages. Consequently, city marketing

has become a strategic instrument and an important part of the city's positioning strategy to attract more residents, visitors, or enterprises so as to enhance the welfare and sustainability of the city concerned. This is achieved by promoting the attractive key attributes of a city (e.g. Braun, 2012; Eshuis & Edwards, 2013; Riza, Doratli, & Fasli, 2012; Waard, 2012), and demonstrating the tangible and intangible innovative or creative power of the city.

By googling 'city marketing', one finds almost 1 billion hits, which illustrates the worldwide popularity of this concept. It is a tool for urban socio-economic policy with a view to the enhancement of urban performance. According to Braun (2008), place marketing may be interpreted as follows: the coordinated use of marketing tools supported by a shared customer-oriented philosophy, for creating, communicating, delivering, and exchanging urban offerings that have value for the city's customers and the city's community at large (p. 43). It is thus clear that if it is decided to put a city on the map its overall performance should be improved, while recognising that a city is a multi-client entity with a variety of interests and attributes. For example, Limburg (1998) distinguished the key attributes of attracting people to a given city by dividing them into four classes: events, history, shops, and entertainment. Clearly, a mix of such attributes helps to enhance the overall dynamism, attractiveness, and quality of life of a city.

It is noteworthy that city marketing is also instrumental in highlighting the unique specificities of a given city. For example, European cities have, in general, a wealth of distinct cultural heritage features, which makes them markedly different from cities in other continents. Thus, in a competing space-economy there is a clear scope for emphasising the 'unique good' in a city image (see also Ashworth & Tunbridge, 1990, Kotler & Gertner, 2002; Ward, 1998), and for visualising 'the invisibility', promoting, and 'selling' the city's uniqueness to various stakeholders (see for a wealth of examples, see Stevens, 2015).

The previous task calls for a smart segmented strategy and the right and high-quality information and data in order to identity the determinants of a successful city marketing approach (see Moilanen & Rainisto 2008; Morgan, Pritchard, & Pride, 2012). City marketing or branding is not only about making the positive characteristics of a city more well-known, but also about creating a positive image that is believable, simple, appealing, and distinctive. Clearly, city marketing is not only a passive public notification of 'what is', but is also a dynamic process of 'what will be', so as to encourage repeat tourism or maintain business investments. In this context, the development of 'flagship' landmarks may be important, as this will create a distinction from competing cities, a sense of structural emotion for the client or visitors, long-run socio-economic benefits for business life, and satisfaction among residents.

Over recent years, city marketing and city branding have developed client-centred approaches to create and offer an attractive and visible image of cities. There is even a City Brands Index, which comprises the following top-10 cities: London, Sydney, Paris, New York, Rome, Washington DC, Los Angeles, Toronto, Vienna, and Melbourne. The City Brands Index ranks cities according to six key P-Principles: Presence, Place, Potential, Pulse, People, and Prerequisites[1] (see also Anholt, 2006).

Cultural and historical heritage can provide a major and unique force of attraction for many cities. This characteristic is shared by many cities in Europe, and consequently city marketing in Europe is taking place on a competitive edge. For example, cities like Rome, Athens, or Paris are competing for the favours of tourists on the basis of the Colosseum, the Acropolis, or the Eiffel Tower, respectively. And Europe has hundreds of cities with a wealth of historico-cultural heritage, representing the legacy of the physical artifacts and intangible characteristics of a city. Consequently, museums, libraries, or heritage sites but also local traditions can be a distinct part of cultural heritage. Threats to this legacy emerge from industrialisation, urbanisation, environmental and climate change, and human behaviour (see also Kourtit, 2015). Consequently, the presence of historico-cultural heritage may be treated as an opportunity for improvement in many respects, and not as a bottleneck for future urban policy.

An example of an analytical approach, with a high involvement of stakeholders, to the assessment of the multiple facets of city marketing can be found in what is called the Spider model, for the valuation of 16 strong dimensions and key values for the city profile (performance and personality) of Amsterdam (see City of Amsterdam, 2004). A presentation of the Amsterdam Spider concept can be found in Figure 12.1, and is now translated by the city officials into the famous city slogan 'I Amsterdam'.

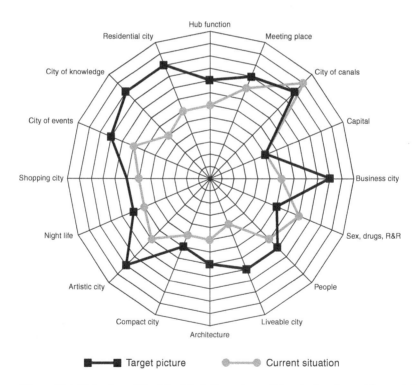

Figure 12.1 Valuation of the 16 critical dimensions of Amsterdam in a spider model.

This Spider model can be used for two purposes, namely as an instrument for comparative benchmarking studies of different cities' performance, and as an instrument for assessing the gap between the actual and the desired situation of a given city. In this way, the benefits of city marketing can be gauged. This possibility calls, of course, for appropriate information and data, and data management. This is discussed further in the next section.

Digital data and information needs and uses in the 'urban century'

Up-to-date information systems are a sine qua non for strategic urban policy. 'Modern cities are becoming strategic data and information systems driven by a multiplicity of interests of actors and stakeholders; they position themselves from different perspectives and are by no means uniform or identical' (Kourtit, 2014, 2015, p. 9). They employ increasingly complex data and information systems for their policy development. Urban policy is no longer blueprint planning, but adaptive, participatory, open-ended, accountable, multi-disciplinary, and cohesive/inclusive. The advent of ICT has prompted a new orientation in urban planning, marketing, and strategy development. Digital data and information have attained a legitimate place in the management and strategy design of modern cities, and smart governance by helping cities in the implementation process, not only as a result of the provision of up-to-date and detailed information provision on a wealth of urban issues, but also due to their capability for direct interaction with citizens (e-governance), businesses, etc.

The newest challenge cities are faced with is the crucial need and use of 'bigger data' driven by 'challenge and response' mechanisms (see Toynbee, 1946) towards the so-called *i*-city (a novel scientific endeavour which seeks to develop and/or advance strong and intelligent management tools for modern cities) supported and stimulated by smart '*i*-dashboards', 'which are adequate to integrate and coordinate complex data bases and information in the form of "signposts" for daily or strategic decisions and actions of urban stakeholders (both public and private), now and in the future'.[2]

> Not only to understand challenges and responses of urban systems, but also to help shape them on the basis of evidence-based research on the important strategic drivers that have an impact on the performance of urban governance systems
>
> (Kourtit, 2014, p. xxi)

and its future-oriented policies. Thus, modern digital bigger data and updated information systems are increasingly of strategic importance and become a key asset in our socio-economic society. They address a variety of distinct urban policy domains, such as population, migration, real estate, land use, infrastructure, mobility, public facilities, workplaces, housing, employment, rehabilitation areas, transport flows, and so forth.

Nowadays, an increasing volume of (time-based) data ('bigger data') is becoming available and can therefore provide various stakeholders with useful information for smart locational decision-making and spatial strategies. According to this research paper, bigger data are larger-sized data sets, often drawn from different sources, with multi-dimensional structures and levels of many characteristics and activities of a complex economic, social, and cultural nature. These data are produced by a multiplicity of actors and stakeholders for the purpose of realising new and sustainable urban development and advanced urban competitiveness and are analysed with powerful tools. However, new raw and bigger data and the large amount of information do not necessarily lead to much better and new insights on policy (strategic) choices. And nor do they lead to 'balanced policy strategies concerning the challenges and the drivers of urban development and action-oriented conditions, as well as the solutions for urban problems for a competitive performance of actors and cities' (see Kourtit, 2015, p. 56) to keep their strategy on track. A balanced urban policy calls for more than this.

All this requires novel scientific insights and policy strategies in order to make 'bigger data' highly valued, useful, and consistent, and which is understandable for its core business and markets by translating complex data into a simple and balanced set of actionable key performance indicators (KPIs) (Brewer & Speh, 2000) and delivering better targeted lists – 'in which different actors have to excel in order to be successful' (Kourtit, 2014, p. xxvi; Melkers & Willoughby, 2005; Waal, Kourtit, & Nijkamp, 2009) – in order to monitor and measure the socio-economic progress. There is an increasingly need for a systematic architecture with a mixed package of tools and methods in order to have a balanced focus on complex data (bigger data) and information as a characteristic of a high-performing system and an important source to improve sustainable competitive advantage and (global) competitive position and performance. 'All these tools – and their combinations – play an important role in identifying, measuring, explaining and comparing (input and output) performance indicators describing the cities' – and their actors' – socio-economic achievements' and value systems (see Kourtit, 2015, p. 22).

The ability to transform and manage bigger data into a high 'source of values' of integrated and high-quality information and knowledge and actionable insights – also called urban or city intelligence – on a city system's (economic and non-economic) performance measures in a comprehensive way, from quantitative data to high-quality information and knowledge, is of increasing strategic importance for the direction and intensity of necessary policy levers: for a city, 'evidence-based and data-driven strategic decision making' (Steenbruggen et al., 2015) is needed for it to become more efficient, smart, and liveable. 'The strategic data performance measures provide a complete view of how a city's system is progressing towards its vision and mission and related strategic goals' (Ho & McKay, 2002; Kourtit, 2015, p. 139), focusing on the highest possible urban quality of life (see Nijkamp, 2008).

The need to make sense of complex or 'bigger data' and information to establish an early warning high-quality information system (based on historical and new information) through the monitoring and measuring (exploring) of data strategic key indicators must be in place, in order to enhance strategic decision-making in various fields, to promote desired changes, and guarantee the accountability of various stakeholders, is leading to a rapid evolution of innovations in (space-time) advanced technologies (for data analysis, visualisation, and management), and the development of new approaches and tools and new skills in order to cope with the challenges of cities in 'post-urban world'.

The next section provides an illustration of what is referred to as the 'Urban Facebook for Urban Facelifts' strategy, supported by high-quality visual assessment tools employed to analyse the intense interactions between different stakeholders, for mapping novel redevelopment initiatives, in order to be able to draw important strategic conclusions and decisions, and so identify and understand specific local needs, values, priorities, and necessary spatial developments in the urban system. This has turned into a demanding and an increasingly important approach in this complex data transformation process, which is beyond the reach of traditional databases and their access and reporting, in order to achieve 'urban management and governance which not only reflects the growing complexity in today's unpredictable, open, diverse and dynamic urbanized world' (Kourtit, 2015, p. 138), but also monitors the urban system's strategic response to today's challenge of a complex operating environment which is a necessary contribution to achieving the city's shared corporate vision. The Facebook mechanism will now be explained in the next section.

Urban Facebooks for urban facelifts[3]

This section provides a brief explanation of the concept of 'Urban Facebook for Urban Facelifts' (details can be found in Kourtit & Nijkamp, 2013). The application of this evaluation framework was actually implemented in several case-study cities: Amsterdam, Naples, Palermo, and Torre Annunziata, which all have an interest in this approach regarding redevelopment strategies of (neglected or low performing) areas which aim to strengthen their socio-economic profile.

The conceptual framework 'Urban Facebook' is a proactive and interactive process which consists of six consecutive steps, not only to collect different kinds of data and information, to evaluate the actual socio-economic performance of cities, and to promote the unique characteristics of the city, but also to identify, understand, and explore problems, opportunities, common future-oriented values and expectations, and strategic goals and choices related to future images and what we call city 'facelifts' (see Kourtit & Nijkamp, 2013), with the involvement of complex interlinked and multiple layers of actors and structures in the city concerned. This approach is closely related to 'mental map' in GIS (see Brennan-Horley, Luckman, Gibson, & Willoughby-Smith, 2010). The systematic architecture of the evaluation framework is illustrated in Figure 12.2. Each step is taken in combination with interactive visualisation methods (e.g. 'geo-imaging tools' to illustrate the current strategic images of the location concerned) for smart and strategic urban planning that may offer a novel contribution and concepts to contemporary urban planning.

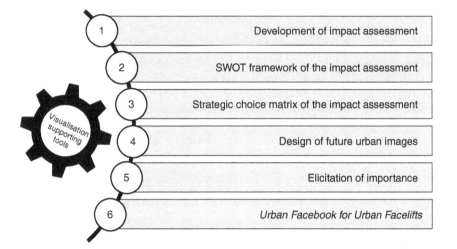

Figure 12.2 The structure of the Urban Facebook approach.

In a stepwise procedure, this evaluation framework helps to collect different data and information, to identify the most effective strategic options and choices, to create possibilities and new opportunities, and to develop successful policy strategies for sustainable development. Furthermore, this approach also brings different forms of expertise together in order to gain trust in (re)developing a positioning strategy with a high level of transparency, and to resolve conflicts between the interests (or values) of a 'multiplicity of stakeholders, with a vision to stimulating economic vitality', while 'meeting social needs and ensuring the conservation of eco-systems in redesigning areas', cities, etc. (see also Kourtit, 2015, p. 38).

Step 1: Development of impact assessment

The first step in this evaluation process starts with the impact assessment of the development of the city's socio-economic positioning, characteristics, and performance in the current situation. A prior broad literature search for possible and tested smart measurement indicators creates a solid basis for a useful impact assessment for the areas concerned. Important in all stages (Step 1–6) is the high involvement and the preference and value system of the different stakeholders at the beginning of (re)designing towards the implementation of the final city positioning strategy (multi-layered bottom-up approach). This process is extensively supported by 'geo-imaging tools', for the high-quality visual assessment of the city, areas, etc. related to the various levels of the revitalisation procedure used in combination with multiple techniques. This procedure relies on common resources and sources provided by the involved stakeholders (e.g. in the form of think tanks, workshops, interviews, surveys, etc.) to improve the attractiveness and vitality of the city, area, etc. These aspects constitute the city's 'urban faces' which are based on photographic material to be judged by the stakeholders (for details, see Kourtit & Nijkamp, 2013; Kourtit et al., 2013). Thus, 'urban faces' are pedagogical interactive material – in a visualised form – that support creativeness and imagination on specific parts or dimensions of the city's future.

Step 2: SWOT framework of the impact assessment

The findings in Step 1 provide a long list of important impacts of the concerned city, area, etc. as input, which adds data and information (derived from various sources) for Step 2. This step contributes to the strategic planning process, and helps to identify and understand the challenges, and develop a systematic overview of most important strengths (S), weaknesses (W), opportunities (O), and threats (T) for the city, area, etc., and their effectiveness. Thereby, past, current, and future effects are assessed from a long-term and broad perspective in order to improve the sustainability of the environment, again extensively supported by the involvement of various stakeholders and the high-quality virtual 'urban faces' of the city areas concerned.

Step 3: Strategic choice analysis of the impact assessment

This stage goes beyond the SWOT analysis by developing strategic planning solutions from the external-internal analysis in Step 2. Based on the integrated and synthesised types of data and information in the SWOT analysis, which also includes the value and preference system of different stakeholders, related to the strategic core domains of cities or areas, a strategic choice analysis (SCA) is employed. A correlation is made between the prioritised most important internal factors (S) and (W) to be used to participate in, or take advantage of, external factors (Strength-Opportunity strategies) and to counter or avoid the prioritised external factors (Strength-Threat-Weakness strategies), with regard to the various levels of revitalisation (from high to low), through the development of effective strategy response choice policies for sustainable development. As mentioned in Step 2, the entire process is extensively supported by the high-quality virtual 'urban faces' of the city areas concerned.

Step 4: Design of future urban images[4]

In this stage, the robustness of the formulated common strategic response choice(s) and development plans, and the evaluated socio-economic position of the 'urban faces' of the concerned city, area, etc., in Steps 1–3, are explored and tested by the impact of various uncertainties and aspects happening simultaneously in the form of future city images (for various recent illustrative applications; see Stevens, 2015). These images are not something happening out of the blue, but are related strategic and thematic urban images of stylised appearances of urban agglomerations in the year 2050, which are based on and connected to the steps followed above using various data and information from the involved stakeholders. Each image is characterised by elements of the '*urban faces*' (Kourtit & Nijkamp, 2013, p. 4396), and tells a story of how various and specific local needs and necessary spatial developments might interact under (un)certain future conditions and interventions, by taking into account the current situation 'in terms of the performance across the different viable future image areas' (Kourtit, 2015, p. 214). The concept of '*urban images*' has shown to be an effective vehicle for mapping out uncertain urban futures (Kourtit, 2015). The 'urban images' may be used as strategic vehicles to determine relevant challenges and foundations for the innovative development of the city, district, area, etc., from different future perspectives, each of which ultimately leads to a new '*urban facelift*' (by backcasting and forecasting approaches) (Kourtit, 2015). Thus, '*urban images*' are long-range and strategically determined scenarios or city mappings that form the possible future contours of the city concerned.

Step 5: Elicitation of importance of stakeholders' views

In the fifth step, the various data and information are derived from the various sources provided by those stakeholders, who are involved in the decision-making process regarding city or urban land-use options. They are asked in different settings (workshops, interviews, surveys, social media (e.g. Facebook, Foursquare, etc.)) to judge pairs of important criteria and conditions (identified and evaluated in Steps 1–4) of each 'urban face' performance (including being given appropriate weights and scores) from different future perspectives that might interact under (un)certain future conditions and interventions, when taking into account the current situation.

Step 6: Urban Facebook for urban facelifts

In this evaluation stage, a practical assessment framework for strategic city or urban policy choice(s) is used which consists of applications of a multi-stakeholder view and a multi-criteria evaluation method, such as a PRO-METHEE method (Brans, 1982; Brans & Mareschal, 1994; Macharis, Brans, & Mareschal, 1998) or an applied regime analysis. The 'Urban Facebook for Urban Facelifts' approach makes use of a mix of various data and information combined in an organised structure and framework in an impact matrix and issues a set of judgement scores to explore the identified and tested conditions cascaded in the composition of each 'urban face'. This approach enables us to determine both which future alternative would have the highest support from most of the interest groups involved, and what level of revitalisation procedure will play a key role in most stakeholders' choice of future image. Such a strategic city policy choice(s) implementation plan would create new possibilities and provide new opportunities to gain and enhance the competitive advantage and strategies for a new 'facelift' in the context of improving and stimulating growth and sustainable development goals. In this final stage of an assessment course conclusions are made, and policy recommendations are drawn.

> This approach improves and increases the ability to recognize the importance of understanding the characteristics of an area and the preferences for socio-economic and environmental values, including the involvement of all stakeholders' interests in a way that brings and keeps them together, and thus offers a broader perspective regarding the district's sustainable development. It is noteworthy that the local authority has to realize that it needs the support of important stakeholders (private companies and, for instance, representatives of civic organizations)
>
> (Kourtit & Nijkamp, 2013, p. 4389)

in the planning process of sustainable development under uncertainty, to make the revitalisation and the implementation of urban facelifts successful.

The successive steps described above in the evaluation framework have been systematically applied, in the following section, for the assessment of a range of cities, notably Amsterdam, Napoli, Palermo, and Torre Annunziata, including the conversion and transforming of various data and information, originating from different places and actors, into meaningful information quality and delivery with added value. By doing this, the cities may act as good showcases for other cities that want to evaluate their city strategy and to (re)develop effective policy strategies, including building around it a high-quality information warning system, to work with 'intelligence' and to learn competencies in pursuit of more sustainable development. We now provide an outline of the comparative systematics of the Facebook approach in our study, based on a systematically designed common template.

Illustrations of Urban Facebook mechanism for rehabilitation plans

This section reflects on a diversity of experiences using the 'Urban Facebook' framework, messages, methods, observations, and empirical findings of a range of city case studies in Europe. The added value of these case studies is the accurate evaluation of city achievements, not only from an economic context but also from a multi-dimensional, partly non-economic, valuation perspective, in order to identify and to suggest strategic policy directions and the related actions for cities to have a competitive edge in the global spatial network economy (see also Kourtit, 2015, p. 12).

Table 12.1 provides a broad overview of the use of various Facebook mechanisms in several European cities. These cases are quite diverse in terms of population size, economic prosperity, and political culture. Nevertheless, despite this heterogeneity the conceptual framework of a Facebook approach to strategic urban planning is interesting, and offers promising results. Next, it is noteworthy that there is not a single Facebook approach. Each of the case studies is centred

Table 12.1 An overview of 'Facebook' applications in various European cities

Summary **Amsterdam** case-study[5]	
Aims and scope	• To further develop the multi-layered stakeholder-based framework by introducing and elaborating what we call the 'urban Facebook for urban facelifts', an approach that is extensively supported by high-quality visual assessment tools for mapping novel redevelopment initiatives, in order to be able to identify and understand specific local needs and necessary spatial developments. It offers a basis for interventions that tackle present and future urban problems, foundations, challenges, and consequences (in combination with urban scenarios, which are essentially strategic future image experiments based on, for example, the imagining of future port cities' positions) designed to achieve the desired goals related to urban strategic visions, while, in addition, this approach may encourage the urban economy to stay (internationally) competitive.
Description of problem case	• The empirical study is carried out in and around the NDSM-area, a former dockyard in Amsterdam, the Netherlands.
	• This study was undertaken in the context of transitional urban port systems for sustainable urban development, from a forward-looking long-term strategic policy perspective (a combination of backcasting and forecasting approaches), which meets the needs, and addresses the concerns, of its various users, where vision and strategy have to fit well with their environment.
	• The future form of the NDSM-Safari is already taking shape. However, it lacks both long-term strategies (e.g. a solid and integrated breeding place policy) to meet the important needs and preferences of the various stakeholders and guarantees by the local authority to create a sustainable home for various professionals, businesses, and artists. And it should not remain only as a temporary 'project', but become a new part of a future productive urban landscape instead of an isolated breeding place.
Appropriate methods	• Using an analytical framework that links the opportunities provided by traditional port areas/cities to achieve creative, resilient, and sustainable urban development.
	• Using evidence-based research, findings are presented from a case study by employing a stakeholder-based model – with interactive visual support tools as novel analysis methods – in a backcasting and forecasting exercise for sustainable development.
	• Various future images were used – in an interactive assessment incorporating classes of important stakeholders – as strategic vehicles to identify important policy challenges, and to evaluate options for converting historical-cultural urban port landscapes into sustainable and creative hotspots, starting by reusing, recovering, and regenerating such areas.
	• A bottom-up approach is, inter alia, based on information collected, during interviews, from different stakeholders with a wide range of interests in relation to the area, followed by the use of a strength-weakness opportunities-threats (SWOT) analysis methodology with visual support tools. All this is done in order to develop a collective and quantitative evaluation of the socio-economic performance of the NDSM, which focuses on its physical use, characteristics, and historical landscape attributes.
	• Viable strategic options have to be interpreted and discussed in an integrated multi-layered framework in order to provide a sound basis for the possible preparation of conditions for the further redevelopment of the NDSM location as a district for the production of urban culture. There, place-based characteristics and opportunities, and historical landscape attributes may draw (more) creative minds and innovative business models to certain sites, where they can share and combine their (international) knowledge and expertise with challenging socio-economic opportunities. This requires an understanding of more than just the commercial side of this district or the decrease of the 20 sub-clusters located there, in order to realise their common interests in the NDSM vision and come to a general strategic core policy.
Results	• This study has provided, on the basis of structured interviews, an overview of experience and findings that address the socio-economic impacts of the NDSM district in a broader context.
	• The results indicate that the interactive policy support tools developed for the case study are fit for purpose, and are instrumental in designing sustainable urban port areas.
General lessons and policy relevance	• This approach helps to identify successful policy strategies, and to bring together different forms of expertise in order to resolve conflicts between the interests (or values) of a multiplicity of stakeholders, with a view to stimulating economic vitality in combination with meeting social needs and ensuring the conservation of eco-systems in redesigning old port areas.
	• Novel ways of thinking are increasingly required and linked to new, efficient, and effective urban planning, governance, and management processes in order to finally ensure broad stakeholder acceptance.
Summary **Napoli** case-study[6]	
Aims and scope	• To build a long-term common goals and shared strategic vision for the sustainable urban development of Naples, from a forward-looking long-term strategic policy perspective.
	• To understand better the driving forces and processes of urban redevelopment and city development initiatives through a bottom-up approach by exploring the preference and value system of various stakeholders (e.g. social groups), as inputs for the urban policy decision-making process.
	• To explore the quality of the urban landscape in Naples with the support and use of visual supporting tools.

Description problem case	• The need to recover (redevelopment) the relationship (physical reconnection) between the port area and the historic centre of the city, through an integrated and shared strategy, through bottom-up processes to create the conditions to improve the livability of the area (for e.g. restoring buildings of historical and cultural interest, stimulating activity related to culture and entertainment, redeveloping the urban voids, creating activities related to trade and crafts, improving information systems, roads, and the public transport system for residents) and to increase job opportunities arising from the tourism revival and the subsequent resumption of the commercial and high-quality artisan activities that characterise it. • A specific part of the central area of the waterfront in Naples faces different problems and positive values which illustrate the weak relationship between the waterfront and the historic centre. • A lack of solid strategic policies for governance and innovative development plans and initiatives (e.g. social services and facilities) for reconnecting the historic centre and the port area. • Lack of managerial knowledge and skills and experiences to deal with challenges emerging from various social, economic, and environmental issues and the continuity of local community and stakeholders involvement in the area in the planning process.
Appropriate methods	• The methodological framework is a process which combines several techniques and tools to the case study research from a cultural and socio-economic perspective, with the strong involvement of different stakeholders (using multi-actor multi-criteria analysis and visual support tools) in the decision-making process in order to explore and systematise positive and negative aspects and action priorities of the present relationship and unique characteristics and strategic positioning future alternatives of the areas (pairwise comparisons) in order to reconnect the historic centre and the waterfront of Naples (based on a shared vision) for sustainable development. • Semi-structured interviews have been used in the field to collect data on the areas and prioritise values and the preferences system and beliefs of different actors regarding their expectations and experiences in and surrounding the area and its policies in order to highlight priority issues, based on cooperation and agreement, to be integrated in the city development.
Results	• The multi-criteria analysis was able to identify a list of priority actions, problems, and conflicts among the homogeneous areas within the study district, supported by visual tools, and their unique elements (better visual quality) that are of real help in the processes to develop or reformulate policy for sustainable development. • The systematisation of data through appropriate indicators is useful for recognising the interrelationship between the various aspects of sustainability and the consequent need for a multi-dimensional approach in defining the choices for sustainable urban development. • This assessment was able to explain the main factors that can affect, in a significant way, the development of sustainable future strategic choices and alternatives in order to enhance the perception and value system of actors (e.g. monuments, architecture, urban landscape) and the need for priority intervention for the improvement of the visual perception of the district (safety, environment, public transport).
General lessons and policy relevance	• The analysis of social preferences highlights the unsolved socio-economic gaps in the municipal planning for the city of Naples to reconstruct the historic relationship by e.g. improving the accessibility between the coastline and the town, based on a shared vision and values, through the active participation of all the forces of its community. • An urban redevelopment plan for Naples has to implement new and innovative community engagement tools to identify the key values of the city's different stakeholders, set common goals, and develop shared visions of the future. • The guiding principle of the existing plan lacks an integration of various planning tools and suffers from an extremely conservative attitude that tends to isolate the historic city and ignore any possible transformative intervention based on a mix of territorial capital (e.g. economic, ecological, cultural, social and human capital). • The methodological approach proved to be a powerful tool in assessing the preference and value system of stakeholders and increasing their awareness of the various implications of actions involved in a city transformation (e.g. spatial or urban qualities, economic activity), as a starting point to assess and implement urban development policies from a long-term strategic perspective.

Summary **Palermo** case-study[7]

Aims and scope	• To map out the specific characteristics of Palermo and opportunities in order to highlight effective transformation and action strategies for the areas concerned, supported by (digital) social networks such as Facebook and face to face relationships. • To achieve a coherent and appropriate picture of the future positioning strategy of Palermo by means of an effective and efficient transformation, based on a better appreciation of the multicultural character of the city, that leads to a minimisation of conflicts between the various stakeholders. in order to make Palermo a reference point for the development of dialogue in the Mediterranean.

continued

Description problem case	• The port of Palermo represents an important source of income and city growth, but after the industrial revolution, its polarity from the ancient city system has disappeared progressively, reducing the integrated structure of the port city, hence the need to provide interventions that generate scenarios of continuous interchange with the city. • The environment is increasingly becoming an expression of a modified nature, conditioned by human activity so that the existing historical and cultural heritage require more identification, especially through promotional activities such as integrated conservation. • The need to save resources and also identify of new targets of environmental sensitivity for technologies and architectures, which are careful about the health of users and about the existing resource saving. • The start of public programmes for the conservation of urban areas, and in particular those areas of historical and architectural interest, relates to the need to assess *ex ante* operational models of land use so that, on the basis of shared choices, they can attract new long-term investments.
Appropriate methods	• The case study of Palermo is based on a multi-disciplinary and integrated approach, using the 'Urban Facebook' concept (see Kourtit & Nijkamp, 2013), reflecting the principles of a multi-criteria evaluation strategy on the possible effects of strategic planning with a strong involvement of different social groups. • To collect data this research conducted field research which involves a combination of participant observations and semi-structured interviews (traditional channels) and using an experimental channel supported by visual tools, through a powerful social media tool for public participation such as Facebook that allows the expansion of the network of contacts, the construction of a map of geo-referenced images of the city and the achievement of a better understanding of and interaction with stakeholders to share their idea and preferences (residents, worker, firms, tourists, migrants, policymakers) and the collection of updated information (clarifying the characteristics and needs of the renewal process, functions, and the socio-economic activities, analysing the role of the stakeholders) on the potential of the *places of dialogue* or *architectures of dialogue* concerned. • The use of the 'Urban Facebook' concept with Checkland's CATWOE tool to improve the identification of important intangible conditions and criteria and future opportunities and alternatives in the urban transformation process (called '*Urban Facelift*' management) with the involvement of various stakeholders in terms of active participation and access to the decision-making process (bottom-up strategy reclassification of an urban area, considering the degree of desirability of the alternatives in relation to a parametric scale) of urban renewal strategies for Palermo.
Results	• The risk of homogenising and destabilising the process and procedures of architectural solutions and prosperity has been induced with the high interaction and strong involvement of different stakeholders. The working together approach is the tool to preserve the identity through an integration process. • The methodology makes it possible to bring out in particular the 'unknown' intrinsic historical values of the city in the urban transformation process with the strong involvemnt of different stakeholders and shared values and criteria for the transformation, together with a better understanding of the redevelopment strategy of the city and tthe construction of a map from which shared future images of *Palermo Pioneer City* emerges. • The use of social media such as Facebook has facilitated to strengthen the participation of different stakeholders and to improve the interaction among them, supported by visual tools, in order to test criteria and alternatives for future strategies in the city transformation process.
General lessons and policy relevance	• The methodology has helped to increase the involvement of stakeholders in the decision-making process to define shared future strategies, actions, and alternatives (e.g. clarifying the characteristics and needs) of the city as a 'pioneer' city (learning process). Thus, stakeholders in the planning and level of transformation (including, for example, values, preferences, conditions, criteria) process (urban management process) played a central role (bottom-up approach). • Using social networks and media (interactive approach) to reach different stakeholders has helped to increase the access to 'unknown' knowledge, information, and the value system of actors (with different backgrounds and cultures) in the city. • Learning process in the construction of an interactive methodology based on transparency and multi-level knowledge is used to identify different values, preferences and needs, evaluate and solve conflicts, trust and miscommunications, and used as an input to formulate shared beliefs and ambitions for the city's sustainable development, socio-economic growth, and attractiveness. • The transformation process in this case study refers to the assessment of the areas concerned. However, the following steps in the transformation process can also be extended in the entire decision-making process of any urban site with, for instance, strong historical and cultural connotations and different values and outcomes.

Summary **Torre Annunziata** case-study[8]

Aims and scope	• To assess the opportunities and strategic actions in the repositioning process for the urban waterfront in order to enhance the regeneration, growth, development, and promotion of transformation areas in the port city.
	• To develop an assessment tool to explore socio-economic impacts generated by a diversity in the 'spatial quality' of areas in the context of attractiveness of port cities.
	• To assess whether and how visual features and choices by various stakeholders play an important role regarding the attractiveness and image in and around the waterfront districts.
	• To process a participative and transparent tool for the development of a shared long-term strategy and to manage conflicts due to the different needs and priorities of public and private sectors to formulate the most effective regeneration strategies for the sustainable development of the urban coastline and enhance the attractiveness of waterfront areas.
	• To develop a bridge between the physical and visual quality of the areas concerned and their socio-economic attractiveness.
Description of problem case	• The unique attractiveness of the charming landscape and historical amenities in the industrial port area and waterfront in the city of Torre Annunziata is neglected and outperformed by the commercialisation and pro-active role of located shipyards.
	• The underdevelopment of the waterfront district due to, for example, criminality, population reduction, high youth unemployment, corruption in the system, lack of urban planning, physical barriers (i.e. railways and roads) between the city and the sea that create a negative image of the waterfront district.
	• The decreasing industrial activities now led to a decrease of port activities and attractiveness (losing the city's identity) for various stakeholders.
	• A lack of social, cultural, leisure, and accommodation and sports facilities in the tourism system and policy to attract and retain the tourist flows and improve the residents' quality of life.
	• The youth unemployment level is very high although various productive activities are present in the city.
Appropriate methods	• The research method is based on a participative process able to build a shared long-term strategy for the enhancement of the visual quality of the areas concerned in and around the port district, based on the evaluation of the identified urban quality of the Torre Annunziata waterfront.
	• In-depth interviews have been used extensively for data collection from various stakeholders in order to assess and to understand better the general values, perceptions, and image (intangible values) of the area in terms of its economic and cultural attractiveness and competitiveness (using a logit model for the evaluation and analysis of statistic data).
	• A mix of tools and approaches (e.g. SWOT Analysis, interviews, survey (on a Likert scale), scenarios/future images, strategic choice matrix, multi-actor analysis) were used in the research analysis, with the involvement of different actors, to encourage the optimal collaboration between different actors in order to explore optimal and (long-term) strategic choices, priorities, aspects, and actions regarding the quality of, for example, architecture and urban design, culture, energy and environment, economy, transports, facilities, and services, that influence the attractiveness and competitiveness of the waterfront districts' socio-economic development in Torre Annunziata.
Results	• The results provide an alternative tool to evaluate different 'scenarios' for cities' future development that can support decision-makers, businessmen, citizens, and various stakeholders taking the most effective decisions towards the sustainable development of port cities. The attractiveness of the waterfront of Torre Annunziata is closely connected to the economic performance and environmental features of the district.
	• The high amount of collected data made it possible to create a large database of the stakeholders' value system and different perceptions (e.g. of criminality, cultural heritage, vital economic environment, social cohesion, land and water conservation, energy efficiency) regarding the potential attractiveness of the waterfront district, and to identify the gaps between its current situation (e.g. poor environmental quality) and future-oriented positioning (e.g. achieving a high quality of life in a 'liveable city') of the district concerned.
	• Sustainable development would be possible through the redesign and new functionalisation of the waterfront and port area, improving resilience and creativity and improving entrepreneurial activities in order to integrate economic growth, ecological preservation, and social opportunities.
	• Community participation and involvement in the development (of economic, social, cultural, and environmental) processes can reduce the investment risk in regeneration areas.

continued

General	• The proposed method is a tool to support policymakers, with the involvement of different
lessons and	stakeholders, to assess and develop effective strategic policies, and to prioritise strategic actions
policy	and public investments leading to a sustainable development and effective waterfront
relevance	regeneration projects (based on achieved common goals).
	• The actual policies and the related strategic choices influence the future-orientation of the city
	and need clear and transparent tools to manage the conflicts and build trust between public and
	private interests.
	• The changes in the economic attractiveness of the waterfront depend largely on the physical and
	visual quality of the districts. Common goals and actions to improve the conditions of the port
	and seaside areas may result in the enhancement of urban design of public spaces.
	• The multi-criteria evaluation tool is essential to find optimal strategic solutions to improve the
	socio-economic attractiveness of the waterfront district, with a high involvement of, for
	example, professionals, residents, administrators, firms, associations retailers, and policymakers
	in the strategic planning process.

on a similar conceptual framework, but its specific application of tools differs greatly. Consequently, the Facebook planning tool is not a straight jacket, but an amalgam of various techniques oriented towards an advanced interactive decision-making process among different stakeholders for 'understanding the emerging complexity of urban systems, using modern accessible databases at the interface of physical and virtual flows and stocks',[9] while respecting the specificities of a local planning culture.

Retrospect and prospect

Cities are agents in transition. Their evolution needs to be carefully monitored and governed in order to ensure a high degree of sustainability and resilience. Responsive governance and adaptation are needed to help cities overcome downturns and to remain on course for a balanced future. The Facebook mechanism – a multi-actor tool for addressing a multiplicity of driving forces and consequences – provides an operational tool to keep a city on course.

Our four illustrations – based on an evidence-based, concise, and systematic assessment – have brought to light various important lessons:

• Systematic information systems design and data collection is of great importance.
• Information sharing with all stakeholders involved is essential for avoiding biases in evaluation exercises.
• Sophisticated tools for decision support are needed in order to offer the city concerned sufficient scope to reach the smart city's goals.
• Interactive design experiments (e.g. Imagineering methods) may become critical approaches in consensus building.

Strategic analytical vehicles, through a multi-layered bottom-up approach, avoid the danger of transforming the city's cultural footprint into a historical 'Las Vegas' or a happy 'Disneyland' setting (i.e. cultural heritage and historic assets are in danger of commercialisation or of being sacrificed to commercial needs in the form of souvenir shops, non-authentic replicas, etc.) or destroying the city's historical footprint. What is needed is a fair balance of old and new elements to create the most intelligent strategic (re)development plans for cities, and to preserve selectively the city's important old treasures, architecture, and history for the next generations with a view to understand and experience the past which is linked to the future.

A coherent approach to the great diversity of messages, needs, and values of various classes of stakeholders related to urban socio-economic forces is strategically important for effective policy actions on sustainable urban futures.

The basis for the toolbox for managing complex urban cyberplaces is formed by interactive communication and planning tools, which have recently been developed in the spatial sciences. In this context, the development of the strategic planning tool 'Urban Facebooks' is based on: (i) the assessment of visual images of a given urban area; (ii) interactive communication on systematically designed urban images (e.g. through social media such as 'Facebook'); (iii) the design of attractive spatial alternatives through multicriteria and strategic choice methods.

The cornerstone and operational feature of the 'Facebook' tool (linking the present performance of urban areas to various future perspectives and urban future images for cities at different transition levels) may act as an operational navigation instrument for urban stakeholders and policymakers. It should be added that geo-science methods are not developed in a wonderland of no urban dimensions. A thorough knowledge of the urban living climate, the creative classes, and entrepreneurial development is also needed, as well as a deep familiarity with institutional and decision-making processes in the city. This approach is also helpful in the context of new challenges, such as crowd management, public security, or traffic management.[10]

Our study concludes that becoming a smarter sustainable city involves more than deploying new technological approaches, tools, and solutions. It means connecting, involving, and managing stakeholders and a better alignment of planned and more informed policies, projects, programmes, facilities, and services across a wide range of communities, fields, and areas, oriented towards a common vision. Our study has made an attempt to highlight that sustainability of cities – or urban agglomerations – in the 'New Urban World' calls for smart, proactive, and stakeholder-based planning approaches based on intelligent data management in order to pave the road towards a 'waking city' (see Ginkel & Verhaaren, 2015) stimulating engagement of the different actors involved in the city system, with the support of intelligent governance instead of a total control from above.

Notes

1 See website: www.simonanholt.com/Research/research-city-brand-index.aspx.
2 Source: This idea was inspired by the Regional Science Academy (2016), in its 1st Advanced Brainstorm Carrefour (ABC) meeting on 'It's a Small World' – Big Data and Beyond', in Stockholm, Sweden. www.regionalscienceacademy.org/site/events/advanced-brainstorming-carrefour-workshop-its-a-small-world-big-data-and-beyond/.
3 Here, we do not provide a detailed description of the concept and the various steps involved, but the details can be found in Kourtit and Nijkamp (2013).

4 For the details and description of the urban images, see also: Kourtit and Nijkamp (2013) and Nijkamp and Kourtit (2013).

5 The information in this section of the table stems from Kourtit and Nijkamp (2013) (see, e.g., pp. 4381, 4382, 4384, 4379).

6 The information in this section of the table stems from Attardi, De Rosa, and Di Palma (2015) (see, e.g., pp. 256, 268, 269) and De Rosa and Di Palma (2013) (see, e.g., pp. 4278, 4281).

7 The information in this section of the table stems from Nicolini and Pinto (2013) (see, e.g., pp. 3942, 3943, 3956, 3955) and Borriello, Carone, Nicolini, and Panaro (2015) (see, e.g., pp. 100).

8 The information in this section of the table stems from Gravagnuolo and Angrisano (2013) (see, e.g., pp. 3906, 3908, 3912) and Gravagnuolo, Franco Biancamano, Angrisano, and Cancelliere (2015) (see, e.g., pp. 56, 59, 63, 64, 83).

9 Source: This idea was inspired by the Regional Science Academy (2016), during its 1st Advanced Brainstorm Carrefour (ABC) meeting on *'It's a Small World' – Big Data and Beyond"*, in Stockholm, Sweden.

10 Source: This was inspired by the Regional Science Academy (2016), the 1st Advanced Brainstorm Carrefour (ABC) meeting on 'It's a Small World – Big Data and Beyond' in Stockholm, Sweden.

References

Anholt, S. (2006). The Anholt-GMI City Brands Index: How the world sees the world's cities. *Place Branding and Public Diplomacy, 2*(1), 18–31.

Ashworth, G. J., & Tunbridge, J. E. (1990). *The tourist-historic city*. London: Belhaven Press.

Attardi, R., De Rosa, F., & Di Palma, M. (2015). From visual features to shared future visions for Naples 2050. *Applied Spatial Analysis and Policy, 8*(3), 249–271.

Borriello, F., Carone, P., Nicolini, E., & Panaro, S. (2015). Design and use of a Facebook 4 Urban Facelifts. *International Journal of Global Environmental Issues, 14*(1/2), 89–112.

Brans, J. P. (1982). L'ingénièrie de la décision; Elaboration d'instruments d'aide à la décision. La méthode PROMETHEE. In R. Nadeau & M. Landry (Eds.), *L'aide à la décision: Nature, instruments et perspectives d'avenir* (pp. 183–213). Québec, Canada: Presses de l'Université Laval.

Brans, J. P., & Mareschal, B. (1994). The PROMETHEE-GAIA decision support system for multicriteria investigations. *Investigation Operativa, 4*(2), 107–117.

Braun, E. (2008). *City marketing: Towards an integrated approach.* Dissertation. Erasmus University, Rotterdam. ISBN 978-90-5892-180-2.

Braun, E. (2012). Putting branding into practice. *Journal of Brand Management, 19*(4), 257–267.

Braun, E., Kavaratzis, M., & Zenker, S. (2013). My city – my brand: The role of residents in place branding. *Journal of Place Management and Development, 6*(1), 18–28.

Brennan-Horley, C., Luckman, S., Gibson, C., & and Willoughby-Smith, J. (2010). GIS, ethnography, and cultural research: Putting maps back into ethnographic mapping. *The Information Society, 26*(2), 92–103.

Brewer, P., & Speh, T. (2000). Using the balanced scorecard to measure supply chain performance. *Journal of Business Logistics, 21*, 75–93.

Cheshire, P., & Gordon, I. (2006). Resurgent cities? Evidence-based urban policy? More questions than answers. *Urban Studies, 43*(8), 1231–1438.

City of Amsterdam. (2004). *The making of ... The city marketing of Amsterdam.* Amsterdam: Joh. Enschede.

De Rosa, F., & Di Palma, M. (2013). Historic urban landscape approach and port cities regeneration: Naples between identity and outlook. *Sustainability, 5*(10), 4268–4287.

Eshuis, J., & Edwards, A. (2013). Branding the city: The democratic legitimacy of a new mode of governance. *Urban Studies, 49*(1), 153–168.

Ginkel, J. C. van, & Verhaaren, F. (2015). *Werken aan de wakkere stad – langzaam leiderschap naar gemeenschapskracht.* Deventer: Vakmedianet.

Gravagnuolo, A., & Angrisano, M. (2013). Assessment of urban attractiveness of port cities in Southern Italy: A case study of Torre Annunziata. *Sustainability, 5*(9), 3906–3925.

Gravagnuolo, A., Franco Biancamano, P., Angrisano, M., & Cancelliere, A. (2015). Assessment of waterfront attractiveness in port cities: Facebook 4 Urban Facelifts. *International Journal of Global Environmental Issues, 14*(1/2), 56–88.

Ham, van P. (2008). Place branding: The state of the art. *The Annals of the American Academy of Political and Social Science, 616*, 126–159.

Ho, K. S., & McKay, R. B. (2002). Innovative performance measurement; balance scorecard-tow perspectives. *The CPA Journal, 72*(3), 20–25.

Hospers, G. (2004). Place marketing in Europe: The branding of the Oresund Region. *Intereconomics, 39*(5), 271–279.

Insight. (2014). EU consortium on Innovative Policy Modelling and Governance Tools for Sustainable Post-Crisis Urban Development, Part D2.2 (Urban Planning and Governance: Current Practices and New Challenges), Madrid.

Ishikawa, N., Kourtit, K., & Nijkamp, P. (2015). Urbanization and quality of life: An overview of the health impacts of urban and rural residential patterns. In K. Kourtit, P. Nijkamp, & R. Stough (Eds.), *The rise of the city: Spatial dynamics in the urban century* (pp. 259–317). Cheltenham, UK: Edward Elgar.

Kavaratzis, M., & Ashworth, G. J. (2008). Place marketing: How did we get here and where are we going? *Journal of Place Management and Development, 1*(2), 150–165.

Koglin, T. (2009). Sustainable development in general and urban context: A literature review. *Bulletin* 248, Lund University, Lund Institute of Technology.

Kotler, P., & Gertner, D. (2002). Country as brand, product, and beyond: A place marketing and brand management perspective. *Journal of Brand Management, 9*(4), 249–261.

Kourtit, K. (2014). *Competitiveness in urban systems: Studies on the urban century.* PhD Dissertation. Amsterdam, Netherlands.

Kourtit, K. (2015). *The New Urban World, economic-geographical studies on the performance of urban systems.* PhD Dissertation. Poznan, Poland.

Kourtit, K., & Nijkamp, P. (2013). The use of visual decision support tools in an interactive stakeholder analysis: Old ports as new magnets for creative urban development. *Sustainability, 5*, 4379–4405.

Kourtit, K., Nijkamp. P., & Suzuki, S. (2013). Exceptional places: The rat race between world cities. *Computers, Environment and Urban Systems, 38*, 67–77.

Limburg, B. (1998). City marketing: A multi-attribute approach. *Tourism Management, 19*(5), 415–417.

Macharis, C., Brans, J. P., & Mareschal, B. (1998). The GDSS PROMETHEE procedure: A PROMETHEE-GAIA based procedure for group decision support. *Journal of Decision Systems, 7*, 283–307.

Melkers, J., & Willoughby, K. (2005). Models of performance-measurement use in local governments: Understanding budgeting, communication, and lasting effects. *Public Administration Review, 65*(2), 180–190.

Moilanen, T., & Rainisto, K. (2008). How to brand cities. In T. Moilanen & K. Rainisto (Eds.), *Nations and destinations: A planning book for place branding*. Basingstoke, UK: Palgrave Macmillan.

Moilanen, T., & Rainisto, S. (2009). *A planning book for place branding*. Hampshire, UK: Palgrave Macmillan.

Morgan, N., Pritchard, A., & Pride, R. (2012). *Destination brands*. London: Taylor & Francis.

Nicolini, E., & Pinto, M. R. (2013). Strategic vision of a Euro-Mediterranean port city: A case study of Palermo. *Sustainability, 5*, 3941–3959.

Nijkamp, P. (2008). XXQ factors for sustainable urban development: A systems economics view. *Romanian Journal of Regional Science, 2*(1), 1–34.

Nijkamp, P., & Kourtit, K. (2013). The 'New Urban Europe': Global challenges and local responses in the urban century. *European Planning Studies, 21*(3), 1–25.

Nijkamp, P., Kourtit, K., & Westlund, H. (2016). The urban economy. In A. M. Orum (Ed.), *Encyclopedia of urban and regional studies*. New York: Wiley-Blackwell (forthcoming).

Paddinson, R. (1993). City marketing, city reconstruction and urban regeneration. *Urban Studies, 30*(2), 339–350.

Preston, J., & Rajé, F. (2007). Accessibility, mobility and transport-related social exclusion. *Journal of Transport Geography, 15*, 151–160.

Riza, M., Doratli, N., & Fasli, M. (2012). City branding and identity. *Procedia – Social and Behavioral Sciences, 35*, 293–300.

Smyth, H. (1994). *Marketing the city: The role of flagship developments in urban regeneration*. London: Taylor & Francis.

Steenbruggen, J., Beinat, E., Smits, J., van der Kroon, F., Opmeer, M., & van der Zee, E. (2015). *Strategische verkenning 'big' data*. The Hague: Rijkswaterstaat.

Stevens, Q. (Ed.). (2015). *Creative milieux*. London: Routledge.

Toynbee, A. J. (1946). *A study of history abridgement*. London: Oxford University Press.

Waal, A.A. de, Kourtit, K., & Nijkamp, P. (2009). The relationship between the level of completeness of a strategic performance management system and perceived advantages and disadvantages. *International Journal of Operations & Production Management, 29*(12), 1242–1265.

Waard, M. de. (2012). *Imagining global Amsterdam: History, culture and geography in a world city*. Amsterdam: Amsterdam University Press.

Ward, V. (1998). *Selling places: The marketing and promotion of towns and cities 1850–2000*. London/New York: E & FN Spon/Routledge.

Westlund, H. (2014). Urban futures in planning, policy and regional science: Are we entering a post-urban world? *Built Environment, 40*(4), 447–457.

13 Accentuate the regional[1]

Edward Soja

Introduction

Never before have regional approaches been more important in urban research, and urban emphases more influential in regional development theory and planning. This increasing fusion of the urban and the regional in theory, empirical analysis, social activism, planning, and public policy is creating many new pathways for innovative critical and comparative research, some of which I will identify and discuss in this chapter. I reverse the usual convention of putting urban first to signal the increasing absorption of the urban into regional studies, or at least the growing inseparability of the two terms and concepts, as signaled in such terms as city-region, regional city, and what I will call regional urbanization. If we are entering a "new urban age," as some proclaim, it is a distinctly regionalized urban age.

The new regionalism

A starting point for this effort is to recognize that regional studies have changed radically over the past few decades. Building on the so-called spatial turn, the transdisciplinary diffusion of critical spatial perspectives, a new regionalism (NR) has emerged and generated a radical reconceptualization of the nature and importance of regions and regionalism.[2] The most forceful presentation of this reinvigorated regionalism, even if it never uses the term new regionalism, is *The Regional World: Territorial Development in a Global Economy* (Storper, 1997).[3] Storper asserts that regions are vitally important social units, on a par with social formations based on kinship and culture, economic exchange and markets, and political states and identities, the traditional foci of the social sciences. Moreover, Storper argues, primarily through the stimulus of urban agglomeration, cohesive regional economies, especially those in city-regions, emit a powerful generative force for economic development, technological innovation, and cultural creativity that is comparable to, if not stronger than, market competition, comparative advantage, and capitalist social relations. Even at its most hyperbolic, traditional regional development theory never went this far in its assertive regionalism.[4]

Unfortunately, the new regionalism in an explicit and assertive sense has remained poorly articulated in the wider literature and not well developed empirically, even by some of its most forceful proponents. One consequence has been a widespread difficulty in distinguishing between the old and the new regionalism. Many on the left dismiss the NR as just another deceptive neoliberal ploy, while others see only a renewed and economistic regional science or a lightly disguised version of growth pole theory, leading to little more than tired demands for entrepreneurial regional government and city-regional marketing.[5] Still others welcome the NR but define it too narrowly, focusing only on multinational trading blocs. Without a sufficiently clear explanation of the new regionalism, it is no wonder that contemporary regional studies often appear so confused and uncritical to non-regionalists.

What then are the distinctive features of the NR? What makes the regional question so important in the contemporary academic and political worlds? Most clearly distinguishing the new from the old regionalism is the NR's much more powerful and far-reaching theoretical foundation, as exemplified by Storper and related works by Allen Scott (1998, 2001, 2008) on city-regions and the world economy. Regions in the past were viewed primarily as places in which things happen; background repositories of economic and social processes. Today, regions are seen as powerful driving forces in themselves, energizing regional worlds of production, consumption, and creativity, while at the same time shaping the globalization of capital, labor, and culture.

As networks of urban agglomerations, cohesive regional economies have come to be seen as the primary (but not sole) generative force behind all economic development, technological innovation, and cultural creativity. In another twist derived mainly from the work of Jane Jacobs (1969), this generative force may go back more than 10,000 years to the origin of cities and the development of full-scale agriculture.[6] The NR is built on these far-reaching premises and promises.

The generative power of cities and regions

This amazing "discovery" of the generative power of cities and regions is, in my view, not just a ground-breaking idea in urban and regional studies; it may be the most important new idea in all the social sciences and humanities. We have only begun to explore this subject and there remains significant resistance to its implied urban spatial causality, especially among geographers who fear a return to the embarrassing environmental determinism of the 19th century. At this time, research and writing on this stimulus of urban agglomeration, what I have called synekism (Soja, 2000),[7] has been monopolized by a creative if stiffly quantitative cadre of geographical economists, including several Nobel prize winners, as well as by a few opportunistic spatial entrepreneurs selling superficial notions of economic clusters or creative cities.

Blunting the development of more comprehensive and critical research has been the almost complete absence in the Western literature of any effective recognition and analysis of the generative power of urban spatial organization. All there is to refer back to is *The Economy of Cities* by Jane Jacobs (1969) and the much earlier work of Alfred Marshall (1890) on agglomeration economies. Just recognizing that such an urbanization effect exists, which I believe is now beyond doubt, points to an extraordinary lacuna in the Western social science and humanities literature.

Here then is one of the greatest challenges: to encourage the conceptual broadening and more acute critical interpretation of research and writing on the generative force of urbanization and regional development. We still know very little about how this generative effect works, whether big agglomerations always generate more than small ones, whether networks of smaller agglomerations generate more development impulses than one large agglomeration, whether specialization or diversity is more important to economic clusters. What is the role of face-to-face contact (what is called "buzz" in Storper and Venables, 2004)?[8] Has the internet made location and other spatial variables more or less relevant and influential? Does the clustering of profit-motivated firms differ from the logic of cultural clusters of artists or musicians?

Even more challenging and less recognized is the question of how agglomeration also generates negative effects, something that the geographical economists have thus far largely ignored. Accepting Jane Jacobs' argument that this generative effect goes back more than 10,000 years to the very first urban settlements, it becomes possible to trace how urban agglomeration stimulated the development of social hierarchy and power differentials in human society, from the early rise of patriarchy and empire-building states to more contemporary exploitative class relations and racism. We know a little about how capitalism, racism, and patriarchy shape urban space, but almost nothing about how these social processes are shaped by the organization of urban and regional space, a necessary component of what I long ago called the socio-spatial dialectic (Soja, 1980).

There is also the issue of environmental degradation and climate change. Has the concentration of the world's population in cities and megacity-regions been more or less conducive to sustainable ecologies? Are the largest agglomerations more energy efficient than much less urbanized areas, and does this matter? Is networking among city-regions becoming more important than international organizations in developing effective environmental policies? Given the anti-urban biases of the past and the theoretical weaknesses of the old regionalism, it will take a great deal of effort to put these issues of urban spatial causality and regional synekism on the research agenda.

Regional urbanization

Another defining (if not definitive) feature of the NR is the increasing intermixture of urban and regional concepts and forms that is at the foundation of what I describe as regional urbanization. This hybridizing process I argue is leading to a paradigmatic transformation of the modern metropolis, an epochal shift in urban form and "ways of life," to use the old Chicago School phrase coined by

Louis Wirth. In its wake, much of traditional urban and regional theory is being shattered as regional urbanization opens up many alternative arenas for urban–regional (regional–urban?) research.

Within metropolitan areas, for example, regional urbanization is erasing the once fairly easily identifiable boundary between urban and suburban and, as a new literature suggests, between urban and rural, city and countryside. As "outer cities" take shape through a complex process of decentralization and recentralization, a new "inner city" is also emerging, creating new challenges to urban planning and policymaking. Many downtowns have been divested of their domestic populations and partially filled with suburban-like homes, while some inner-city areas have attracted vast numbers of migrants from nearly every country on earth. An unstable and unpredictable inner city is emerging, often filled with tensions and conflicts between domestic and immigrant populations, as well as among urban planners confused by declining central-city densities and new minority majorities.

At the same time, there has been a growing peripheral urbanization, as high-density development covers what was once sprawling low-density suburbia. An expanding glossary of new terms has been generated from this mixture of the urban and the suburban, and the mass urbanization that is "filling in" the entire metropolitan area. Included are edge cities, outer cities, boomburgs, in-between cities, hybrid cities, rurban areas, urban villages, citistates, metroburbia, and exopolises. Although these new forms are frequently crammed back into old metropolitan typologies, it is clear that suburbanization is not continuing in the same way as it did in the postwar decades. Traditional suburbia is slowly disappearing as the once relatively homogeneous suburbs are feeling the effects of mass regional urbanization, opening up a rich frontier for comparative research on the differentiation – the many different ways of life – of what some now call post-suburbia.

Some former suburbs, such as Orange County and Silicon Valley in California, have become large urban-industrial complexes, with as many jobs as bedrooms. Combining increasingly dense outer cities with mass migration into the inner city, the five-county Los Angeles city-region surpassed New York City's 23-county metropolitan area in the 1990 census as the densest "urbanized area" in the US, a remarkable transformation given that Los Angeles was the least dense major US metropolis 60 years ago. Indicative of its extraordinary peripheral urbanization, the City of Los Angeles is surrounded today by 40 cities of more than 100,000 inhabitants.

Despite the urbanization of suburbia and outer-city development happening to some degree around almost every major city in the world, many areas have been able to fight in new ways to maintain their old suburban densities and lifestyles, often based on private residential governments and gated communities, as well as specialized zoning laws. Peripheral urbanization and the growth of outer cities has been noted for decades – it has been an integral part of the urban restructuring process generated by the urban crises of the 1960s – but we still know very little of its dynamics; too many scholars refuse to recognize the magnitude and transformative significance of the changes taking place, and still cling to the old and declining metropolitan model and mentality.

The end of the metropolis era

Regional urbanization and the rise of polycentric city-regions and regional cities (I think the term regional cities will become much more widely used in the future) are the core concepts of the new regionalism (see Hall & Pain, 2006).[9] In several recent writings (Soja, 2010a, 2011a, 2011b), I have taken the regional urbanization concept one step further, arguing that it is not just an extension of the modern (or postmodern) metropolis but an indicator of an epochal shift in the nature of the city and the urbanization process, marking the beginning of the end of the modern metropolis as we knew it. Such a radical shift also suggests the need for radically new approaches to urban and regional theory and practice.

The "metropolis era" as it is used here began in the late 19th century, growing out of an earlier, more centralized, and denser version of the industrial capitalist city. Unlike that earlier city, with its unplanned concentricities that the Chicago School adapted from Engels' view of Manchester, the metropolis was more centrifugal than centripetal, growing primarily by suburban expansion, at least in North America. In the interwar years, the modern metropolis ceased growing by accretion (e.g., incorporating adjacent and already dense "streetcar suburbs") and instead spawned an expansive suburbia filled with a constellation of little "almost cities." This created a pronounced dualism, two very different ways of life that became embedded in popular as well as academic notions of urban form and function. The urban studies literature reflected this dualism, being categorically divided into urban and suburban emphases. Furthermore, the metropolitan model came to be thought of by many as a kind of end-state, an ultimate equilibrium that could never become anything else, making the notion of regional urbanization almost inconceivable. One of the tasks of new research on regional urbanization is to rethink this rigid dual model of the metropolis, and recognize the paradigmatic shift that is taking place from a metropolitan to a regional model of urbanization. Now, to be sure, this shift is (like all social processes) happening unevenly, more intensely evident in some areas, much less so in others. With some effort, however, evidence of peripheral urbanization and outer-city growth, as I have noted, can be found in almost every large city-region. This widespread impact of peripheral urbanization accentuates the demand for rigorous comparative analysis at the national and international scales.

The relation between peripheral urbanization and sprawl is particularly complicated and needs to be clarified, especially given the negative connotations attached to such notions as "periurbanization" in Europe, where it is associated with unsustainable sprawl beyond hinterland boundaries. Regional urbanization does not just involve moving outward from inner to outer metropolitan rings. Urbanization in what was once suburbia can take place almost anywhere, close to or far away from the old city center, and brings with it much higher densities than before. That it strains public services (especially mass transit), often worsens pollution and public health, and creates many other problems (including aggravating income inequalities), needs to be seen and responded to, not as an extension of the metropolitan model but of the new processes associated with regional urbanization. Again, the need for good comparative analysis is vital.

In the US, regional urbanization is probably most advanced in the city-regions of Los Angeles, the San Francisco Bay area, and Washington, DC, with Chicago catching up rather quickly. New York's very extensive suburbanization contains a large number of edge cities but remains relatively less dense than the other city-regions mentioned. The spread of Greater London, the extended regions around Milan, Barcelona, and Berlin, and the multi-centered Dutch Randstad are European examples, as is the almost entirely new "Grand Region" surrounding the financial center of Luxemborg and including the German Saar, the French Lorraine, and other parts of Germany and Belgium. The Gauteng region of South Africa, containing Johannesburg, Pretoria, and the Witwatersrand, was the first officially proclaimed "global city-region."

Extended regional urbanization

Another collection of new terms and concepts has arisen from what can be called extended regional urbanization, stretching beyond the outer limits of the metropolis (see Soja & Kanai, 2007). Included here are the endless city, megacity regions, megaregions, megalopolitan regions, regional constellations and galaxies, and more. Growing out of the computer games empire created by SimCity, for example, the latest version of the OpenSimulator focuses on creating megaregions, assiduously keeping the world of simulation up-to-date with the new regionalism.

Although a new regional lexicon has not yet been established, the most general term in use today is city-region, with or without a dash (although city-region as one word is not used); those with more than a million inhabitants are either millionaire city-regions or megacity-regions. Megacity is also widely used for city-regions with populations exceeding 5 million, while megaregions (occasionally megalopolitan or megapolitan regions) usually refer to giant regional units of more than 20 million inhabitants. The UN claims that the first and now largest megaregion combines Shenzhen, Guangzhou, and Hong Kong in southern China's Pearl River Delta, with a population of 120 million. En route to an urbanization of the world, some say the scale of urbanization is getting even larger with continental-sized urban regions identifiable in North America, Europe, and East Asia, where an urban zone stretching across China, Korea, and Japan is home to more than 400 million people.

Chinese planners expect 200 million new inhabitants in what they officially call extended urban regions, or alternatively *chengzhongcun*, meaning areas where village and city mix together. Some Chinese scholars use the term periurbanization, but without the negative connotations associated with its use in Europe. Led by China, the entire world is becoming enmeshed in a network of polycentric and expansive city-regions, absorbing and generating a dispropor-tionate share of the world's wealth and innovative capacity. A recent UN report on the state of the world's cities claims that the 40 largest megaregions, contain-ing 18% of the world's population, today concentrate two-thirds of the world's wealth and more than 80% of its technological and scientific innovations (UN Habitat, 2010; see also Florida, 2009).

Globalization itself is being redefined, around the spread of industrial urban-ism in some form everywhere – the Amazon rainforest, the Sahara desert, the Siberian tundra, even the Antarctic icecap – after more than a century of being confined to the core capitalist and socialist countries. Five hundred megacity-regions of more than 1 million inhabitants (a fifth of them in China) sit atop this worldwide web of regional urbanization, coordinating all planetary activities. Not only has there been a globalization of the urban, giving rise to the most culturally and economically heterogeneous cities the world has ever known (an important research focus in itself), there has also been occurring an urbanization of the world, what some are now calling planetary urbanization, demanding recognition, attention, and further research from an avowedly regional perspective.

In addition to noting the importance of megaregions, the United Nations now lists urban size by city-region, not metropolitan area or "Greater so-and-so." In the US census, increasingly complex metropolitan area definitions are side-stepped in a relatively new category of "urbanized area," defined by local density levels. Incidentally, it is this measure that has made Los Angeles, perhaps the leading-edge exemplar of the regional urbanization process, surpass New York City as the densest urbanized area in the US.

Multiscalar regionalism

Extended regional urbanization is indicative of another distinctive feature of the NR: its expression at multiple scales. The old regionalism focused almost entirely on sub-national regions like New England, Quebec, Catalonia, Appala-chia. Sub-national regionalism remains important in the NR and has seen a resurgence in recent years, stimulated by many different goals: political, eco-nomic, cultural, strategic. Examples abound in Belgium, Italy, all of the former Yugoslavia and Soviet Union, China, India, Brazil, Argentina, Eritrea, Somalia, and Sumatra. But the new regionalism is more formatively characterized by the expansion of supranational regionalism, from everything associated with the European Union to the proliferation of regional trading blocs such as NAFTA, MERCOSUR, and ASEAN.

The European Union, as the first attempt to unite advanced industrial nation-states, has probably been the most vigorous promoter of regionalism and regional policies, new and old, in the world today. Through the EUREGIO program and the European Spatial Development Perspective (four words that would never have been combined this way 20 years ago, yet now official policy across all the EU states), new cross-border regions have been created throughout

Europe where there used to be confronting antagonistic forces. Related to these developments, more advanced forms of spatial and regional planning are recognizing and fostering "innovative regions" (e.g., Rhone-Alpes, Catalonia, Baden-Wurtemburg) and greater interconnections between the largest city-regions. The search for a United States of Europe, as well as what is called a Europe of the regions, is a form of supranational coalition-building aimed, like locally based community coalitions, at achieving for strategic purposes a sufficient size to compete with other giant entities like China, Russia, and the USA.

Uncritical approaches to supranational regional training blocs, seen only as efficient state coalitions for competing in global markets, have unfortunately diverted attention away from nearly everything else in the NR. As the first exercise in my class on regional planning, I ask students to enter "new regionalism" in their search engines and choose three pages of hits to analyze how the NR is being defined and discussed. Usually, there are more than 150,000 hits, but the vast majority are concentrated on regional trading blocs, leading to a biased picture of the NR (and loads of confusion for students).

For many political scientists, international relations specialists, economists, and some geographers, regionalism and hence the new regionalism is seen as an alternative to bilateralism and multilateralism in trade relations, and defined only as a coming together of nation-states. It takes some effort to convince students, as well as a few urban and regional scholars, that there is something more to the NR than ASEAN, NAFTA and MERCOSUR. At the same time, it must also be said that there is a need for more critical research on trading blocs and their potential for adding more progressive political, environmental, and economic equity goals to their focus on trade regulation.

The NR thus needs to be seen as stretching across many scales. At the global level, in addition to the European Union and trading blocs, there has been a complex restructuring of what has been called the international division of labor, or most simplemindedly the North–South divide. What was once the Third World has disintegrated, with the Asian "tigers" or NICs (newly industrialized countries) joining the developed world, and the poorest countries being relegated to another categorical world of deepening poverty. For the most part, the socialist–communist Second World has disappeared (although it is not entirely clear whether the formerly communist states have entered the First World or Third World in their old sense). New regionalists such as Kenichi Ohmae (1995, 1996) have suggested that, as the world becomes increasingly "borderless," three great regional power blocs have emerged: one in the Western hemisphere dominated by the US; another in Europe, the Middle East, and Africa dominated by the European Union; and the third in South and East Asia led by China.

Another area of interesting debate remains unresolved: the significance of the differences in urbanization processes between North and South, developed and developing worlds. I have argued that regional urbanization is happening everywhere, albeit unevenly. That more people live in the cities of the developing South than in those of the developed North, and that this disproportion will increase in the future, takes nothing away from the global process. What the globalization of the urban suggests is that the differences between urbanization in the developed versus the developing world are decreasing. They have certainly not disappeared entirely, but more than ever before their similarities make it possible for London to learn from Lagos as much as Lagos can learn from London. It is this global balance that must inform contemporary urban and regional studies, not some categorical Eurocentrism or Third Worldism.

Similarly, I think it is becoming unacceptable to speak of typically European or North American cities, especially when this refers to compact versus sprawling cities. To some degree, every city on earth is experiencing some similar developmental forces shaped by globalization, the new economy, and the revolution in information and communications technology. At the same time, each experiences these general processes in unique ways, rooted in local history and geography. What is needed is not some confrontation between Northern and Southern perspectives but rigorous and open-minded comparative analysis, based on an appropriate and contemporary theorization of cities and regions.

What have just been described are examples of scalar restructuring and its regional implications. Closer to the bottom of the scalar structure has been another, still poorly understood, tendency that forms an attractive focus for urban and regional research.[10] I refer to another kind of scalar fusion, as metropolitan regions seem to be blending into larger subnational regions, creating something like region-states. Barcelona blending into Catalonia is one example. Berlin, Hamburg, and Singapore (plus the old Hong Kong) already exist as regional city-states. To some degree, however, all megacity-regions have experienced some of this scalar coalescence. Almost by definition, the city-region is larger than the metropolitan region. A major problem here is the absence or weakness of regional authority, as the restructuring of economic relations has proceeded much faster than the adaptation of governmental administration. This brings us to another research frontier.

Regional governance and planning

Another aspect of the NR worthy of more detailed study is the governance crisis generated by the expansion of megacity-regions, and the deepening political and economic tensions caused by the tendencies towards income inequality and social polarization that seem to be built into regional urbanization. Several studies in the US have suggested that income inequalities tend to be lower in city-regions where there is some effective regional authority.[11] If this is true, then there is an extraordinarily strong case for introducing more effective regional governance and planning in all the world's city-regions.

In the old regionalism, regional planners argued that regional planning, usually involving some variant of growth pole/growth center policy, was necessary to reduce income inequalities and prevent widespread social unrest. A similar argument can be made from the perspective of the new regionalism, but this argument is reinforced by a new form of spatial planning focused on the generative effects of urban agglomerations, industrial clusters, and cohesive regional economies. The key challenge here becomes how to take maximum advantage of the positive effects of agglomeration while also recognizing and dealing with the perhaps inevitable accompanying negative effects on social justice and environmental quality.[12]

Never before has the necessity for effective regional governance and planning been so great. This intensified demand does not necessarily revolve around the creation of formal regional governments, a primary focus of the old regionalism. A more adaptive and flexible regionalism is needed, focusing on particular issues such as mass transit, environmental management, regional equity, housing, and social justice. One interesting example of such adaptive and flexible regionalism is the new "metropolitics" promoted by the politician-lawyer-regionalist Myron Orfield (1997, 2002, 2010).

Orfield's initial work focused on the Twin Cities (Minneapolis–St. Paul) area of Minnesota and revolved around the formation of a metropolitan regional coalition, consisting of suburban municipalities and inner-city communities willing to pool their tax resources to invest in urban and regional redevelopment. The regional coalition was relatively successful in Minnesota, and attempts continue to transplant the idea to other city-regions.

Other examples of more flexible regional associations and coalitions include various innovative alliances between industry and community groups in Silicon Valley, where regionalism has played a key role in weathering various economic crises,[13] and the growth of community-based regionalism, as practiced by several successful labor–community coalitions in Los Angeles.[14] The largest and most successful of these regional alliances is the Los Angeles Alliance for a New Economy (LAANE), which consists of around 120 organizations grouped in different ways for different projects. An additional effect of community-based regionalism has been the growing connection between community development specialists and regional planners, a connection that was almost non-existent 10 years ago.

Seeking regional democracy

An open theoretical frontier growing out of the debates on regional governance and planning involves the application of critical regional and spatial approaches to the study of citizenship, democracy, justice, human rights, and social movements. The development of community-based regionalism, as mentioned above, provides one interesting example of struggling for regional democracy. Closely related has been the "regionalization" of the right to the city movement, based on an idea initially presented by Henri Lefebvre as *le droit à la ville*.

The right to the city idea has been expanded to at least the right to the city-region if not to the right to occupy space everywhere, a moot point in a sense if one recognizes that the entire world is being urbanized to some degree. In any case, there is now a World Charter for the Right to the City, many UNESCO meetings and publications on the subject and, most pertinent here, the formation in 2007 in Los Angeles (and later more formally in Atlanta) of a national Right to the City Alliance, led by regional coalitions from Los Angeles, Washington, DC, and Miami. Struggles over the right to the city and community-based regionalism, and (with some careful qualification) the Occupy Movement of recent years, all revolve in one way or another around fomenting and promoting more participatory democracy, especially with regard to questions of equity, citizenship, and hierarchies of social power.

Conclusion

Eight broad themes have been identified, each stimulated by new spatial insights and brimming with innovative research possibilities. We are witnessing an unprecedented period in which the urban and the regional, formerly quite distinct from one another, are blending together to define something new and different, an evolving regional–urban synthesis that demands new modes of understanding.

Notes

1 Edward Soja, "Accentuate the Regional," first published in the *International Journal of Urban and Regional Research* (*IJURR*), Wiley, Volume 39, Issue 2, March 2015, pages 372–381. Reproduced by kind permission from Edward Soja and *IJURR*.
2 For a discussion of the spatial turn, see Soja (2008). A brief discussion of the new regionalism framed within a discussion of the evolution of regional planning ideas can be found in Soja (2009).
3 Territory and territorial are often used as a substitute for region and regional, a practice I hope will not continue in the future, if used at the expense of asserting the regional.
4 Regionalism is defined as advocating the usefulness of regions for any particular purpose, for theory building, identity formation, political action, or just economic efficiency. A simple definition of region is an organized space with some shared qualities. The term comes from the Latin *regere*, to rule, from which also come regal, regime, and regulate.
5 See Lovering (1999) for an early critique of the new regionalism (using Wales as an example). See also Hadjimichalis and Hudson (2006).
6 Some have claimed Jacobs deserved a Nobel Prize for her "discovery" of the stimulus of urban agglomeration. Economists now call these urbanization economies Jane Jacob's externalities.
7 The term synekism is taken from the Greek *synoikismos*, literally coming together to live under one roof, a reference to the stimulating formation of the *polis* or city-state.
8 The original subtitle of this article was closer to "the generative effect of cities," but the journal editors claimed their readers would not understand this and recommended a change to incorporate "buzz."
9 For a look at the megacity-regions of the US, see Nelson and Lang (2011).
10 The scale issue and the process of rescaling can take us to a micro level – from neighborhood, to building, to the body – the so-called geography closest in, a (mobile) nodal region at the base of all nodal (territorial) regions. The NR can thus be seen as extending from the body to the planet.
11 A leading figure in this area is Manuel Pastor Jr., professor of Geography and American Studies and Ethnicity and director of the Program for Environmental and Regional Equity at the University of Southern California (see Pastor, Benner, & Matsuoka, 2009; Pastor, Dreier, Grigsby, & Lopez-Garza, 2000).
12 For more on the old and new regional planning, see Soja (2009).

13 For the opinions of a leading figure studying Silicon Valley regionalism, see Saxenian (2006).
14 The concept of community-based regionalism was developed first by Martha Matsuoka, a co-author of Pastor et al. (2009). LAANE and other labor–community coalitions are discussed in Soja (2010b).

References

Florida, R. (2009). Foreword. In C. Ross (Ed.), *Megaregions: Planning for global competitiveness*. Washington, DC: Island Press.

Hadjimichalis, C., & Hudson, R. (2006). Networks, regional development and democratic control. *International Journal of Urban and Regional Research, 30*(4), 858–872.

Hall, P., & Pain, K. (2006). *The polycentric metropolis: Learning from the mega-city regions of Europe*. Abingdon and New York: Earthscan.

Jacobs, J. (1969). *The economy of cities*. New York: Random House.

Lovering, J. (1999). Theory led by policy: The inadequacies of the "new regionalism." *International Journal of Urban and Regional Research, 23*(2), 379–395.

Marshall, A. (1890). *Principles of economics*, book 4. London: Macmillan and Company.

Nelson, A., & Lang, R. E. (2011). *Megapolitan America: A new vision for understanding America's metropolitan geography*. Chicago and Washington, DC: American Planning Association.

Ohmae, K. (1995). *The borderless world: Power and strategies in the interlinked economy*. New York: The Free Press.

Ohmae, K. (1996). *The end of the nation-state: How regional economies will soon reshape the world*. New York: The Free Press.

Orfield, M. (1997). *A regional agenda for community and stability*. Washington, DC and Cambridge, MA: Brookings Institute and Lincoln Land Institute.

Orfield, M. (2002). *American metropolitics: The new suburban reality*. Washington, DC: The Brookings Institute.

Orfield, M. (2010). *Region: Planning the future of the twin cities*. Minneapolis: University of Minnesota Press.

Pastor, M., Benner, C., & Matsuoka, M. (2009). *This could be the start of something big: How social movements for regional equity are reshaping metropolitan America*. Ithaca, NY and London: Cornell University Press.

Pastor, M., Dreier, P., Grigsby, E., & Lopez-Garza, M. (2000). *Regions that work: How cities and suburbs can grow together*. Minneapolis: University of Minnesota Press.

Saxenian, A. (2006). *The new Argonauts: Regional advantage in a global economy*. Cambridge, MA: Harvard University Press.

Scott, A. J. (1998). *Regions and the world economy*. Oxford: Oxford University Press.

Scott, A. J. (Ed.). (2001). *Global city-regions: Trends, theory, policy*. Oxford: Oxford University Press.

Scott, A. J. (2008). *Social economy of the metropolis: Cognitive-cultural capitalism and the global resurgence of cities*. Oxford: Oxford University Press.

Soja, E. (1980). The socio-spatial dialectic. *Annals of the Association of American Geographers, 70*, 207–225.

Soja, E. (2000). *Postmetropolis: Critical studies of cities and regions*. Oxford: Blackwell Publishers.

Soja, E. (2008). Taking space personally. In B. Warf & S. Arias (Eds.), *The spatial turn: Interdisciplinary perspectives*. New York and London: Routledge.

Soja, E. (2009). Regional planning and development theories. In R. Kitchin & N. Thrift (Eds.), *International encyclopedia of human geography*. New York: Elsevier.

Soja, E. (2010a). Regional urbanization and the future of megacities (extended version). In S. Buijs, W. Tan, & D. Tunas (Eds.), *Megacities: Exploring a sustainable future*. Rotterdam: 010 Publishers.

Soja, E. (2010b). *Seeking spatial justice*. Minneapolis: University of Minnesota Press.

Soja, E. (2011a). Regional urbanization and the end of the metropolis era. In G. Bridge & S. Watson (Eds.), *The new Blackwell companion to the city*. Oxford and Chichester: Wiley-Blackwell.

Soja, E. (2011b). From metropolitan to regional urbanization. In T. Banerjee & A. Loukaitou-Sideris (Eds.), *Companion to urban design*. London and New York: Routledge.

Soja, E., & Kanai, J. M. (2007). The urbanization of the world. In R. Burdett & D. Sudjic (Eds.), *The endless city*. New York: Phaidon.

Storper, M. (1997). *The regional world: Territorial development in a global economy*. New York: Guildford Press.

Storper, M., & Venables, A. (2004). Buzz: Face-to-face contact and the urban economy. *Journal of Economic Geography, 4*(4), 351–370.

UN Habitat. (2010). *State of the world's cities report*. New York: UN Habitat.

14 Commodity or commons?

Knowledge, inequality, and the city

Fran Tonkiss

The importance of knowledge in contemporary urban economies is now well-established. While its role in post-industrial and service-intensive economies is especially critical, the ways in cities which generate, organise, and enhance knowledge is an enduring feature of urban life. Cities have always been 'smart'. The current focus on networked, digital, and data-driven urbanisms should not obscure the fact that urban environments are by their nature systems of collective intelligence; information-rich and highly conducive to social as well as individual learning. The production and circulation of knowledge is the basis for urban innovation, key to urban competition, and central to urban productivity – not to say crucial to the cultural intensity of urban experience. Creating knowledge, simply, is one of the things that cities do, and they tend to do it well.

If knowledge is good for cities, then, it is also the case that cities are good for knowledge. Urban environments are (among other things) complex systems for producing, refining, and dispersing ideas, skills, and information. 'Knowledge', as Molotch (2014, p. 220) has it, 'tends to be a distributed good', and cities are exemplary distribution systems, with their dense networks of hard, soft, and human infrastructures to circulate knowledge across extended territories and large populations. Like other resources, however, the ways in which knowledge is distributed is crucial to the structuring of opportunities and inequalities in contemporary cities. The discussion that follows explores two primary and contrasting approaches to the organisation of knowledge in urban economies. In the first of these, knowledge is individualised in the form of skills which are sorted and priced in urban labour markets. This competitive model of knowledge grades aptitude, experience, and capabilities through market exchange – knowledge, that is, is a marketised element of human capital. In the second, it is managed as a common resource in the form of information – while this may carry a price, it is not necessarily set by competitive markets; and while knowledge may be privately produced, its distribution and access is socialised in various ways. The distinction between these two modes of organising knowledge in cities is a stylised one – and it does not exhaust the ways in which knowledge is generated and allocated in urban settings – but the aim is to highlight the complex character of knowledge as an urban good, and to underline the different choices cities have to make about how resources are produced, distributed, and valued in social as well as economic terms. My interest as a sociologist is less in the technical solutions, systems, and strategies that are central to models of smart urbanism than in the social relations of knowledge in the city: the ways in which people develop, use, and access knowledge, ideas, and information through forms of social interaction and economic exchange. The double life of knowledge as private asset and as collective good has implications for the structuring of inequalities in cities and for attempts to promote greater urban equity, and social and economic inclusion.

Such a focus on knowledge offers insights into the production and distribution of other resources, assets, and services in the city, in part because knowledge is so distinctive in this context. As Foray (2004, pp. 15–16) points out, knowledge is – at least in principle – a 'nonexcludable' good: it is hard to stop people from using it. It is, furthermore, a 'nonrival' good – different people can use it at the same time without diminishing the overall stock; on the contrary, knowledge is a 'cumulative' good which tends to be developed and enhanced through use, especially use by different people (see also Malecki, 2010). Knowledge is also, however, 'dispersed and divided', and it is this quality which makes questions of distribution so vital. 'Given the peculiar properties and features of knowledge as an economic good', Foray (2004, p. 18) goes on, 'most of the resource allocation mechanisms used in the world of tangible goods do not work properly to maximize knowledge creation and diffusion'. This may be so, but the structuring of knowledge economies in cities makes evident the ways in which forms of knowledge – skill, information, ideas, data – are rendered excludable through privatisation and commodification, and constructed in rival terms. There is a case to be made that such competitive processes can be good for knowledge creation; it is much less clear that they are effective in maximising the diffusion of knowledge most efficiently or equitably.

Given the basic properties of knowledge as nonexcludable, nonrival, and cumulative – that is, as fundamentally *collective* in character – it is rather striking that as urban economies get smarter (more knowledge-intensive, more information-centric, more data-driven) they also seem to be getting more unequal. There is a prevailing rhetoric around the dynamism of contemporary urban economies but deepening inequality is a keynote of recent trends in urbanisation – whether in the expanding cities of the global south or the post-industrial cities of the global north. Viewed through an economic lens, inequality can appear less as an urban problem than an index of urban productivity – cities sort large numbers of people in economic terms and the most competitive cities may do this in particularly uncompromising ways (see Behrens & Robert-Nicoud, 2014a, 2014b; Florida, 2015). Inequality is hardly a new feature of urban life, and worsening disparity does not appear to be a barrier to the economic growth of cities or to the pull of urban in-migration. But there is surely something perverse about the way in which urban economies that are increasingly organised around intangible and 'nonexcludable' knowledge resources are also increasingly structured around substantive inequalities and persistent exclusions. How are these dynamics of inequality being embedded in urban knowledge economies, and how might cities be 'smarter' in distributing knowledge and its benefits in more equitable ways?

Marketising knowledge: skill, economy, and inequality

Let us begin with the good news about knowledge and skill in the city. Urban economies – with their thick labour markets and agglomerations of enterprise – are crucibles for innovation, creativity, and productive spillovers from the accumulation of human capital (Andersson, Burgess, & Lane 2007; Carlino, Chatterjee, & Hunt, 2007; Ciccone & Hall, 1996; Florida, 2002; Florida, Mellander, Stolarick, & Ross, 2012; Glaeser, 1994; 2011; Glaeser & Gottlieb, 2009; Glaeser & Resseger, 2010; Glaeser, Kallal, Scheinkman, & Shleifer, 1992; Knudsen, Florida, Stolarick, & Gates, 2008; Rauch, 1993; Storper & Venables, 2004). Denser market concentration in cities promotes not only competition but also collaboration, imitation, diffusion, and social learning. There are, moreover, "dynamic advantages to urban diversity" (Duranton & Puga, 2001, p. 1455); positive economic and social returns generated by the circulation of knowledge, innovation, expertise, and market opportunities between different kinds of enterprise in a dense urban economy (see Jacobs, 1969; Quigley, 1998).

Cities – the economists agree – are leading sites of creativity and knowledge production, and the benefits are legible in higher rates of innovation and productivity in cities, particularly in larger cities. It is also visible in the pricing of skill in urban labour markets. The concentration and development of human capital is a key part of cities' economic dynamism, and contemporary cities support dense and diverse markets for skill. Economists have for some time recognised the existence of an urban wage premium under which workers tend to earn more in larger urban economies across different national contexts (D'Costa & Overman, 2014; De La Roca & Puga, 2017; Glaeser & Maré, 2001; Yankow, 2006). A number of factors are seen as relevant here, but the value placed on skill in urban labour markets is key: there is generally a greater concentration of skill in dense urban economies, higher skills are linked to greater productivity, and competitive urban labour markets reward these productive forms of human capital. Combes, Duranton, and Gobillon (2008, p. 737) put it plainly: an urban wage premium can be attributed in large part to the fact that '[w]orkers with better labour market characteristics tend to agglomerate in the larger, denser and more skilled local labour market'.

While the urban wage premium holds at the broader city scale, however, the economic returns to skill appear increasingly skewed around polarising urban labour markets. Detailed analysis points to a dispersion of skill and a sharp divergence in wages in urban economies (Berry & Glaeser, 2005). Research in US cities suggests that 'the urban wage premium is greater for workers with high cognitive and people skills, but not for workers with high levels of motor skills' (Bacolod, Blum, & Strange, 2009, p. 150; see also Bacolod & Blum, 2010). It follows, Bacolod et al. (2009, p. 150) argue, that 'the salient economic policy issue today is inequality, in particular, the increase in inequality in labor income' between those who make their living from 'thinking and social interaction' and those who undertake physical work. Eeckhout and his colleagues concur. 'Big cities' in the US, they argue, 'have big real inequality' (Eeckhout, Pinheiro, & Schmidheiny, 2014, p. 601; see also Baum-Snow & Pavan, 2013). What is more, these authors find that there is an 'urban inequality "premium"' for large cities in which the complementarity and functional interdependence between high and low-skilled (and high and low-waged) workers enhances overall urban produc-tivity. Highly paid workers in advanced services support labour markets in low-paid services for those who drive their cars, secure their buildings, wait their tables, and clean their houses: a model of social polarisation outlined in older accounts of the informational or 'global' city but becoming more evident across broader urban geographies (see Castells, 1989; Sassen, 1991).

These patterns of skill and wage polarisation have been evident in US cities for a number of years. Urban inequalities are produced in complex ways, but the restructuring of urban economies around service and knowledge industries has been a leading driver of 'unequalisation' in 21st century cities. Researchers have tracked the widening of income disparities in US metros over more than three decades, as workers in professional and knowledge-based sectors (including medicine and law, accounting and financial services, IT and management con-sulting) take an increasing income share in urban labour markets, with decreas-ing returns to lower-skill and less-educated workers (see Baum-Snow, Freedman, & Pavan, 2014; Behrens & Robert-Nicoud, 2014b; Choi & Green, 2015; Florida & Mellander, 2016; Glaeser, Resseger, & Tobio, 2008; Wheeler, 2005). It has long been conventional to attribute urban inequalities to the concentration of poverty in cities, but some of the most pronounced recent trends have been steered by the accelerated growth at the top end of urban income curves. Cities with advanced knowledge sectors – notably in finance and tech – have seen sharp rises in inequality since the 1980s, with some of the richest, 'smartest' cities in the United States (San Francisco, Boston, New York, or New Haven) ranked among the nation's most unequal (Holmes & Berube, 2016; see also Sommeiller, Price, & Wazeter, 2016).

This point is worth underlining. Research on inequality in North American cities has tended to correlate higher average incomes with lower levels of inequality: more affluent cities, that is, are usually less unequal (Florida & Mel-lander, 2016; Glaeser et al. 2008; for Canada, see Bolton & Breau, 2012). As the highest earners take an increasing share of the urban spoils, however, this basic association has weakened, and in certain stand-out cities growing affluence has gone in lockstep with deepening disparity. Meanwhile, urban America has seen the hollowing of its middle classes, with the share of middle-income populations falling in over 95% of the 229 urban areas tracked by the Pew Research Center (2016) between 1999 and 2014. During the same time frame almost 70% of US metros saw increases in their low-income population share, with around 75% seeing a growth in their upper-income share. Such a pulling-apart of urban incomes is evident in cities with quite distinct economic trajectories; playing out in different ways but with similar polarising effects in cities such as Detroit which have seen significant losses in skilled manufacturing jobs as they deindustrialised, and in wealthy tech economies where jobs and skills have diverged around high- and low-wage services – San Francisco again appears as a poster child for this kind of post-industrial polarity.

While these trends are well-documented in the US they are not confined to it, with similar (if less stark) patterns evident in European and Canadian contexts (see Bolton & Breau, 2012; Breau, Kogler, & Bolton, 2014; Combes et al., 2008; De La Roca & Puga, 2017; Lee, 2011; Lee & Rodríguez-Pose, 2013; Lee, Sissons, & Jones, 2016). Neither is this a matter only for rich-world economies. Such patterns of economic restructuring and social polarisation might also be seen in China's rapidly developing urban economy, with widening wage gaps between higher and less-skilled workers. The income disparities and enhanced returns to certain kinds of human capital that researchers in the US have traced since the 1980s have been paralleled in China in the post-reform period, with higher-skilled urban workers taking the greater share of income growth as the expansion of Chinese cities has gone together with accelerating degrees of inequality (Chen, Liu, & Lu, 2017; Gan, 2013; Liu, Park, & Zhao, 2010; Meng, 2004; Meng, Gregory, & Wang, 2005; Pan, Mukhopadhaya, & Li, 2016; Whalley & Xing, 2014; Zhang, Zhao, Park, & Song, 2005). These polarising logics are exacerbated by the situation of the sizeable population of migrant workers in Chinese cities; rural-to-urban migrants tend to be less educated, work in lower-skill jobs, and earn lower hourly wages than established urban residents (Chen et al., 2017; Pan et al., 2016). Such labour market effects, moreover, are compounded by systematic non-income and welfare inequalities – unregistered migrants are marginalised in urban housing markets (and largely excluded from public housing provision), they have limited recourse to social assistance or health insurance, and their children have restricted access to urban public schools and universities (Lai et al., 2014; Logan, Fang, & Zhang, 2009; Park & Wang, 2010; see also Solinger, 2006).

This last point underscores the way that income inequalities structured by urban labour markets intersect with other vectors of disadvantage in contemporary cities. The reliance of migrant workers in urban China on private sector and informal employment, private and irregular housing markets, unlicensed and unregulated health clinics, and privately run 'migrant schools' may represent an extreme form of state abandonment, but it shows up in high relief the sense in which public and social interventions can both offset and augment unequal labour market outcomes. While the legal protections for private sector workers have markedly improved in China in the last decade, and reforms to the household registration system should enhance access to municipal provision and social support for rural-urban migrants, the dual system which has prevailed since the late 1980s has seen this notionally 'socialist' system support stark welfare inequalities and increasing consumption inequalities. Established urban populations are advantaged not only in taking higher wages out of segmented urban labour markets, but because their welfare and consumption costs are subsidised and secured by social insurance and public provision. This is a particularly severe but hardly a unique instance of how market and state mechanisms work in tandem in contemporary urban economies to distribute income and welfare in ways which produce and reinforce inequalities along different lines of advantage and disadvantage. Widening income disparities in the United States have also been linked to expanding consumption inequalities (Aguiar & Bils, 2015; Attanasio, Hurst, & Pistaferri, 2015; JP Morgan Chase Institute, 2016; see also Attanasio & Pistaferri, 2016) in a context where social transfers which might redress welfare inequalities have been steadily shifting away from the poorest households (Moffitt, 2015). As cities strive to develop knowledge-based industries and to attract highly skilled workers in finance and business services, technology, and communications, they are competing for those sectors and populations that are driving inequality at the top end of the urban income scale. At the same time, and across different urban contexts, welfare retrenchment at national and local levels, patterns of residential and commercial gentrification, and the marketisation of urban services all work to magnify welfare and consumption inequalities in cities where many find themselves earning less but having to pay more (Donald, Glasmeier, Gray, & Lobao, 2014; Lees, Shin, & López-Morales, 2015; Peck, 2012).

Socialising knowledge: information and the open-source city

The discussion so far has focused on one of the primary ways in which knowledge is distributed in contemporary cities: through the sorting of skill in urban labour markets. Such an approach constructs knowledge in terms of cognitive and creative human capital which is accumulated, circulated, and exchanged in competitive market settings with powerful effects for income inequality. The restructuring of urban economies around knowledge-intensive sectors has seen cities as distribution systems work effectively – if rather mercilessly – to capture, commodify, and capitalise knowledge in the form of human capital; to sort the skills they want most from those they want less, or can pay less for. Yet a great deal of the literature on urban economies stresses the untraded aspects of knowledge in the city: the positive spillovers that promote learning across firms, industries, and sectors; that see innovations around certain products or processes spur advances in quite different domains; and which mean rising tides of creativity and ingenuity can float many cognitive boats. For all the efforts to render knowledge excludable and rival as a good – not only in competitive labour markets but in efforts to patent, copyright, and brand forms of knowledge as intellectual property – it is very difficult to stop ideas and information from spilling over in the city. And there are good arguments for public, private, and civic actors to go with these kinds of knowledge flow.

As systems for distributing knowledge across space, cities are excellent 'machines for learning' (McFarlane, 2011). Urban populations, furthermore, tend to be good learners. The density of information, intensity of interpersonal communication, and the power of demonstration effects make urbanites particularly open to social learning, behavioural change, and adaptation. As Edward Glaeser (1999, p. 255) has written, however 'impressive ... the role of cities in generating new innovations may be, the primary informational role of cities may not be in creating cutting edge technologies, but rather in creating learning opportunities for everyday people'. In important and quite fundamental ways, knowledge in the city is *socialised* – produced and distributed through collective and cooperative means. This is to think about knowledge in the city as a different sort of economic object – not as commodity or intellectual property, but as common resource. Urban knowledge economies, it follows, are not simply the locational headquarters for cognitive capitalism, but are engaged in the circulation of ideas, information and expertise as non-proprietary goods, opening up the potential for the more equitable allocation of knowledge.

In his work on the economics of knowledge, Dominique Foray (2004, p. 17) argued that proper stewardship of 'the "knowledge commons" requires social regulations that are entirely different to the social arrangements required to regulate ecological systems of exhaustible resources'. If this is the case, it is most obviously true in the sense that the basic aim should be to encourage (rather than to ration or limit) consumption and appropriation of this common resource. Knowledge may be inexhaustible, but it can be lost through under-use. These questions concerning the management of knowledge are especially salient in the context of 'data-driven urbanism' (Kitchin, 2015). The potential to address information inequalities through digital networks is substantial, but the extent to which the 'smart' agenda for cities has been driven by technology companies and the consulting industry means that market and information capture have been central to these developments (see, *inter alia*, Hollands, 2008, 2015; Kitchin, Lauriault, & McArdle, 2015; Marvin, Luque-Ayala, & McFarlane, 2016).

There has been a gathering awareness on the part of city governments that networked urbanism provides opportunities for social and economic returns that go beyond the balance-sheets of Big Tech, and that there may be scope for urban innovation outside the trademarked 'smart' solutions of corporate providers. An emerging paradigm for the distribution of knowledge involves public agencies making big urban data accessible to smaller scale users. Large centres such as New York, Chicago, and London have well-established data-sharing portals that create a digital public domain for and about their city. This model of data-sharing, though, remains fairly one-way; with well-resourced and well-informed cities providing data to their residents, and inviting them in turn to 'talk back' through curated calls for DIY data solutions and strategies (Sassen, 2011). A more open source model is to be found in other urban settings where collaborative knowledge is generated by a range of different actors – individuals, citizen groups, NGOs, and non-profits as well as public and private agencies; including in contexts of government restriction or incapacity. The Open Data Hong Kong network, for example, is run by a network of volunteers seeking to source and share data and to promote greater government transparency (https://opendatahk. com/). The synAthina network in Athens is supported by a city government with severely weakened capacity, providing an open source forum for the autonomous civil initiatives which have emerged under conditions of austerity (Eurocities, 2016; www.synathina.gr). In this sense, addressing information inequality forms part of a broader set of social responses to worsening welfare inequalities. Such strategies for making the city 'hackable' might be seen as the basis for more participatory or progressive approaches to the co-production and social distribution of urban knowledge in and about the city (Hollands, 2008, 2015; Kitchin, 2014).

Initiatives such as these are also instructive in highlighting the fact that the distribution of knowledge in cities is not simply reducible to state or market mechanisms. While the sorting and pricing of skill in urban labour markets may be seen as a critical means by which knowledge economies entrench patterns of inequality, these market effects are compounded or mitigated by government action in respect of social transfers, public provision, and legal protections, as well as by forms of social organisation and intervention (it is worth noting here that higher levels of trade unionisation in cities is still associated with lower levels of income inequality; see Florida & Mellander, 2016; Volscho, 2007). Similarly, 'socialised' approaches to the production and distribution of knowledge go beyond conventional models of the state to take in a broader range of civic actors and organisations; indeed, the knowledge economy may be a privileged context for thinking about the social stewardship of an urban commons in more general terms. What is more, and as the economic literature on innovation spillovers suggests, markets are often important sites of collaboration; while competition around knowledge and innovation takes place outside market settings – from spheres of academic combat to the cut and thrust of hackathons, design sprints, and data challenges.

From a narrowly economic standpoint, urban inequalities can be seen as a possibly regrettable but generally functional effect of the productivity of cities. The most dynamic urban economies are structured around thick markets for labour, information, and services, and these produce more or less severe inequalities of income, access, and consumption. In knowledge-intensive economies, the 'smartest' will thrive and others may find it increasingly hard to get by (Behrens & Robert-Nicoud, 2014a, 2014b). However, even if one gives priority to economic explanations and objectives, information inequalities represent a barrier to economic development in foreclosing economic opportunities, and restricting the potential for innovation and enterprise. If knowledge and skill are central to dynamic urban economies, how optimal is an urban system in which significant parts of the population have unequal access to education, employment, market entry, and other opportunities – especially insofar as these urban exclusions continue to be reproduced along lines of gender, race, or ethnicity, or class position? Two decades ago, Edward Glaeser (1999, p. 275) averred that the 'important informational role of the city means that if we are entering an informational age, then the city will not die but flourish'. The question remains who – and how many – will be able to flourish in it?

References

Aguiar, M., & Bils, M. (2015). Has consumption inequality mirrored income inequality? *The American Economic Review, 105*(9), 2725–2756.

Andersson, F., Burgess, S., & Lane, J. I. (2007). Cities, matching and the productivity gains of agglomeration. *Journal of Urban Economics, 61*(1), 112–128.

Attanasio, O. P., Hurst, E., & Pistaferri, L. (2015). The evolution of income, consumption, and leisure inequality in the US, 1980–2010. In C. D. Carroll, T. F. Crossley, & J. Sabelhaus (Eds.), *Improving the measurement of consumer expenditures* (pp. 100–140). Chicago: University of Chicago Press.

Attanasio, O. P., & Pistaferri, L. (2016). Consumption inequality. *The Journal of Economic Perspectives, 30*(2), 3–28.

Bacolod, M. P., & Blum, B. S. (2010). Two sides of the same coin: US 'residual' inequality and the gender gap. *Journal of Human Resources, 45*(1), 197–242.

Bacolod, M., Blum, B. S., & Strange, W. C. (2009). Skills in the city. *Journal of Urban Economics, 65*(2), 136–153.

Baum-Snow, N., Freedman, M., & Pavan, R. (2014). Why has urban inequality increased? Working paper, June. Retrieved 3 July 2017, from www.mcgill.ca/economics/files/economics/nathaniel_baum-snow.pdf.

Baum-Snow, N., & Pavan, R. (2013). Inequality and city size. *Review of Economics and Statistics, 95*(5), 1535–1548.

Behrens, K., & Robert-Nicoud, F. (2014a, 24 July). Urbanisation makes the world more unequal. *Centre for Economic Policy Research.* Retrieved 3 July 2017, from http://voxeu.org/article/inequality-big-cities.

Behrens, K., & Robert-Nicoud, F. (2014b). Survival of the fittest in cities: Urbanisation and inequality. *The Economic Journal, 124*(581), 1371–1400.

Berry, C. R., & Glaeser, E. L. (2005). The divergence of human capital levels across cities. *Papers in Regional Science, 84*(3), 407–444.

Bolton, K., & Breau, S. (2012). Growing unequal? Changes in the distribution of earnings across Canadian cities. *Urban Studies, 49*(6), 1377–1396.

Breau, S., Kogler, D. F., & Bolton, K. C. (2014). On the relationship between innovation and wage inequality: New evidence from Canadian cities. *Economic Geography, 90*(4), 351–373.

Carlino, G. A., Chatterjee, S., & Hunt, R. M. (2007). Urban density and the rate of invention. *Journal of Urban Economics, 61*(3), 389–419.

Castells, M. (1989). *The informational city: Information technology, economic restructuring, and the urban-regional process* (p. 15). Oxford: Blackwell.

Chen, B, Liu, D., & Lu, M. (2017). City size, migration, and urban inequality in the People's Republic of China. *ADBI Working Paper, 723.* Tokyo: Asian Development Bank Institute. Retrieved 3 July 2017, from www.adb.org/publications/city-size-migration-and-urban-inequality-prc.

Choi, J. H., & Green, R. (2015, 22 December). Income inequality across US cities. http://dx.doi.org/10.2139/ssrn.2707439.

Ciccone, A., & Hall, R. E. (1996). Productivity and the density of economic activity. *American Economic Review, 86*(1), 54–70.

Combes, P.-P., Duranton, G., & Gobillon, L. (2008). Spatial wage disparities: Sorting matters! *Journal of Urban Economics, 63*(2), 723–742.

D'Costa, S., & Overman, H. G. (2014). The urban wage growth premium: Sorting or learning? *Regional Science and Urban Economics, 48*, 168–179.

De la Roca, J., & Puga, D. (2017). Learning by working in big cities. *The Review of Economic Studies, 84*(1), 106–142.

Donald, B., Glasmeier, A., Gray, M., & Lobao, L. (2014). Austerity in the city: Economic crisis and urban service decline? *Cambridge Journal of Regions, Economy and Society, 7*(1), 3–15.

Duranton, G., & Puga, D. (2001). Nursery cities: Urban diversity, process innovation, and the life cycle of products. *American Economic Review*, 1454–1477.

Eeckhout, J., Pinheiro, R., & Schmidheiny, K. (2014). Spatial sorting. *Journal of Political Economy, 122*(3), 554–620.

Eurocities. (2016). Athens engages citizens in reform. Retrieved 3 July 2017, from http://nws.eurocities.eu/MediaShell/media/2016%20Awards_Cities%20in%20action_Athens.pdf.

Florida, R. (2002). The economic geography of talent. *Annals of the Association of American Geographers, 92*(4), 743–755.

Florida, R. (2015, 6 January). The connection between successful cities and inequality. *CityLab*. Retrieved 3 July 2017, from www.citylab.com/politics/2015/01/the-connection-between-successful-cities-and-inequality/384243/.

Florida, R., & Mellander, C. (2016). The geography of inequality: Difference and determinants of wage and income inequality across US metros. *Regional Studies, 50*(1), 79–92.

Florida, R., Mellander, C., Stolarick, K., & Ross, A. (2012). Cities, skills and wages. *Journal of Economic Geography, 12*(2), 355–377.

Foray, D. (2004). *The economics of knowledge*. Cambridge, MA: MIT Press.

Gan, L. (2013). *Income inequality and consumption in China*. Retrieved 3 July 2017, from https://international.uiowa.edu/sites/international.uiowa.edu/files/file_uploads/incomeinequalityinchina.pdf.

Glaeser, E. L. (1994). Economic growth and urban density: A review essay. *Working Papers in Economics*, E-94–7. The Hoover Institution, Stanford University.

Glaeser, E. L. (1999). Learning in cities. *Journal of Urban Economics, 46*(2), 254–277.

Glaeser, E. L. (2011). *Triumph of the city*. New York: Penguin.

Glaeser, E. L., & Gottlieb, J. D. (2009). The wealth of cities: Agglomeration economies and spatial equilibrium in the United States. *Journal of Economic Literature, 47*(4), 983–1028.

Glaeser, E. L., Kallal, H. D., Scheinkman, J. A., & Shleifer, A. (1992). Growth in cities. *Journal of Political Economy, 100*(6), 1126–1152.

Glaeser, E. L., & Maré, D. C. (2001). Cities and skills. *Journal of Labor Economics, 19*(2), 316–342.

Glaeser, E. L., & Resseger, M. G. (2010). The complementarity between cities and skills. *Journal of Regional Science, 50*(1), 221–244.

Glaeser, E. L., Resseger, M. G., & Tobio, K. (2008). Urban inequality (No. w14419). *National Bureau of Economic Research*. Cambridge, MA: National Bureau of Economic Research.

Hollands, R. G. (2008). Will the real smart city please stand up? Intelligent, progressive or entrepreneurial? *City, 12*(3), 303–320.

Hollands, R. G. (2015). Critical interventions into the corporate smart city. *Cambridge Journal of Regions, Economy and Society, 8*(1), 61–77.

Holmes, N., & Berube, A. (2016, 14 January). *City and metropolitan inequality on the rise, driven by declining incomes*. Brookings Institution. Retrieved 3 July 2017, from www.brookings.edu/research/city-and-metropolitan-inequality-on-the-rise-driven-by-declining-incomes/.

Jacobs, J. (1969). *The economy of cities*. New York: Random House.

JP Morgan Chase Institute (2016). Consumption inequality: Where does your city rank? Spending by the top income quintile. Retrieved 7 July 2017, from www.jpmorganchase.com/corporate/institute/document/consumption-inequality010816.pdf.

Kitchin, R. (2014). The real-time city? Big data and smart urbanism. *GeoJournal, 79*(1), 1–14.

Kitchin, R. (2015). Networked, data-driven urbanism. *The Programmable City Working Paper 14.* http://dx.doi.org/10.2139/ssrn.2641802.

Kitchin, R., Lauriault, T. P., & McArdle, G. (2015). Knowing and governing cities through urban indicators, city benchmarking and real-time dashboards. *Regional Studies, Regional Science, 2*(1), 6–28.

Knudsen, B., Florida, R., Stolarick, K., & Gates, G. (2008). Density and creativity in U.S. regions. *Annals of the Association of American Geographers, 98*(2), 461–478.

Lai, F., Liu, C., Luo, R., Zhang, L., Ma, X., Bai, Y., … & Rozelle, S. (2014). The education of China's migrant children: The missing link in China's education system. *International Journal of Educational Development, 37*, 68–77.

Lee, N. (2011). Are innovative regions more unequal? Evidence from Europe. *Environment and Planning C: Government and Policy, 29*(1), 2–23.

Lee, N., & Rodríguez-Pose, A. (2013). Innovation and spatial inequality in Europe and USA. *Journal of Economic Geography, 13*(1), 1–22.

Lee, N., Sissons, P., & Jones, K. (2016). The geography of wage inequality in British cities. *Regional Studies, 50*(10), 1714–1727.

Lees, L., Shin, H. B., & López-Morales, E. (Eds.). (2015). *Global gentrifications: Uneven development and displacement.* Bristol: Policy Press.

Liu, X., Park, A., & Zhao, Y. (2010). Explaining rising returns to education in urban China in the 1990s. *IZA Discussion Paper, No. 4872.* Bonn: Institute for the Study of Labour.

Logan, J. R., Fang, Y., & Zhang, Z. (2009). Access to housing in urban China. *International Journal of Urban and Regional Research, 33*(4), 914–935.

McFarlane, C. (2011). The city as a machine for learning. *Transactions of the Institute of British Geographers, 36*(3), 360–376.

Malecki, E. J. (2010). Everywhere? The geography of knowledge. *Journal of Regional Science, 50*(1), 493–513.

Marvin, S., Luque-Ayala, A., & McFarlane, C. (Eds.). (2016). *Smart urbanism: Utopian vision or false dawn?* Abingdon: Routledge.

Meng, X. (2004). Economic restructuring and income inequality in urban China. *Review of Income and Wealth, 50*(3), 357–379.

Meng, X., Gregory, R., & Wang, Y. (2005). Poverty, inequality, and growth in urban China, 1986–2000. *Journal of Comparative Economics, 33*(4), 710–729.

Moffitt, R. A. (2015). The deserving poor, the family, and the US welfare system. *Demography, 52*(3), 729–749.

Molotch, H. (2014). *Against security: How we go wrong at airports, subways, and other sites of ambiguous danger.* Princeton, NJ: Princeton University Press.

Pan, L., Mukhopadhaya, P., & Li, J. (2016). City size and wage disparity in segmented labour market in China. *Australian Economic Papers, 55*(2), 128–148.

Park, A., & Wang, D. (2010). Migration and urban poverty and inequality in China. *China Economic Journal, 3*(1), 49–67.

Peck, J. (2012). Austerity urbanism: American cities under extreme economy. *City, 16*(6), 626–655.

Pew Research Center. (2016, 11 May). *America's shrinking middle class: A close look at changes within metropolitan areas.* Retrieved 3 July 2017, from www.pewsocialtrends. org/2016/05/11/americas-shrinking-middle-class-a-close-look-at-changes-within-metropolitan-areas/.

Quigley, J. M. (1998). Urban diversity and economic growth. *The Journal of Economic Perspectives, 12*(2), 127–138.

Rauch, J. E. (1993). Productivity gains from geographic concentration of human capital: Evidence from cities. *Journal of Urban Economics, 34*(3), 380–400.

Sassen, S. (1991). *The global city: New York, London, Tokyo*. Princeton, NJ: Princeton University Press.

Sassen, S. (2011). Talking back to your intelligent city. Retrieved 3 July 2017, from http://voices.mckinseyonsociety.com/talking-back-to-your-intelligent-city/.

Solinger, D. J. (2006). The creation of a new underclass in China and its implications. *Environment and Urbanization, 18*(1), 177–193.

Sommeiller, E., Price, M., & Wazeter, E. (2016, 16 June). Income inequality in the US by state, metropolitan area, and county. *Economic Policy Institute*.

Storper, M., & Venables, A. J. (2004). Buzz: Face-to-face contact and the urban economy. *Journal of Economic Geography, 4*(4), 351–370.

Volscho, T. W. (2007). Unions, government employment, and the political economy of income distribution in metropolitan areas. *Research in Social Stratification and Mobility, 25*(1), 1–12.

Whalley, J., & Xing, C. (2014). The regional distribution of skill premia in urban China: Implications for growth and inequality. *International Labour Review, 153*(3), 395–419.

Wheeler, C. H. (2005). Cities, skills, and inequality. *Growth and Change, 36*(3), 329–353.

Yankow, J. J. (2006). Why do cities pay more? An empirical examination of some competing theories of the urban wage premium. *Journal of Urban Economics, 60*(2), 139–161.

Zhang, J., Zhao, Y., Park, A., & Song, X. (2005). Economic returns to schooling in urban China, 1988 to 2001. *Journal of Comparative Economics, 33*(4), 730–752.

Part III

Emerging cultures in a post-political and post-urban world

15 Toward a new urban paradigm

Laura Burkhalter and Manuel Castells

Introduction

We live in a chronic urban crisis that affects the major metropolitan areas of the world, impacting at least 25% of the global population. In this chapter we argue that the kind of planning and governing practices that characterize the modern metropolis have become obsolete to confront this urban crisis. We explore alternative strategies that could open the way for a new urban paradigm for the 21st century.

Some of the ideas in this text originated in a presentation and paper we delivered at the 4th International Conference of the International Forum on Urbanism (IFoU), Amsterdam/Delft in 2009. The original paper was named "Beyond the Crisis: Towards a New Urban Paradigm."

The failure of the functional city

Urban planning methods of the last 75 years or so around the globe have been largely based on ideas defined by a group of modernist European men in the 1930s that very much reflected the consciousness and knowledge of the era. In essence, their approach boils down to the analogy that the city functions like a machine. In this analogy, it follows that the whole is made up of parts that can be dissected, separated, fixed, and reassembled in ways that would create the "Functional City."

It made rational sense in this line of thinking to divide different uses and aspects of the city into physically separated parts so that they may be controlled and directed better. And different governmental controlling agencies would be set into place to oversee these neatly separated functions of the city. In theory, when added up, all parts would be well controlled and directed and therefore in assembled form, create a perfectly "Functional City."

This concept was the foundation and the beginning of the widespread introduction of zoning regulations that very fundamentally have been shaping our built and social environment.

The exact expression of the "Functional City" has varied greatly from one culture and ideology to the next, but the fundamental analysis and mindset from which to implement planning strategies has been the same. Some ideologically contrasting, idiosyncratic examples for the "living" zones are well exemplified by the hugely expansive areas zoned for single family dwellings in post-war US metropolitan areas according to the "American Dream" ideology of the time; the massive living tower zones so emblematic of modern Asian metropolitan regions, especially China; the rectangular living blocks indicative of the Soviet era and the two-story townhouse-style living clusters typical of Western Europe.

The point is, the ideology that informed the ideal "function" for living in this example has been culturally distinct. But the principles of spatially separating the zones has been consistent in most post-World War II urban planning efforts around the globe.

It is noteworthy that totalitarian regimes throughout the world and on both ends of the post-World War II iron curtain have found great affinity toward this particular machine-like urban paradigm. In its very essence it serves to control, separate, and divide its parts (and its participants, namely its people) and structurally introduces a controlling, top-down hierarchical approach to urbanism into the very fabric and physiology of everyday life.

Separating living from working then universally meant the need for the daily commute, which brought with it the necessity for transportation and usually, quite quickly, its dark shadow, the inevitable congestion. Furthermore, it brought with it the cyclical desolation of entire zones. Work areas are abandoned at night and therefore feel scary and unsafe. Living zones are desolated during the day and feel isolated and dead. Some people, however, are inevitably left behind in those isolated dwelling units: the people who don't work and don't go to school. Mostly, those people have been old people, young children, and of course, in many cultures and times, the women. In postwar America the women who had been employed during World War II, often in highly technical fields that were previously reserved for men only, were now deployed again to make space in the workforce for the returning (male) veterans. The postwar propaganda of the full-time homemaker housewife took full force, and combined with the suburban American Dream setting, it secured an environment for the women and the nonworking left-behinds that was utterly isolating. Homemaking of the single-family houses became an energy- and resource-intensive endeavor and women became, once again, completely dependent on the male breadwinners. Despite the strong propaganda and the baby boom that resulted from the stay-at-home mom push, and the lack of societal acceptance of a female identity outside of being a full-time homemaker, eventually American women started asking for liberation and equality. It was clear that this postwar model of reality, this American Dream, did not work for everybody and had, since the beginning, left out huge parts of the population.

Over time, via civil rights movements and women's liberation movements, the LGBT rights movement and more, the socioeconomic realities and the values and ideas of our urbanized population have changed, yet the planning ideas that shape our urban realities have not.

Our zoning and planuse ordinances have basically remained unchanged since their postwar beginnings and continue to serve as the fundamental building block of today's city. This planning stagnation and incoherence with current reality is in large part responsible for the chronic urban crisis and fundamentally what we are addressing in this chapter.

We would like to point out that the urban crisis is present in recognizably similar form in each differing variation of the "Functional City," and although we are using the US model as our point of departure due to the fact that we are both based in Los Angeles, the principles presented in this chapter are applicable, with adaptation, to other variations.

What we are calling for is a fundamental revisit of the validity of those building blocks and the possibility that another type of city is possible.

A new paradigm

We propose that the city is concentrated life. It is the eco-system of millions of living beings. Thus it follows that the laws of physics and biology that apply to living organisms would apply to cities in self-similar ways. How could it be any different? When will we stop applying Newtonian physics to living systems and expect to design a desired, predictable outcome?

As long as our urban planning theories are still based on linear thinking and the Newtonian clockwork universe, or the "Functional City" we are regarding cities as a series of dead parts with a quantifiable mass index per unit that can be puzzled together to create some supposedly functional machine-like infrastructure that we now call a city. However, this theory completely missed the fact that what makes cities is not their dead body mass index (also known as bricks and mortar), but their living ecosystem of organisms (also known as humans, plants, animals, and microorganisms). We can look at any of the many Chinese ghost towns (in their home turf or one of their African "colonies") to recognize the inherent validity of this argument.

In practical terms, what that means is that if we regard the city as a living organism, an ecology of scale, then we approach the planning process completely differently.

If we want to grow a healthy ecosystem, we don't divide and dissect it. Because we will quickly find out that the parts will grow stale, sick, and eventually die.

Instead, we nurture it. We add beneficial ingredients to the ecosystem that create positive feedback loops and aid its intelligent self-organization. We look for catalysts that will help diversity and a peaceful symbiotic relationship between its parts. And very importantly, we observe. Without observation, the subtle changes that make a system thrive or retract will easily be missed. In this living ecology, we easily recognize the inherent participation and co-authorship of all its parts.

Fundamentally, the proposed urban paradigm puts life at its center

The organizing principle of urban "planning" (or better, urban "nurturing") then becomes life-affirming.

One might also name this paradigm a feminine urban paradigm. We would dare to say that ultimately, humans by and large, when given a true choice, feel better in life-affirming environments than stale, divided, and controlled environments.

Fear is the age-old mechanism of controlling and dividing people.

Community, freedom, interpersonal connectivity, and belonging are the antithesis of the fear-based urban model.

In a life-centric urban model, the aim is to make a city not just functional, but also lovable. Not in a formalistic way, but in a life-affirming way.

Neither physical nor nonphysical interventions need to necessarily fulfill a "function" in the old machine-analogy way of thinking. They can be there just for the sake of making life more happy, healthy, and joyful. For the sake of celebrating community and diversity and creating a sense of togetherness and belonging. For the sake of making the city lovable.

Again, we want to point out the difference between lovable and impressive. Totalitarian-style governance has always loved impressive boulevards and statues and large, open assembly plazas. Their purposes are to impose a sense of authority and power, to control and to divide spaces. The boulevards and plazas, even when public, lack any sense of intimacy.

Rarely do people fall in love with those cities, or at least those aspects of a city. What makes people fall in love with a city is the sense of community, the freedom of expression and choice, the immense diversity, the opportunities to thrive personally and collectively, to feel integrated and connected, the freedom of mobility and communication, the connective physical fabric, and, simply, the creative pulse, its energy. That is the fertile ground where new ideas and opportunities grow and thrive.

People-centered infrastructural possibilities

In our 2009 article we proposed a specific design integrating different models of transportation specifically focused around people. We would like to present it here again, as we still regard it as a crucial connective tissue for creating the new urban paradigm.

Because infrastructure is the most financially and bureaucratically daunting of tasks, it has generally been the least explored. The propositions outlined in this article therefore may seem radical or utopian even. The truth is that they are no more radical and arguably more doable than any of the past great infrastructural interventions, such as the building of freeways, train, and subway systems. It is to be understood that no feasibility studies of the following proposals have been done at this point in time and that these types of proposals could only come into

Figure 15.1 Proposed Hollywood bicycle highway.

existence if people and subsequently the politicians were to subscribe to the ideas on a massive scale.

Since mobility and connectivity are central to a healthy urban and economic ecosystem, looking at cities across the globe, we can see that the most miserably ineffective ones are the ones that rely on a single mode of transportation, usually the surface street catering to the automobile with the bus as its only alternative. Usually the cities that either exclusively or very heavily rely on surface street transportation tend to be the ones that have made little or no investments to make the surface streets safe for sharing by transportation modalities other than cars including motorcycles, bicycles, and pedestrians. Incidentally these mono-transportational cities have the most gridlocked streets, and therefore the idea of removing lanes from an oversaturated system of streets to provide space for alternate surface transportation modalities would mean to aggravate the already deficient situation even more and would most likely gain little support from people or politicians. In contrast, the cities that have at least two existing modalities, such as surface streets and a thorough subway or light rail systems already function exponentially better than their mono-transportation counterparts. Cities with dual systems are able to absorb higher urban densities without collapse and they provide residents with options that fit and include a more diverse range of social classes and personal circumstances. The higher urban density allows for people to live closer to work and the transportation options help people effectively avoid unnecessary financial and personal hardship over their mobility. This is a key factor in giving a city its competitive edge and providing its region with economic prosperity.

The infrastructural interventions we propose here are a mere extension of this line of reasoning. They are the creation of a multi-modal transportation network. This new network is to be superimposed over the existing infrastructure, so not to inflict major additional cuts through the city and stresses on the existing structures, yet to provide an array of new options of transportation modalities to the city dwellers. In other words, existing cuts through the city fabric (major roads, freeways, train tracks, storm drains, etc.) would now be utilized for multiple purposes, rather than the current monofunction, in a multi-tiered approach.

What is important about this proposal is that bicycles and similar low-impact modes of individual transport are given their fair share. This means more than the creation of bike paths, because the distances to be traveled in most large metro regions, even with increased density, are still considerable. Therefore bicycles need safe, pleasant bicycle freeways where no traffic lights are hindering their speed of travel. In some instances, such freeways could be created on the ground along existing rivers and storm drains that already carve a car-free space through a city. In few cities, it may be conceivable to close an entire thoroughfare to traffic permanently and designate it a bicycle freeway with under- and over- passes getting traffic from one side to the other. In most cases though, this would be unfeasible. Rivers and storm drains do exist in most cities, and even though they could not take care of an entire network, they could for relatively small investments cover some grounds with the potential of added beauty of the riparian landscape, that in most cities would have to be reestablished out of the existing concrete channels. As ideas of reusing water channels for pedestrian use have been explored by others already (see the LA river proposals as examples), we will not elaborate these proposals in further detail in this chapter but rather focus on and illustrate the multi-modal highway and freeway solutions that will, with the appropriate investment and planning, work for most cities in one form of adaptation or another.

In this proposal, the alternate modalities are to be superimposed over large thoroughfare streets and freeways by creating an upper-level street in a way to maximize the benefits and minimize the disadvantages of each mode. For example, the most pleasant modalities in terms of least noise and pollution and greatest esthetic value get the most privileged position, the top. These include bicycles, pedestrians, and any other fitting mode of transport. Below that, a suspended, monorail system connects the citizens with mass transit in places where subways are nonexistent and/or not feasible. Below that again still continues car and bus traffic as usual, although hopefully in revised forms of vessels that minimize pollution and noise. Clearly intelligent, high and low tech noise and pollution mitigation systems should be developed and used beyond the vegetation above and along the transportation-arteries.

The point of this multi-tiered, multi-modal transportation infrastructure is to elevate people to the top of the food chain, rather than the bottom. People and people-powered transportation means will now have an elevated, safe, esthetical, efficient, and panoramic parkway system to move around the city.

© by Laura Burkhalter 2009

Figure 15.2 Proposed downtown Los Angeles bicycle highway.

Figure 15.3 Underside of the proposed bicycle highway above the 101 Hollywood Freeway, Los Angeles.

Figure 15.4 Night view of proposed Wilshire corridor bicycle highway in Los Angeles, view of high-speed monorail and station in background.

The point of these superimposed structures is that in most cases, with a single approach often cheaper or more feasible than a tunneling a new subway system through an existing metropolis, multiple modes of sustainable transportation could be served beyond just mass transit. Also, the layering system makes it easy to transition from one mode to another at any given nodal point.

Moreover, these new bicycle highway structures will also serve as distributed public parks, with the bike paths lined by trees, softscape, and hardscape for relaxation, walking, and playing. The parkways will also lift real estate values along those busy thoroughfairs and freeways as people in tall office buildings usually lining those roads are now looking down at a park rather than noisy car traffic.

Buildings may also gain direct access to the elevated parkways via private catwalks. The building floors may change their importance, with the floor level at the parkway height becoming the major public and retail interface.

It is easy to discard or severely underestimate the potential number of cyclists who would choose this mode of transport for their daily commutes. The fact is that now in most megacities the percentage of cycling commuters is very small. But the opposing fact is that in cities where urban policies have made cycling attractive and safe, the number is huge. In Amsterdam for example, 30% of people use their bicycles for their daily commute and another 40% use the bicycle sometimes for commuting. In the same city slightly more trips are made every day by bicycle than by car. And to put it in perspective, Amsterdam is not blessed with perfect year-round weather, so these numbers could be even higher in the sunbelt cities of the world. In many other European cities bicycles make up 20% or more of the commuter trips, so Amsterdam is not so much an exception as it is an illustration of highly effective planning policies. China's cities on the other hand used to have an 80–90%+ share of bicycle commutes until the last three decades slowly deteriorated the safety and thus desirability of bicycle

Figure 15.5 Proposed Hollywood bicycle highway over the 101 Hollywood Freeway, Los Angeles.

commuting. At the same time, given China's recent interest in sustainable growth policies and its fearless approach to infrastructure projects, the People's Republic could be a prime candidate for introducing a network of bicycle freeways.

To all those that say bicycling is not a practical way to get to work, here are a few facts and a few solutions to alleviate the minor flaws of practicality.

- Bicycle freeways will allow for nonstop flow of cyclist traffic as opposed to bicycle paths on the ground that are subject to traffic lights. This will make bicycle commuting efficient and comparably fast. Average bicycle speed on road with no traffic signals is 15–25 mph depending on the person, but can be 30 mph for trained cyclists. This compares with and often outperforms the speed of freeway traffic during commuter hours. (In comparison the Metro Rapid Bus service on Wilshire Blvd in Los Angeles has an average daytime speed of 11.7 mph, with much slower average speeds during rush hours.)
- The elevated structures (super arteries) can be combined with surface bicycle paths (veins) and neighborhood roads (capillaries) for a complete network.
- The entry/exit points of the arteries will be lined with juice stands, outdoor restaurants, showers and spas, ice cream shops, bicycle repair shops and bicycle-on-demand stands, and major nodes in the transportation network will offer additional amenities to the people and larger areas also for people to gather, take a leisurely evening stroll, dine, shop, etc.
- Shower and spa houses may also offer a rent-a-closet service where people can store their work clothes to change into after a good workout and a shower on the way to the office or home. A cleaning service of workout and business clothes is an obvious extra. Basically, the needs of this new class of commuter, who now has to figure it all out on the fringes, will be serviced in creative and convenient ways which will make the commuting style even more attractive for a much wider array of people.
- Depending on the local climate, the bicycle freeways can be designed covered, partially covered, shaded, and naturally heated or cooled. In line with the ecological ideas outlined by this proposal, heating and cooling should be done by nature, in the form of radiant floor heating generated by solar water heaters on the roof above, or cooling via flowing water curtains and enhanced air ventilation, again powered by solar cells, wind turbines, etc. installed above/along the freeway. Even for climates without the need of temperature enhancement, shading or roof structures may consist of high-tech PV panels that function as a distributed solar power station and power the suspended rail below and the electric charging stations for the EV vehicles on the ground.
- Commuting on a bicycle will makes for happier, healthier, and more effective people. It will also make for a more productive workforce, as daily exercise will keep people healthy and all the endorphins released during

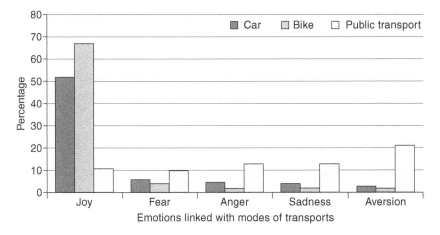

Figure 15.6 Emotions linked with modes of transport.
Source: image from the Dutch bicycle council from a presentation given by Hans Voerknecht.

exercise will leave them in a good mood. In opposition, commuting in traffic makes many people feel anxious, depressed, angry, or resigned and exhausted. If they can replace these negative emotions even for a couple of days a week with positive ones, it will make a big difference in people's personal lives. As studies show, cycling has been rated the highest in the emotion of "joy" in relation to modes of transport even while measuring in noncongested areas, and traffic jams were not considered in the survey.

• Bicycling and walking are the most inexpensive, the healthiest, and the most environmentally sustainable modes of transportation. They are therefore the best candidates to rejuvenate the people without burdening them economically while taking care of the environment.
• To complete the network of bicycle and pedestrian paths for a safe door-to-door connection, surface paths need to be created providing access to the cycle superstructures. Since only secondary neighborhood streets are affected by these feeder paths, most urban settings will be able to accommodate them. How this is done and where is idiosyncratic to the particular city and neighborhood, but here is an outline of a few possible planning methods on how to realize this:
    • Turn low traffic neighborhood streets into one-way streets and designate the other half of the road for pedestrian/bicycle use. To separate the two parts clearly and beautify the roads, trees and landscaping should be planted in the middle.
    • In neighborhoods that are being newly developed and areas where backyard setbacks are clear of structures, a pedestrian pathway can be placed along the backyard line, thus creating a parkway system between

people's yards, totally separate from car traffic. This would be a very idyllic path but in existing neighborhoods it would mean people have to give up a piece of their backyard to designate it for the common good.

- In neighborhoods with very wide, low traffic streets, such as some industrial park areas and suburban areas, the center of the street, at least 12′ in width, may be designated for pedestrian use. Again, this would need to be separated from car traffic via landscaping and trees. Being in the center, cyclists would not be interfered with and endangered by parking cars as they are in typical side-of-the-road bike paths. Plus, the double-width path separated by landscaping creates a better quality space than regular side-of-the-road paths.

- Remove parking lanes for narrower streets and turn the extra space, preferably in the center, into bike paths and make the parking spaces into neighborhood parking structures.

After publishing the above proposal of the "multi-modal transportation system" with bicycle freeways and high-speed monorail systems in our previous 2009 article, critics said that such ideas were utopian, unrealistic, and not economically sound. Eight years later, we would argue that the critics lacked the imagination to embrace a radically different, people-centric approach to infrastructure building. In this time period, proposals in some cases more "utopian" than ours, are in the process of being actualized.

Infrastructure in our modern history, and for the most part, in our human history, has served a direct "functional" purpose. Whether it is to transport goods, move armies or human workforces from point A to point B, there seemed to be a direct return on the inevitably large investment. A linear, above-ground pedestrian parkway system and bicycle freeway, in some sense still serves a very functional purpose. Many people would arguably choose to move from point A to point B by bike when given a safe, panoramic, and practical means to do so, which means less traffic and congestion on the regular roads, more health and wellness for the citizens, etc. But since there is no highly funded bicycle industry lobbying for it, the argument easily gets lost.

However, in June 2014 Copenhagen opened the first elevated bicycle highway to the public and Northwestern Germany is in process of building a 100 km-long bicycle freeway through the region.

The Copenhagen–Albertslund route is the first of a planned network that when completed will comprise 28 Cycle Super Highways, covering a total of 500 km. The network will increase the number of cycle lanes in Greater Copenhagen by 15% and is predicted to reduce public expenditure by €40.3 million annually thanks to improved health (source: "The Official Website of Denmark.")

Also, Minneapolis has introduced a bicycle freeway and Los Angeles is finally realizing a continuous bike highway along the LA River while re-introducing natural habitat and biodiversity into sections of the river that were concreted in and chain-linked off for decades. New York opened its elevated linear park, the "Highline" in sections since 2009 and has proven not only its lovability but also its high economic success for the adjacent area. Also, Sir Norman Foster in 2014 unveiled renderings for a bicycle highway system through London quite similar to the ones proposed above.

On the suspended monorail end, the first Hyperloop pod prototype just took levitation in October 2016. The Hyperloop, a SpaceX/Elon Musk pet project, aims to create futuristic high-speed transportation pods that travel through low-pressure vacuum tubes, mostly in an above-ground superstructure. Combining the Hyperloop with the bicycle freeway/linear park superstructure seems more feasible now than ever.

Lastly, the spread of electric vehicles has started to grow exponentially in the last few years, and with it, the charging infrastructure in metropolitan areas, which has made it a practical, economic, and desirable alternative to the gasoline car for more and more people.

The fact is, times are changing at exponential rates.

Larry Page, co-founder of Google, reflected on the reason even very large businesses fail at increasing speed, and concluded "because they missed the future."

We either learn and adopt and evolve in our thinking as well as our building and governing of physical and shared environment, or we too, collectively, miss the future and head toward a steady, slow, and probably at times implosive decline of potential for our mostly urbanized human family.

The reality is, our recurrent urban crisis is just that. The slow, steady decline of potential.

Ultimately, what is functional depends on the definition of functionality and on the eye of the beholder. If the function is to support a life-affirming urban environment, then rooftop vegetable gardens and chicken coops, urban farm cooperatives and farmers' markets, pedestrian streets and bicycle freeways, and shared economical models all make a lot of "functional" sense.

We propose it is time to turn this around and be open to radically new ways of dwelling, moving, working, learning, earning, growing, evolving, and playing together.

The creative city

As the advances in automation keep leaping forward, it is clear that in the foreseeable future, a large number of today's jobs throughout the global workforce will be obsolete. We do not here within the scope of this chapter try to predict the socioeconomic and political impact such a shift will have on our urbanized environments. However, we do suggest that the creative city, will, without a doubt, suffer the least amount of growing pain and setbacks and offer the most appeal and opportunities during and post shift. The fact is that people need to learn how to reinvent themselves and their realities in increasing numbers and at increasing speed. There are environments that nurture the embrace of the unknown and environments that stifle it.

It is almost superfluous to state that the top-down, hierarchic, controlling, and fear-based environments do not foster creative thinking. But a more subtle suffocator of creativity is connected to affordability, or lack thereof. It is well documented that many of the most affordable cities attract and foster the most creative urban environments. It is also well documented that a vibrant, creative urban beat attracts further "creative capital" that eventually attracts global investment capital and, at some point, erodes affordability.

For people to be creative they cannot be overly burdened by excessive costs of living, health compromises, or lengthy commuting time required for basic survival in a particular city. When life becomes too unaffordable and/or commuting/transportation too time consuming due to congestion and inefficiency or too risky due to environmental hazards or crime, the city's creative capital quickly begins to decline. Creativity on a large scale is possible when the cost of life is in a good balance with the economic potential of its individuals.

In order for creativity to exist, people have to charter unknown territories and take risks. Risks inevitably bring a high chance of failure with them, and when a system (be it on an individual level or a macro/urban scale) is overburdened, there is no space for error as any failure would mean the eminent collapse of the system. Often, creatives hold a day job to keep a roof over their head and work the rest of the time on their creative endeavors. However, when that day job no longer pays the bills, the creative endeavor dies in the name of getting a second job to supplement basic survival needs. Effectively, this puts the system (micro or macro) into survival mode and creative thinking is greatly diminished, if not killed.

Los Angeles, for example, has risen out of its severe real estate and financial crisis since the time of writing the previous article on the theme, into another real estate bubble. However, this does not mean it has recovered from its urban crisis. In fact, the city has become more unaffordable than ever, with housing prices for both renting and ownership well above a level that gives the middle class access to reasonable choices. And although the city is putting some effort into building more "affordable housing units," it is only a drop in the bucket. The fact is that a lot of creative capital, including many creative individuals, companies, and startups are leaving the city, while global capital is buying up the city at a massive scale.

The question is whether the affordability-creativity-popularity-unaffordability-creative decline cycle is inevitable. To some extent, it might be. But arguably, a framework of a sharing economy, combined with a densification and symbiotic layering of spatial occupation and a continuous, holistic, intelligent reinvestment into the creative social, natural, and physical environment may very well help foster a lasting positive feedback loop in which the creative decay is not an inevitable part of the cycle.

The reality is, the creative decline happens when the city has less to offer than the energy/effort it takes to create a life there. In an open, creative, self-organizing intelligent system, that pivotal point is not inherently necessary and, by attentive observation and necessary action and fine-tuning, also reversible.

The sharing economy

Contemporary society has been on a steady path of alienation and fragmentation, and the spatial policies in place today are enforcing that it will continue on this course.

There is an acute need for a new dwelling typology associated with the culture and functions of the 21st century city. In our perspective, to define new dwelling forms we need to define new social forms, because dwellings serve as people's habitat. As it is now, people have to fit in rigid, preexisting dwelling forms that are either the expression of obsolete forms of living or, more often, the product of speculative calculations that force people to fit in whatever dwelling forms are most profitable for the developers and easier to control for the bureaucrats. New dwelling forms may require the reengagement and reinvention of forms of living based on sharing resources.

Planning policies today are mainly concerned about the size of houses and sizes of lots and front and side yards but not at all at the performance of a house. Los Angeles, for example, adopted the anti-mansionization law "reducing the ratio of square feet to lot size, and therefore reducing the opportunity of supersizing a single family home."

The question is whether the ratio of lot size to house size is the real problem or whether the underlying problem is much deeper. We argue that the biggest problems of "supersized single family homes" is, on the one hand, the unsustainable construction practices developing these homes, and on the other, the very concept of "single family," a shrinking entity in our time. The fact is that large houses make for great places for communal living. Of course these houses may have different features than the standard supersize mansion, and to perform well and truly respect the idea of shared resources, they have to be built sustainably and should provide their own energy, as well as a garden for outdoor enjoyment and food growing. But a large, completely sustainably built house with a just as large roof garden on a not so large lot, occupied by a sizable number of people who may share resources beyond the house, will add up to a much smaller carbon footprint per person than a small house on a large lot occupied by only two people who spend most of their time at work or commuting in traffic. It is time for the planners to start tackling deeper issues of landuse rather than finding quick fixes that only address the tip of the iceberg.

With people today involved in a dense network of activities, sharing home labor and space actually can liberate one from many time-consuming tasks and financial stresses.

In addition to sharing a living space, there are many types of resources that can be successfully shared. They may include anything from real estate, finances and investments, to services of all kinds, gardening and food growing, cooking and meals, clothes, office spaces and equipment, transportation, child care, education, elderly care, energy as well as social and emotional matters such as giving each other company, sharing laughter and sorrow, protests and celebrations.

Many of these forms of sharing resources are common practice already and, for the most part, these forms of communal association don't require a change in spatial policies. Nevertheless they would greatly benefit from a change. Fragmented space tends to create a fragmented social structure. Thus we can reverse the process, creating by design more cohesive spatial patterns that will help amalgamate and solidify social structures.

We would like to denote at this moment that since the writing of our last article on the theme, there have been a few very insightful developments in the arena of the sharing economy:

The founding and rapid and seemingly irreversible success of Uber and Airbnb (and the likes) have shown us in very clear and tangible terms that the sharing economy is not a marginalized potential between a few outsiders, but a solution on a mass scale. The success of these sharing platforms illustrates the impact that small shifts can have, when scaled up. And for the purpose of this chapter, we use the term "sharing and shared" even though services and payments are exchanged. Because what we are talking about in an economy of sharing is the sharing of private resources, in many cases in exchange for a fee, but not always.

The electric vehicle (EV) driver community for example has created a subculture in which people are happy to help each other out often for no charge as they are believers in the greater good that gasoline-free vehicles can bring to the world. Many members of the community go out of their way and support other participants in this movement by providing their personal outlets in their private driveway to other EV drivers at no charge and even when the owners aren't present, and they let drivers know of the availability of their outlet through an EV charger community app.

Eight years ago it would have seemed unimaginable to most that non-professional, part-time drivers, who are strangers, would give you rides in their personal cars anytime, anywhere. Yet it turns out that there is more trust in our metropolitan environment amongst strangers than previously suspected. In fact, Uber, Lyft, and the likes have impacted circulation patterns and commuting habits in just a few years on a massive scale. Even in spreadout cities like Los Angeles people are starting to not own cars out of choice because they no longer depend on them the way they used to. Also, it has added millions of part-time jobs for people who need flexible schedules, often artists, students, and creatives, while giving both the riders and the drivers diverse cultural exposures and interpersonal connections to a vast cross-section of people. We realize that some of these points that make these ridesharing platform great today will be obsolete again tomorrow when automation takes place, like the self-driven car fleet Uber intends to use in the future.

On the short-term housesharing front, Airbnb and the likes have given many people a chance to make an unaffordable life more affordable by hosting traveling strangers in their own home. Again, it would have been hard to imagine the widespread acceptance of people willing to trust and host strangers in their own home, and yet the concept has spread like wildfire. In many cases people establish personal connections between hosts and guests, sometimes even creating lasting friendships. The downfall of the vacation rental platforms have been their own huge economic success. The large income potential for people doing vacation rental has caused many people to start full-time renting out entire dwellings, thus aggravating the affordability problem in desirable neighborhoods rather than solving it. Some cities are now restricting the vacation rental practice to housesharing only to avoid its undesirable shadow. As with all new things, there will be some problems that need to be addressed and some kinks to be ironed out in order to create the most beneficial, symbiotic sharing economy for all the constituents affected.

As much as these new platforms are not flawless or have solved our traffic or housing problems, they have proven the viability of sharing resources and creating a culture of interpersonal trust within the metropolitan context.

Also, these platforms have shown that even when laws and regulations are not set up in favor of a sharing economy, when there is massive economic pressure and widespread public acceptance of a new concept, the laws and regulations will eventually yield to the will of the constituents.

In conclusion, sharing private resources, such as space, goods, time, knowledge, skills, money, meals, care, education, and transportation can make life easier and less resource depleting to both the individual and the collective and create distributed and flexible employment opportunities for a great number of people. Thanks to the success of these share-for-fee platforms described above, we expect a lot of future development in the urban sharing economy in the years to come.

Urban self-reliance: from shopping malls to urban farming

It is often overlooked that access to food is still the primary concern of everyday life. And we believe insufficient attention is paid to the fact that chemically grown/processed and genetically modified food is associated with a whole range of illnesses, from cancer to cardiovascular diseases, and from obesity to migraines. Yet, even when people are aware of the dangers of what amounts to be little more than poisoned food, they have few practical alternatives, particularly if their budget does not allow them to buy high priced organic produce. So, growing their own food is fast becoming a way to create a healthy lifestyle at a more affordable budget. Furthermore, beyond the individual benefits, there are extraordinary payoffs for the environment and for the economy. Increasing the share of agricultural land in a congested metropolis sets the path for a balanced landuse pattern that benefits the proper functioning of the local eco-system. Reducing the amount of industrial food that has to be manufactured, conserved, transported (often from the other side of the world), stored, and distributed would represent a major contribution to the fight against global warming and to energy conservation. Eating your own food and making the physical effort necessary to plant it, cultivate, and harvest it, may yield extraordinary benefits in terms of preventive healthcare, thus contribute to alleviate the health costs that have reached an unsustainable level because the emphasis has been placed on machines, pills, and corporate hospitals geared toward the sophisticated care of serious illnesses, often when it is too late. Furthermore, there is not much that so effectively brings people together and also connects people to nature as communal food growing and then the related preparation and sharing of meals.

Urban farming on a scale large enough to make a difference in the city and in society is not just a matter of individual vegetable gardens. It is a communal venture. While it is commendable that people use their own balconies, window sills, and front and back yards to grow vegetables rather than tending an immaculate lawn at great cost of energy, pollution, and time, urban farming requires dedicating small tracts of land throughout the metropolis for cooperatives of part-time or full-time farmers, with proper financing and skills. There is an abundance of vacant land in most metropolitan areas. In most cases this relates to speculative schemes, as this is land waiting to be entitled for residential and commercial uses, when the conditions are matured for developers, and when they are able to put pressure on the planning agencies to spur new growth. With sufficient political will, and a new comprehensive planning strategy, numerous tracts of idle land, in different points of the metropolis, can be converted to urban farms. Some of these tracts should be permanent in nature. Others can be specifically set up as nomadic urban farms. In average, it takes a larger project in the US metropolitan areas between 3 and 10 years to be fully entitled and permitted and ready for construction. This means, these idle pieces of land end up creating a negative impact on their environment. Usually they're fenced in and littered with garbage. To the community they are damaging because they attract garbage dumping and criminal activities; they're dark at night and unsightly during the day and make the street less safe. To the developers, they represent a costly liability, as they require maintenance, taxes, and sometimes create legal problems due to illegal activities going on at the properties by gangs, etc. The nomadic urban farm strategy thus creates a win-win situation for everyone: The community receives, for a number of years, an urban farm and associated vegetable stand with the super-local produce harvested on site, while enjoying a safer, cleaner street and a place to meet neighbors and potential jobs. The developer is relieved of the headache and expenses associated with dealing with criminal activity and cleaning up an illegal trash dump; the nomadic farmer cooperative receives a rent-free plot of land in exchange for maintenance in the middle of their consumer market, removing the need for storage and transportation of the harvested goods. Although not without some limitations, growing vegetables and even fruit trees and vines in movable containers is entirely manageable and in many ways even beneficial so that the soil can be carefully managed and kept clean of environmental hazardous substances that may be found on many vacant urban lots.

The urban farming strategy could in fact go beyond self-consumption. If the harvest of permanent and nomadic urban farming and individual vegetable gardens can amount to even a fraction of total food consumption of a city, it would mark a great deal of ecological progress. Plus, urban farms may generate jobs and revenues by providing organic food to nearby households, to local restaurants, and even to an extended area, using home delivery and multiplying the locations of farmers' markets.

The urban farms may be accompanied by urban villages housing the farmers and volunteers as well as produce stores, restaurants, and other commercial activates.

Thus, the metropolis could become dotted with numerous farms and villages that coexist with the manufacturing and services functions of the city. The diversity of uses allows for the metropolis to adapt to the changing conditions of the market and society, following the evolution of people's needs and desires.

People-centered landuse patterns

As discussed in the beginning of this chapter, we build cities today based on governing laws and ideas that were put in place often close to a century ago. In most places, such governing laws have been modified incrementally, yet minimally. However, the laws have not been fundamentally examined for their validity and their reflection of today's needs and values. It was not within the capacity of the founding fathers of modern city planning laws to predict the social and technological advances nor the accelerated rate at which some of those advances are happening. When the governing laws were originally created, they were created to address current problems of the time with the tools and understanding they had at that time. It goes without saying that they did not yet have 70 years (+) of empirical data to show what the results of such governing laws would be.

Today, those values reflected in those landuse laws don't represent the majority of the metropolitan constituent's views, lifestyle, or needs. In fact they are to many, arguably a majority, in direct contrast with their actual values and beliefs.

It has been accepted that technology changes constantly, yet the physical environment of the city and its functionality essentially stays constant. However, it isn't the nature of the city to be the way it is. It is the nature of the governing laws, interacting with its constituents that shape the "nature" of the city.

Therefore, the city could be completely different with different governing laws and different interactions by the city's constituents.

We propose that the fundamental building blocks of 20th century urban planning be reexamined for their intent, purpose, and their actual measurable track record of results.

We don't suggest deregulation. As shown by many metropolitan cities in parts of the world where there have been no laws to regulate the development of private properties, no space or investment is set aside for the common good, thus no sidewalks are built and little public infrastructure and pedestrian safety exists. What we suggest is a framework of regulations that can be modified as needed, that is transparent, inherently flexible, and self-intelligent, meaning that it has mechanisms in place that keep adding collected data to the information matrix so that better decisions and conclusions can be made based on multidisciplinary empirical data.

In that spirit, in our previous article, we enumerated the following changes in landuse patterns as part of the Urban Rescue Plan "Planning and Landuse Policies for Urban Quality of Life" that we still consider valuable:

1   Zoning laws are turned into performance guidelines. This eliminates restrictions on landuse as long as the established performance requirements are fulfilled as well as existing safety building standards. Performance guidelines may be based on the following criteria:
    • Ecological performance/sustainability
    • Social quality to the local community
    • Economic performance/employment opportunity
    • Creative value

Replacing zoning laws with performance guidelines would singlehandedly address many of our current urban problems, especially in North American cities. It could transform a monotonous suburban landscape into vibrant, thriving communities. It would turn every community into mixed use, not from a top-down master planned approach of apartment living above a shopping mall, but in a spontaneous, diverse, and grassroots way. The fact that one can now open a business anywhere as long as the performance criteria are respected means the beginning of a new chapter of community entrepreneurism creating flourishing local economies based on real added values. This gradual transformation would automatically tailor itself to each and every community and give places a unique identity rather than the master planned or zoned "one size fits all" solutions currently making up our urban fabric.

Moreover, it would no longer exempt factories and polluting industries from performance standards. Regardless of the use of a building, performance standards would have to be met.

The points 2–5 specifically address the landuse patterns changes of the typical US cities:

2   Front yard and side yard setbacks are eliminated. (Seismic separation may be required between structures.) Natural light and natural ventilation and emergency access must be provided for each structure. Each structure is required to provide a certain amount of accessible and usable garden space that may be located anywhere within, around, or above the building for each dwelling unit.
3   The minimum lot size is eliminated.
4   The legal process to subdivide and join land is freed from its current red tape procedures.

These three points together would have a fundamental impact on the urban fabric. Under these new rules, each property owner could decide to sell portions of her property. For example two neighbors may agree to sell their adjacent side yards and partial front yards to a new owner by creating a new property out of these strips of land. The new lot may be quite narrow, but wide enough for the new owner to build an infill structure. Let us look at the benefits from various perspectives.

Economic benefits: By selling off a portion of their property both existing owners get a considerable financial relief. It also creates opportunities and economic accessibility for new ownership as small, more affordable parcels would be available on the market. Ecological benefits: The denser communities with a mixed use program ensure that a good portion of the local residences can also work in the immediate community, thus reducing transportation needs and associated pollution and traffic gridlock. Denser neighborhoods allow for smaller city footprints and more opportunities for open space. Furthermore, small infill lots make for smaller structures which can help reduce carbon footprints and pollution associated with property maintenance. Removing the status quo of the front lawn means reducing very considerable amounts of toxins currently polluting our soil and water with pesticides, herbicides, and fertilizers, reducing the wasteful water use as well as the loud and highly polluting lawn mowers and leaf blowers. Instead, yards would be encouraged to include vegetable gardens and compost and would be allowed to include small chicken coops, etc. as outlined by the performance requirements. Social benefits: The new spatial density allows for a much more integrated social structure. For one it makes it feasible for extended family and friends to be neighbors and thus attend to each other's needs. This means taking care of each other's children, cooking for each other, and generally more time to exchange and socialize. The many new community businesses, such as community cafes and mini restaurants, daycare centers, etc. create places for people to meet and commune and give people a sense of belonging. Spatial benefits: The infill projects will piece by piece transform the visual disconnect of the suburban street face by providing the visual glue between the parts. Eventually the street face will gain continuity within diversity of expression and grow suburban monotony into attractive urban villages.

5   Onsite parking requirements are eliminated and made voluntary (currently in US metropolitan areas every single family home must provide a garage for at least two cars). Loading zones and offsite designated parking facilities are established instead.
6   Every neighborhood designates at least one street as a pedestrian zone.

This is one of the simplest surefire ways to create a vibrant neighborly feel and a long-term, local economic boost as has been shown in every living example of a pedestrian zone. Moreover, it adds significant quality of life to the neighborhood. The pedestrian zone becomes the vital core of the neighborhood, hosting weekly farmers' markets and other occasional street fairs and festivities. The businesses along the pedestrian street, especially restaurants, cafes, and retail, will have an instant and permanent boost in business and all the residences in the surrounding area will see an increase in property value. This is an easy, inexpensive, and permanent economic stimulus that can be applied anywhere.

7   Restore existing rivers, storm drains and seasonal runoffs into connective urban parks.

Most cities in the US and across the world have a sizeable number of fenced off and concrete encased water channels that represent a natural and financial opportunity to be uncovered. Every one of these cuts through the city should become part of the connective tissue rather than a divide and include bicycle paths and nature walks that connect and supplement the network of bike paths as outlined in the multi-modal transportation section. These linear parks will physically and psychologically tie neighborhoods together, bring natural resources to the communities, create sanctuaries for natural habitat, and, with today's improved understanding of flood control, keep adjacent neighborhoods safe.

8   Easy processing of licenses to operate small, homecooked food and beverage service businesses. This point would create a whole new entrepreneurial class of small-scale food businesses, giving people of all backgrounds economic opportunities. It would also create access for citizens to many convenient, healthy, homecooked food choices within walking distance from their house and work. It would create a real competition with fast food chains, which, under the performance guidelines, would clearly have to clean up their act to open new businesses and would get taxed after a certain grace period if they kept existing facilities running in the current depleting manner, thus disadvantaging such unsustainable operations economically. (Currently the exact opposite is the case.)

Since zoning laws have been replaced with performance standards, small-scale homecooked food businesses could be located anywhere, from within private homes to roof tops, courtyards to front yards, thus creating lively neighborhoods and social places for exchange and to meet neighbors. It would also give the opportunity for food establishments to be located in attractive areas and have outdoor seating away from busy through streets, which, in cities across the US are currently the only places zoned for commercial/restaurant use. In essence it would create nicer places to eat on a daily basis, with more, better and healthier choices of food and in closer vicinity to the users.

9   Percentage of property sales tax of each parcel (including portions of previous parcels), as well as a percentage of business tax of any business goes directly into the local community fund that is 100% managed by the local community and serves as a direct reinvestment into the neighborhood and the people. This would give the local community a budget and a voice for self-determination. Whether it's to plant trees, create a community center, a playground, or improve a neighborhood parking structure, or introduce new youth programs that help kids stay out of trouble and keep the neighborhood safe, the priorities of each community would be implemented in a direct fashion and without the financial waste of top-down bureaucracy. The selected improvement project would also reinvest into the local community by employing locals to direct and construct the projects whenever possible. This then creates a positive feedback loop with the area getting more valuable, thus attracting more businesses and residents and then again collecting more money to reinvest into the community. And since every

community would work this way, every community would have the opportunity for positive feedback loops leading to true economic prosperity based on real values.

To conclude this part, we want to point out the intrinsic interrelationship of density and a multi-modal transportation system. One cannot function without the other. A very low-density suburban model has an extraordinary amount of area designated for streets. Therefore, at an unsustainably high economic and environmental cost, it enables cars to move around relatively freely. With added density comes the inevitable traffic congestion. Out of this dilemma all metro regions eventually suffer from the congestion symptoms. Despite low-density zoning, metro regions over time grow tighter than they were originally designed for, with very few exceptions. Instead of fighting this inevitable trend of densification, our suggestion is to embrace it and design for it. On the flip side multi-modal transportation requires manageable distances for many of its modes. Manageable distances again require added density. This does not mean a necessity for verticality, simply a necessity for using space wisely, maximizing its qualities and creating what we call densified urban villages.

Urban intelligence gathering

Intelligence gathering has long been one of the driving economic forces online. Its power has been greatly recognized in the arena of commercialism and has greatly improved the target marketing for selling you stuff. However, its potential for generating emergent and synergetic models of urban patterns has not been used on a significant scale. With all the technology available today, we should be able to access anonymous empirical data that measure the patterns and trends of pedestrian and bicycle traffic, vehicular traffic and occupancy, mass transportation usage, traffic safety and personal safety (both statistical and subjectively perceived safety), communication, interpersonal connectivity, trust, health (both personal and environmental), food options, educational options, real estate and rental values, typology and sizes of businesses, etc. so we may start to truly understand the links between these different patterns and can start making informed decisions on effectively nurturing the complex, living system that makes up our urban environment.

It is important to more holistically understand the interconnected, true effects of new entities and trends like new businesses, transportation hubs, parks, density increases, commercial and educational centers, etc. on their immediate and larger surroundings so communities may learn to introduce specific growth catalysts that attempt to bring about their desired progression of trends.

To truly enable the idea of intelligent, informed urban growth, regulations need to be intention based and inherently adaptive and flexible, so that they continue to evolve alongside the growing empirical data and intelligence as well as the constituents' changing needs and demands.

Lastly, the constituents of a community need to feel directly represented in those governing laws, thus allowing different communities to express themselves, by all means, differently within the context of their physical and organizational environment. Only by developing contrasting models and a local sense of self-determination can we evaluate the successes of different models and catalysts and allow the freedom of choice for people with different preferences to live in different environments, thus creating a truly vibrant and multi-dimensional polycentric city.

Conclusion

What we aim to do here is to propose that there are other ways, in fact a myriad of other ways, in which humans may co-inhabit in geographic vicinity creating a certain density and size, considered a metropolitan region or city.

We suggest thus, that it is time to look for the sand under the pavement and reevaluate and re-system-design patterns of human co-habitation and interaction that are flexible to change, open to creativity, are based on evolving intelligence and continuously growing empirical data, and created by and for humans and living systems in holistic, life-affirming ways. We propose considering the human needs for togetherness and interpersonal connections, creativity and diverse expression, as well as belonging to the earth and integrally participating in the planetary ecosystem at large, the need for peacefulness and tranquil retreat, health and wellness, as well as rituals and celebrations, sounds, creative chaos, and rebellious forces that are as necessary to the cycle of life as fire is.

We propose, that in this new urban paradigm, there is ample space for it all. And that through the means of community-based self-determination and city-wide connective, people-centric infrastructure and parks, the expressions of the polycentric city can become as pluralistic, creative, and diverse as life itself.

16 Buying pieces of cities?

Saskia Sassen

Cities are complex entities. Yet in today's world they risk being shaped by a few very basic logics; this fact is often camouflaged, or not easy to see, due to the enormously diverse visual and social orders of cities. Among these rising logics, two stand out: aggressive profit seeking and indifference to the environment. Their effects range from empowerment of the global corporation to enfeeblement of local democracy, and from the proliferation of megaprojects to the erasure of streets, squares, and open-air markets.

This unsettling of older urban formats also means that today empirical research and conceptual recoding must happen together – they need each other.[1] Empirically a phenomenon may look urban but may in fact be merely a massive complex of privately owned buildings and privately owned "streets." It signals that the visual markers of an earlier era – such as the notion that if it is densely built it must be a city – are far less useful today to identify a city. We need other markers to understand what is urbanity in our epoch.

Here I will focus on one particular trend that has emerged with great force and a capacity to privatize cities and displace large numbers of workers and enterprises that may long have lived and operated in these cities. It is the large-scale buying of buildings by national and foreign private and corporate entities, and their transformation mostly into high-end expensive properties. Data on major acquisitions in the top hundred cities globally (as ranked by the value of such acquisitions) shows such acquisitions reached well over $1 trillion in 2015; this figure includes only properties with a minimum price of $5 million, and includes many properties with a far higher value than that.[2] These numbers exclude investment in new developments and site development, both also the object of considerable national and foreign investment.

My organizing question is what this means for cities and the notion of urbanity. In what follows I posit that much of this built density does not quite contribute to the urbanity of a city center. Indeed, at its most extreme, there is a de-urbanizing of the city. It also tempts me to ask somewhat provocative questions. Might urbanity be shifting partly to the neighborhoods – places often seen as parochial and homogeneous? And is the center of the city becoming de-urbanized even as it raises its density? In short, would the dense but de-urbanized urban core actually be the non-city? That is to say, what used to mark the limits or edge of the city is now at its center, so that entering that corporate center means exiting the city? (Sassen, 1991, ch. 7; Sassen, 2016).

The specifics of the current period

Already in my earlier work on the global city I examined such acquisitions (Sassen, 1991). But I detect a difference between that earlier phase and the current one. In that earlier period the utility function was very high. For instance, it made enormous practical sense for non-European, and even European firms to locate in the financial center of London because it was a great platform to access the riches of the rest of Europe.

The current phase of buying, which took off a few years after the 2008 financial crisis, is characterized by a weak utility function: many of these buildings are under-utilized, and it looks like the buyers are storing their capital for some new type of future possibility. The question, then, is whether this buying might point to a new type of project: the corporate buying of significant stretches of urban land (Sassen, 2014, 2016).

Thus this massive foreign and national corporate buying of urban buildings and urban land that took off after the 2008 crisis signals an emergent new phase in major cities. And the overall levels of investment keep rising, even if some cities may see a decline in these levels. Taking just the two most recent years, from mid-2013 to mid-2014, corporate buying of existing properties reached over $600 billion in the top 100 recipient cities, and, as already mentioned, over a trillion from mid-2014 to mid-2015 (Cushman & Wakefield, 2016; Sassen, 2015b). This figure includes only major acquisitions (e.g., $5 million dollars in the case of New York City) and it excludes large amounts spent on the buying of urban land for site development.[3]

At the same time, in a growing number of countries there have been massive foreclosures on low and modest income households, especially in the US, but also in countries such as Hungary and Germany; one result has been an abundance of empty urban land.[4]

The current scale of acquisitions points to a systematic transformation in the pattern of ownership in cities. And this has deep and significant implications on equity, democracy, and rights. It is particularly so because what was small and/ or public is becoming large and private, even if often with local government support. Some of the most noxious developments of "site assembly" happen when one or two whole city blocks are bought by a single owner, either local or foreign, and the city authorities cave in to their requirements. These often involve elimination of streets, squares, public buildings, and such, as well as a sort of wall-like enclosure, often in the name of enhanced security.

This privatizes and de-urbanizes city space. Such a proliferating urban gigantism is strengthened and enabled by the privatizations and deregulations that took off in the 1990s across much of the world, and have continued since then with only a few interruptions. The overall effect has been a reduction in public buildings and an escalation in the amount of ownership by large, mostly powerful private enterprises. This brings with it a reduction in the texture and scale of spaces previously accessible to the public – a space that was more than just a bunch of public buildings. Where before there was a government office building handling the regulations and oversight of this or that public economic sector, now there might be a corporate headquarters, a luxury apartment building, or a mall.

Next I examine these trends and then begin to conceptualize what we can think of as the making of a new urban landscape, which goes well beyond the notion of a new visual order. It is also partly a new ownership and control order as well as a frontier zone where the powerless and the powerful actually get to have an encounter.

An emergent new phase in major cities?

Why does this type of development matter? Are not cities about density and built-up terrain? I will argue that not all densities are the same, and that some actually de-urbanize the city by eliminating urban tissue (little streets and squares, mixed small-scale uses, etc.) and turning whole sections of a city into basically office enclaves and luxury apartment towers. Importantly, cities are the spaces where those without power get to make a history and a culture, thereby making their powerlessness complex. We will lose this type of making that has given our cities their cosmopolitanism if the current large-scale buying continues.

We might ask, What is a city if it cannot be simply identified by its density of built environments? But London, for instance, has long been home to one of the leading financial centers in the world, yet it has low density.[5] Density matters but it is increasingly a failing indicator of urbanity. A large privately owned and controlled office park is a dense environment, but it is not marked by urbanity. In that regard, I argue that the key is that a city is a complex but incomplete system: in this mix lies the capacity of cities (across histories and geographies) to outlive far more powerful but fully formalized systems (from large corporations to national governments). London, Beijing, Cairo, New York, Johannesburg, Bangkok, to mention just a few, have all outlived multiple types of rulers and of firms.

Further, in this mix of complexity and incompleteness also lies the possibility for those without power to be able to assert "we are here," "this is also our city." Or, as the legendary statement by the fighting poor in Latin American cities puts it, "estamos presentes" – "We are present, we are not asking for money, we are just letting you know that this is also our city." It is in cities to a large extent where the powerless have left their imprint – cultural, economic, social – even if mostly in their neighborhoods; eventually each one of these imprints can spread to a vaster urban zone as an "ethnic" something – food, music, therapies, and more. And with time, some of this enters the more abstract space of cosmopolitanism, even it gets dressed in fancier clothing and there is an erasure of the origins in the neighborhood subcultures (see Sassen, 2013).

None of this can happen in an office park, no matter its density; these are privately controlled spaces where low-wage workers can work, but not make. Nor can they in our increasingly militarized plantations and mines, though in the past these were spaces where powerless workers could gain that complexity in their powerlessness by the sheer concentration of their numbers. Thus today it is in cities where that possibility of gaining complexity in one's powerlessness and leaving a historic trace can happen – in our large messy and somewhat anarchic cities because nothing can fully control such diversity of peoples and engagements.

When I ask myself where is today's frontier zone, my answer is: in our large cities. The frontier is a space where actors from different worlds have an encounter for which there are no established rules of engagement. In the old historic frontier this led to either negotiation with indigenous peoples or, mostly, to their persecution and oppression. The frontier space that is today's large, mixed city offers far more options. Those with power to some extent do not want to be bothered by the poor, and the mode is often to abandon them to their own devices. In some cities (for instance US and Brazilian cities) there is extreme violence by police, and yet, this can often become a public issue, which is something, perhaps a first step in longer trajectories of gaining at least some rights. It is in cities where so many of the struggles for vindications have taken place and have, in the long run, partly succeeded.

This possibility of complexity in one's powerlessness, the capacity to make a history, a culture, and so much more, all of this is today threatened by the surge in large-scale corporate redevelopment of cities. Such developments often push long-established modest neighborhoods out of their space and produce a scramble for modest housing and a massive loss of that urban tissue they had built in their neighborhood.[6]

It is with this larger context in mind that I turn to the "innards" of this new phase in city buying.

Buying pieces of cities

While foreign acquisitions may have received much of the attention in some cities, the process is far broader, and in many cities is mostly shaped by domestic investors and developers. The key issue is not the foreign vs. national buyers, but the shifts in ownership mode – from modest or small to large and expensive, and from modest public properties to expensive private. Examples of scale-ups in private ownership are Gurgaon in Delhi, Santa Fe in Mexico City, or Sandton in Johannesburg.

Foreign acquisitions of buildings in a city are not a new development. In *The Global City*, I documented the large-scale acquisition of buildings and urban land plots in the late 1980s, especially by foreign firms, in the three leading global cities in that early global phase – New York, London, and Tokyo.[7] These acquisitions included iconic buildings, especially in New York and London, that would have shocked the average resident at the time had they known: Harrods in London, the Rockefeller Center and Sachs Fifth Ave in New York, and more. In

London, over half of the buildings in the City were foreign owned – especially by Continental European and by Japanese entities.

It is not the novelty of it all that I seek to emphasize but rather its scale and impact on urban fabric, on daily life in the city, and even on social cohesion in an urban area. In short, the effect goes well beyond functional use. These acquisitions are not simply about buying an office building and a home that are needed if a firm and its employees are to live and work in that city. These are, to a large extent, just acquisitions – they can be a safe or speculative investment, a second or third or nth home, and more. For instance, according to the *Financial Times* (Brooker, 2017; O'Murchu, 2014) a good many residential and business properties in central London and residential properties in central Oxford, the two cities they studied, have been bought by foreign firms, investors, or households over the last few years.

A share of the foreign owned residential properties tend to be underutilized, and in some documented cases, never used (see for instance the extreme examples in the Hampstead area of London [Booth, 2014]). This then also means that they contribute to a sort of de-urbanizing, especially if they are large and have been constituted by combining several buildings on a block. This removes the texture and porosity, as Richard Sennett would call it (Sennett, 1996), of the urban built environment. They do not contribute to cityness, but rather kill it.

Most recently, a so-called "super-prime" real estate market has been launched (Sassen, 2014, ch. 3). This is a made – an invented – market, where properties are given minimum prices – 8 million, 20 million, often de facto 100 million US dollars in cities such as New York, London, and Hong Kong. As far as I can establish, these properties are not worth that much money: setting these minimums is a form of gating via exclusionary criteria rather than self-evident walls. But it is above all a mechanism for super-profits. It is also the making of a cross-border geography that connects particular spaces of major cities across the world and strengthens the new geographies of wealth and privilege that cut across the old historic divides of North and South, East and West.[8]

The leading cities in this super-prime market include major European and major Asian cities.[9] A key feature is properties above the minimum levels which can move into 20 million dollars. Most of these minimum prices are in fact well below the asking price. Further, the mixes of nationalities do vary across these cities, with Dubai and Hong Kong perhaps the two most different cases of the 10 listed.

Finally, the new wave of foreign acquisitions in New York City, for instance, includes among others, buyers from Kazakhstan and from China. Among the largest are Chinese acquisitions. The economy in China is slowing down, Europe's is not in top shape, and South America's is unstable. In this context, New York has become an attractive destination for Chinese real estate investment. It is seen as a safe haven for investors, as the law definitely protects the rich.[10]

These investments are massive, and include the biggest construction company in China, China State Construction Engineering Corp. The latter has bought New York-based Plaza Construction, which builds commercial and residential developments across the US. The largest of these recent investments is from Shanghai-based Greenland Holding Group: in December of 2013 they acquired a 70% stake in the vast Atlantic Yards project in Brooklyn for $200 million. The project will include 14 apartment buildings, in addition to the Barclays Center Arena. The investors expect to complete the entire project within eight years – that is about 2020.

What is different in today's corporate buying of urban properties

It is easy to explain the post-2008 investment surge as more of the same. After all, also the late 1980s saw rapid growth of national and foreign buying of office buildings and hotels, especially in New York and London. I already wrote about this in *The Global City* (1991, 2001 ch. 7), notably, that a large share of buildings in the City of London were foreign owned at the height of that phase.[11] Financial firms from countries as diverse as Japan and the Netherlands found they needed a strong foothold in London's City to access Continental European capital and markets.

There is, then, something familiar in this current post-2008 surge in acquisitions.

But an examination of the current trends shows some significant differences and points to a whole new phase in the character and logics of foreign and national corporate acquisitions. Let me add that I do not see much of a difference in terms of the urban impact between national and foreign investment. The key fact here is that both are corporate and large scale: this is what is critical.

Six features stand out.

One is the sharp scale-up in the buying of buildings, even in cities that have long been the object of such investments, notably New York and London. The Chinese have most recently emerged as mayor buyers in cities such as London and New York. Today there are about a hundred cities worldwide that have become significant destinations for such acquisitions. Indeed the rates of growth are far higher in some of these than they are in London and New York, even if the absolute numbers are still far higher in the top tier cities. For example, foreign corporate buying of properties from 2013 to 2014 grew by 248% in Amsterdam/Randstadt, 180% in Madrid, and 475% in Nanjing. In contrast, the growth rate was relatively lower for the major cities in each region: 68.5% for New York, 37.6% for London, and 160.8% for Beijing (see Sassen, 2015b).

The second feature that stands out is the extent of new construction. In the older period of the 1980s–1990s it was often about acquiring buildings: notably high-end Harrods in London and Sachs Fifth Ave in New York, and trophy buildings, such as Rockefeller Center in New York. There were however also some massive new developments, notably in London and Tokyo. In the post-2008 period, much buying of buildings is to destroy them and to replace them with far taller and far more corporate and luxurious types of buildings – basically, luxury offices and luxury apartments.

The third feature is the spread of mega-projects with vast footprints that inevitably kill much urban tissue: little streets and squares, density of street level shops and modest offices, and such. These mega-projects raise the density of the city, but they actually de-urbanize it. Thereby they bring to the fore the fact, easily overlooked in much commentary about cities, that density is not enough to have a city.

A fourth emergent feature for now confined to a limited number of countries, is the foreclosing on modest properties, owned by modest income households. This has reached catastrophic levels in the US, with the Federal Reserve data showing over 14 million households have lost their homes (see Sassen, 2014, ch. 3). One outcome is a significant amount of empty or under-occupied land. How this land might be used is unclear, but there it is.

A fifth feature is the development of a whole new market for high-end housing. This is an invented market, with minimum prices and it functions in a limited number of cities.[12] It represents yet another claim on urban land.

A sixth feature is the acquisition of whole blocks of underutilized or dead industrial land for site development. Here the prices paid by buyers can get very high. One example is the acquisition of a vast stretch of land in New York City (Atlantic Yards) by one of the largest Chinese building companies for $5 billion. It was land occupied by a mix of modest factories and industrial services, modest neighborhoods, and more recently artists' studios and venues as these were pushed out of lower Manhattan by large-scale developments of high-rise apartment buildings. This very urban mix of occupants will be thrown out and be replaced by 14 formidable luxury towers for residences. Also here we see this sharp growth of density that actually has the effect of de-urbanizing that space. It will be a sort of de facto "gated" space with lots of people. It will not be the dense mix of uses and types of people we think of as urban. This type of development is taking off in many cities, mostly with virtual walls, but sometimes also with real ones. I would argue that with this type of development the virtual and the actual walls have similar impacts on de-urbanizing pieces of a city.

This proliferating urban gigantism has been strengthened and enabled by the privatizations and deregulations that took off in the 1990s across much of the world, and have continued since then with only a few interruptions. The overall effect has been a reduction in public buildings and an escalation in large corporate private ownership. This brings with it a thinning in the texture and scale of spaces previously accessible to the public – a space that was more than just public buildings. Where before there was a government office building handling the regulations and oversight of this or that public economic sector, or addressing the complaints from the local neighborhood, now there might be a corporate headquarters, a luxury apartment building, or a mall.

Conclusion: how do we interpret these trends?

There are familiar concepts that come to mind promptly, notably gated communities and gentrification. They contribute to explain some of this. But I am interested in going beyond these in order to get at what we might think of as constitutive elements of the city. One of these is urban land. Another one is the larger spatial formations within which inter-urban transactions and shifts take place.

The large acquisitions of urban land – whether by foreigners or locals – bring urgency to the work of actively making the public and the political in urban space. Today's large complex cities, especially if global, are a kind of new frontier zone. Where the historic frontier, as seen from imperial centers, was in the far stretches of the "colonies," today it is deep inside global cities, some of which are those erstwhile imperial centers. Actors from different worlds meet there, but there are no clear rules of engagement. These actors come from multiple diverse settings. Chinese investors are not the same as British investors, and these in turn are not the same as Dutch or Kazhakstani investors. Similarly, those making new, modest, neighborhood economies are also diverse: Jamaicans are not the same as Bangladeshi, and so on. Nor are the long-time residents and old leading firms the same as the neighborhood enterprises or as the new foreign moguls investing in global cities. It is the world that moves into the city.

These cities, whether in the global north or south, have become a strategic frontier zone for global corporate capital. Much of the work of forcing deregulation, privatization, and new fiscal and monetary policies on the host governments had to do with creating the formal instruments to construct their equivalent of the old military "fort" of the historic frontier. Now the "fort" is the regulatory environment needed in city after city worldwide to ensure a global space for their operations.

Under these conditions, the work of making the public and the political in urban space becomes even more critical. There are multiple actors and multiple perspectives – that of the citizen, the foreign investor, the immigrant entrepreneur, the old oligarchy, the grandmother, professional men and women, and many more. Let me illustrate my point with one type of actor, major developers. The challenge here is how to contain or govern major developers, both local and foreign, who consider urban space a commodity, a good to be bought and traded. City residents, no matter where they live, should have a voice when major developments in a city center absorb what was once public space, streets, urban tissue, into a privately built and owned mega-building.

The mantra of "economic development" might be enough for some major developments but it should not be enough of a justification for all major building projects. Gerald Frug's argument in "A Rule of Law for Cities" (Frug, 2010, p. 63) comes to mind, that

> we need to open up the contestability of economic development policy ... to a democratically organized institution. I think that the institution should represent people city-wide ... The participants should be empowered to establish the city's strategy for economic growth, with the experts advising the decision makers rather being the decision makers. The goal is to include the very people left out in the reigning economic development strategy.

Having a robust urban public space is critical at a time when national political space is increasingly dominated by powerful actors, both private and public, only minimally accountable to a city's and a country's people. There is a kind of "public-making" work that can happen in urban space and helps us see the local and the silenced. Our (still) large complex global cities are one key space for this making: they are today a strategic frontier zone for those who lack power, those who are disadvantaged, outsiders, minorities who are discriminated against. The disadvantaged and excluded can gain presence in such cities, presence vis-à-vis power and presence vis-à-vis each other.[13] This signals the possibility of a new type of politics, centered on new types of political actors. It is not simply a matter of having or not having power. These are new hybrid bases from which to act, spaces where the powerless can make history even when they do not get empowered.

This emergent frontier-space at the heart of major global cities arises in a context of increasingly hardwired borderings inside cities and across cities. Gated communities are but the most visible representation of these borderings. The uses that global corporate capital makes of "our" cities are also part of that hard bordering. The common assertion that we are a far less bordered world than 30 years ago only holds if we consider the traditional borders of the interstate system, and then only for the cross-border flow of capital, information, and particular population groups. Far from moving toward a borderless world, let me argue that even as we lift some of these barriers for some sectors of our economies and society, these same sectors are actively making new types of borderings that are transversal and impenetrable. It is in this context that the complex global city becomes a frontier space with political consequences.

Notes

1 This proposition underlies "The Quito Papers" project (Clos, Sennett, Burdett, & Sassen, in process). See e.g. Greenspan (2016).
2 Cushman & Wakefield (2016), also based on information from Real Capital Analytics, Oxford Economics, Guardian News and Media Ltd., The World Economic Forum, Urban Land Institute.
3 The acquisition of Atlantic Yards in New York is one instance; see generally Sassen (2015b).
4 The Making of Empty Urban Land: Foreclosures in the United States and in Europe. These data come from the Federal Reserve (the US central bank). In Sassen (2014, ch. 3), I present them in a simpler format provided by Realty Track.
5 London's low density stands out when compared to the density of major global cities (see The Urban Age Archives [n.d.]).
6 See e.g. Sassen (2015a) for a visualizing of this loss of urbanity that can be read to children!
7 See Sassen (1991, pp. 185–189) and Sassen (2001, pp. 190–195).
8 I develop this in chs. 3 and 9 of *Cities in a World Economy* (Sassen, 2012).
9 See Sassen (2014), ch. 3, and the chart on p. 139.
10 See generally Sassen (2015b).
11 One distinct aspect in the 1980s is that the price of land in central London and central New York appeared to be increasingly unrelated to the conditions of the overall national economy. Further, the bidding for space was confined to specific locations and did not necessarily spread to all available space in these cities. High bidders, often foreign, were willing to pay extremely high prices for a central location and were not

258 *S. Sassen*

interested at all in other parts of London or New York. For a fuller account of these trends see Sassen (2001), "The International Property Market" in ch. 7, see also Table 7.13 for a distribution of nationalities. See also *Cities in a World Economy* (Sassen, 2012). Today's investments mostly are not quite as narrowly confined.

12 The Super-Prime Market; see ch. 3 in Sassen (2014).

13 Elsewhere (Sassen, 2011) I have examined the importance of indeterminacy in our cities: cities need indeterminate spaces. The street, broadly understood, is one of the key spaces providing indeterminacy – unlike a building, a zoo, an amusement park, and such. Thus the elimination of what were once streets via megaprojects, is a deeply problematic development.

References

Booth, R. (2014, January 31). Inside "Billionaires Row": London's rotting, derelict mansions worth £350m. *Guardian*. Retrieved July 4, 2017, from www.theguardian.com/ society/2014/jan/31/inside-london-billionaires-row-derelict-mansions-hampstead.

Brooker, N. (2017, February 10). London's prime property bargains for foreign buyers. *Financial Times*. Retrieved July 14, 2017, from www.ft.com/content/47d30872-e89e-11e6-967b-c88452263daf.

Clos, J., Sennett, R., Burdett, R., & Sassen, S. (in process). *Towards an open city: The Quito papers and the New Urban Agenda*. Retrieved July 14, 2017, from https://files. lsecities.net/files/2017/01/Quito-Papers-Preview-Version2.3.pdf.

Cushman & Wakefield (2016). Cushman & Wakefield named to the Global Outsourcing 100. Retrieved July 12, 2017, from www.cushmanwakefield.com/en/news/2016/06/ cushman-and-wakefield-named-to-the-global-outsourcing-100.

Frug, G. (2010). A rule of law for cities. *Hagar, 10*(1), 63.

Greenspan, E. (2016, October 19). Top-down, bottom-up, urban design. *The New Yorker*. Retrieved July 4, 2017, from www.newyorker.com/business/currency/top-down-bottom-up-urban-design?intcid=mod-latest.

O'Murchu, C. (2014, July 31). Tax haven buyers set off property alarm in England and Wales. *Financial Times*. Retrieved July 14, 2017, from www.ft.com/content/6cb11114-18aa-11e4-a51a-00144feabdc0.

Sassen, S. (1991). *The global city*. Princeton, NJ: Princeton University Press.

Sassen, S. (2001). *The global city* (2nd ed.). Princeton, NJ: Princeton University Press.

Sassen, S. (2011). The global street: Making the political. *Globalizations, 8*(5), 573–579.

Sassen, S. (2012). *Cities in a world economy* (4th ed.). Beverly Hills, CA: Sage Publications.

Sassen, S. (2013). Does the city have speech? *Public Culture, 25*(2), 209–221. Duke University Press. Retrieved July 4, 2017, from www.saskiasassen.com/PDFs/publications/ does-the-city-have-speech.pdf.

Sassen, S. (2014). *Expulsions: Brutality and complexity in the global economy*. Cambridge, MA: Harvard University Press.

Sassen, S. (2015a). "A monster crawls into the city" – an urban fairytale by Saskia Sassen. *Guardian*. Retrieved July 4, 2017, from www.theguardian.com/cities/2015/ dec/23/monster-city-urban-fairytale-saskia-sassen?CMP=twt_gu.

Sassen, S. (2015b, November 24).Who owns our cities – and why this urban takeover should concern us all. *The Guardian*. Retrieved July 4, 2017, from www.theguardian. com/cities/2015/nov/24/who-owns-our-cities-and-why-this-urban-takeover-should-concern-us-all.

Sassen, S. (2016). The global city: Enabling economic intermediation and bearing its costs. *City & Community, 15*(2), 97–108.

Sennett, R. (1996). *Flesh and stone: The body and the city in Western civilization.* New York: W.W. Norton & Company.

The Urban Age Archives. (n.d.). LSE Cities. https://urbanage.lsecities.net/.

17 Resilience and justice[1]

Susan Fainstein

The term "resilience" has become extraordinarily popular. A *New York Times* headline asserts: "Forget sustainability. It's about resilience." According to this article, the purpose of developing resilience is to help vulnerable people adapt to unforeseeable disruptions: "Where sustainability aims to put the world back into balance, resilience looks for ways to manage in an unbalanced world' (Curry, 2013; Zolli, 2012). Another journalistic piece on the recent widespread use of the term inquires whether it has just become one more buzzword like synergy or social capital (Carlson, 2013; see also Davoudi, 2012) – or, one might add, like creative cities or, long ago, comprehensive planning (a once discredited concept that has returned with the aim of planning for resilience). The surge of interest in resilience responds to the damage wrought by hurricanes and earthquakes in the last decade even while it is being stretched beyond natural disasters to encompass economic crisis and social misery.

The mandate for the 2013 joint meeting of AESOP and ACSP[2] illustrates the breadth of aims the term has come to cover. Resilience was the conference's unifying theme, defined as the means "to sustain the urban and rural viability and improve the quality of life for their residents amidst the global economic and socio-political crisis and climate change." Using the term to cover so many laudable objectives disguises the trade-offs involved and the resulting distributions of costs and benefits. For example, efforts to achieve resilience in relation to climate change through developing natural buffers against sea level rise will likely result in the displacement of populations. Who will be displaced and what measures will be taken to replace lost housing and community are crucial questions not captured by the term resilience. The issue becomes whether, by using this word, policymakers are, as with sustainability, seeking an innocuous label to justify controversial actions. The term has been deployed by elite groups to prevent development that encroaches on privileged territories, while at the same time progressive elements regard it as an appealing label under which they can press for more equitable outcomes. One can only wonder, though, whether the effort to, as it were, sneak in considerations of justice amounts to more than self-delusion. The argument for resilience mainly acts as a rhetorical device that fits with a bland language of planning in which every challenge produces a win-win solution. Strategies that aim at producing just outcomes, however, require clear statements regarding who benefits; accept that some groups will bear losses; are not usually based on consensus and direct resources toward the most vulnerable as demarcated by their social situation.

This chapter first examines how resilience is currently being defined, then discusses the way in which it obscures power relations, notes the strengths of a Marxist framework, and critiques progressive attempts to circumvent power hierarchies through calls for participation. I argue that, in current usage, resilience derives from an idealist formulation of social processes that leads planners to propose responses to crisis divorced from reality. I further argue, however, that neither Marxism nor the conventionally acceptable approach of evolutionary resilience provides a guide to practice. As will be discussed below, efforts at developing resilient practices typically involve sophisticated risk analysis based on big data, justified within complexity theory. These exercises give practitioners much to do, but their results do not prescribe specific actions any more than do identifications of underlying conflicting interests.

What is meant by resilience?

C. S. Holling (1973) is generally given credit for developing the model of evolutionary resilience and arguing that resilience means not a return to a previous equilibrium but rather to system transformation. As Richard Forman (2008, p. 89) comments:

> Ecologists have basically dropped "balance of nature" and equilibrium community from their vocabulary. Instead they emphasize the non-equilibrium nature of nature, since the scientific evidence overwhelmingly highlights change as the norm ... Indeed the prevention of disturbance, rather than disturbance itself, is the threat.

In this view humans and the physical world are part of an interactive system rather than one in which nature is objectified and humans are the masters of it. D. E. Alexander (2013, p. 2710), citing the United Nations definition of resilience, notes that various meanings have been incorporated into the term and that "it should be evident ... that some of the meanings are potentially contradictory, such as restoring equilibrium and getting away from it by moving to a new system state."

The incorporation of evolution into planning for resilience undermines the assumptions of a steady state on which the linear extrapolations of planners often rely (Davoudi, 2012). In this interpretation, whether applied to nature or the economy, the implicit argument is that unavoidable events (earthquakes, storms, property bubbles, stock market crashes, etc.) will inevitably produce system change. Having resilience requires accommodating to these jolts not preventing them. Significantly, in terms of public policy, because they result from the interaction of multiple, uncoordinated factors, no agent has the power to control them.

This view of ungovernability, along with a faith that accepting risk is less harmful than attempting to avoid it, actually long predates the recent discussions of evolutionary resilience. Well before Holling's (1973) article, Norton Long, an American political scientist, published a widely cited article entitled "The Local Community as an Ecology of Games." In it he argued:

> Observation of certain local communities makes it appear that inclusive overall organization for many general purposes is weak or non-existent. Much of what occurs seems to just happen with accidental trends becoming cumulative over time and producing results intended by nobody. A great deal of the communities' activities consist of undirected co-operation of particular social structures, each seeking particular goals and, in doing so, meshing with others … As in the natural ecology, random adjustment and piecemeal innovation are the normal methods of response [to breakdown]. The lack of over-all institutions in the territorial system and the weakness of those that exist insure that co-ordination is largely ecological rather than a matter of conscious rational contriving.
>
> (Long, 1958, p. 252)

This analysis prefigures Gunderson and Holling's (2002) concept of panarchy; that is, non-hierarchically directed adaptation. Long's viewpoint reflects the sophisticated pluralistic analysis of his time, embodied also in the works of Robert Dahl and his followers. The thrust was to debunk those like C. Wright Mills and Floyd Hunter who identified power elites who could control development. The pluralists ignored the way in which capitalism sets the overall structure in which the social ecology exists and in which the relationship between society, nature, and the built environment is formed and reproduced. Without fully adopting a Marxist framework, we can still glean from it insights into the theoretical questions raised by resilience scholarship and also see some of the obstacles to planning in practice more clearly. The two principal theoretical questions to be discussed in the next sections are: (1) the political question of power, and (2) the epistemological question of describing complex systems. They point to issues in using resilience as the basis for planning, including the danger that the terminology of resilience engenders either passivity or a favoring of the already advantaged.

Politics and power

A number of theorists, when discussing the paradigm of social ecology from which the argument for resilience derives, critique it for inadequately addressing the questions of political power and the role of the state, and for incorporating a conservative political bias (see e.g. Swanstrom, 2008; Wilkinson, 2012). When looking at Figure 17.1, which maps the interconnections between various types of risks using an ecological approach, we can easily see how the issue of power is evaded. Developed for the World Economic Forum (2013) – the meeting of

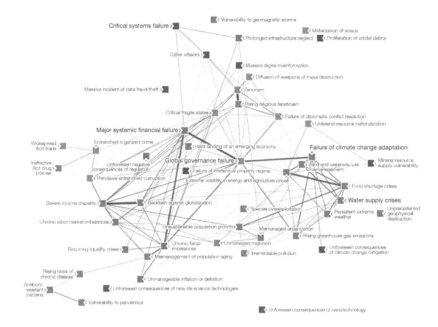

Figure 17.1 The risk interconnection map.

governmental and corporate leaders that occurs each year at Davos – the chart presents a view of crisis that will not discomfit these elites.

When interactive processes are portrayed in this fashion, whereby everything is connected to everything else, there appear to be no overriding logic, no agents, and no targets for effective action. In the words of Brendan Gleeson: "If left to natural interpretation alone, the tropes of evolution and equilibrium suggest a law bound urban ecology that makes social intervention meaningless or self-defeating ... Naturalism, of course, disavows and therefore misrepresents human agency and social possibility" (Gleeson, 2013, p. 13).

Examining social phenomena through the lens of complexity leaves the analyst with enormous mapping jobs and model-building challenges but provides little in the way of decision rules. Eric Swyngedouw (2010, p. 303) comments: "Unforeseen changes are seen either as the effect of 'externalities' ... or as a catastrophic turbulence resulting from initial relations that spiral out in infinitely complex and greatly varying configurations such as those theorized by Chaos or Complexity Theory." For Swyngedouw, this perspective amounts to a denial of the socio-ecological relationships of dominance that are upheld by the hidden, conservative ideology of environmentalism.

Marxist analysis explains crisis through analyzing the logic of capital. Although Marx himself saw crisis in purely economic terms and accepted the view that humans could, and should, dominate nature (Harvey, 1996, p. 126), more recent theorists working within the Marxian tradition reject that perspective. Instead, they extend the analysis to share with the complexity theorists an interactionist understanding of the relations between humans and the "natural" world, but they interpret that interaction quite differently. Neil Smith (1984), for instance, asserts that nature is entirely a social creation produced within the capitalist mode of production. David Harvey (1996, p. 131) contends that 18th-century political economy (and, equally, contemporary neoliberalism) disguises the question of humans' relationship to nature as "a technical discourse concerning the proper allocation of scarce resources (including those in nature) for the benefit of human welfare." He argues that programs which are not profitable or protective of private property rights will be neglected, regardless of their environmental or social impact. The American refusal to institute a carbon tax is a case in point.

Key to the intellectual outlook formed by the Marxian tradition is a focus on class relations rather than communication as the determinative factor in explanation. David Harvey critiques Habermas for treating communicative action "as a linguistic discursive problem," thus providing "a very weak understanding of how the discursive 'moment' … internalizes effects of power, of material practices, of imaginaries, of institutions, and of social relations" (Harvey, 1996, p. 354). A recent, highly publicized book by Bruce Katz and Jennifer Bradley of the Brookings Institution reflects this obliviousness to structural conflict, business domination, and a Panglossian view of consensus building:

> Four years after the recession's official end, it is clear that the real, durable reshaping [of the American economy] is being led by networks of city and metropolitan leaders – mayors and other local elected officials, for sure, but also heads of companies, universities, medical campuses, metropolitan business associations, labor unions, civic organizations, environmental groups, cultural institutions, and philanthropies. These leaders are measuring what matters, unveiling their distinctive strengths and starting points in the real economy: manufacturing, innovation, technology, advanced services, and exports … [They are] using business planning techniques honed in the private sector. They are remaking their urban and suburban places as livable, quality, affordable, sustainable communities and offering more residential, transport, and work options to firms and families alike. And they are doing all these things through coinvention and coproduction.
>
> (Katz & Bradley, 2013, p. 3)

From this perspective there are no structural conflicts within metropolitan areas and cooperation among all the various interests – capital and labor, white and black, industrialists and environmentalists – will insure resilience, sustainability, and economic development.

In sharp contrast, the Marxist viewpoint identifies contradictions in the capitalist mode of production that make environmental despoliation inevitable and points to the power of capitalists as the underlying cause of ecological crisis. This thinking accepts the argument, espoused by non-Marxists as well, that there is no such thing as a natural disaster, in that human activity always underlies environmental crisis (see Hartman & Squires, 2006). Marxists, however, differ from liberals in that they are much more willing to assess blame. Unlike complexity theory, Marxist thought is deeply political. Its weakness, from the perspective of planners, is that it offers relatively little, beyond political mobilization in defense of the weak, for responding to threat in the present. Furthermore, and with little supporting evidence, it assumes that under socialism contradictions resulting in environment crisis would be eliminated. It cannot, however, on these grounds be simply dismissed, since its depiction of the consequences of capital accumulation is largely valid. In fact, complexity theory, with its multiplicity of variables and numerous feedback effects, offers no greater practicality; rather its political acceptability and scientific trappings protect it from being disregarded or treated contemptuously.

Ideological frameworks and theories of change

Davoudi (2012, pp. 302–303) comments that the concept of evolutionary resilience means that "small-scale changes in systems can amplify and cascade into major shifts" in a process of creative destruction. This picture of what, in Hegelian thought, is characterized as the qualitative leap, captures also the understanding of social change within the Marxist dialectic, although for Marx the jump is materialist rather than ideational. Within dialectical materialism nothing ever remains the same in history, and although changes may be imperceptible, eventually they result in systemic transformation. Thus, the accumulation of wealth by a merchant trading class eventually gave rise to the capitalization of industry, leading to the jump from a rural-agricultural mode of production to the urban-industrial one. Within the present epoch, the fiscal crises of the 1970s in the West stimulated a new international division of labor under which manufacturing moved to developing countries. Along with the outsourcing of production also came the outsourcing of pollution, as regulation in the West and poverty in the rest caused dirty industries to move to places where they could profitably continue their activities. Thus, reforms in the major industrial countries aimed at environmental protection and public welfare cumulated during the postwar years until they produced a crisis of profitability and a major transformation in the relations of production, characterized by a new international division of labor, the globalization of production, and a new geography of environmental harm.

The term "creative destruction" is frequently used by both Marxists and their critics to characterize processes resulting in new sets of ecological relationships. The difference between the Marxian and Schumpeterian understandings of "creative destruction" lies in the normative evaluation of its effects. In the latter, the emphasis is on creativity and innovation as the driving forces of progress. In the Marxian view it is on the destruction of communities and ways of life. Thus, Marx laments the loss of independence of the skilled craftsman, and Harvey (2003) mourns the destruction of the working-class quarters of Paris under the aegis of Haussmann. At the same time the process is attributed to the logic of the capitalist drive for profit, and the set of interactions as a whole produces a dynamic that undermines the system. Consequently industrial production and high-level consumption lead to massive employment of energy and water sources with consequent global warming and depletion of water supplies.

Similarly, the global financial crisis of 2007–2008 can be interpreted through the lens of complexity theory as a consequence of unpredictable externalities and feedback effects flowing out of financial innovation. From this viewpoint it was the attempt to contain risk rather than accept it through the development of financial derivatives that exacerbated the crisis. From a Marxist perspective it resulted from the financialization of capitalist relations and increased reliance on debt leading to a crisis of accumulation.

Dialectical materialism allows the identification of new qualitative stages. It is part of a critical social science that regards social relationships as conflictual and inherently power-driven rather than consensual or the product of an invisible (and implicitly beneficent) hand. In the latter part of the 20th century, theorists in the Marxist tradition developed regulation theory to explain changes in capitalism in response to crises of profitability. While not involving a leap into a post-capitalist stage, these changes nevertheless marked a substantial shift from the preceding years. According to this theory, the Keynesian welfare state, mass production for mass consumption, and manufacturing dominance ("Fordism") characterized the wealthy countries of the West during the years immediately following World War II. Under the "post-Fordist" regime of accumulation that commenced during the 1970s, finance capital became dominant within a globalized economic system, a new international division of labor was imposed, and privatization and deregulation reduced the role of the state in maintaining social well-being (Amin, 1994). The labeling of the supportive ideology of post-Fordism as neoliberalism derives from this kind of approach, which considers that the continuing acceptance of capitalist accumulation results from its embeddedness in a system of regulation involving cultural, social, and political conventions (Brenner & Theodore, 2002). Regulation theorists thus consider conventional thinking to be a mechanism that supports a particular regime of accumulation. The current attempt to use market mechanisms as the means for environmental protection, as in the establishment of markets for the right to pollute (i.e., "cap and trade"), illustrates the way in which neoliberal thinking limits the range of acceptable policy responses to ones that will benefit capital. Similarly the recapitalization of banks with government funds in response to financial crisis along with the failure to halt mortgage foreclosures represents a highly biased adaptation to the crisis.

Marxist analysis leads to the identification of the contradictions and crisis-prone nature of capitalism. The negative environmental effects of commodity production – what mainstream economists call market failures – arise from such contradictions, are inevitable, and do indeed cause crisis. What is remarkable about capitalism, however, and not predicted by Marx, is its extraordinary resilience. Marx considered that the contradictions of capitalism would cause crisis, the breakdown of the system, and the empowerment of the working class. And indeed, the crises of over-accumulation, environmental disaster, and rebellion have occurred. Since its inception capitalism has been characterized by financial bubbles and their subsequent puncture, by the destruction of environments embodied in ghost towns and London fogs, by the spread of diseases engendered by poor sanitary conditions within cities, and by inequality giving rise to antagonistic classes and nations. Yet there has been adaptation and the defeat of socialism as it really existed (and which suffered from its own contradictions). Dialectical thought allows the observer to see the relationships within a system, but it does not, any better than complexity theory, allow us to know the ultimate outcome – and in fact, in the absence of Marx's teleology, we should not expect any final outcome.

Ideology, resilience, and planning

The depoliticizing character of standard ecological analysis legitimates the term resilience – hence, its appeal to defenders of the socioeconomic status quo. Protecting bucolic suburban areas from high-density housing becomes justified as maintaining green spaces that will absorb run-off. These are the same suburban areas that feature mowed lawns and golf courses even while their negative impacts on the water table and water quality are widely known. What exists is seen as normal, and resilience is commonly defined as the creation of a new normality after a disruption. Normality tends to be what is in the interests of property owners: thus, the effort to re-create Berlin as it was before the Wall (expressed in the terms "we are a normal city again") or to reduce social housing in Amsterdam (where the director of planning informed me that Amsterdam was finally becoming "a normal city"). What appears "normal" produces ontological security for many, even while exacerbating the insecurity of others.

Planning for resilience generally is conducted as an exercise in risk assessment followed by a calculation of alternative responses. Risk calculations, however, cannot tell us what level of risk is tolerable, nor do they break down the question into that of risk for whom? Instead, they aim at giving precise numbers, despite the actual uncertainty involved:

> The clearest message from the changing evidence base over the last decade concerns the dangers of false precision … With regard to flooding, the data appears to be particularly subject to rapid and fundamental change and raises questions as to the extent to which it can be distilled to a probabilistic figure or clear spatial delineation between "safe" areas and those "at risk."
>
> (White, 2013, p. 110)

These numbers, however, are demanded by insurers so that they can develop underwriting criteria and calculate premiums and by planners so that they can decide on desirable levels of density. They fit into the current fad of "evidence-based planning." Similarly, economic forecasters provide precise figures for expected growth and inflation so that national banks can adjust interest rates to accommodate them. But changed interest rates produce winners and losers (e.g., holders of variable rate mortgages) whose welfare is not taken into account.

Patsy Healey (2012) refers to "traveling ideas" and warns us to be careful about applying models or best practices that work well in one place but may be inappropriate elsewhere. There are two such ideas currently prevalent in regard to making cities more resilient to natural disasters, one dealing with outcomes and the other with process: (1) going along with rather than trying to defeat ecological processes – for example making room for water, allowing forest fires to burn away undergrowth; (2) arriving at a participatory, consensual agreement on what is to be done. In conclusion, I address and critique these two ideas within the framework already laid out, then advance some modest proposals.

Accommodating to natural processes

The Dutch have pioneered the approach of making room for water, which involves accommodating flooding rather than using barriers to protect low-lying land. Of course, there is really nothing new about this strategy except within the context of a country that previously relied on massive public works to fend off the surrounding seas. In fact, less developed countries have traditionally relied on annual flooding as the basis for agricultural productivity. Therefore, it is its social-historical positioning that makes the approach novel. We hear similar calls in the United States, where the Army Corps of Engineers is dismantling some dams and rebuilding wetlands in the Mississippi Delta. When we are speaking of unbuilt areas, little harm will be done, but even there some land owners will benefit while others will lose out. In cities the potential hardships are much greater when inhabited neighborhoods are marked for inundation. Moreover, even the Dutch will continue to rely primarily on engineered barriers to water flows and the use of high-technology-based emergency responses; they are modifying rather than leaving behind the mastery of the nature model.

Most notoriously, in New Orleans, making room for water was the basis for the "green dot" map where certain impoverished parts of the city were designated by planning experts as appropriate locations to return to open space. The resulting furor caused the withdrawal of the plan and a willingness to allow any neighborhood to rebuild if its former residents could find the will and finances to do so (Nelson, Ehrenfeucht, & Laska, 2007). The New Orleans case highlights the politics of making room for water in already built-up areas. Since the most environmentally challenged land is typically inhabited by low-income residents who initially had few choices, returning the land to its pre-inhabited state places the cost burden of relocation on those least able to sustain it. Where waterfront land has been colonized by upper-income residents seeking views, the effort has largely been to protect them and keep them in place. Hypothetically a poor community could be moved "en bloc" to a more salubrious area, but this approach is very costly and seldom applied to marginalized communities. Simple compensation to individual households for the loss of their land would not supply the amount of money needed for former residents to settle in a decent home in more environmentally beneficial surroundings, nor would it reconstruct the community relations that had been severed. This situation, within the standard view of social ecology, is simply a dilemma of governance; within a more radical theory, it is the consequence of capitalism under neoliberalism, where the resources to support everyone in a decent home and suitable living environment are withheld.

A progressive approach would use the criteria of use values in determining strategies. If poor communities ought to move, then they should not have to do so until a new location is developed, and members should be able to move together. Dealing with environmental threat should not be considered in isolation from the broader question of producing affordable housing. Conventional thinking regards government production of housing as inefficient and limiting choice, but empirical investigation shows that only countries that have had large-scale production of social housing provide adequate shelter for low-income households. Just outcomes require a move away from reliance on market processes and a return to a dominant state role in housing provision (Marcuse & Keating, 2006).

Participatory processes: do they produce better outcomes than expert-driven ones?

The New Orleans example points also to the process issue. Participation led ultimately to a resolution whereby the city would be rebuilt pretty much as it was for those with resources, while many of those lacking in financial and social capital were unable to return or rebuild – although they were not prohibited from doing so. Participants at the local level, even while their participation resulted in their being allowed to stay in place, were unable to command funding in relation to need. Although considerable federal money did flow into New Orleans, calculations of property values were based on exchange values not use values, as was the case for private insurers as well. The hurricane was also used as the rationale for demolishing all the public housing in the city, leaving poor residents with even fewer options than formerly. Rather than top-down expert-imposed strategies determining the shape of rebuilding, a combination of participation and market forces produced a result as favorable to the well-off as the green-dot map. A few poor neighborhoods were able to muster sufficient organization and political resources to rebuild; most never recovered. The outcome shows that participation without financial resources is an empty promise.

In conclusion, I will illustrate my argument with the case of New York City. New York has been at the epicenter of three recent crises: the World Trade Center attack of September 11, 2001; the implosion of financial markets in 2007–2008; and Hurricane Sandy in 2012. A book published in 2005 that analyzed the impact of the first of these events on the city's economy was entitled *Resilient City* (Chernick, 2005). Mayor Michael Bloomberg's plan for dealing with future storm threats was entitled "A Stronger, More Resilient New York." In truth, New York has proved resilient in particular ways, but these ways have strongly benefited financial sector executives and real estate owners and developers. Reacting to 9/11, the federal government poured money into the city in a fashion quite different from after the 1975 fiscal crisis, when it was begrudging in its response; in fairness, a substantial sum gave recompense to the families of those killed in the towers, and although the amount was calibrated according to the individuals' earnings, even low-paid workers received fairly generous sums. The big winner, however, was the developer Larry Silverstein, who was protected from any financial loss and given the right to rebuild on the site (Sagalyn, 2005). After the collapse of the secondary mortgage market in 2007, the federal government stepped in with the Troubled Assets Relief Program (TARP), to the benefit of the financial institutions headquartered in the city (Gladstone & Fainstein, 2013). Since then, New York's rich have become richer, and everyone else has become poorer (US Bureau of the Census, 2013). Bloomberg's proposal for a more resilient New York involves the construction of a giant new real-estate development on the East River adjacent to the downtown financial district. Allegedly this megaproject will simultaneously act as a buffer against rising waters and be an economic driver which will supposedly pay for itself (New York City, Office of the Mayor, 2013). A more just approach would focus on the areas of the city, primarily the barrier islands off of Queens and the Brooklyn waterfront, with large numbers of low-income households in fragile housing, retrofit that housing to the extent possible, or move the inhabitants to new construction on higher ground.

A proposal more sensitive to issues of justice, in both New York and elsewhere, would start with examining the situation of the most vulnerable populations and develop alternatives that would best protect them in the event of a major storm. In terms of financial crisis it would begin with figuring out how to make whole those who have lost their homes and jobs. I commented earlier that Marxian analysis offered important theoretical insights into the causes of crisis but not much in terms of how to plan for it in the here and now. Marxist terminology is very unstylish; it sounds too radical and is unacceptable to the dispensers of social science grant money. It points, however, to important facts about how issues of disaster recovery are normally addressed – that without radical questioning they devolve into a consensual agreement to value growth over equity and to encourage growth by directly benefiting those who already are most advantaged. If, instead of starting with the question of how to normalize the situation and assuming that there are not underlying conflicts of interest in terms of a desirable post-disaster situation, we started with the question of how best to make the lives better of the most vulnerable, we would move toward different policies.

Local planners have limited capacity to force the redistribution of resources since the national level is the principal source of revenues. Nevertheless, the planning of capital budget priorities, mapping of transportation systems, and zoning are within their purview (Fainstein, 2010, ch. 6). A city that is more just would respond to rising water levels by moving low-income residents to higher ground or else investing in either raising their buildings or creating buffers to protect against inundation. If poor households agree that they need to move and accept that the likeliest location is a distance from the center, then transit systems to improve access, social services, and local amenities have to be developed along with housing.

The Rockefeller Foundation recently put out a request for proposals (RFP) to city governments that stated:

> public and private sector leaders are expressing an increasing desire to build greater resilience, yet many have neither the technical expertise nor the financial resources to create and execute resilience strategies on a city-wide scale, in a way that addresses the need of the poor or vulnerable people.
>
> (Rockefeller Foundation, 2013)

It is doubtful, however, that either technical expertise or financial resources are the primary explanation for the failure to address the need of poor or vulnerable people. Rather it is their lack of political power that explains why building a real-estate megaproject would be a priority for developing resilience.

Proposals that require spending a great deal of money on poor people are generally regarded as politically impossible and therefore are evaded. The discourse of evolutionary resilience, the apparent scientific precision of risk analysis, and the glamor of complexity theory allow conversations that fail to confront the real issue of which groups of the population will actually benefit from the expenditure of public resources. These conversations avoid divisiveness by assuming that everyone will benefit if resilience is enhanced, and the allusion to the great complexity involved in achieving resilience creates a cloud of obfuscation around the question of who is getting what. Planners can contribute to a more just city by using the information at their disposal to show clearly what are the stakes in any particular decision regarding environmental protection or economic development and advocate for policies that are more equitable. They may not succeed in overcoming the obstacles to more just outcomes, but by challenging the feel-good rhetoric characteristic of discussions of sustainability and resilience, they can contribute to enlarging the boundaries of the politically possible.

Notes

1 Susan Fainstein, "Resilience and Justice," published in the *International Journal of Urban and Regional Research* (*IJURR*), Wiley, Volume 39, Issue 1, January 2015, pages 157–167. Reproduced by kind permission from Susan Fainstein and the *IJURR*.
2 These acronyms refer to the European and American associations of planning faculty members. AESOP stands for Association of European Schools of Planning; ACSP is the US Association of Collegiate Schools of Planning.

References

Alexander, D. E. (2013). Resilience and disaster risk reduction: An etymological journey. *Natural Hazards Earth Systems Science, 13*, 2707–2716. Retrieved May 3, 2014, from www.nat-hazardsearth-systsci.net/13/2707/2013/doi:10.5194/nhess-13-2707-2013.

Amin, A. (Ed.). (1994). *Post-Fordism: A reader*. Oxford: Blackwell.

Brenner, N., & Theodore, N. (Eds.). (2002). *Spaces of neoliberalism*. Oxford: Blackwell.

Carlson, S. (2013, May 10). After catastrophe. *The Chronicle Review*. Retrieved June 16, 2014, from http://chronicle.com/article/After-Catastrophe/138927/.

Chernick, H. (Ed.). (2005). *Resilient city*. New York: Russell Sage.

Curry, J. (2013, May 29). Forget sustainability – it's about resilience. *Climate Etc.* Retrieved July 2017, from https://judithcurry.com/2013/05/29/forget-sustainability-its-about-resilience/.

Davoudi, S. (2012). Resilience: A bridging concept or a dead end? *Planning Theory & Practice, 13*(2), 299–307.

Fainstein, S. S. (2010). *The just city*. Ithaca, NY: Cornell University Press.

Forman, R. T. T. (2008). *Urban regions*. Cambridge, UK: Cambridge University Press.

Gladstone, D., & Fainstein, S. S. (2013). The New York and Los Angeles economies revisited. In D. Halle & A. Beveridge (Eds.), *New York and Los Angeles: The uncertain future*. New York: Oxford University Press.

Gleeson, B. (2013). Resilience and its discontents. *Research Paper, No. 1*, Melbourne Sustainable Society Institute. Retrieved May 3, 2014, from www.sustainable. unimelb. edu.au/content/pages/mssi-research-paperbrendan-gleeson-resilience-and-its-discontents.

Gunderson, L. H., & Holling, C. S. (Eds.). (2002). *Panarchy: Understanding transformations in systems of humans and nature*. Washington, DC: Island.

Hartman, C., & Squires, G. D. (Eds.). (2006). *There is no such thing as a natural disaster*. New York: Routledge.

Harvey, D. (1996). *Justice, nature and the geography of difference*. Oxford: Blackwell.

Harvey, D. (2003). *Paris: Capital of modernity*. New York: Routledge.

Healey, P. (2012). The universal and the contingent: Some reflections on the transnational flow of planning ideas and practices. *Planning Theory, 11*(2), 188–207.

Holling, C. S. (1973). Resilience and stability of ecological systems. *Annual Review of Ecology and Systematics, 4*, 1–23.

Katz, B., & Bradley, J. (2013). *The metropolitan revolution*. Washington, DC: Brookings Institution.

Long, N. E. (1958). The local community as an ecology of games. *American Journal of Sociology, 64*(3), 251–261.

Marcuse, P., & Keating, W. D. (2006). The permanent housing crisis: The failure of conservatism and the limitations of liberalism. In R. Bratt, M. Stone, & C. Hartman (Eds.), *A right to housing: Foundation for a new social agenda*. Philadelphia: Temple University Press.

Nelson, M., Ehrenfeucht, R., & Laska, S. (2007). Planning, plans, and people: Professional expertise, local knowledge, and governmental action in post-hurricane Katrina New Orleans. *Cityscape, 9*(3), 23–52.

New York City, Office of the Mayor. (2013). A stronger, more resilient New York. Retrieved May 3, 2014, from http://nytelecom.vo.llnwd.net/o15/agencies/sirr/SIRR_ singles_Hi_res.pdf.

Rockefeller Foundation. (2013). 100 resilient cities centennial challenge. Retrieved May 3, 2014, from www.rockefellerfoundation.org/our-work/currentwork/100-resilient-cities.

Sagalyn, L. B. (2005). The politics of planning the world's most visible urban redevelopment project. In Mollenkopf, J. H. (Ed.), *Contentious city*. New York: Russell Sage.

Smith, N. (1984). *Uneven development*. Oxford: Basil Blackwell.

Swanstrom, T. (2008). *Regional resilience: A critical examination of the ecological framework*. Working Paper 2008–07. Macarthur Foundation Research Network on Building Resilient Regions. Retrieved July 12, 2017, from http://brr.berkeley.edu/brr_workingpapers/2008-07-swanstrom-ecological_framework.pdf.

Swyngedouw, E. (2010). Trouble with nature: "Ecology as the new opium for the masses." In P. Healey & J. Hillier (Eds.), *The Ashgate research companion to planning theory*. Farnham, UK: Ashgate.

US Bureau of the Census. (2013). American fact finder. Retrieved May 3, 2014, from http://factfinder2.census.gov/faces/nav/jsf/pages/searchresults.xhtml?refresh=t#none.

White, I. (2013). The more we know, the more we know we don't know: Reflections on a decade of planning, flood risk management and false precision. *Planning Theory & Practice, 13*(1), 106–113.

Wilkinson, C. (2012). Urban resilience: What does it mean in planning practice? *Planning Theory & Practice, 13*(2), 319–324.

World Economic Forum. (2013). *Global risks 2013* (8th ed.). Geneva: World Economic Forum.

Zolli, A. (2012, November 2). Learning to bounce back. *New York Times*. Retrieved June 17, 2014, from www.nytimes.com/2012/11/03/opinion/forget-sustainability-its-about-resilience.html?pagewanted=all&_r=0.

18 Neighborhood social diversity and metropolitan segregation

Emily Talen

The story of 20th century urbanism is a story of manifest social division. Rising affluence and the growth of the middle class, cheap oil, highways and government subsidies, and centralized notions of cultural authority combined with racial and class intolerance to create the conditions leading to extraordinary social sorting within cities along racial, ethnic, and economic lines. Urban planners, policymakers, and community activists have often tried to counter these trends, but they are forced to confront a competing public attitude that is fearful of the "other," and often actively resistant to social change if it means an increase in social diversity in their neighborhood.

As an empirical matter, there is evidence that, especially in the U.S., economically diverse neighborhoods are being lost (Fry & Taylor, 2012). This loss is exacerbated by the stability of homogeneity: rich neighborhoods stay rich, poor neighborhoods stay poor, and middle-income neighborhoods change up or down, with race determining to a large degree the direction of change (Hwang & Sampson, 2014). Lower-income households who live mostly around others with low incomes increased from 23% to 28% between 1980 and 2010; higher-income households who live mostly around others with high incomes doubled from 9% in 1980 to 18% in 2010. In addition, the data show that most economically diverse neighborhoods do not remain so, either because they become more uniformly rich or they become more uniformly poor. Only 18% of neighborhoods that were economically integrated in 1970 remained integrated in 2000. These changes are exasperated by income inequality overall; between 1980 and 2010, there was a significant increase in the percentage of lower-income households living in majority lower-income tracts, and upper-income households living in majority upper-income tracts (Fry & Taylor 2012; Tach, Pendall, & Derian, 2014). The segregation of the affluent is especially problematic because it translates to a reduction in support for public investment in cities and neighborhoods that are less well off. Income inequality perpetuates wealth inequality, as higher-income Americans drive higher housing prices in affluent neighborhoods (Albouy & Zabek, 2016; Reardon & Bischoff, 2011).

Unfortunately, the decline of diversity is accelerated in neighborhoods that are also walkable – unfortunate because commensurate with the decline of neighborhood diversity are the well-documented benefits of living in walkable neighborhoods (Riggs, 2014). A recent summary of hundreds of peer-reviewed articles published in the last decade provides evidence that components of the walkable, diverse neighborhood have positive resident-level effects, in terms of health, social interaction, and safety (Talen & Koschinsky, 2014). For the walkability component, surveys of the literature have found consistent links between walkable neighborhoods and physical activity (Durand, Andalib, Dunton, Wolch, & Pentz, 2011).[1] The majority of studies find important relationships between walkable neighborhood form and walking, physical activity, and ultimately, obesity and other health measures. Walkable places tend to have high access (to goods and services), which has been shown to lower obesity, improve mental health, and increase brain function (Brown, Khattak, & Rodriguez, 2008; Erickson et al., 2010; Jack & McCormack, 2014; Kloos & Shah, 2009; Saelens & Handy, 2008). Brian Saelens and James Sallis have authored multiple studies documenting these neighborhood-based differences in physical activity. Walkability is also associated with higher rates of social interaction and place attachment, as well as sense of community (Kim & Kaplan, 2004; Pendola & Gen, 2008; Saelens, Sallis, Black, & Chen, 2003; Sallis, Kraft, & Linton, 2002; Wood, Frank, & Giles-Corti, 2010). Surveys have utilized Robert Putnam's scale measuring social capital to show the link between walkable neighborhoods and higher levels of social capital, social engagement, and sociability. Walkable places often also include public spaces that support casual or spontaneous interaction that promotes social ties and can have positive effects on social interaction, especially in mixed-income areas (Brown & Cropper, 2001; Leyden, 2003; Putnam, 2007; Roberts, 2007; Rogers, Halstead, Gardner, & Carlson, 2010; Skjaeveland & Garling, 1997; Wood, Frank, & Giles-Corti, 2010). Mixed uses (related to walkability) facilitate the exchange of information, services, and goods. Mixing public and quasi-public facilities and neighborhood-level commercial enterprises is considered essential for sustaining socially mixed communities. *Increased serviceability underlies the finding that long-term residents of gentrifying neighborhoods are able to see positive gains, despite rising rents and the threat of displacement.* Frequent destinations help to create "safe and social" neighborhoods (Carlino, Chatterjee, & Hunt, 2006; Freeman, 2005; Glaeser, 2011; Hall & Hesse, 2012; Levasseur et al., 2015; Myerson, 2001; Nyden, Lukehart, Maly, & Peterman, 1998; Wood et al., 2008).

Why should we value neighborhood diversity?

The importance of income diversity is based on concepts and theories about place vitality, economic health, social equity, and sustainability. There is expansive writing, in both the scholarly and more popular literature, laying out the conceptual arguments that social diversity is a mode of existence that enhances human experience in all of these ways. There is a pervasive view among urbanists that diversity is a positive force in a global society, a mode of existence that enhances human experience. Partly this has to do with place vitality. The city is revered precisely because it is the locus of difference and diversity. Allan Jacobs and Donald Appleyard wrote a widely cited manifesto in which they argued that diversity and the integration of activities were necessary parts of "an urban fabric for an urban life" (Jacobs & Appleyard, 1987, p. 117). What counted for Jane Jacobs was the "everyday, ordinary performance in mixing people," forming complex "pools of use" that would be capable of producing something greater than the sum of their parts (Jacobs, 1961, pp. 164–165).

Lewis Mumford wrote about the importance of social and economic mix often, citing the "many-sided urban environment" as one with more possibilities for "the higher forms of human achievement" (Mumford, 1938, pp. 485–486. Planners, in their plans for the physical design of cities, were supposed to foster this wherever possible to achieve the mature city: "A plan that does not further a daily intermixture of people, classes, activities, works against the best interests of maturity" (Mumford, 1968, p. 39). These ideas were strongly influenced by Patrick Geddes, and both men saw the advantage and positive stimulation of cities as a way to accommodate "the essential human need for disharmony and conflict" (Mumford, 1968, p. 485). Baumgartner's study of the "moral order of a suburb" revealed the negative implications of homogenized, privatized social world where communal conflict is internalized or avoided rather than dealt with openly (Baumgartner, 1991).

Diversity is seen as the primary generator of urban vitality because it increases interactions among multiple urban components. A "close-grained" diversity of uses provides "constant mutual support," and planning must, Jacobs argued, "become the science and art of catalyzing and nourishing these close-grained working relationships" (Jacobs, 1961, p. 14). Thus the separation of urbanism into components, like land use categories, miles of highways, square footage of office space, park acreage per capita – all of these abstracted calculations lead to, as Mumford termed it, the "anti-city" (Mumford, 1968, p. 128). Jacobs similarly berated planners for treating the city as a series of calculations and measurable abstractions that rendered it a problem of "disorganized complexity," and made planners falsely believe that they could effectively manipulate its individualized parts (Jacobs, 1961, p. 14).

Diversity is usually not thought of as being chaotic or random. For Jane Jacobs, social, economic, and physical diversity effectively coexisted within an underlying system of order, which she termed "organized complexity." Similarly, Eliel Saarinen thought the diversity of urban elements could be brought into "a single picture of rhythmic order" (Saarinen, 1943, p. 13). Melvin Webber's "Order in Diversity" essay lamented the mistaking of complexity for chaos. He believed that plans, to accommodate diversity, must be designed "to accommodate the disparate demands upon land and space made by disparate individuals and groups" (Webber, 1963, pp. 51–52).

A sub-category of "place vitality" is economic health. Urban diversity, the "size, density, and congestion" of cities, was considered by Jacobs to be "among our most precious economic assets" (Jacobs, 1961, p. 219). Scholars have investigated how income diversity plays a role in stimulating economic networks of interconnected relations and "exchange possibilities," where a "richly differentiated neighborhood" is considered more resilient against economic downturn. There has been disagreement over the role of diversity in generating knowledge spillovers, but the view that diversity of industries in close proximity generates growth, rather than specialization within a given industry, is generally accepted. The richness of human diversity is an economic asset because innovation within firms can come from spillovers outside of the firm. Spillovers depend, to some degree, on spatial proximity, since distance affects knowledge flows. The scale at which diversity is able to create spillovers that contribute to innovation and vitality depends on the scale at which cross-cultural knowledge spillovers are likely to occur (Florida, 2005; Glaeser, 2000; 2011; Glaeser, Kallal, Scheinkman, & Shleifer, 1992; Montgomery, 1998; Quigley, 1998; Sohn, Moudon, & Lee, 2012).

Richard Florida has been particularly explicit in arguing for the importance of diversity in economic terms, but his argument is structured differently (Florida, 2002a). His creative capital theory states that high densities of diverse human capital (the proportion of gay households in a region is one measure), not diversity of firms or industries in the conventional economic view, is what promotes innovation and economic growth. Cities that are open to "diversity of all sorts" are also the ones that "enjoy higher rates of innovation and high-wage economic growth." Cities should therefore attract human capital, focusing on what's good for people rather than on, more conventionally, what's good for business. This naturally leads to an elevation of the qualities of place, since "talent does not simply show up in a region" (Florida, 2002b, p. 754).

Diversity promotes economic health because it fosters opportunity. In Jacobs' words, cities, if they are diverse, "offer fertile ground for the plans of thousands of people" (Jacobs, 1961, p. 14). Non-diversity offers little hope for future expansion, either in the form of personal growth or economic development. And in fact class segregation has been shown to lower a region's economic growth. Nor are non-diverse places able to support the full range of employment required to sustain a multi-functional human settlement. Diversity of income and education levels means that the people crucial for service employment, including local government workers (police, fire, school teachers), and those employed in the stores and restaurants that cater to a local clientele, should not have to travel from outside the community to be employed there (Ledebur & Barnes, 1993).

There is also the idea that a diverse neighborhood is better able to take care of itself. The "richly differentiated neighborhood" is more "durable and resilient" against economic downturn (Jacobs, 1961, p. 14). But interaction among diverse peoples also helps generate the contacts needed for individual success. Where there is less social diversity and more segregation, there is likely to be less opportunity for the creation of these wider social networks. While mixed-income neighborhoods involving public housing have revealed weak social ties and a sense of vulnerability (Chaskin, 2013; Clampet-Lundquist, 2010), these dynamics are likely to be less of a factor in places with long-term (stable) diversity. Income-diverse neighborhoods have been shown in some cases to increase feelings of safety among low-income residents who were previously living in concentrated poverty (Briggs, 2010). Place diversity is important because it may help build social capital of the "bridging" kind by widening networks of social interaction (Putnam, 2000).

A different motivation is to link neighborhood diversity to social equity (Talen, 2008). The idea is that social diversity is equitable because it ensures better access to resources for all social groups – it nurtures what is known as the "geography of opportunity" (Briggs, 2005). Lack of income diversity translates to neighborhoods that experience concentrated poverty, leading to disinvestment in the built environment. Moreover, as Sampson, Mare, and Perkins (2015) argue, as these extremes remain concentrated, the advancement of mixed-income neighborhoods may be more of a challenge than anticipated. Poor physical conditions and lack of facilities play a role in perpetuating an "American Apartheid" since it is unlikely that higher-income social groups will be attracted to places with bad physical qualities and few facilities.

In a related, second sense, diversity is seen as a utopian ideal – that mixing population groups is the ultimate basis of a better, more creative, more tolerant, more peaceful and stable world. Under one objective, distribution and access to resources is a matter of fairness. Under the second, even those in higher-income brackets can take advantage of the creativity, social capital, and cross-fertilization that occurs when people of different backgrounds, income levels, and racial and ethnic groups are mixed. The former speaks to functionality and material need, the latter to the nurturing of the human spirit.

The idea of calculated social mixing in cities and towns – deliberately attempting to put people of different means and backgrounds in the same general area – was born in the 19th century by idealists and social critics who deplored the living conditions of the poor. The Settlement Houses and Co-Partnerships of Samuel and Henrietta Barnett, Octavia Hill, Jane Addams, and others were aimed at educating and socializing the poor, but also sensitizing the rich through deliberate social mix in urban places. Others focused on constructing utopian communities that deliberately mixed people of different social and economic classes through spatial planning and housing design. Examples include company towns like Bournville or Ebenezer's Garden Cities of Letchworth, Welwyn Garden City, and Wythenshawe. They were meant to include all social groups, although in varying degrees of physical closeness. Whereas Howard's idea of mix was more segregated on a micro-level, Bourneville's mix was fine-grained. But even Howard's idea included a level of mix that far exceeded conventional American patterns: places to work, shop, and recreate were to be within a short walking distance. Raymond Unwin, the architect who gave physical form to Howard's theory of Garden Cities, stated that town planning must "prevent the complete separation of different classes of people" (Unwin, 1909, p. 294). Of course, there were limits: "close enough, but not too close" as Hall describes Unwin's attempt at social mix (Hall, 2002, p. 104).

Sociologists argue that if people are confined to a social environment with concentrated problems, a variety of life chances are diminished, such as access to health care and employment information. Social scientists often focus on the strong links that can be made between social and spatial isolation, emphasizing neighborhood as the context of social problems. Children growing up in neighborhoods of diminished resources are negatively impacted because student achievement is significantly influenced by classmates and their families, not just teachers. Researchers have concluded that the concentration of social disadvantage leads to an increase in crime rates (Sampson, Raudenbush, & Earls, 1997; see also Burtless, 1996; Chetty, Hendren, & Katz, 2015; Jargowsky, Crutchfield, & Desmond, 2005). Concentrated poverty also correlates with economic dislocation and the loss of jobs, something William Julius Wilson protested in *The Truly Disadvantaged* (Wilson, 1987).

Because of concentrated social conditions like joblessness, the segregated neighborhood will experience property disinvestment, housing abandonment, and the withdrawal of commercial activity. Kefalas' study of a working class neighborhood showed how racism was being driven by the deterioration of place, where the physical decay of the ghetto was used "as irrefutable evidence of widespread social breakdown" (Kefalas, 2003, p. 52). Loss of consumer income means loss of consumer demand and a depleted retail sector. Rich and poor communities will have different tax structures resulting in different resource levels. High-income residents will seek lower property tax rates, while low-income neighborhoods will have to tax themselves at a much higher rate to receive a comparable level of service (Massey & Fischer, 2003).

Integration also creates a basis for "pluralist politics" based on shared benefit, whereas non-diverse, exclusively poor neighborhoods compete for public expenditures on their own. Neighborhood-based diversity provides the basis for shared concern, a "coalition politics based on geographically structured self-interest" (Massey & Denton, 1993, pp. 14, 157). Diversity is thus essential for making sure that groups can share interests and build political effectiveness. Social segregation, by limiting this power, limits the degree to which physical improvements – facilities like schools and parks – are likely to be funded. Supporting this are findings that neighborhood public facilities play a role in reducing crime, which is important for sustaining mixed-income communities (Myerson, 2001; Peterson, Krivo, & Harris, 2000).

What explains neighborhood diversity?

In the U.S., there has long been a certain acceptance of the inevitability of differentiation and segregation of the kind Park, Burgess and McKenzie identified almost a century ago, when they proclaimed that "competition forces associational groupings." Leveraging the extraordinary work of the Local Community Research Committee, which merged tract-level data by community area starting in 1920, Park and the Chicago School made clear that the result of "continuous processes of invasions and accommodations" was a subdivided residential pattern of varying classes and associated land values, mores, and degrees of "civic interest." Where one neighborhood might be "conservative, law-abiding, civic-minded," another would be "vagrant and radical." Such differentiation and segregation developed along racial, linguistic, age, sex, and income lines, forming units of communal life that they termed "natural areas" (Park, Burgess, & McKenzie, 1925, pp. 78–79).

Thus began the tradition of defining neighborhoods based on segregation. Zone, sector, and wedge models were constructed to explain similarity and patterning, looking for areas that could be considered to be organically unified and, it might be assumed in many cases, internally integrated. As the decades progressed, spatial patterning models became more complex, although the search for social homogeneity was always paramount. In the 1970s, Hawkes brought in the question of distance from the city center in an effort to explain the social patterning of 351 census tracts in Baltimore. His model achieved what subsequent researchers have sought: finding "the spatially systematic variation" of people in neighborhoods" (Hawkes, 1973, p. 1234). A standard geographer's definition of neighborhood is not dissimilar. One reads: "A neighborhood *sensu stricto* is a defined area within which there is an identifiable subculture to which the majority of its residents conform."[2]

The important point is that the Chicago School did not provide much support for the idea that neighborhoods could be viably mixed. It was the village – a freestanding neighborhood, not an urban one – that, according to R. D. McKenzie, represented the "dominance of neighborhood over kinship as a bond of union" (McKenzie, 1924, p. 344). There was something universal and hardwired about the social make-up of the village, the result of "common human nature responding to common stimuli" (McKenzie, 1924, p. 348) so it was imbued with a natural form of social integration. City neighborhoods, in contrast, did not have it: they instead thrived on differentiation along economic, racial, or cultural lines.

As a result of this ethos, our understanding of the factors that underlie diverse neighborhoods is mostly theoretical (Grant & Perrott, 2011; Tomer, Kneebone, Puentes, & Berube, 2011). Yet we can postulate three sets of factors that are likely to increase neighborhood diversity: (1) built environment and zoning; (2) housing and economic development policy; and (3) governance and institutions. The list below pays special attention to factors that are related to diversity as well as walkability.

Built environment and zoning. The built environment is believed to contribute to diversity if it permits a mix of housing types – i.e., variation of sizes, tenures, and building ages, which would permit a mix of rents and prices and thus enable income diversity. The mix might be accomplished where larger or more expensive housing is developed in lower-income areas through demolition and replacement or by restoring housing previously divided into smaller apartments. A mix of lot sizes, shapes, and positioning relative to the street might also encourage the mixing of unit sizes and types and therefore prices. A longstanding theory posits that diversity will be more stable if the outward variation of housing type is minimized (e.g., by making apartment dwellings look like large single-family homes), with minimal difference in the design and quality of housing for different income categories. Density is believed to play a role in maintaining diversity and walkability as well, although the relationship for diversity is unlikely to be linear (density may exacerbate segregation because high density enables serviceability and stimulates demand). On the other hand, lack of density poses a significant problem for low-income people when it comes to the provision of neighborhood-level facilities and access to jobs and urban services. Zoning can encourage both walkability and income diversity by allowing mixed housing types, mixed uses, and eliminating rules that homogenize development (minimum lot size, maximum density, minimum setbacks, and other barriers to diverse development types) (see Brophy & Smith, 1997; Hughes & Seneca, 2004; Jacobs, 1961; Lang & Danielson, 2002; Pendall & Carruthers, 2003; Talen, 2010, 2012).

Housing and economic development policy. A wide range of policies and programs might play a role in fostering stable, mixed-income, and well-serviced neighborhoods. Housing-related policies include: new mixed-income neighborhoods, scattered-site housing, vouchers, community land trusts, inclusionary housing requirements, tax credits, bonus densities, transfer of development rights, condominium conversion ordinances, and limits on the use of restrictive covenants. Some policies are designed to limit gentrification which may have the effect of encouraging stable income diversity, including rent control and strategies for subsidizing low-income housing in high- or middle-income neighborhoods. Economic development policies that may promote healthy, equitable neighborhoods include tax increment financing, enterprise zones, business improvement districts, community facilities funding; or policies that support neighborhood-scale businesses via tax incentives or grants. Policies promoting small-scale infill (e.g., adaptive reuse, infill on reclaimed land, or niche housing for seniors or students) may promote "partial/small-scale gentrification" resulting in stable, mixed-income neighborhoods. Infrastructure policies that support public transportation and economic development policies that support employment have also been tied to income diversity. Former industrial sites replaced by luxury townhomes, condominiums, and shopping malls may become the basis of income diverse tracts (Kennedy & Leonard, 2001; see also Freeman & Braconi, 2004; Lee & Leigh, 2004; Orfield, 2002; Polese & Stren, 2000; Vigdor, 2002; Zuk & Chapple, 2016).

Governance and institutions. There are well-developed theories about the essential role of neighborhood-based empowerment in sustaining social diversity and place quality. One view is that lack of resident empowerment translates to an inability to inform decision-making toward positive, neighborhood-sustaining investments. Some neighborhoods have adopted revitalization strategies that are small scale, scattered, shaped by residents, and intended to promote stable diversity. Studies consistently document that successful improvement-without-displacement efforts are a matter of "residents rallying together," a mobilization forged by an ability to organize and activate a local constituency and stimulate participation in a neighborhood-based group. Some stress the importance of neighborhood-based political representation, including privately or government-sanctioned neighborhood associations, advisory neighborhood councils, or district-level election of city council. The long-term diverse neighborhood may be a place that has been able to capitalize on "collective efficacy," where diversity has engendered bridging social capital. Sociologists argue the importance of an "organizational infrastructure" (a diversity of nonprofits and collective enterprises) and the importance of a neighborhood's "institutional base" extends to diverse neighborhoods, too, seen as especially important for creating "strong cross-status ties" in mixed-income areas. Neighborhood legal tools (taxing powers of business improvement districts, code enforcement, neighborhood service centers, neighborhood councils) provide empowerment, reduce urban alienation, maintain accountability, and can stimulate interest in walkability (Clampet-Lundquist, 2010; Curran & Hamilton, 2012; McKnight, 2013; Miller, 2012; Morrish & Brown, 2000; Pearsall, 2012; Putnam, 2000; Rose, 2000; Sampson, 2011; Sampson, Morenoff, & Earls, 1999; Wenger, 2015; Wolch, Byrne, & Newell, 2014).

What are alternatives to neighborhood diversity?

Several proposals have been put forward that run counter to the promotion of neighborhood-scale diversity. One is to focus on a homogeneous neighborhood's external connection. In this view, what matters is how well neighborhoods connect to a larger metropolitan or even global domain, such that their internal homogeneity becomes less of an issue. For marginalized social groups, failure to make these external linkages can be devastating. In France, the segregated *banlieue* have no physical or social connection to the existing boroughs surrounding the city, making the neighborhoods "marginal, irrelevant," and there is now an urgent call to reintegrate each neighborhood as "a tile of the great urban mosaic" (Picone & Schilleci, 2013, pp. 356, 363).

Researchers at the Washington, D.C.-based Urban Institute made a related case, arguing that neighborhoods themselves should be defined as districts composed of smaller homogenous blocks clustering together. They termed their scheme the "mosaic district." The district-neighborhood would share larger facilities like parks, schools, and commercial streets – assets that would act as social seams to encourage important, though weaker social ties. Such ties would not be the same as those that could occur among proximal neighbors at the sub-neighborhood scale, where residents would be bonded by income, ethnicity, or race (Tach et al., 2014).

Another response to the neighborhood diversity imperative is to normalize the ethnically concentrated neighborhood. Neighborhood segregation in the form of concentrated poverty cannot be good – but what about neighborhood segregation in the form of a thriving ethnic enclave? The ethnic enclave is shorthand for the self-selected clustering of people according to cultural, ethnic, or religious similarity. Can the ethnic neighborhood be viewed positively because it is self-selected, and therefore much different from the ghetto, slum, or other instance of imposed segregation? Can it be viewed positively because it is likely to be mixed on other dimensions, such as age and income?

Conclusion

Efforts to promote neighborhood diversity are not always welcomed. Social mix policies are sometimes met with claims about a "hidden social cleansing agenda," where words like "renaissance," and "sustainability" stand in for gentrification (Lees, 2008, pp. 2451, 2452). The resistance is felt on the ground, and well reported. In New York City, Mayor de Blasio's seemingly progressive housing mix policies produced "screaming matches" aimed at halting development entirely. Any investments – whether affordable housing, or street upgrades – were resisted. Residents seemed highly attuned to the problem of gentrification, and simply wanted affordable housing to be preserved. Newly constructed units ostensibly aimed at diversifying the neighborhood would, in some residents' views, only increase height, density, and housing prices (Yee & Navarro, 2015).

Other critics argue that there is simply not enough empirical support that mixed neighborhoods actually achieve what they are supposed to: more resources for the neighborhood, improved social networks, and strengthened local economies. Critics find the evidence backing claims about social mix "rather thin," and that living in a neighborhood with "resource-rich people" does not help poor people find jobs or increase their social capital (Bolt & Van Kempen, 2011, p. 362). Where the increased mix is the result of gentrification, poorer, longtime residents might value the increase in safety and amenities that newcomers seem to attract, but they feel alienated. Long-timers miss the home-grown services their neighborhoods used to have (for example, see Dastrup et al., 2015). Residents of gentrified neighborhoods seem to lack their own sense of neighborhood – both in terms of belonging to a shared place, and in terms of being able to leverage neighborhood for shared purposes.

Robert Sampson summarized the "theoretical assumptions" underlying mixed-income neighborhoods and found them to be suspect: that low-income residents benefit from high-income neighbors as models of behavior and educational attainment; that positive interaction and social support is dependent on residential proximity; that higher-income residents are willing to provide this social support via informal social control or organizational involvement; and that these improvements in social engagement and role-model provision will offset neighborhood instability resulting from attempts to mix up the population of a neighborhood. In addition, mixed-income policy "assumes a static equilibrium with regard to intervention effects," it does not account for "interdependencies" among neighborhoods in terms of "social mechanisms," and it ignores the macro-level political and social realms (Sampson, 2014).

Beyond the usual arguments about the value of neighborhood diversity as a moral imperative – arguments that have been made for a century now – there are two important counter points to make in response to criticisms about the value of neighborhood diversity and policies aimed at achieving it. First, the vast majority of poor neighborhoods are still suffering from the opposite problem – too little investment – and are not, by any stretch, at risk of gentrification and displacement. Poor neighborhoods are caught in cycles of disadvantage that are entrenched and extremely difficult to break. While it is true that gentrification has been displacing some people in some neighborhoods, overall the issue is limited to a relatively small percentage of neighborhoods. Less than 10% of high poverty neighborhoods in 1970 had reduced their poverty rate to below the national average by 2010 (Cortright & Mahmoudi, 2014). It would seem that any increase in investment via social mixing would be a welcomed turn.

Second, too much of the criticism is aimed at neighborhood level social inter-action, rather than basic neighborhood functionality. Because the social neigh-borhood over-shadows so much of the neighborhood discourse, arguments against neighborhood social mixing policy tend to get reduced to an inability to attain social interaction and "community" goals,[3] when the more important aim of neighborhood social mixing might be to garner improvements in basic neigh-borhood serviceability and livability. Mixed-income housing, when viewed as a matter of affordances and all that implies – functionality, access, safety, identity, beauty – contributes to a number of objectives that lie outside the terrain of social mechanisms. There is an argument to be made, then, that the social mixing debate need not devolve into dismissals of "spatial solutions to poverty," as if place and the opportunities it affords are irrelevant – where the physical neigh-borhood is seen as no longer mattering.[4] To the extent that social mixing improves a neighborhood's form and functionality via an influx of investment and political capital, perhaps this is strong enough backing for social mixing policies.

When social mixing and serviceability goals are combined, this is framed as the "sustainable" city. Beatley and Manning (1997, p. 36) define a sustainable place as one where separation by income and race is "nonexistent," and where residents have equal access to "basic and essential services and facilities" (see also Steiner, 2002). Policymakers have sought to implement sustainability in cities as far-reaching as Cape Town, Beijing, and Santiago, although so far, most of the evaluation research is U.S. based. Opinions on likely success are mixed. Some have concluded that mixed-income neighborhood policies do not work as well as containment policies (like urban growth boundaries) when it comes to racial desegregation. Opposing studies argue that containment pol-icies increase housing prices, and as a result, can't be good for social mixing.[5] One researcher seeking to understand whether containment adequately con-fronts segregation – therefore helping America become "the country it ought to be" – argued that it really isn't possible to find a single answer. Achieve-ment varies by density, region, politics, and position along an urban-to-rural continuum (Dierwechter, 2014).

Probably everyone agrees that when it comes to socially mixed neighbor-hoods, there could be more nuance, sensitivity, and adjustment. We need to learn from our decades of attempting to create mixed neighborhoods – whether via new high-end condos constructed in poor neighborhoods, or subsidized housing in otherwise wealthy neighborhoods – and refine accordingly. Physical forms have been less than helpful – awkwardly placed new developments where the wealthy quickly retreat inside their homes, public space that is not accessible and badly designed, or services that never materialize.[6] Many still hold out hope that these missteps should not signal complacency about the inter-related problems of all-wealthy and all-poor neighborhoods. As Joe Cortright argued, we should "stop demonizing the very changes that are, however slowly and awkwardly, moving us in the right direction" (Cortright, 2015).

We have learned that proximity alone does not achieve a plural, integrated society. People in a diverse setting find other, non-spatial ways of maintaining what Robert Park called "social distance." In an earlier time this took the form of "upstairs/downstairs, as in Haussmann's Paris, back of streets and front of streets, as in Engels' Manchester, front building/back building, as in Berlin's Mietskasernen" (Marcuse & van Kempen, 2002, p. 23). In our time, social distance is maintained via homeowner association rules that prohibit the aesthetics and functionality of low-income and nonwhite neighborhoods: materials (for siding, roofing) cannot be "cheap," no clotheslines for laundry (which is a public display of private items), no pickup trucks in front yards or parked on the street (working-class accoutrements are to be kept hidden), no signs of "visible commerce," no basketball courts (Maher, 2004). Small physical elements can be substantial human barriers too: home security systems, walls, gates, fences and even cyberspace are the "discourse of urban fear" that encode class separation (Ellin, 1997; Low, 2003).

And we have learned that the desire for social mix varies widely depending on cultural background. For example, claims are made that Latinos seek sociability in a neighborhood that is way above the average American, since "community interaction is a vital element of the Latino lifestyle" – creating a need for "active and animated community gathering spaces." For Latinos, "the more the dynamic the diversity" the better, preferring neighborhoods with the "multi" effect – multicultural, multisocial, multigenerational, multiincome, multitenure, multiuse, multihouse types, multidensity, multiarchitectural styles, multitechnology (Cisneros & Rosales, 2006, pp. 90, 95).

Notes

1 For recent reviews, see Carlson et al. (2016); Grasser, Van Dyck, Titze, and Stronegger (2013); Kerr et al. (2014).
2 U.S. Department of Commerce, Bureau of the Census, 1980 Census of Population and Housing, Census Tracts. For current tract definition see www.census.gov/geo/reference/gtc/gtc_ct.html; "Defining Neighborhood." *National Civic Review, 73*, no. 9 (1984), 428–429. doi:10.1002/ncr.4100730902. p. 429.
3 This is the main basis of the rather acerbic critique of social mixing advanced by Lees (2008). See also Cheshire (2006).
4 For a very anti-space and place argument, see Goetz and Chapple (2010). The quote is from p. 229.
5 Contrast Nelson (2013), and Pozdena (2002). See also Dierwechter (2014, p. 692), paraphrasing Dreier, Mollenkopf, and Swanstrom (2013).
6 These design limitations were clear in this study: Davidson (2010).

References

Albouy, D., & Zabek, M. (2016). *Housing inequality* (No. w21916). National Bureau of Economic Research. Social Science Research Network. http://ssrn.com/abstract= 2721777.

Baumgartner, M. P. (1991). *The moral order of a suburb*. New York: Oxford University Press.

Beatley, T., & Manning, K. (1997). *The ecology of place: Planning for environment, economy, and community*. Washington, DC: Island Press.

Bolt, G., & Van Kempen, R. (2011). Successful mixing? Effects of urban restructuring policies in Dutch neighbourhoods. *Tijdschrift voor economische en sociale geografie, 102*(3), 361–368.

Briggs, X. de Souza. (2005). *The geography of opportunity: Race and housing choice in metropolitan America*. Washington, DC: Brookings Institution.

Briggs, X. de Souza. (2010). *Moving to opportunity: The story of an American experiment to fight ghetto poverty*. New York: Oxford University Press.

Brophy, P. C., & Smith, R. N. (1997). Mixed-income housing: Factors for success. *Citiscape: A Journal of Policy Development and Research, 3*(2), 3–31.

Brown, A. L., Khattak, A. J., & Rodriguez, D. A. (2008). Neighbourhood types, travel and body mass: A study of new urbanist and suburban neighbourhoods in the US. *Urban Studies, 45*(4), 963–988.

Brown, B. B., & Cropper, V. L. (2001). New urban and standard suburban subdivisions: Evaluating psychological and social goals. *Journal of the American Planning Association, 67*(4), 402–419.

Burtless, G. (1996). *Does money matter: The effects of school resources on student achievement and adult success*. Washington, DC: Brookings Institution.

Carlino, G. A., Chatterjee, S., & Hunt, R. M. (2006). *Urban density and the rate of invention*. Working Paper, No. 06–14, Federal Reserve Bank of Philadelphia.

Carlson, J. A., Remigio-Baker, R. A., Anderson, C. A., Adams, M. A., Norman, G. J., Kerr, J., ... & Allison, M. (2016). Walking mediates associations between neighborhood activity supportiveness and BMI in the Women's Health Initiative San Diego cohort. *Health & Place, 38*, 48–53.

Chaskin, R. J. (2013). Integration and exclusion: Urban poverty, public housing reform, and the dynamics of neighborhood restructuring. *The Annals of the American Academy of Political and Social Science, 647*(1), 237–267.

Cheshire, P. C. (2006). Resurgent cities, urban myths and policy hubris: What we need to know. *Urban Studies, 43*(8), 1231–1246.

Chetty, R., Hendren, N., & Katz, L. F. (2015). The effects of exposure to better neighborhoods on children: New evidence from the Moving to Opportunity experiment. *The American Economic Review, 106*(4), 855–902.

Cisneros, H. G., & Rosales, J. (2006). *Casa y comunidad: Latino home and neighborhood design*. BuilderBooks.com.

Clampet-Lundquist, S. (2010). "Everyone had your back": Social ties, perceived safety, and public housing relocation. *City & Community, 9*(1), 87–108.

Cortright, J. (2015, October 29). Truthiness in gentrification reporting. *City Observatory*. Retrieved July 5, 2017, from http://cityobservatory.org/truthiness-in-gentrification-reporting/.

Cortright, J., & Mahmoudi, D. (2014). Lost in place: Why the persistence and spread of concentrated poverty – not gentrification – is our biggest urban challenge. *City Observatory*.

Retrieved July 5, 2017, from http://cityobservatory.org/wp-content/uploads/2014/12/LostinPlace_12.4.pdf.

Curran, W., & Hamilton, T. (2012). Just green enough: Contesting environmental gentrification in Greenpoint, Brooklyn. *Local Environment, 17*(9), 1027–1042.

Dastrup, S., Ellen, I., Jefferson, A., Weselcouch, M., Schwartz, D., & Cuenca, K. (2015). *The effects of neighborhood change on New York City Housing Authority residents.* New York: NYC Center for Economic Opportunity, Office of the Mayor.

Davidson, M. (2010). Love thy neighbour? Social mixing in London's gentrification frontiers. *Environment and Planning A, 42*(3), 524–544.

Dierwechter, Y. (2014). The spaces that smart growth makes: Sustainability, segregation, and residential change across Greater Seattle. *Urban Geography, 35*(5), 691–714.

Dreier, P., Mollenkopf, J. H., & Swanstrom, T. (2013). *Place matters: Metropolitics for the twenty-first century* (2nd rev. ed.). Lawrence: University Press of Kansas.

Durand, C. P., Andalib, M., Dunton, G. F., Wolch, J., & Pentz, M. A. (2011). A systematic review of built environment factors related to physical activity and obesity risk: Implications for smart growth urban planning. *Obesity Reviews, 12*(5), 173–182.

Ellin, N. (1997). *Architecture of fear.* Princeton, NJ: Princeton Architectural Press.

Erickson, K. I., Raji, C. A., Lopez, O. L., Becker, J. T., Rosano, C., Newman, A. B., ... & Kuller, L. H. (2010). Physical activity predicts gray matter volume in late adulthood: The Cardiovascular Health Study. *Neurology, 75*(16), 1415–1422.

Florida, R. (2002a). *The rise of the creative class.* New York: Basic Books.

Florida, R. (2002b). The economic geography of talent. *Annals of the Association of American Geographers, 92*(4), 743–755.

Florida, R. (2004). The great creative class debate: Revenge of the squelchers. *The Next American City, 5.*

Florida, R. (2005). *Cities and the creative class.* New York and London: Routledge.

Freeman, L. (2005). *There goes the hood: Views of gentrification from the ground up.* Philadelphia: Temple University Press.

Freeman, L., & Braconi, F. (2004). Gentrification and displacement: New York City in the 1990s. *Journal of the American Planning Association, 70*(1), 39–53.

Fry, R., & Taylor, P. (2012). The rise of residential segregation by income. *Pew Research Center's Social & Demographic Trends Project.* Retrieved January 28, 2015, from www.pewsocialtrends.org/2012/08/01/the-rise-of-residential-segregation-by-income/.

Glaeser, E. (2000). The future of urban research: Nonmarket interactions. *Brookings-Wharton Papers on Urban Affairs*, 101–150.

Glaeser, E. (2011). *Triumph of the city: How our greatest invention makes us richer, smarter, greener, healthier, and happier.* New York: Penguin Press.

Glaeser, E. L., Kallal, H. D., Scheinkman, J. A., & Shleifer, A. (1992). Growth in cities. *Journal of Political Economy, 100*(6), 1126–1152.

Goetz, E. G., & Chapple, K. (2010). You gotta move: Advancing the debate on the record of dispersal. *Housing Policy Debate, 20*(2), 209–236.

Grant, J., & Perrott, K. (2011). Where is the café? The challenge of making retail uses viable in mixed-use suburban developments. *Urban Studies, 48*(1), 177–195.

Grasser, G., Van Dyck, D., Titze, S., & Stronegger, W. (2013). Objectively measured walkability and active transport and weight-related outcomes in adults: A systematic review. *International Journal of Public Health, 58*(4), 615–625.

Hall, P. (2002). *Cities of tomorrow: An intellectual history of urban planning and design in the twentieth century* (3rd ed.). Oxford: Blackwell.

Hall, P. V., & Hesse, M. (2012). *Cities, regions and flows* (Vol. 40). London: Routledge.

Hawkes, R. K. (1973). Spatial patterning of urban population characteristics. *American Journal of Sociology, 78*(5), 1216–1235.

Hughes, J. W., & Seneca, J. J. (2004). *The beginning of the end of sprawl?* Rutgers Regional Report, Issue Paper No. 21. New Brunswick, NJ: Edward J. Bloustein School of Planning and Public Policy.

Hwang, J., & Sampson, R. J. (2014). Divergent pathways of gentrification racial inequality and the social order of renewal in Chicago neighborhoods. *American Sociological Review, 79*(4), 726–751.

Jack, E., & McCormack, G. R. (2014). The associations between objectively-determined and self-reported urban form characteristics and neighborhood-based walking in adults. *International Journal of Behavioral Nutrition and Physical Activity, 11*(1), 71.

Jacobs, A., & Appleyard, D. (1987). Toward an urban design manifesto. *Journal of the American Planning Association, 53*(1), 112–120.

Jacobs, J. (1961). *The death and life of American cities.* New York: Vintage Books.

Jargowsky, P. A., Crutchfield, R., & Desmond, S. A. (2005). Suburban sprawl, race, and juvenile justice. In D. F. Hawkins & K. Kempf-Leonard (Eds.), *Our children, their children: Confronting racial and ethnic differences in American juvenile justice.* Chicago: University of Chicago Press.

Kefalas, M. (2003). *Working-class heroes: Protecting home, community, and nation in a Chicago neighborhood.* Berkeley: University of California Press.

Kennedy, M., & Leonard, P. (2001). *Dealing with neighborhood change: A primer on gentrification and policy choices.* A discussion paper prepared for the Brookings Institution Center on Urban and Metropolitan Policy. Washington, DC: The Brookings Institution.

Kerr, J., Norman, G., Millstein, R., Adams, M. A., Morgan, C., Langer, R. D., & Allison, M. (2014). Neighborhood environment and physical activity among older women: Findings from the San Diego Cohort of the Women's Health Initiative. *Journal of Physical Activity and Health, 11*(6), 1070–1077.

Kim, J., & Kaplan, R. (2004). Physical and psychological factors in sense of community: New urbanist Kentlands and nearby Orchard Village. *Environment and Behavior, 36*(3), 313–340.

Kloos, B., & Shah, S. (2009). A social ecological approach to investigating relationships between housing and adaptive functioning for persons with serious mental illness. *American Journal of Community Psychology, 44*(3–4), 316–326.

Lang, R. E., & Danielson, K. A. (2002). Monster houses? Yes! *Planning, 68,* 24–26.

Ledebur, L. C., & Barnes, W. R. (1993). *All in it together: Cities, suburbs and local economic regions.* Washington, DC: National League of Cities.

Lee, S., & Leigh, N. G. (2004). Philadelphia's space in between: Inner-ring suburbs evolution. *International Journal of Suburban and Metropolitan Studies, 1*(1), 13–30.

Lees, L. (2008). Gentrification and social mixing: Towards an inclusive urban renaissance? *Urban Studies, 45*(12), 2449–2470.

Levasseur, M., Généreux, M., Bruneau, J. F., Vanasse, A., Chabot, É., Beaulac, C., & Bédard, M. M. (2015). Importance of proximity to resources, social support, transportation and neighborhood security for mobility and social participation in older adults: Results from a scoping study. *BMC Public Health, 15*(1), 503.

Lewis, M. (1938). *The culture of cities.* London: Secker & Warburg.

Leyden, K. M. (2003). Social capital and the built environment: The importance of walkable neighborhoods. *American Journal of Public Health, 93*(9), 1546–1551.

Low, S. M. (2003). The edge and the center: Gated communities and the discourse of urban fear. In S. M. Low & D. Lawrence-Zuniga (Eds.), *The anthropology of space and place: Locating culture* (Vol. 4). Oxford: Blackwell.

Maher, K. H. (2004). Borders and social distinction in the global suburb. *American Quarterly, 56*(3), 781–806.

Marcuse, P., & van Kempen, R. (2002). *Of states and cities: The partitioning of urban space*. Oxford: Oxford University Press.

Massey, D. S., & Denton, N. A. (1993). *American apartheid: Segregation and the making of the underclass*. Cambridge, MA: Harvard University Press.

Massey, D. S., & Fischer, M. J. (2003). The geography of inequality in the United States, 1950–2000. In W. G. Gale & J. R. Pack (Eds.), *Brookings-Wharton Papers on Urban Affairs* (pp. 1–40). Washington, DC: The Brookings Institution.

McKenzie, R. D. (1921). The neighborhood: A study of local life in the city of Columbus, Ohio. II. *American Journal of Sociology, 27*(3), 344–363.

McKnight, J. (2013). Neighbourhood necessities: Seven functions that only effectively organized neighbourhoods can provide. *National Civic Review, 102*(3), 22–24.

Miller, S. R. (2012). Legal neighborhoods. *SSRN Scholarly Paper*. Rochester, NY: Social Science Research Network.

Montgomery, J. (1998). Making a city: Urbanity, vitality and urban design. *Journal of Urban Design, 3*(1), 93–116.

Morrish, W. R., & Brown, C. R. (2000). *Planning to stay: Learning to see the physical features of your neighborhood*. Minneapolis, MN: Milkweed Editions.

Mumford, L. (1938). *The culture of cities*. London: Secker & Warburg.

Mumford, L. (1968). *The urban prospect*. New York: Harcourt, Brace & World.

Myerson, D. L. (2001). Sustaining urban mixed-income communities: The role of community facilities. A Land Use Policy Report prepared for The Urban Land Institute, *Charles H. Shaw Annual Forum on Urban Community Issue*, October 18–19. Chicago.

Nelson, A. C. (2013). *Reshaping metropolitan America: Development trends and opportunities to 2030*. Washington, DC: Island Press.

Nyden, P., Lukehart, J., Maly, M. T., & Peterman, W. (1998). Chapter 1: Neighborhood racial and ethnic diversity in US cities. *Cityscape*, 1–17.

Orfield, M. (2002). *American metropolitics: The new suburban reality*. Washington, D.C.: Brookings Institution.

Park, R., Burgess, E. W., & McKenzie, R. D. (1925). *The city: Suggestions for the study of human nature in the urban environment*. Chicago: University of Chicago Press.

Pearsall, H. (2012). Moving out or moving in? Resilience to environmental gentrification in New York City. *Local Environment, 17*(9), 1013–1326.

Pendall, R., & Carruthers, J. I. (2003). Does density exacerbate income segregation? Evidence from US metropolitan areas, 1980 to 2000. *Housing Policy Debate, 14*(4), 541–589.

Pendola, R., & Gen, S. (2008). Does "Main Street" promote sense of community? A comparison of San Francisco neighborhoods. *Environment and Behavior, 40*(4), 545–574.

Peterson, R. D., Krivo, L. J., & Harris, M. A. (2000). Disadvantage and neighborhood violent crime: Do local institutions matter? *Journal of Research in Crime and Delinquency, 37*, 31–63.

Picone, M., & Schilleci, F. (2013). A mosaic of suburbs: The historic boroughs of Palermo. *Journal of Planning History, 12*(4), 354–366.

Polese, M., & Stren, R. (Eds.). (2000). *The social sustainability of cities: Diversity and the management of change*. Toronto: University of Toronto Press.

Pozdena, R. J. (2002). *Smart growth and its effects on housing markets: The new segrega-tion.* Washington, DC: The National Center for Public Policy Research.

Putnam, R. D. (2000). *Bowling alone: The collapse and revival of American community.* New York: Simon & Schuster.

Putnam, R. D. (2007). E pluribus unum: Diversity and community in the twenty-first century: The 2006 Johan Skytte Prize Lecture. *Scandinavian Political Studies, 30*(2), 137–174.

Quigley, J. M. (1998). Urban diversity and economic growth. *The Journal of Economic Perspectives, 12*(2), 127–138.

Reardon, S. F., & Bischoff, K. (2011). Income inequality and income segregation 1. *American Journal of Sociology, 116*(4), 1092–1153.

Riggs, W. (2016). Inclusively walkable: Exploring the equity of walkable housing in the San Francisco Bay Area. *Local Environment, 21*(5), 527–554.

Roberts, M. (2007). Sharing space: Urban design and social mixing in mixed income new communities. *Planning Theory & Practice, 8*(2), 183–204.

Rogers, S. H., Halstead, J. M., Gardner, K. H., & Carlson, C. H. (2011). Examining walk-ability and social capital as indicators of quality of life at the municipal and neighbor-hood scales. *Applied Research in Quality of Life, 6*(2), 201–213.

Rose, D. R. (2000). Social disorganization and parochial control: Religious institutions and their communities. *Sociological Forum, 15*, 339–358.

Saarinen, E. (1943). *The city. Its growth. Its decay. Its future.* New York: Reinhold Pub-lishing Co.

Saelens, B. E., & Handy, S. L. (2008). Built environment correlates of walking: A review. *Medicine and Science in Sports and Exercise, 40*(7 Suppl), S550.

Saelens, B. E., Sallis, J. F., Black, J. B., & Chen, D. (2003). Neighborhood-based differ-ences in physical activity: An environment scale evaluation. *American Journal of Public Health, 93*(9), 1552–1558.

Sallis, J. F., Kraft, K., & Linton, L. S. (2002). How the environment shapes physical activity. *American Journal of Preventive Medicine, 22*(3), 208.

Sampson, R. J. (2011). Neighborhood effects, causal mechanisms, and the social structure of the city. In P. Demeulenaere (Ed.), *Analytical sociology and social mechanisms* (pp. 227–250). Cambridge and New York: Cambridge University Press.

Sampson, R. J. (2014). Notes on neighborhood inequality and urban design. *The City Papers, 7*(23).

Sampson, R. J., Mare, R. D., & Perkins, K. L. (2015). Achieving the middle ground in an age of concentrated extremes: Mixed middle-income neighborhoods and emerging adulthood. *The Annals of the American Academy of Political and Social Science, 660*(1), 156–174.

Sampson, R. J., Morenoff, J. D., & Earls, F. (1999). Beyond social capital: Spatial dynamics of collective efficacy for children. *American Sociological Review, 64*(5), 633–660.

Sampson, R. J., Raudenbush, S., & Earls, F. (1997). Neighborhoods and violent crime: A multilevel study of collective efficacy. *Science, 277*, 918–924.

Skjaeveland, O., & Garling, T. (1997). Effects of interactional space on neighbouring. *Journal of Environmental Psychology, 17*(3), 181–198.

Sohn, D. W., Moudon, A. V., & Lee, J. (2012). The economic value of walkable neigh-borhoods. *Urban Design International, 17*(2), 115–128.

Steiner, F. R. (2002). Foreword. In F. Ndubisi (Ed.). *Ecological planning: A historical and comparative synthesis* (pp. ix–xi). Baltimore: Johns Hopkins University Press.

Tach, L., Pendall, R., & Derian, A. (2014, January 24). Income mixing across scales: Rationale, trends, policies, practice, and research for more inclusive neighborhoods and metropolitan areas. *The Urban Institute*. Retrieved July 5, 2017, from www.urban.org/publications/412998.html.

Talen, E. (2008). *Design for diversity: Exploring socially mixed neighborhoods*. London: Elsevier.

Talen, E. (2010). The context of diversity: A study of six Chicago neighborhoods. *Urban Studies, 47*(3), 486–513.

Talen, E. (2012). *City rules: How regulations affect urban form*. Washington, DC: Island Press.

Talen, E., & Koschinsky, J. (2014). Compact, walkable, diverse neighborhoods: Assessing effects on residents. *Housing Policy Debate, 24*(4), 717–750.

Tomer, A., Kneebone, E., Puentes, R., & Berube, A. (2011). *Missed opportunity: Transit and jobs in metropolitan America*. Washington, DC: The Brookings Institution.

Unwin, R. (1909). *Town planning in practice: An introduction to the art of designing cities and suburbs*. London: T. Fisher Unwin.

Vigdor, J. L. (2002). Does gentrification harm the poor? *Brookings-Wharton Papers on Urban Affairs* (pp. 133–182). Washington, DC: The Brookings Institution.

Webber, M. M. (1963). Order in diversity: Community without propinquity. In L. Wingo (Ed.), *Cities and space: The future use of urban land* (pp. 23–54). Baltimore: Johns Hopkins University Press.

Wenger, Y. (2015, May 10). Saving Sandtown-Winchester: Decade-long, multimillion-dollar investment questioned. *Baltimoresun.com*. Retrieved July 5, 2017, from www.baltimoresun.com/news/maryland/baltimore-city/west-baltimore/bs-md-ci-sandtown-winchester-blight-20150510-story.html.

Wilson, W. J. (1987). *The truly disadvantaged: The inner city, the underclass and public policy*. Chicago: University of Chicago Press.

Wolch, J. R., Byrne, J., & Newell, J. P. (2014). Urban green space, public health, and environmental justice: The challenge of making cities "just green enough." *Landscape and Urban Planning, 125*, 234–244.

Wood, L., Frank, L. D., & Giles-Corti, B. (2010). Sense of community and its relationship with walking and neighborhood design. *Social Science & Medicine, 70*(9), 1381–1390.

Wood, L., Shannon, T., Bulsara, M., Pikora, T., McCormack, G., & Giles-Corti, B. (2008). The anatomy of the safe and social suburb: An exploratory study of the built environment, social capital and residents' perceptions of safety. *Health & Place, 14*(1), 15–31.

Yee, V., & Navarro, M. (2015, February 3). Some see risk in de Blasio's bid to add housing. *New York Times*. Retrieved July 5, 2017, from www.nytimes.com/2015/02/04/nyregion/an-obstacle-to-mayor-de-blasios-affordable-housing-plan-neighborhood-resistance.html.

Zuk, M., & Chapple, K. (2016). *Housing production, filtering and displacement: Untangling the relationships* (Urban Displacement Project). Berkeley, CA: Institute of Governmental Studies.

19 Simplexity, complicity, and emergent collectivities

Informal urbanism in Rome

Michael Neuman and Nadia Nur

Introduction

As cities continue to grow worldwide, with many booming and others struggling and/or shrinking – and the same goes for districts and neighborhoods within cities – issues of equity and sustainability increasingly define the domains of politics, policy, and economics in the urban realm. While making plans, policies, and designs for cities has become more sophisticated, and more successful and effective when aligned with growth and economic development, there remain many instances where poverty, decline, economic and social disparities, pollution, etc. stubbornly resist improvement. This latter holds true for a wide range of policy and planning tools, whether carrot or stick (incentive or disincentive), including infrastructure investment, design improvements, and social programs (incentives); or regulations and tariffs (disincentives). Is there something as (or more) effective than planning and policymaking in institutional arenas to address these problems?

One way has been for active and activist citizens and groups to take matters into their own hands by making change themselves. Grassroots efforts at urban change, including urban social movements, have been documented for generations (Castells, 1983). Yet much has changed since these earlier movements: globalization, climate change, terrorism, refugee and other migration, the internet, inequality, and other trends have all made strong imprints on cities and city life. Megacities and unprecedented degrees of urbanization define the 20th and 21st centuries as urban centuries. Slow-moving planning, policy, politics, and governing institutions have a hard time keeping up, and the evidence suggests that they are falling behind and increasingly failing their citizens.

In this vacuum, citizens have become more likely to fashion their own futures, as well as their immediate locale's. This occurs in spite of some success attributable to statutory participatory planning, where citizens and interest groups cooperate with official planning processes (Healey, Khakee, Motte, & Needham, 1997; Innes, Gruber, Neuman, Thompson, 1994). Citizen direct action also occurs in spite of, or perhaps due to, the failures of participatory planning, where dominant interests co-opt citizens, or government makes a mere show of participation yet does not take it into account in its decision making (Huxley & Yftachel, 2000; Legacy, 2016; Neuman, 2000).

The new types of direct citizen action – tactical urbanism, do-it-yourself urbanism, Better Block, and many more – are leading the way, breaking new ground. Cities such as Dallas, San Francisco, New York, and Amsterdam, to name a few, have taken notice and follow, in part, the citizens' lead. This movement, if it has risen to such a level, takes different shape depending on local conditions. These conditions include culture, politics, civil society, existing institutions' effectiveness, leadership, and more. Given the track record and promise of citizen-led planning and design, it is worthwhile to explore these cases closely, to see how, why, and under which conditions they can produce more sustainable and effective outcomes.

This chapter highlights the response of activist citizens in one city, Rome, Italy, to the multiple crises confronting them. Since the onset of the crisis in 2007/2008, Italy has been rocked by multiple, overlapping, and mutually reinforcing circumstances that have kept its economy in decline. These include its political economy, especially unemployment, poverty, homelessness, debt, in-migration of refugees, and outmigration of youth and professional talent, and their attendant crises of politics at all levels of government, including their fiscal conditions. This situation has continued unabated for a decade, and prospects remain bleak. Among the consequences of these crises, the resources government has to act are ever more scarce, and trust in government and its ability to act in the interests of the people is at an all-time low. As such, people tend to believe that politics as usual, even in unusual Italy, is futile, and reform has led nowhere.

For people under 30 years of age in 2007 at the outset of the crisis, their general responses to these drastic circumstances have been multifold. Given their lack of income, assets, and prospects, the youth have opted to:

1   live with their parents;
2   live in small, shared, and often substandard housing in crowded conditions;
3   move to another country to seek work or higher education;
4   move to rural areas to start another type of life;
5   remain in or return to higher education and thus out of the workforce;
6   design an entirely new way of living in situ in their city.

This chapter reports on and analyses this sixth approach because all the other approaches are seen by these protagonists as non-solutions, or short-term and precarious solutions. Moreover and more importantly, none of the first five approaches, despite being the ones predominantly chosen, is believed to address the underlying causes of the crisis conditions, nor do they propose any long-term, sustainable solutions.

These underlying conditions are deeply entrenched in the mainstream institutions and thus are difficult to change or improve in a significant way. Yet in Rome there are many passionate, dedicated, and creative individuals acting in concert through overlapping networks who create new types of work, new types of living arrangements and housing, and new spaces for collective and individual production, consumption, and enjoyment. In other words, they are creating fundamentally new modes of urban living and new modes of urbanism. "Commoning" is one term in use, which we describe in the case studies of Rome in this chapter.

Their modus operandi exhibits several features worth noting. They collaborate pragmatically, they share collectively, they make operational important values such equity, justice, solidarity, and sustainability. Their hallmark is to deliberately operate outside the mainstream by creating a viable alternative. The collective vocabularies – both literally in terms of terminology and figuratively in terms of new practices – that these social entrepreneurs employ as they shape their new lives are untested, fragile, and fraught with conflict and insecurity. Yet they move forward undaunted, their experimentation perseveres, even while encountering setbacks along the way, and push-back from government and other mainstream institutions, including the media. This is so because they see no other viable option (for them), and they are dedicated and committed to their cause.

In Rome as in Italy and other northern Mediterranean cities and towns, youth are at the vanguard in recognizing that politics and institutional reform have not offered real change, and thus have not offered hope for a better future. Their reply: to take matters into their own hands. Not merely do-it-yourself (DIY) urbanism, but do-it-yourself living.[1] The rest of this chapter illustrates and analyses a range of the activities recently and currently under way in Rome that may illuminate practices elsewhere. At the least, what is happening in Rome today may turn out to be significant because the crisis conditions in Rome, while perhaps not widespread in so-called advanced societies, are widespread elsewhere, and because they may be a harbinger of conditions to come in many more cities, including those of advanced societies. As such, it is metaphorically a canary in the coal mine.

Scup! A grassroots organization that provides training for the people

To understand Scup!, and indeed any grassroots urban social movement in Rome over the last decade, it is critical to understand its context. This was dominated by the crisis of 2008 to an extent not experienced in any other nation, save Greece and Spain. In Italy the crisis was comprehensive in nature, with financial, economic, social, political, and ecological dimensions. The first occupation of Scup! (Sport e Cultura Popolare) occurred in 2012, when the crisis was deep and continuing. Popular distrust of local government was soaring. At that time connections between the right-wing mayor and organized crime were increasingly evident (namely the Mafia Capitale[2] scandal two years later). Social conflicts within the city were intensifying. The political aspect of the crisis is ongoing, despite the changes in the political composition of the city council as a result of subsequent elections, including the latest in 2016.

Increasingly uneven wealth distribution and its resulting class polarization led to the shrinkage of the middle class, which attempted to cope with the ambiguity of its newly precarious position. The middle class had been active in society, yet now it is being marginalized by it. This polarization was marked by financial capital being increasingly captured by the wealthy, while at the same time the middle class reduced its consumption.

The ongoing economic crisis is not only affecting the GDP rate and purchasing power, but in a broader sense it is a crisis of the whole political system that is progressively jeopardizing the social and economic balance of society. The government, in particular the local administration, has almost completely lost its capacity to serve many emergent public (non-market) needs. Furthermore, political participation on which democracy is (still) grounded is no longer taken for granted. Sustainable and equitable growth seems to be just a pale aspiration. Thus, the State, from local administration to national welfare system, has lost its connection with the people.

In this new and volatile context, created and compounded by the ongoing crisis, the attitude toward civic engagement and self-determination gained in the era of postwar democracy is now turning into a powerful tool for constructing a radically alternative politics. This is being expressed by new social movements, of which Scup! is the first of our two chosen examples that we analyze. The other is Communia.

Unlike the old-style occupations and squats in Rome, that were clearly based on more radical leftist ideology, Scup! represents a landmark in the new wave of actions of reappropriation of spaces that spread mainly after the crisis began in 2008.

Although the Social Centers (CSOA – Centri Sociali Occupati Autogestiti) movement represented for decades a response to the commercialization of the city and its uneven and inequitable development, it eventually failed to extend cooperation with the broader network of non-insurgent activists, and failed to engage non-politicized citizens.[3] Since the beginning of the crisis, the landscape of the "alternative city" has changed and new realities have emerged. Barricades against the political system have been replaced by the claim for a better life against austerity measures. In exercising these claims, a wide range of citizens took direct action in new modes. Squats transformed into experimental multi-ethnical laboratories trying to solve both housing and migration issues simultaneously (Nur & Sehtman, 2016). Traditionally politicized Social Centers have progressively evolved to include the broader population: common citizens, workers, and local residents. Together, they confronted the lack of public services and spaces by fighting against privatization of public assets and real estate speculation (Della Ratta, 2013).

This new pragmatism evinced in Rome's urban social movements was apparent in the first building occupied by Scup! It was located between the San Giovanni neighborhood, a residential and commercial district very close to the city center, and Esquilino, an ethnically mixed neighborhood. The area has a heterogeneous and often contradictory social fabric, composed basically by middle-class residents living along with different socio-economic segments of the population such as upper-class managers, community-based organizations, tourists, pilgrims, and workers. In addition, due largely to its central location, the area attracts many homeless and Roma people (Romani gypsies). Moreover, it is also the site of real estate speculation and commercially oriented urban policies that consequently affected not only the weakest sectors of the resident population (elderly and migrants), but also the living conditions of the middle-income inhabitants.

The former administrative headquarters for motor vehicle registration, owned by the Minister of Transportation, on Via Nola, was abandoned at the time of its occupation by Scup!. The occupation was led by a group of young activists, sports instructors, and residents of the neighborhood, who decided to clean it up and restore it.

In 2004 this public building was included in the Public Real Estate Fund for its "valorization" and selling of public properties. The building was sold in 2010 to a private real estate company that was established just for that purpose, and then left vacant until the occupation in 2012. Since then it was re-appropriated and given a new life as a common urban resource, as well as other vacant buildings in the same district. For example, a building belonging to Banca d'Italia has been occupied since 2005 by the CSOA Sans Papier, and another building was occupied by Action and hosted 300 people until their eviction in 2015.

The occupation of Scup! represented the response of the citizens to the lack of public spaces and the increasing privatization of urban space, but it was above all symptomatic of the impact of the crisis on the daily life of the middle class. Basic needs such as housing, transportation, food, education, and welfare still remain as the basis of most urban social struggles. Yet for the newly impoverished middle urban class in Rome (as a result of the ongoing crisis), social and cultural activities, sport, wellness, and leisure were the first items to be cut in the list of household expenses. As "extra needs" they are no longer considered fundamental by public policies in this new age of extreme austerity. As a result, they were remanded to the private sector, therefore making them unaffordable to most people.

It was not only the austerity-driven shortage of public funds that led to the lack of basic and "extra" services. The political crisis that led to a lack of citizen participation in the making of public policy, and the incapacity of policymakers to meet citizens' demands in terms of communication, accessibility, reliability, and trust also must be taken into account. In this context, Scup! sparked citizen awareness and action by initiating and spreading civic dialogue on the collective use of urban commons as a tool to achieve wellbeing.

Against this background, the people who occupied the vacant building were a group of sports trainers, students, un- and under-employed persons, activists, and occupiers from other social centers. Their projects and aspirations merged into a new type of collective action. Acting as a "community of practices," they gave birth to a multifunctional and intercultural laboratory aimed at the "production of community based welfare and services, self-income and the promotion of accessible sport and affordable cultural activities, the realization of a public space for meeting, discussion and organization within the same urban collective space" (Costanza, 2016, p. 256).

The collective management of Scup! organized a set of activities that attracted people from various social classes and ages, thus contributing to the social recomposition of the neighborhood population. Moreover, Scup! activists worked in cooperation with the residents of other occupied spaces in the neighborhood, acting as a mediator with the residents in negotiating their presence and facilitating the integration of squatters and immigrants. They played a critical role in creating a common space for interaction.

The numerous activities carried out by Scup!, all free or extremely low cost, encompass a wide range of needs related to wellbeing, from the material to intellectual to leisure, from the essential to the superfluous ones, including:

- a popular gym with classes for yoga, tai chi, capoeira, boxing, bio-energetics, kickboxing, etc.;
- a public library with 5,000 volumes, managed in agreement with a network of self-managed libraries;
- cultural events, book presentations, concerts, public assemblies, debates, seminars, and workshops;
- psychological assistance and self-help groups;
- language courses;
- a recreational space for children;
- music and dance classes;
- Radio Sonar, a web radio station, managed in cooperation with the activists of Sans Papier social center;
- a free internet point;
- a tavern and bar;
- Ecosolpop, a monthly market of organic food, handicraft, and recycling, in cooperation with the urban laboratory Reset (Riconversione per un'Economia Solidale, Ecologica e Territoriale).

The ability to manage such heterogeneous activity led Scup! to position itself as a reference point in the neighborhood. Despite being illegal, it was perceived as a cross-class and intercultural container where people could experiment the practices of "commoning," the sharing economy, and new welfare.

> In this collaborative world, people are self-consciously engaged in a process of commoning: the bottom-up coordination, disputation, negotiation, social practices and ethics needed to create functioning commons. As social systems, these commons resemble, but go well beyond, the commons archetypes described by [Elinor] Ostrom.
>
> (Bollier, 2016)

Given the variety of activities, Scup!'s main achievement is to contribute to the development of a potentially transformative "common sector" (Bollier, 2016), that operates beyond the schematics of market vs. solidarity, essential vs. leisure, and public vs. private. Scup! functions within a network of activists, associations, and people aimed at reappropriating the city without necessarily belonging to an insurgent movement.

In 2015 Scup! was evicted[4] and the community of activists decided to occupy another building near Tuscolana Station, not far from the previous building, but far enough to cause a sensible loss in the relation with the territory. The eviction caused a massive campaign in support of Scup! and other threatened occupied places. Citizens, residents, associations, collectives, and occupiers gathered in Nola street to oppose the eviction in various forms: a spontaneous rally, a collective lunch, art and sports performances, a street book exchange, a campaign on social media posting their portraits with #iosonoscup written on them, asking the City Council of Rome to suspend the eviction. Scup!'s re-occupation was enhanced by a great part of "social Rome" – a grassroots network of activists and organizations – that enabled collective support to resilience and resistance.

Although all the activities and services initiated by Scup! are currently ongoing, the social and territorial environment is different from the one that existed in the San Giovanni district beforehand. It is now characterized by a more evident situation of social exclusion and deprivation. Since it is more distant from the city center and close to a minor railway station, and as it is basically residential, the neighborhood is now less attractive for tourists or non-residents. In consequence, its broader connection to the city has been weakened, as has Scup! itself.

Communia: mutual aid against austerity

In recent years squatting has re-emerged as a political practice in order to confront austerity policies, lack of welfare plans, and neoliberal urbanism. The right to housing is indeed the main issue raised by squatter movements that in 2013 enacted the so called "Tsunami Tour." The "tour" was a wave of occupations coordinated by Action-Diritti in Movimento, Blocchi Precari Metropolitani, Coordinamento di Lotta per la Casa that targeted more than 30 publicly and privately owned abandoned buildings in Rome that provided shelter for almost 2,000 people. As part of this initiative, a group of activists occupied an abandoned warehouse owned by the municipality in the San Lorenzo neighborhood and called it Communia, to recall the famous slogan by Thomas Muntzer "Omnia sunt communia."

The occupation of Communia is just one step on the pathway started with Ripubblica,[5] a network of social collectives grounded on the experience of the national campaign for Public Water, and continued with the occupation of Cinema America in Rome. The aim of the activists was to make that space a public space once again, following the model of the worker-owned factories in Argentina, and avoiding the activation of a speculative real estate process. After a few months, the activists decided to move to the former Bastianelli Foundries, after discovering that the previous building had toxic materials. The new occupation was supported by activists, students, volunteers, neighbors, and above all, by the Free Republic of San Lorenzo Network (more below) that contributed to the reshaping of the space. Yet after a few months, they were evicted. Mobilization resumed in the neighborhood, and Communia activists squatted another location, in agreement with the Free Republic of San Lorenzo, other associations, local groups, and the residents. The former Piaggio garage occupied now by Communia is located in a part of the district where a speculative real estate project has been launched to build new luxury residences. The garage has been totally modernized in the renovation by the squatters.

San Lorenzo, at the eastern border of the city center, is a neighborhood with a longstanding tradition of political engagement. Because it was a stronghold of antifascist resistance, it is still perceived as a leftist or communist district. Once a working-class quarter, now it is inhabited mainly by long-time residents and students coming from other parts of Italy, due to the presence of Sapienza University, which is one of the largest in Europe by enrollments. Despite the changes in the social composition, the increases of real estate value, and its transformation to a nightlife destination, the neighborhood still retains its political character with an inclusive and participatory attitude towards the emergence of autonomous spaces. Moreover, students are increasingly involved in the activities of social centers, and they conceive squatting as a solution to unaffordable rentals, which generally leads them to rely on black market rents (Martinez, 2013). Squatting is often considered as a way (sometimes the only one) to remain in the big city after graduation (Di Feliciantonio, 2016a), instead of going back to their hometown. A big percentage of students are from the south of Italy, where there are few possibilities to be employed after graduation. In addition, the economic crisis affecting their families back home reduces their chances of completing their studies in Rome.

Communia serves as a connection among students, the squatter movement, and social centers, since many activists and occupiers are themselves students. Almost 80% of the respondents to a survey conducted by Di Feliciantonio on Communia militants (Di Feliciantonio, 2016b) identified themselves as undergraduate or postgraduate students. Austerity policies, lack of housing, economic distress, and cuts in student services provided by the University are just some of the reasons that made students and squatters merge in the same movement. In this context of increasing precariousness,[6] the autonomous space of Communia represents a collective response to the deterioration of material conditions of students and young people in general.

The space of Mutual Aid in the Scalo di San Lorenzo street provides:

- services to students, such as a library, a reading/studying room open until midnight, managed by students;
- a tailor shop managed by refugees, with the aim of self-producing and distributing apparel within the "fuori mercato" sales channel (e.g., local self-organized markets);
- an information desk on citizenship and labor rights, within the project "Info-futuro" with the cooperation of various associations and labor unions;
- a theater laboratory;

- Italian classes for foreigners and other language laboratories;
- a bar where self-produced drinks are served (e.g., Ri-moncello, produced in the self-managed factory Rimaflow).

Providing a wide range of self-managed services, Communia engaged the people of the neighborhood in a process of communing, enabling them to create new communal resources to resist austerity and thus opening up a new communal thinking (Di Feliciantonio, 2016b). The idea of mutual aid on which Communia activities are based turned into a wider national program of mutual aid and a laboratory for self-production "apart from the market" (*fuori mercato*) and spread into Communia Network, that includes various associations, groups, committees, individuals, squatters, and students.

The idea of producing out of the market schemes, reactivating the economy of the area through the revitalization of the spaces of production, is at the basis of the network Fuorimercato, formed mainly by Commnia, SOS Rosarno, and Rimaflow. The challenge is to construct a sustainable (both socially and economically) alternative to the market system, based in an "equonomic" (equal and self-managed) point of view.

As demonstrated with the Communia network experience and with the other networks connected to it, the practice of commoning, that is mainly developed at a urban level, encompasses a diverse range of claims connected to the progressive deterioration of material conditions of everyday life. Thus, its political potential goes beyond the local scale, although in the Italian case it has not developed into a more broadly organized protest against national austerity policies.

Networking: the way to resilience

The networks within which Scup! and Communia act are composed primarily by other occupied spaces, social centers, associations, and collectives that join common projects with the aim of shaping a pathway for reappropriating urban spaces in order to transform them into "commons." Networking is also a way for redesigning the politics and planning of urban movements, enhancing their capacity of resilience, by which we mean the ability to resist hostile policies, to adapt to the volatile institutional environment, to reframe objectives and ideals, to reshape the patterns of reappropriation, and to act in a temporary frame.

Occupations in Rome have been cyclically attacked by the city government through resolutions that enable evictions. Attacks alternate with reconciliation through agreements on the use of vacant spaces. At the time of writing this chapter many occupied and "commoned" spaces are threatened by city council deliberation n. 140/2015, approved by the previous mayor, that has the aim to reorganize municipally owned properties and to evaluate the profitability of this real estate. The wave of evictions that could spread as a consequence of this resolution, which has precedent in the past, can seriously, and probably intentionally, undermine and deconstruct the exceptional network of associations, social centers, and autonomous communities that has risen recently in response to both the crisis and the austerity measures that have been put in place because of the crisis.

This occurs in the face of public policy that seems to be unable to manage neither the deep change in the political and social structure of the city (but also of the country) nor the new post-political forms of resistance and activism, that catalyze all the sectors of population affected by the crisis, activating autonomous forms of welfare in the absence of traditional public sector welfare. In this context, autonomous communities and occupied spaces sometimes "solve problems that might otherwise appear as classical market failures or state failures" (Bowles & Gintis, 2002) such as insufficient provision of local public goods such as neighborhood amenities.

Distant from the romantic idea of the civil society opposing the power of institutions, the purpose of these networks in Rome that we have reported on is to extend the democratic capacities of ordinary people, showing them that there is still a "possibility" to construct a new politics, although in an extra-institutional, and perhaps "illegal" environment. Occupation is illegal according to Italian law.

As we can read in the Charter for Roma Comune, written in the framework of the "Decide Roma" campaign[7] (www.decideroma.com), the right is not to be considered as a product of the authority of the State, but rises from practices and uses. Thus, it should be recognized as legitimate by public institutions. The charter is a work in progress aimed at setting the basis to rule the city according to the principles and the practices of the commons. As such, it is a radical re-imagining of a new urban politics.

Other attempts at institutionalization (Costanza, 2016) of the practices of commoning are those once enabled by the network DeLiberiamo Roma and Patrimonio Comune. The previous was grounded on a set of proposals to the Municipal Council, addressing a series of issues: water management, land use, knowledge and education, and finance. The latter was started as a campaign of pressure focused on the commons that could be described as a network of networks for a social enterprise economy and the "new welfare" by Scup! and others. These movements seek the right to housing, to establish local committees, to create collectives promoting art and culture, etc.

Our analysis reveals that the engagement with the neighborhood is fundamental for the resistance to the city government and the resilience of the self-managed spaces. The Repubblica di San Lorenzo played a crucial role in the resilience of Communia by organizing a public assembly, organizing rallies in the district, and providing consensus and practical support for the occupation. The network composed by squatters, residents, activists, the neighborhood committee, and other social organizations together set up an opinion movement claiming self-governance (*autogoverno*) was formed by the activists of Nuovo Cinema Palazzo, that has been for a few years one of the most lively self-organized social and cultural spaces in Rome. Its occupation in 2011 was supported by the neighborhood committee of San Lorenzo, that participated actively against the transformation of this old cinema into a community-based casino and social center.

The Communia network (www.communianet.org) is grounded on the experiences of occupation and recovery of factories and abandoned spaces, such as Ri-Maflow in Milan and the original Communia itself in Rome. The network represents the meeting point of various collectives against rising debt and economic precariousness, and has fused together with feminist and LGBT movements. This network operates at a national level, even as its nodes are mainly local.

The Communia network itself provides a framework for resilience since it releases the communities of activists from the "productivistic" approach that is central to the mainstream economy. Generally, movements tend to have a life-cycle (Prujit, 2003). Yet that does not necessarily imply that a movement must end, but the evidence throughout the rest of Italy suggests that it may weaken the insurgent impulse. Rome seems to be an exception, since the new network of grassroots movements and collectives is resilient, despite structural changes, fragmentation, and adaptation to the social and political context. The network seems not to want to reject institutions or representative democracy as a whole. Instead, it has introduced important new practices where politics can be understood in a more proactive and participative way, and in a stronger bond with the territory itself, independent of their extra-institutional nature.

Notes

1 Unless urbanism itself is understood "as a way of life." See Wirth (1938).
2 The scandal of Mafia Capitale exploded in 2014 when a Judicial Inquiry discovered a network comprised of criminals, public officers, and policymakers that was actually "governing" Rome and managing social emergencies (Mondo di mezzo inquiry). The main accusations were related to the mafia: including corruption, fraud, and collusive tendering. Citizens responded by organizing a two-day-long rally called "Spazziamoli" (let's wipe them out), promoted by two associations operating against the mafia: Libera and DaSud.
3 Two trends characterized Italian CSOAs: their integration into the metropolitan society by the recognition of their political and cultural roles, yet on the other hand, they chose to be a sort of ghetto.
4 In 2016, the occupation of Action in the same area was also evicted, and the 300 persons moved to other housing facilities. The result of this operation is the eradication of spaces of autonomy in the district of San Giovanni. At the time of writing this chapter, only the Sans Papier Social Center is still working in the San Giovanni district, although it is threatened with eviction, according to the deliberation n. 140 of the Council of Rome.
5 Ri-pubblica is a play on the word *repubblica* – republic – ri meaning once again, pubblica meaning public.
6 Precariousness is understood not only as a condition of labor uncertainty, but it involves many aspects of daily life, such as housing conditions, social relations, and trust in the future.
7 A previous attempt of institutionalization of "commoning" has been the Constitution of the Teatro Valle bene comune, that still represents a milestone. For more information, see www.teatrovalleoccupato.it.

References

Bollier, D. (2016). Transnational republics of commoning. Retrieved July 5, 2017, from http://bollier.org/blog/transnational-republics-commoning.

Bowles, S., & Gintis, H. (2002). Social capital and community governance. *The Economic Journal, 112*(483), F419–F436.

Castells, M. (1983). *The city and the grassroots: A cross-cultural theory of urban social movements* (No. 7). Berkeley: University of California Press.

Costanza, S. (2016). *Economic crisis, role of public authorities and the commons: Rome and the governance of urban resources.* PhD Thesis at Sapienza University, Faculty of Political Science, Rome.

Della Ratta. D. (2013, February 20). "Occupy" the Commons. *Al Jazeera.* Retrieved July 5, 2017, from www.aljazeera.com/indepth/opinion/2013/02/2013217115651557469.html.

Di Feliciantonio, C. (2016a). Students, migrants and squatting in Rome at times of austerity and material constraints. In P. Mudu & S. Chattopadhyay (Eds.), *Migration, squatting and radical autonomy: Resistance and destabilization of racist regulatory policies and b/ordering mechanisms.* London: Routledge.

Di Feliciantonio, C. (2016b). The reactions of neighborhoods to the eviction of squatters in Rome: An account of the making of precarious investor subjects. *European Urban and Regional Studies.* doi:10.1177/0969776416662110.

Healey, P., Khakee, A., Motte, A., & Needham, B. (Eds.). (1997). *Making strategic spatial plans: Innovation in Europe.* London: University College London Press.

Huxley, M., & Yftachel, O. (2000). New paradigm or old myopia? Unsettling the communicative turn in planning theory. *Journal of Planning Education and Research, 19*(4), 333–342.

Innes, J., Gruber, J., Neuman, M., & Thompson, R. (1994). Coordinating growth and environmental management through consensus building. *Report to the California Policy Seminar.* Berkeley, CA.

Legacy, C. (2016). Is there a crisis of participatory planning? *Planning Theory.* doi:10.1177/1473095216667433.

Martinez, M. A. (2013). The squatters movement in Europe: A durable struggle for social autonomy in urban politics. *Antipodes, 45*(4), 866–887.

Neuman, M. (2000). Communicate this: Does consensus lead to advocacy and pluralism? *Journal of Planning Education and Research, 19*(4), 343–350.

Nur, N., & Sehtman, A. (2016). Migration and mobilization for the right to housing: New urban frontiers? In P. Mudu & S. Chattopadhyay (Eds.), *Migration, squatting and radical autonomy: Resistance and destabilization of racist regulatory policies and b/ordering mechanisms.* London: Routledge.

Prujit, H. (2003). Is the institutionalization of urban movements inevitable? A comparison of the opportunities for sustained squatting in New York City and Amsterdam. *International Journal of Urban and Regional Research, 27*(1), 133–157.

Wirth, L. (1938). Urbanism as a way of life. *The American Journal of Sociology, XLIV*, 1.

20 Resilience and design

Post-urban landscape infrastructure for the Anthropocene

Nina-Marie Lister

For the first time in history, more than half the world's 7.4 billion humans live in urban settlements. *Homo sapiens sapiens* has become the single dominant species shaping the planet, from surface lands and waters to climate, and by extension, to the future of all other species on earth. The Anthropocene Era has arrived, defined by unprecedented, rapid social and technological changes that have transformed urban spaces, from patterns of settlement and morphology to their meanings and representations in virtually every city across the globe. With these changes, many urban spaces have lost their previous functions and in some cases, their forms. These social, technological, and built-form changes are being exacerbated, tied inexorably through positive feedback to large-scale ecosystem and climate change. In short, the post-urban world is upon us, and new modes of planning and design are needed.

On December 21, 2013, the city of Toronto and its metropolitan area of 5,000,000 inhabitants – along with a sizeable portion of southern Ontario and northern New York – experienced an unseasonably warm winter storm. The storm dropped more than 30 millimeters of freezing rain on the city. Temperatures hovered around freezing for almost 36 hours and then rapidly plummeted to –25 °C and stayed there, locking the city under a blanket of ice for almost two weeks and leaving more than half a million residents in the frozen dark following the Winter Solstice. Under the weight of the ice, more than 20% of the city's 10,000,000 trees were felled, bringing down power lines and cables in the process and leaving thousands of homes without power, heat, or light through Christmas and the holiday season. With an estimated cost of C$106,000,000 to the city of Toronto alone in clean-up and emergency services, the eastern North American ice storm of 2013 is recorded as one of the worst natural disasters in Canadian history (City of Toronto, 2014). Yet, notably, this figure does not account for the loss of the green infrastructural value and the attendant ecosystem services of the loss of one-fifth of the city's mature tree canopy. The city will continue to suffer long-term related impacts of the ice storm through increased soil erosion, decreased flood protection, carbon sequestration, urban heat mitigation, and so on.

The ice storm, however, was not an isolated incident. In February 1998, a similar ice storm caused a massive power outage throughout Québec that lasted more than two weeks, affecting more than 50,000 homes in the middle of a deep freeze. The Red River floods of 1998 and 2012 crippled the cities of Winnipeg, Minneapolis, and St. Paul, while Alberta's Bow River flood of 2012 virtually shut down the city of Calgary and the Trans-Canada highway for more than a month. These are but a few of many recent, locally catastrophic storm events. The better-known "monster storms" such as Hurricane Katrina which devastated New Orleans in 2005, and Superstorm Sandy in 2011, which left half of midtown Manhattan without power for more than a week, are globally significant events. By virtue of their reach and effect in major urban centers, these storms have catalyzed a new wave of research into urban environmental planning, coastal defense, urban vulnerability, and related policy responses that link urbanism, planning, and ecology.

In addition to the economic, social, and environmental costs of such storms, there is growing recognition that these events pose significant challenges to the post-urban condition and largely outdated systems of governance and planning. Cities throughout the globe are facing the reality that the increasing magnitude and frequency of major storm events are evidence of human-induced global climate change, and with this reality has come a range of increasing challenges to our systems of survival, including a need for new design approaches to cope with ecological change and vulnerability (see, for example, Steiner, 2011). Identified as a global threat by the *International Panel on Climate Change* and grounded in a wide range of policy-related research linked to long-term sustainability, climate change is now an accepted phenomenon for which adaptation strategies must be developed and implemented from municipal to national scales.[1]

Long-term environmental sustainability demands the capacity for resilience – the ability to recover from a disturbance, to accommodate change, and to function in a state of health. In this sense, sustainability refers to the inherent and dynamic balance between social-cultural, economic, and ecological domains of human behavior that is necessary for humankind's long-term surviving and thriving. Ann Dale has described this dynamic balance as a necessary act of reconciliation between personal, economic, and ecological imperatives that underlie the primordial natural and cultural capitals on Earth (Dale, 2001).[2] With this departure from conventional "sustainable development," Dale has set the responsibility for long-term sustainability squarely in the domain of human activity, and appropriately removed it from the ultimately impossible realm of managing "the environment" as an object separate from human action.

A growing response to the increasing prevalence of major storm events has been the development of political rhetoric around the need for long-term sustainability and, specifically, resilience in the face of vulnerability. As a heuristic concept, resilience refers to the ability of an ecosystem to withstand and absorb change to prevailing environmental conditions. In an empirical sense, resilience is the amount of change or disruption an ecosystem can absorb, by which, following these change-inducing events, there is a return to a recognizable steady state in which the system retains most of its structures, functions, and feedbacks

(Holling, 1973). In both contexts, resilience is a well-established concept in ecological systems research, with a robust literature related to resource management, governance, and strategic planning. Yet, despite more than two decades of this research, the development of policy strategies and planning applications related to resilience is relatively recent. While there was a significant political call for resilience planning following Superstorm Sandy in 2011 and the ice storm of 2013, there remains a widespread lack of coordinated governance, established benchmarks, implemented policy applications, and few (if any) empirical measures of success related to climate change adaptation.[3] In this context, there has been little critical analysis of and reflection on the need to understand, unpack, and cultivate resilience beyond the rhetoric. In this chapter, I argue that concomitant with the language of resilience is the need to develop nuanced, contextual, and critical analyses coupled with a scientific, evidence-based understanding of resilience; that is, we need an evidence-based approach that contributes to adaptive and ecologically responsive design in the face of complexity, uncertainty, and vulnerability. Put simply: What does a resilient world *look* like, how does it *behave*, and how do we plan and design for resilience in a post-urban world?

Why resilience? Why now?

The emergence of resilience as a rhetorical idea is tied not only to the emerging reality of climate change, but to an important and growing synergy between research and policy responses in the fields of ecology, landscape architecture, and urbanism – a synergy that is powerfully influenced by several remarkable and coincidental shifts since the turn of the second millennium. Most notable is the global population shift, in which our contemporary patterns of settlement are tending towards large-scale urbanization, a hallmark of the Anthropocene. The last century has noticeably been characterized by mass-migration to ever-larger urban regions, resulting in the rise of the "mega-city" and its attendant forms of suburbia, exurbia, and associated phenomena of the modern metropolitan landscape.[4] For most of the world's population, the city is fast becoming the singular landscape experience.[5]

In North America and the United States, in particular, this shift in urbanism has come, paradoxically, with a widespread decline in the quality and performance of the physical infrastructure of the city. The roads, bridges, tunnels, and sewers that were built during the late 19th and early 20th centuries to service major urban centers are now aging and crumbling, in some cases, while both the political will and the public funds to rebuild this outdated but essential public infrastructure are disappearing. More significantly, these infrastructures continue to decay, and they are increasingly vulnerable to catastrophic failure in the face of more frequent and severe storm events, thus compounding the cost of their loss and the extent of impact (Figure 20.1).

The emergence of a new direction and emphasis ecology represents another significant and concomitant shift with a change in urbanism and the reality of

Figure 20.1 Four views of a washed-out section of a major arterial roadway in Toronto after heavy rain and flooding of the Don River followed Hurricane Katrina, which was downgraded to a tropical storm when it hit Toronto on August 29, 2005.

Source: photo-collage by Carmela Liggio and Nina-Marie Lister, 2005.

climate change. During the last few decades, the field of ecology has moved from a classical, reductionist concern with stability, certainty, predictability, and order in favor of more contemporary understandings of dynamic, systemic change and the related phenomena of uncertainty, adaptability, and resilience. Increasingly, these concepts in ecological theory and complex systems research are found useful as heuristics for decision-making generally and, with empirical evidence, for landscape design in particular (Lister, 2008). This offers a powerful new disciplinary and practical space; one that is informed by ecological knowledge both as an applied science and as a construct for managing change within the context of sustainability. As a practice of planning *for and with* change resilience is, in itself, a conceptual model for design (see, for example, Reed & Lister, 2014).

With this new ecological approach has come another important shift in creating the synergy necessary for resilience-thinking: the renaissance of landscape as both a discipline and praxis throughout the last two decades and its (re)integration with planning and architecture in both academic and applied professional domains. Landscape scholars have identified the rise of post-industrial urban landscapes coupled with a focus on indeterminacy and ecological processes as catalysts for the reemergence in landscape theory and praxis.[6] Understood today as an interdisciplinary field linking art, design, and the material science of ecology, landscape scholarship and application now includes a renewed professional field of practice within the space of the city (Reed & Lister, 2014).

Considered together in the era of climate change and vulnerability, these shifts in our collective understanding of urbanism, landscape, and ecology have created a powerful synergy for new approaches in planning and design to the contemporary metropolitan region. This synergy has been an important catalyst for the emergence of resilience as a rhetorical idea, but much work remains to be done to move towards evidence-based implementation of strategies, plans, and designs for resilience. The scale and impact of North American mega-storms such as Hurricane Katrina in 2005 and Superstorm Sandy in 2011 have been effective triggers for a new breed of policy and planning, initiatives in disaster preparedness, in general, and flood management plans, in particular. Conventional policy and planning approaches to natural disasters have long been rooted in the language of *resistance* and *control*, referencing coastal defense strategies such as fortification, armoring, and "shoring up" by using brute-force engineering responses designed to do battle with natural forces.[7] By contrast, emerging approaches in design and planning reference the language of *resilience* and *adaptive management*, terms associated with elasticity and flexibility, leading to the use of hybrid engineering of constructed and ecological materials that adapt to dynamic conditions and natural forces (see, for example, Lister, 2009). Recent coastal management policies and flood management plans following the major storm events abound in this language of resilience, including New Orleans's *Water Management Strategy*, Louisiana's *Coastal Management Plan*, New York City's *Rebuild by Design* program, and Toronto's *Wet Weather Flow Master Plan*. These examples are notable as responses (reactive and proactive) to catalytic storm events and climate change, yet they remain, for the most part, speculative, untested, and unimplemented, relying on a language of resilience that is heuristic and conceptual rather than experiential, contextual, or scientifically derived.

The general concept of resilience has origins across at least four disciplines of research and application: psychology, disaster relief and military defense, engineering, and ecology. A scan of resilience policies reveals that the concept is widely and generally defined with reference to several of the original fields and is universally focused on the psychological trait of being flexible and adaptable; for example, of having the capacity to deal with stress, the ability to "bounce back" to a known normal condition following periods of stress; to maintain well-being under stress; and to be adaptable when faced with change or challenges.[8] The use of resilience in this generalized context, however, begs important operational questions of how much change is tolerable, which state of "normal" is desirable and achievable, and under what conditions is it possible to return to a known "normal" state. In policies that hinge on these broadly defined, psychosocial aspects of resilience, there is little or no explicit recognition that adaptation and flexibility may result in transformation and, thus, require the *transformative capacity* that is ultimately necessary at some scale in the face of radical, large-scale, and sudden systemic change. Using sea level as an example,

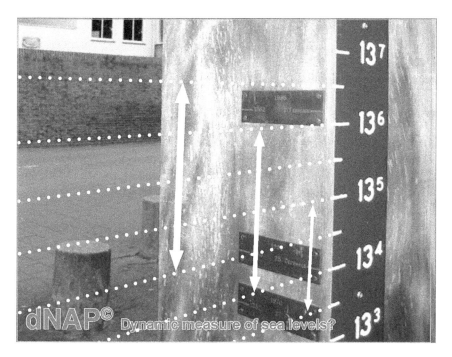

Figure 20.2 The Normaal Amsterdams Peil (NAP) is a measure used to gauge the rise in sea-level and to establish national policies, laws, and regulations on the basis of a fixed, "normal" water level. In contrast, the Dynamic Normaal Amsterdams Peil or d(NAP), shown here, is a proposed measure of sea-level for the Netherlands Delta Region that acknowledges dynamic water levels to address better changing hydrological regimes; for example, to reflect seasonal flooding.

Source: diagram courtesy of Kimberly Garza and Sarah Thomas, 2010.

if we accept that waters naturally rise and fall within a range of seasonal norms, we might be better off to embrace a gradient of acceptable "normal" conditions rather than a single static – and ultimately brittle state – that is unsustainable (Figure 20.2). A more critical and robust systems-oriented discussion of resilience will force all concerned to confront a difficult but essential question: How much can a person, a community, or an ecosystem change before it becomes something unrecognizable and functions as an altogether different entity?[9] If resilience is to be a useful concept in application and, in particular, to inform design and planning strategies, it must ultimately instruct us *how* to change safely rather than how to resist change completely. Current policies and eventual design strategies will risk the potential power of resilience by emphasizing a misguided focus on "bouncing back" to a normal state that is, ultimately, impossible to sustain.

Unpacking resilience

Before one can implement applied strategies and associated indicators for resilience in design and planning, it is useful and, arguably, necessary to unpack the history, theory, and conceptual development of resilience as it emerged in ecology. We can do so critically with reference to a well-established social-scientific literature derived principally from ecosystem ecology and, in particular, with research applications in natural resource management. Decades of research related to complex systems ecology and thinking about and practice of social-ecological systems offers both broad heuristic and empirical contexts for the study and application of resilience. As such, both the construct and measures of resilience are important to embed, apply, and test within policies and designs for long-term sustainability. As an essential capacity for sustainability, applications of resilience are derived from research in complex systems ecology, first published by the American ecologist Howard T. Odum and later developed by the Canadian ecologist, Crawford Stanley ("Buzz") Holling.[10] Yet it should be noted that the foundations of resilience thinking were laid much earlier. Well before the language of complex systems was embraced within ecological science, the early 20th-century conservationist movement was already concerned with the health of natural systems, which was conceptualized variously, from self-renewal to healing and balance with implications for management practices. For example, Aldo Leopold used the concept of "land health" to refer to the land's capacity for self-renewal – essentially resilience – which he saw as threatened by and at odds with unchecked exploitation of land and resources for economic growth.[11] Similarly, Gifford Pinchot's perspectives on the need for cautious resource extraction, however utilitarian, gave rise to an early version of adaptive management to accommodate changes in nature and the landscape.[12] By the 1960s, with the birth of modern environmentalism, there were more urgent calls for caution. Notable among these was Rachel Carson's characterization of nature as resilient, changeable and unpredictable: "the fabric of life … on the one hand delicate and destructible, on the other miraculously tough and resilient, capable of striking back in unexpected ways" (Carson, 2002, p. 297).

The late 1970s and early 1980s marked the beginning of a significant theoretical shift in the evolving discipline of ecology. In general, ecological research at all scales has moved toward a more organic model of open-endedness, indeterminacy, flexibility, adaptation, and resilience and away from a deterministic and predictive model of stability and control, based on engineering models for closed (usually mechanical) systems. Ecosystems are now understood to be open, self-organizing systems that are inherently diverse and complex and behave in ways that are, to some extent, unpredictable.

This shift, influenced by the early ecosystem analyses of the Odum brothers (Eugene P. and Howard T.), followed the rise in complexity science and the groundbreaking work of Ilya Prigogine, Ludwig Von Bertalanffy, C. West Churchman, Peter Checkland, and other systems scholars throughout the latter half of the 20th century. Ecological research came into its own discipline, distinct from biology and zoology, by focusing on large-scale and cross-scale (connected) functions and processes of an ecosystem. As an outgrowth of research in complex systems coupled with the emerging new discipline of landscape ecology and associated spatial analyses – made possible by new tools, such as high-resolution satellite imagery – ecosystem ecology led to multi-scaled, cross-disciplinary, and integrated approaches in land-use planning. Beginning in the 1970s with F. Herbert Bormann's and Gene Likens' first ecosystem-based study of the Hubbard Brook watershed, long-term ecological research programs (known as LTERPs) became established, influencing, throughout the 1980s and 1990s, a growing recognition of the dynamic processes inherent and essential to living, layered landscapes and the understanding of ecosystems as open, complex systems within which structure and function are interrelated and scale-dependent (Bormann & Likens, 1979).[13]

The dynamic ecosystem model has been an important development in ecology and a significant departure from the conventional, linear model of ecosystems that dominated scholarly 20th-century thought. Resilience is an important concept that emerged from this development. Defined by the process of ecological succession, the linear model held that ecosystems gradually and steadily succeed into stable climax states from which they will not routinely move unless disturbed by a force external to that system.[14] An old-growth forest is the typical example, in which a forest matures and then remains in that state permanently such that any disturbance from that state is considered an aberration. Yet we now know that not only is change built into these systems, but, in some cases, ecosystems are dependent on change for growth and renewal. For example, fire-dependent forests contain tree species that require the extreme heat of fire to release and disperse seeds and to facilitate a forest's renewal and, sometimes, a shift in the complement of a species following a major fire. The dynamic ecosystem model, based on long-term research in a variety of global contexts, asserts that all ecosystems go through recurring cycles with four common phases: rapid growth, conservation, release, and reorganization. Known as the adaptive cycle, or the Holling Figure 8, this generalized pattern is a useful conceptual description of how ecosystems organize themselves over time and respond to change.[15] The adaptive cycle of every ecosystem is different and contextual; how each system behaves from one phase to the next depends on the scale, context, internal connections, flexibility, and resilience of that system (Figure 20.3).

Ecosystems are constantly evolving, often in ways that are discontinuous and uneven, with slow and fast changes at small and large scales. While some ecosystem states appear to be stable, stability is not equated in a mathematical sense but rather in a human-scale or time-limited perception of stasis. C. S. Holling pioneered this concept in application to resource management, in which he described ecosystems as "shifting steady-state mosaics," implying that stability is patchy and scale-dependent and is neither a constant nor a phenomenon that defines a whole system at any one point in time or space (Holling, 1992). The key point is that ecosystems operate at many scales, some of which are loosely and others tightly connected, but all subject to change at different rates and under different conditions. An ecosystem we perceive as stable in a human lifetime may, at a longer scale, be

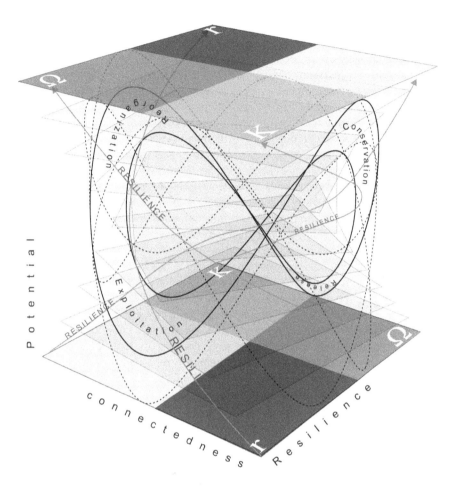

Figure 20.3 Resilience visualized as a function of the adaptive cycle: Holling's Modified
        Figure 8.

Source: reinterpreted by Thomas Folch, Chris Reed, and Nina-Marie E. Lister, reproduced from
Reed and Lister (2014).

ephemeral, and this realization has profound implications for how we choose to
manage, plan, or design for that system (Figure 20.4).

There is an important connection between stability, change, and resilience –
a property internal to any living system and a function of the unique adaptive
cycle of that system. Resilience has both heuristic and empirical dimensions,
arising from its origins in psychology, ecology, and engineering. As a heuristic
or guiding concept, resilience refers to the *ability* of an ecosystem to withstand
and absorb change to prevailing environmental conditions and, following these
change-events, to return to a recognizable steady state (or a routinely cyclic set
of states) in which the system retains most of its structures, functions, and

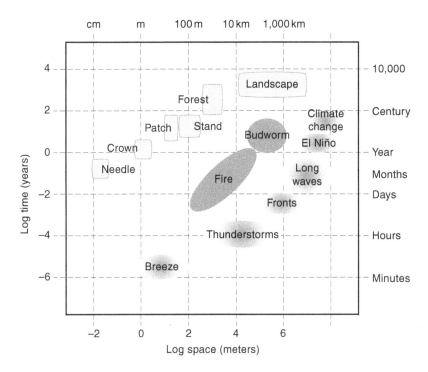

Figure 20.4 Ecosystem dynamics are observed here across multiple scales of time and space.

Source: redrawn by Marta Brocki and adapted from Holling (2001, p. 393).

feedbacks. As an empirical construct in engineering, resilience is the *rate* at which an ecosystem (usually at a small scale, with known variables) returns to a known recognizable state, including its structures and functions, following change-events. Such events, considered disturbances – which Holling strategically referred to in the vernacular as "surprises" – are usually part of normal ecosystem dynamics, yet they are also unpredictable, in that they cause sudden disruption to a system (Holling, 1986). These can include, for example, forest fires, floods, pest outbreaks, and seasonal storm events.

The ability of a system to withstand sudden change at one scale assumes that the behavior of the system remains within a stable regime that contains this steady state in the first place. However, when an ecosystem suddenly shifts from one stable regime to another (in the reorganization phase, via a flip between system states or what is called a "regime shift"), a more specific assessment of ecosystem dynamics is needed. In this context, *ecological resilience* is a measure of the *amount of change* or disruption that is required to move a system from one state to another and, thus, to a different state of being maintained by a different set of functions and structures than the former (Figures 20.5, 20.6,

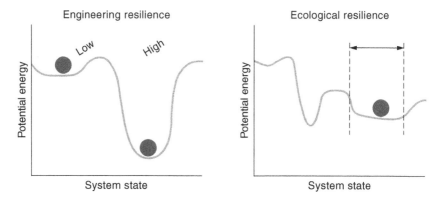

Figure 20.5 Shown here are two contrasting perspectives on resilience: (left) Engineering Resilience in closed systems (limited uncertainty and known variables) versus (right) Ecological Resilience in open systems (inherent uncertainty and infinite variables).

Source: redrawn by Nina-Marie Lister and Marta Brocki and adapted from Holling (1996, p. 35).

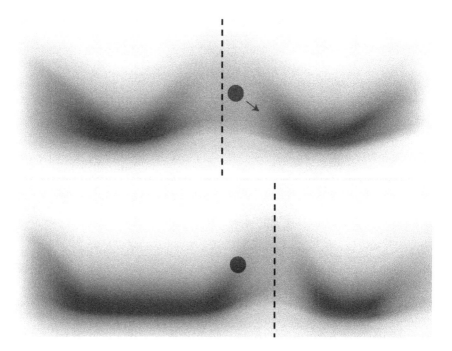

Figure 20.6 Resilience, seen here as a function of social-ecological system conditions, is described metaphorically as a (red) ball in a changing basin. The basin represents a set of states that share similar functions, structures, and feedbacks. Though the location of the ball remains the same, changes in the surrounding conditions bring about a shift in state.

Source: redrawn by Marta Brocki and adapted from Walker et al. (2004, p. 4).

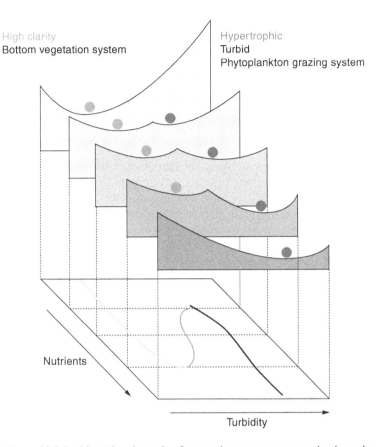

High clarity
Bottom vegetation system

Hypertrophic
Turbid
Phytoplankton grazing system

Nutrients

Turbidity

Figure 20.7 In this early schematic of a complex systems perspective in ecology, we visualize multiple states – all possible – in a fresh-water ecosystem.

Source: Courtesy of James J. Kay, as sketched in lectures from a course, "Systems Design Engineering," at the University of Waterloo, 1994, in which the author was a student. Redrawn by Marta Brocki and adapted from Kay and Schneider (1994).

20.7).[16] Each of these nuanced aspects of resilience are important, because they underscore the social-cultural and economic challenges inherent in defining what "normal" conditions are and, in turn, how much change is acceptable at what scale.

It becomes critical to understand the ecological systems in which we live, and, given their inherent uncertainty, we ought to do so through a combination of ways of knowing: experiential, observational, and empirical. Indeed, if there are multiple possible states for any ecosystem, there can be no single "correct" state – only those we choose to encourage or discourage. Notably, these are not questions of science but of social, cultural, economic, and political dimensions – they are also questions of design and planning. The trajectory of research in resilience has been instrumental in exploring the paradoxes inherent within living systems – the tensions between stability and perturbation, constancy and change, predictability and unpredictability – and the implications of these for management, planning, and design of the land. Resilience, in short, as Brian Walker declares, "is largely about learning *how* to change in order not to *be* changed."[17]

From rhetoric to tactic: towards resilient design

More recently, applied ecology has been focused on trying to understand what are the ecosystem states that we perceive to be stable; at what scales do they operate; and how are they are useful to us. It is important to recognize that stability can be positive or negative, just as change is neither universally good nor bad. Thus, while designers want to encourage a desirable stability (such as access to affordable food or a state of health for a majority of citizens), they also wish to avoid pathological stability (such as chronic unemployment, a state of war, or a dictatorship). This approach has significant implications for management, planning, and design, as it rests on the recognition that humans are not outsiders to any ecosystem but, rather, participants in its unfolding, and agents of its design.

In this context, the sub-science of urban ecology developed during the 1990s has created a new niche for resilience (see, for example, Pickett, Cadenasso, & Grove, 2004). Related practices of urban design, environmental planning, and landscape architecture have cross-pollinated in the service of design and planning for healthier cities within which connected vestiges of natural landscapes might thrive. The work of environmental scholars (such as William Cronin, Carolyn Merchant, and David Orr), together with the practice of landscape architects (such as Anne Whiston Spirn, Frederick R. Steiner, and James Corner) effectively brought nature into the embrace of the city, challenging the hierarchical dualism of humans versus nature (Corner, 1997; Cronin, 1996; Merchant, 1981; Orr, 1992; Spirn, 1984; Steiner, 1990). The once-discrete concepts of "city" and "country" grew tangled and hybridized and the boundaries between the urban and the wild blurred. This blurring of boundaries, coupled with the contemporary ecological paradigm of nature as a complex, dynamic open system in which diversity is essential and uncertainty the norm, represented a significant break from ecological determinism and its slavish pursuit of perpetual stability underpinned by the illusion of the balance of nature.[18] The increasing hybridization of cultural and natural ecologies has created a powerful aperture for the development of resilience in thought and practice – and with it a new realm for design developed formatively through the interdisciplinary study of social-ecological systems science, in which coupled systems of humans *within* nature are the norm.[19]

What does design for resilience look like? What tactics do post-urban planners and designers need to engage in for attaining resilience? To activate such a model for design, one can summarize key principles of adaptive complex systems, generally, and of resilience, specifically.[20] First, change can be slow and fast, at multiple scales. This means that it is essential to look beyond one scale in both space and time and to use various tools to understand the ecological system. Slow variables are arguably more important to understand than fast ones, as they provide necessary stability from which to study change at a distance, safely. Yet there can be no universal point of access or ideal vantage point. Mapping, describing, and analyzing the system from multiple perspectives, using different ways of knowing and with a diversity of tools, is critical. If uncertainty is irreducible and predictability is limited, then the role of the traditional expert is also limited – and the role of designer is more akin to a facilitator or curator.

Second, some connectedness, or modularity, across scales is important, and feedback loops should be both tight and loose. Resilient systems are not so tightly coupled that they can't survive a shock throughout the system that moves rapidly and destructively. For example, children need some limited exposure to viruses to develop immunities but at not too large a scale of impact so as to endanger long-term health. In the same way, design strategies for resilience must consider novelty and redundancy in terms of structures and functions. A useful example is a trail system in a park, which is somewhat connected using a hierarchy of paths that is legible and efficient and yet not so tightly connected that it compromises habitat, folds in on itself, or prohibits spontaneous exploration.

Third, even as there are multiple states in which an ecosystem can function, there is no single correct state. It is important to determine where, in the adaptive cycle, the system of interest is, such that decision-makers and designers can learn patterns and anticipate change (if not predict it). Eventually, perceived stability in any phase will end, and the system will move to a new phase in its adaptive cycle. A non-linear approach to design that encompasses oscillating or changing states within various phases of a system's development will help facilitate change. For example, it may be desirable to design for seasonally flooded landscapes or along a gradient of water that changes rapidly in a short period of time.

Finally, resilient systems are defined by diversity and by inherent but irreducible uncertainty. Successful strategies for resilient design should use a diversity of tactics through in-situ experimental and ecologically responsive approaches that are safe-to-fail, while avoiding those erroneously assumed to be fail-safe (Lister, 2008). This distinction is important, for conventional engineering relies on prediction and certainty to assume an idealized condition of fail-safe design. Yet this is impossible under dynamic conditions of ecological and social complexity in which predictability is limited at best to one scale of focus. Even knowing one scale exhaustively and managing for it specifically and exclusively may compromise a system's overall function and resilience. The reductionist caveat of "scaling up," using knowledge gained at one scale and applying it to the whole system, cannot work in complex systems in which scales are nested. Design strategies that support and facilitate resilience should, for example, model its attributes, using living infrastructures that mimic ecological structures and their functions, and to design them to be tested and monitored, from which learning and adaptation to changing conditions are built into the design. When design experiments fail, they should fail safely, at a scale small enough not to compromise long-term health.

These and other emerging approaches to design for resilience tend to reflect the characteristics of the theoretical paradigm shifts that have laid its foundation. They are often interdisciplinary, integrating architecture, engineering, and ecology, specifically, and art and science, broadly. They cross-pollinate freely across scales and hybridize in surprisingly novel ways.[21] The growing use of living "blue" and "green" infrastructures (see, for example, Green, 2015) to soften sea walls, anchor soils, provide rooftop habitats, clean storm water, soak and hold flood water, and move animals safely across highways[22] are a collective and optimistic testament to the emergence of a new breed of urban and landscape designers whose creative work mimics, models, and manifests the living systems that inspire and sustain us. Yet activating resilience requires a subtle and careful approach to design: one that is contextual, legible, nuanced, and responsive, one that is small in scale but large in cumulative impact. In designing for change with this sensibility, we have begun to cultivate a culture of resilience and the adaptive, transformative capacity for long-term sustainability – thriving beyond merely surviving – with change in the post-urban landscapes that now define us.

Acknowledgments

This chapter has been adapted from the original which appears as "Resilience Beyond Rhetoric" (Chapter 13) in *Nature and Cities: The Ecological Imperative in Urban Design and Planning* (F. Steiner, G. Thomson, & A. Carbonell, eds., 2016, published by Lincoln Institute of Land Policy, Cambridge, MA). I am grateful to Marta Brocki, for assistance with research and the collection of illustrations in this chapter, and to my landscape architecture colleagues for discussion and creative design work that helped shape these ideas.

Notes

1 Intergovernmental Panel on Climate Change, *IPCC Fifth Assessment Report (AR5)*, Geneva, Switzerland: IPCC, 2013: www.ipcc.ch/report/ar5/mindex.shtml. Corroborating evidence is published by an independent association of insurance industries in Canada's *Institute for Catastrophic Loss Reduction*: www.iclr.org. Municipal strategies for climate change are evaluated in Robinson and Gore (2015).

2 In this chapter, I use the term "management" in the context of Dale's definition of sustainability; that is, in the context of managing *human activities* within the environment, rather than regarding the environment as an object.

3 See, for example, *The Post-Sandy Initiative: Building Better, Building Smarter – Opportunities for Design and Development* (May 2013), initiated and undertaken by the American Institute of Architects, New York Chapter (AIANY), and the AIANY's Design for Risk and Reconstruction Committee (DfRR), available at http://postsan dyinitiative.org.

4 The United Nations projects that, in 2030, there will be 5,000,000,000 urbanites with three-quarters of them in the world's poorest countries. See United Nations, "World Urbanization Prospects: 2011 Revision," available at http://esa.un.org. In 1950, only

New York City and London had more than 8,000,000 residents, yet today there are more than 20 megalopoli, most in Asia. See Chandler (1987) and Rydin and Kendall-Bush (2009).

5 According to the World Health Organization, the percentage of people living in cities is expected to increase from less than 40% in 1990 to 70% in 2050. See "Global Health Observatory: Urban Population Growth," World Health Organization, available at www.who.int/gho/urban_health/situation_trends/urban_population_growth_text/en/.

6 As articulated and elaborated in Corner (1997, 1999) and Waldheim (2006).

7 This phenomenon is well articulated by Mathur and da Cunha (2009).

8 See, for example, a variety of North American and international examples of resilience policies at http://resilient-cities.iclei.org/resilient-cities-hub-site/resilience-resource-point/resilience-library/examples-of-urban-adaptation-strategies/. The U.S. Department of State's *Deployment Stress Management Program* (www.state.gov/m/med/dsmp/c44950.htm) defines resilience in a psycho-social context, and the same language of resilience is often used in policy documents referencing resilience.

9 Brian Walker, Chair of the Resilience Alliance and research fellow at the Stockholm Resilience Centre, provides an excellent overview of this aspect of resilience in Walker (2013).

10 Seminal references are Holling (1973) and Odum (1983).

11 Discussed in Berkes, Doubleday, and Cumming (2012).

12 Discussed in Johnson (2012).

13 For continuing work based on this pioneering study, see www.hubbardbrook.org.

14 Succession is a process by which one ecosystem's community is gradually replaced by another.

15 The adaptive cycle was first described by Holling (1986); modified in Gunderson and Holling (2002); and, more recently, by Reed and Lister (2014).

16 Holling (1996); further developed in Walker, Holling, Carpenter, and Kinzig (2004).

17 For Brian Walker's view on resilience, see Walker (2013).

18 As discussed by Ellison (2013).

19 The development of social-ecological systems science, supported by case study analyses, can be followed in: Berkes, Colding, and Folke (2008); Gunderson and Holling (2002); and Waltner-Toews, Kay, and Lister (2008).

20 Related versions of these principles – described variously as system attributes, tenets, and characteristics – are elaborated in Gunderson and Holling (2002); Waltner-Toews et al. (2008); and, more recently, in Walker and Salt (2012).

21 See a variety of designed examples in Steiner, Thomson, and Carbonell (2016).

22 A diversity of examples of wildlife crossing infrastructure is available at https://arc-solutions.org/.

References

Berkes, F., Colding, J., & Folke, C. (Eds.). (2008). *Navigating social-ecological systems: Building resilience for complexity and change.* Cambridge, UK: Cambridge University Press.

Berkes, F., Doubleday, N. C., & Cumming, G. S. (2012). Aldo Leopold's land health from a resilience point of view: Self-renewal capacity of social–ecological systems. *EcoHealth, 9*(3), 278–287.

Bormann, F. H., & Likens, G. (1979). *Pattern and process in a forested ecosystem.* New York: Springer-Verlag.

Carson, R. (2002). *Silent spring.* New York: Houghton Mifflin. (Originally published 1962).

Chandler, T. (1987). *Four thousand years of urban growth: An historical census.* Lewiston, NY: St. David's University Press.

City of Toronto (2014, January 8). Impacts from the December, 2013 Extreme Winter Storm Event. Staff Report to City Council: 2. Retrieved July 13, 2017, from www.toronto.ca/legdocs/mmis/2014/cc/bgrd/backgroundfile-65676.pdf.

Corner, J. (1997). Ecology and landscape as agents of creativity. In G. F. Thompson & F. R. Steiner (Eds.), *Ecological design and planning* (pp. 80–108). New York: John & Wiley & Son.

Corner, J. (1999). Recovering landscape as a critical cultural practice. In J. Corner (Ed.), *Recovering landscape: Essays in contemporary landscape theory* (pp. 1–26). Princeton, NJ: Princeton Architectural Press.

Cronin, W. (Ed.). (1996). *Uncommon ground: Rethinking the human place in nature.* New York: W. W. Norton.

Ellison, A. M. (2013). The suffocating embrace of landscape and the picturesque conditioning of ecology. *Landscape Journal, 32*(1), 79–94.

Green, J. (Ed.). (2015). *Designed for the future: 80 practical ideas for a sustainable world.* New York: Princeton Architectural Press.

Gunderson, L., & Holling, C. S. (Eds.). (2002). *Panarchy: Understanding transformations in human and natural systems.* Washington, DC: Island Press.

Holling, C. S. (1973). Resilience and stability of ecological systems. *Annual Review of Ecology and Systematics, 4*, 1–23.

Holling, C. S. (1986). The resilience of terrestrial ecosystems: Local surprise and global change. In W. C. Clark & E. Munn (Eds.), *Sustainable development of the biosphere.* Cambridge, UK: Cambridge University Press.

Holling, C. S. (1992). Cross-scale morphology, geometry and dynamics of ecosystems. *Ecological Monographs, 62*(4), 447–502.

Holling, C. S. (1996). Engineering resilience versus ecological resilience. In P. C. Schulze (Ed.), *Engineering within ecological constraints* (pp. 51–66). Washington, DC: National Academy Press.

Holling, C. S. (2001). Understanding the complexity of economic, ecological, and social systems. *Ecosystems, 4*(5), 390–405.

Johnson, A. (2012). Avoiding environmental catastrophes: Varieties of principled precaution. *Ecology and Society, 17*(3).

Kay, J. J., & Schneider, E. (1994). Embracing complexity: The challenge of the ecosystem approach. *Alternatives Journal, 20*(3), 32–39.

Lister, N. M. (2008). Sustainable large parks: Ecological design or designer ecology. In J. Czerniak & H. George (Eds.), *Large parks* (pp. 31–51). Princeton, NJ: Princeton Architectural Press.

Lister, N. M. (2009). Water/front. *Places, Design Observer Online.* Retrieved July 13, 2017 from https://placesjournal.org/article/waterfront/.

Mathur, A., & da Cunha, D. (2009). *SOAK: Mumbai in an estuary.* Mumbai, India: Rupa & Company.

Merchant, C. (1981). *The death of nature: Women, ecology, and scientific revolution.* San Francisco, CA: Harper and Row.

Odum, H. T. (1983). *Systems ecology: An introduction.* New York: John Wiley & Sons.

Orr, D. W. (1992). *Ecological literacy: Education and the transition to a postmodern world.* Albany, NY: State University of New York Press.

Pickett, S. T. A., Cadenasso, M. L., & Grove, J. M. (2004). Resilient cities: Meaning, models, and metaphor for integrating the ecological, socio-economic, and planning realms. *Landscape and Urban Planning, 69*(4), 369–384.

Reed, C., & Lister, N. M. (Eds.). (2014). *Projective ecologies*. Cambridge, MA: Harvard University Graduate School of Design.

Robinson, P., & Gore, C. (2015). Municipal climate reporting: Gaps in monitoring and implications for governance and action. *Environment and Planning C: Government and Policy, 33*(5), 1058–1075.

Rydin, Y., & Kendall-Bush, K. (2009). *Megalopolises and sustainability*. London: University College London Environment Institute. Retrieved July 5, 2017, from www.ucl.ac.uk/btg/downloads/Megalopolises_and_Sustainability_Report.pdf.

Spirn, A. W. (1984). *The granite garden: Urban nature and human design*. New York: Basic Books.

Steiner, F. R. (1990). *The living landscape: An ecological approach to landscape planning*. New York: McGraw-Hill.

Steiner, F. (2011). *Design for a vulnerable planet*. Austin: University of Texas Press.

Steiner, F., Thomson, G., & Carbonell, A. (Eds.). (2016). *Nature and cities: The ecological imperative in urban design and planning*. Cambridge, MA: Lincoln Institute of Land Policy.

Waldheim, C. (Ed.). (2006). *The landscape urbanism reader*. Princeton, NJ: Princeton Architectural Press.

Walker, B. (2013, July 5). *What is resilience?* The Stockholm Resilience Centre. Retrieved July 5, 2017, from www.project-syndicate.org/commentary/what-is-resilience-by-brian-walker.

Walker, B., Holling, C. S., Carpenter, S., & Kinzig, A. (2004). Resilience, adaptability and transformability in social–ecological systems. *Ecology and Society, 9*(2).

Walker, B., & Salt, D. (2012). *Resilience practice: Building capacity to absorb disturbance and maintain function*. Washington, DC: Island Press.

Waltner-Toews, D., Kay, J. J., & Lister, N. M. E. (2008). *The ecosystem approach: Complexity, uncertainty, and managing for sustainability*. New York: Columbia University Press.

21 Sharing cities for a smart and sustainable future

Duncan McLaren and Julian Agyeman

Introduction

In this chapter we explore the contemporary terrain, contestations, and transformations of sharing in cities and seek to explain how these might be harnessed to rebuild social cohesion in forms suited to a globally interconnected, postmodern, intercultural world. We see new technologies and business models reshaping values and behaviours in ways that could help deliver sustainability and justice: but also in ways that are vulnerable to cooption by destructive and inequitable economic interests. We argue that by learning from the experience and expertise of civic, charitable, and communal sharing, as well as from the commercial sharing economy, cities can adopt a 'sharing paradigm' understanding of urban life and social practices, based on recognition, protection, and development of urban commons, and use this to guide strategy and action.

Around half of the world's population already lives in cities, and by 2050 the share will be over two-thirds. Economic and political inequality between the 'global city' (Sassen, 2001) of increasingly interconnected financial and commercial urban cores; and depressed and declining hinterlands (that nonetheless remain essential to the supply of labour and resources) is already severe. Continuing urbanization is thus both a major challenge, and in light of the sharing paradigm, also a great opportunity. The nature of urban space enables, and necessitates, sharing, and the more we share the more we can – at least in theory – enhance 'just sustainabilities' (Agyeman, Bullard, & Evans, 2003) by decreasing inequalities, increasing social capital, and decreasing resource use. A focus on sharing offers a new way of understanding and designing urban futures.

The chapter proceeds as follows. In the first section, we outline the breadth of sharing practice, its evolutionary roots, and historic emanations in cities. We then describe and theorize current transformations in sharing from traditional evolved communal forms, to intermediated commercial forms. The third section identifies and discusses forms of urban sharing beyond the commercial, highlighting the focus on urban commons in concepts such as social urbanism. In the next section we highlight the ways in which social inclusion and interculturalism, including recognition of and respect for counter-cultures, is central to the shift in values and norms implied in the sharing paradigm. The fifth section explores the new and revived forms of collective politics that become possible in a sharing city (contrasting them briefly with the post-political tendencies of 'smart cities'). In the final section, we outline some of the practical steps necessary to build genuinely smart and sustainable sharing cities.

The roots of sharing

In this section we outline the breadth of sharing practice, its evolutionary roots, and historic emanations in cities. In modern cities – with increasing specialization, ever-longer supply chains, and ever wider environmental footprints – people are more deeply interdependent on one another and in greater numbers than ever. Urban-rural dichotomies are steadily eroding, contributing to what could be called a 'post-urban' condition of spatial interdependence.

The human species' evolved response to interdependence is sharing. From humanity's earliest days as hunter-gatherers, collaborating in the hunt and sharing in its fruits; to neighbours sharing food, seeds, and recipes across garden walls and kitchen tables; sharing has been an intrinsic part of how people live 'together' (Sennett, 2013). Cities have been built around shared spaces – marketplaces, churches, and public squares; shared infrastructures – roads, water supply, and sewerage; and shared services throughout history. These critical 'urban commons' of infrastructure, public spaces and services, social opportunity, and cultural interaction are, however, as much a shared creation of the citizens as the result of city authority planning or investment.

Our understanding of 'sharing' follows dictionary definitions in encompassing processes whereby we divide something between multiple users; or in which we use, occupy, or enjoy something jointly with one or more others. We recognize a broad spectrum of things that can be shared, ranging from material resources and production facilities, to services, experiences, and capabilities. In this we echo real life practice and common usage of the terms 'share' and 'sharing' in which there is also a clear and intended moral undertone of fairness.

In practice, humans share a wide range of things in a remarkable diversity of ways. We share things – like cars or books. We share services like education, healthcare, co-working spaces, or places to sleep. We share our views and values, our activities and experiences (from politics to leisure). Yet we could share much more. Our sharing can be material or virtual; tangible or intangible; it can enable consumption, or production. It can be simultaneous in time, as with public spaces, or sequential as with recycling material; it can be rivalrous like car-sharing, or non-rivalrous like open-source software; and the distribution of shares might be by sharing in parts (as we would share a cake) or sharing in turns (like a bike). Yet we could share more often. We share with other private individuals, in collective groups and as citizens using state provided resources and services, such as green space, sanitation, city bikes, or childcare. Yet we could share more widely.

In all its forms sharing is a product of humans' evolved nature as social animals. But as contemporary evolutionary science explains (Pagel, 2012), it is as much a cultural evolution, as a biological one, rooted in our ability to cooperate in tribes and to trust and reciprocate with others in our social groups. Our evolved sharing nature underlies socio-cultural traditions of sharing that persist to this day, and encompass huge swathes of human interaction. In large parts of the world traditional sharing in extended families remains the norm, and across local communities both rural and urban, gift economies based in reciprocal social obligations underpin the basics of life – water, shelter, food, clothing, and care.

Yet in modern cities – especially in the global North – such socio-cultural forms of sharing have been increasingly undermined, not just by social fragmentation but also by commercialization of the public realm and privatization of shared infrastructures and services. It might be argued that trends of social fragmentation, commercialization, privatization, and individualization represent some sort of 'victory' for capitalism, and public rejection of the large-scale sharing approaches embodied in state communism, and associated with levels of state control and surveillance that many found unacceptable. But the legacies of socialist systems – with agricultural collectives, nationalized industries, and broad public services motivated by concerns to both increase social justice and conserve resources through sharing – persist, with broad public support, notably in Europe. In Scandinavian cities, for example, shared facilities range from children's playgrounds to laundry-rooms and storage areas in apartment blocks, while throughout Europe, welfare states use taxation to fund common services including health and education, that are often free at the point of delivery.

Although the spread of liberal capitalism has triggered changes that have decimated both socio-cultural and state-led sharing, it has also offered new freedoms and potential for greater individual equality. Traditional communities are not without social downsides: often heavily gendered, misrecognizing of difference, and oppressive of minorities. Cities have long offered both economic and social opportunities for people to escape the strictures and oppression of traditional communities, to lose and to find themselves, and to reweave the narratives of their identities. Even so, incomers in cities often form new communities in which traditional sharing remains critical for new arrivals, especially within ethnic and national immigrant cultures. The widespread erosion of social capital (Putnam, 2000), loss of community and public support structures and collective capabilities that support health, learning, and our needs for social affiliation and interaction is therefore a serious problem. Neoliberal, individualist markets simply cannot meet such needs, however hard advertisers and brand managers try to persuade us otherwise.

Sharing transformations

In this section we describe and theorize the current transformations in sharing from traditional evolved communal forms, to intermediated commercial forms.

The emergence of new peer-to-peer and forms of sharing at the intersection of cities' highly networked physical and cyber-spaces is both interesting and exciting. It promises not only more efficient allocation of resources and opportunities, but to also meet basic human needs for interaction and affiliation, and to establish new inter-cultural modes and norms of sharing that can roll out across the whole of society. Contemporary sharing on a grand scale is not dependent on the same social, political, or technological base that prevailed in the mid 20th century, and has the potential to transcend the stale dualism of state and market. Nonetheless, like state-mediated socialist sharing, and in common with most 'online' or web-mediated activity (Bernal, 2014), it too raises concerns about surveillance and privacy, especially when associated with 'smart city' approaches.

Following Botsman and Rogers (2010) we see four enabling and driving factors in the rapid growth of 'collaborative consumption'. First: technological change, in the form of online peer-to-peer social networks and real time technologies. The key new technology is not the internet per se, but the mobile internet, with connected online identities and easy online payment systems. Second: a global recession that provoked serious questioning of consumer behaviours – in particular with respect to behaviours like car ownership. Third: growing concern over unresolved environmental issues, notably climate change, which has driven interest in resource-saving in a 'circular economy', in which materials are shared and recycled repeatedly (Ellen MacArthur Foundation, 2012). And fourth, the revival of community values in new forms, often online, promoted and supported by new approaches to branding and marketing (Cova, Kozinets, & Shankar, 2007).

San Francisco is at the forefront of the collaborative consumption boom, with a proliferation of high-tech sharing companies like Airbnb (accommodation), Dropbox (web-storage), and Lyft (ride-sharing). Such platforms are typically 'intermediaries' in a 'sharing economy' that, in one way or another, bring together peers to more efficiently share resources, access goods, and provide services. Such 'mediated' forms of sharing need not be commercial – governments and not-for-profits can deliver them too. But in San Francisco, the commercial model – utilizing technology and software from Silicon Valley and business models underpinned by risk-hungry venture capital funds – is predominant. The city, following 'smart city' rhetoric (Lee & Hancock, 2012), has been broadly supportive of the sharing economy, but in a fairly hands-off fashion. The predominance of commercial models also makes San Francisco a hotbed of legal and social resistance to the downsides of the commercial sharing economy. Legal challenges to the business models of Uber and Airbnb reflect the very real prospect that sharing businesses might casualize labour and increase precariousness by defining employees as contractors; or take socially useful resources (such as rental housing) out of the reach of the poorest by shifting them into the sharing economy. Concerns extend also to the environmental impacts of sharing where commercial forces can lead to harmful rebound effects, for example, where ride-sharing draws more cars onto the roads.

Yet commercialized sharing can bring benefits as well as risks. It is most socially useful when it draws existing, but socially underused resources into the market. And in already market-dominated societies, it can help renew trust and community values in inclusive or 'cosmopolitan' ways. Such 'cosmopolitan sharing' strengthens bridging social capital between communities as much as bonding capital within communities. It owes more to ideas of 'paying forward' through a community of weak ties than it does to directly reciprocal obligations. Where socio-cultural sharing reflects reciprocal altruism, cosmopolitan sharing could be described as 'karmic altruism' – participants don't know who will do them a good turn or even when, but they expect to be able to call on a wide network of potential aid when in need. Commercial sharing alone cannot build such networks, however, nor the shared public realm or urban commons they depend on, nor the hard and soft infrastructures and resources that are the foundation of all successful urban economies.

Successful entrepreneurial businesses like Airbnb and Uber almost inevitably raise high feelings – on both sides. But we would be mistaken if we were to assume that such companies are all there is to the sharing economy, or that a sharing economy is all there could be in a sharing society. There are both opportunities and risks for sustainability, solidarity, and justice in the changing nature of urban sharing, and these depend on details of the models and institutions involved, as well as the context. For example, the environmental benefits of car- and ride-sharing depend on what it displaces (public transport or private cars), and whether it increases overall mobility and car-use; or by reducing car-ownership and making the marginal cost of car-use more real, reduces use too. Its social impacts depend on who gets access to the new services and whether drivers are empowered or exploited. Both the ownership and business models used by the sharing organizations and the governance models that cities and businesses introduce to guide and regulate the sector are significant. Commercial sharing models driven by venture capital – with the pressure such funding exerts to develop a profitable model ready for a trade sale or a launch on the stock exchange – seem most vulnerable to losing sight of any social purpose, and simply seeking to marketize and sweat their assets: essentially the participants.

However, the cutting edge of the sharing economy is only rarely commercial, combining as it does the anti-corporate spirit of file-sharing and free open source software with the social purpose and altruistic foundations of communal sharing. Many sharing entrepreneurs are social entrepreneurs first and foremost. Moreover, socio-cultural sharing has long informally facilitated the unpaid care, support, and nurturing we provide for one another. Like the blurred margins between sharing and the commercial economy, the fuzzy boundaries between the public sector and sharing are a place where innovative approaches of co-production are multiplying. Cooperative or collective models of sharing platform also offer greater cosmopolitanism with less damage to existing social capital. This is because they provide more power to the participants (and generally) less to the platform owners. Any meaningful concept of Sharing Cities must go beyond the 'sharing economy', and explore approaches that are more cultural than commercial, more political than economic, and that are rooted in a broad understanding of the city as a co-created urban commons.

We propose a 'sharing paradigm' (McLaren & Agyeman, 2015), which recognizes the shift from socio-cultural sharing practices to mediated ones as the central transformation in contemporary cities, but also highlights a second spectrum from communal to commercial models (see Figure 21.1).

Each combination or 'flavour' offers different opportunities, has different circumstances in which it is appropriate, and different implications for governance. Our aim is not to privilege any one category over another, but to trigger new ways of thinking that emphasize sharing resources fairly, rather than by ability to pay; using those resources to directly enhance human capabilities; nurturing the collective commons of culture and society; and treating these resources, those commons, and the natural world as shared heritage and common property. Once the sharing paradigm is understood as offering new ways to create and use collective commons of physical and virtual resources, spaces, infrastructures, and services, a focus on sharing simply as a novel economic tool for allocating access to conventional goods and services is obviously too limited.

Beyond the sharing 'economy'

In this section we identify and discuss forms of urban sharing beyond the commercial, highlighting the focus on urban commons in concepts such as social urbanism.

The predominant language and discourse of the 'sharing economy' is much more significant – and unhelpful – than it might first appear. It frames sharing as

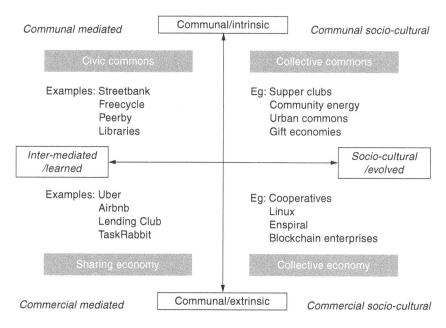

Figure 21.1 The four flavours of sharing.

an economic activity rather than a social, cultural, or political activity. It perpetuates the myth that human society is founded on, and bounded by the economy, rather than vice versa, and that the environment is simply a source of economic resources, rather than the fundamental space in which humans and our societies and cultures evolved and coexist. Moreover, it primes us to seek solutions to our 'problems' in markets, in monetized exchange, in the production and consumption of goods and services, constrained by economic frames and drivers. And it encourages cities to look for expertise on sharing amongst Silicon Valley entrepreneurs and venture capitalists, devaluing the long experience of commoners, cooperatives, and civic managers of public services from libraries to transit systems.

Of course sharing has an economic side: it can deliver utility, providing the services goods provide without having to own them. But this is only a first step in understanding the possible contribution of sharing to human flourishing. Understanding that we can gain the benefit of consumption without ownership allows us to begin rethinking what we mean by needs, well-being, and 'the good life' (see Table 21.1).

Effective economies turn materials into products, and products into services that people value. But the critical issue is how those services transform into human-experienced well-being or happiness, and that – in turn – depends on our capabilities to live our lives in ways we have reason to value (Nussbaum, 2011; Sen, 2009).

Without the capabilities to transform them, neither materials nor goods nor services will necessarily deliver well-being or meet our needs. So the sharing paradigm begins from the question of how sharing approaches and shared resources can more directly enhance capabilities for all.

Table 21.1 The sharing spectrum

Sharing domain (what is being shared)	Concepts	Examples
Material	Industrial ecology	Circular economy, recovery and recycling, glass and paper banks and collection, scrapyards
Production facility	Collaborative production	Fab-labs, community energy, job-sharing, open-sourcing, credit unions, and crowdfunding
Product	Redistribution markets	Flea markets, charity shops, Freecycle, swapping and gifting platforms
Service	Product service systems	Ride-sharing, media streaming, fashion and toy rental, libraries
Experience	Collaborative lifestyles	Errand networks, peer-to-peer travel, couchsurfing, skillsharing
Capability	Collective commons	The internet, safe streets, participative politics, SOLEs, citizens' incomes
Intangible		

But using sharing approaches and shared resources to this end is not simple. It takes more than the sort of facilitating rules and regulations that we are seeing emerge from negotiation between businesses and city authorities in cities like San Francisco. Instead it needs the sort of strong political leadership and active public participation seen in the world's first official 'Sharing City' of Seoul in South Korea. Seoul is actively working to cultivate an inclusive sharing culture – both at the public or civic level and by building public trust in sharing enterprises and organizations – through the city-funded 'Sharing City' project. This project aims to expand physical and digital sharing infrastructure; incubate and support sharing economy startups; and put idle public resources to better use. To make sharing initiatives more socially inclusive, it provides free second-hand smart phones to the elderly and disadvantaged so they can access the same services and apps as others.

Sharing in Seoul reflects the Korean cultural concept of *jeong*, a collective solidarity that motivates "random acts of kindness between people who barely know each other" (The Korean, 2008). This helpfully reminds us that in different cultures, status and recognition are found in different ways. One of the richest possibilities in the sharing society is that we can find identity and recognition in the process of sharing, and who we share with, rather than in what we consume. It might seem that many sharing economy models and platforms actively reinforce consumer norms and brand identities. Rent the Runway, for example, which provides temporary access to top-label fashion brands, appears to simply fuel consumerist desires. Sharing such products, however, does widen choice and also allows those on lower incomes to also more rapidly change image and apparent status compared with ownership. Such a model, allowing people to change their image and identity swiftly to keep up with the rate of change in contemporary life, can be good for our psychological sense of self.

Moreover, commercial sharing that relies on the power of brands is ultimately self-defeating: as the sharing model becomes more popular and well-known, the cachet attached to previously exclusive labels is inevitably diluted. Sharing thus demands that we displace reliance on consumption and possessions to shape our identities. It shifts norms and values, especially where sharing itself is more communal.

From libraries to street carnivals, and from fab-labs to cooperatives, sharing offers new models and norms for living. For example, toy libraries not only cut waste, enhance social inclusion, help parents share values such as sustainability and frugality, and expose children to sharing norms; they also allow children to experiment with and challenge cultural identities – especially those attached to gendered toys (Ozanne & Ballantine, 2010).

Establishing such sharing identities seems more feasible if – as in Seoul – sharing and collaboration extends beyond consumption activities to production and governance. As well as open government and participatory budgeting initiatives, in Seoul co-production between the state and the third sector helps deliver a wide range of public services including childcare, healthcare, library services, and waste management. In these various ways Seoul is feeling its way towards the holy grail of the sharing paradigm: making sharing the city itself, as a whole, the purpose of urban governance.

In Colombia's second city, Medellín, the same goal has been recognized without explicit adoption of the concept or discourse of the 'sharing economy'. Here 'urbanismo sociale' – social inclusion in a shared public realm – has been the critical driving factor behind the remarkable transformation of the once murder capital of the world. After Pablo Escobar, leader of the Medellín Cartel – a violent and powerful drug trafficking organization, was killed in 1993, city leaders, community activist groups, and residents collaborated to give the city a fresh start. Medellín established a focus on empowering citizens, beginning in the poorest neighbourhoods. Library parks such as Parque Biblioteca España have been constructed in marginalized parts of the city, providing free access to computer and information technology, and educational classes, as well as space for cultural activities and recreation. The city has invested heavily in shared public transit and infrastructure – including bus rapid transit, nine cable car links, and a huge outdoor escalator – to connect the poor hillside *comunas* with the centre. Public facilities such as health centres and schools have been developed at the cable car stations. The major projects have been funded with revenue from the city's public services company, Empresas Públicas de Medellín (EPM) and developed through a participatory planning process with the community, which now extends to an online 'city co-creation' platform, Mi Medellín, which has generated over 15,000 citizen proposals.

Sharing, social inclusion, and counter-cultures

Social inclusion has been the driver for Medellín's transformation, where it is not just about class, or income, but also ethnicity and indigeneity. This section highlights the ways in which social inclusion and interculturalism, including recognition of and respect for counter-cultures, is central to the shift in values and norms implied in the sharing paradigm.

In different ways, Amsterdam too has established a shared urban commons founded on tolerance for difference and cultural diversity. Diverse ethnic minorities make up almost half of the Dutch city's residents, yet there are no ghettos – 'a result' of a history of welcoming squatters to bring empty buildings into use, and also from active mixing in social or public housing allocation. Social mixing has helped maintain social capital and neighbourhood trust. In this it reflects the demonstrated effect of positive intercultural interactions in public spaces: they reduce prejudice not only amongst participants, but also amongst onlookers (Allport, 1954; Christ et al., 2014).

Amsterdam highlights the potential of interculturalism for healthy sharing of the city and its public spaces between different cultural and socio-economic groups. This in turn builds trust, and makes the adoption of new mediated sharing practices easier. 'Stranger shock' from exposure to difference – in the relatively safe spaces of integrated cities – helps us widen our perspectives and our moral communities (Sennett, 2013). While traditional socio-cultural sharing strengthens bonds within groups, mediated 'stranger sharing' also promises to broaden our empathy for others, increasing links between social groups and even between societies.

Sadly, in recent years with the rise of far-right politics, Amsterdam has become less institutionally open to immigrants and squatters. Yet informal sharers such as squatters are symbolic for sharing cities, in the same ways as online counter-cultures are transforming sharing societies. Online norms with respect to music and software have shifted rapidly with forms of 'piracy' that challenge consumerism, establish new commons, and redefine identity for those involved. Urban piracy in the form of direct seizure of land and buildings by squatters is typically less widely welcomed, yet widespread, especially in Southern cities, where slum communities typically lack rights to their land, and often depend on informal or even illegal connections to water and power supplies. Innovative approaches to collective community development such as community land-titling offer the prospect of supporting squatters while reinforcing their sharing approaches.

In the North too we concur with urbanist Miguel Martinez (2014) in his conclusion that squats should "be recognized and supported for what they are: vibrant social centers at the very heart of the 'commons', actively including the excluded". In Copenhagen, the history of Christiania illustrates both the conflicts and the possibilities of squatting. For many years practically autonomous, the 'Freetown' of Christiania comprises a disused military district in central Copenhagen squatted since 1971. Initial motivations for the squat included the lack of affordable housing elsewhere in the city. Since 1994, Christiania's 900 or so residents have paid taxes and fees for utility services and in 2012 – as a residents' collective – struck a deal with the Danish government to purchase the site for substantially below market value, raising the money through a form of crowd-funding. In the intervening years residents successfully established an alternative local currency, restored the buildings, built new homes, and regulated the socially and ethnically diverse district according to collective anarchist governance models. Today Christiania is symbolic of the creativity and tolerance of Denmark. As Freston (2013) notes: "these are people who built their own homes, who stood up to the government and criminal elements for decades, who took in the poor and disadvantaged, who were eco-friendly and racially diverse before anyone else."

Counter-cultural sharing behaviours like squatting happen in autonomous or 'interstitial spaces' beyond the reach of the powers that be. As a result they can, as with Christiania, be the birthplace of subversive approaches to social transformation and re-invention. Subversion shifts values through interventions that can win (temporary) support from mainstream interests – such as women's rights backed by employers wishing to expand the potential workforce. Re-invention rather seeks to create alternatives in the margins of the conventional economy. From squatting to time-dollars, in communes and transition towns, re-inventors meet needs in ways that are not subject to the existing norms and rules of the system, but in ways that can obtain cultural momentum. When we argue for the potential for sharing to lead social change, we are not arguing for trickle-down from some newly fashionable niche of 'sustainable consumption' but instead for a subversive, bottom-up – simultaneously counter-cultural and intercultural – re-invention of consumption that is a collaborative, shared, identity-redefining, co-production of services and products supplying fundamental needs.

The politics of the urban commons

In this section we briefly explore the new and revived forms of collective politics that become possible in sharing cities as norms and values shift (contrasting them with the post-political tendencies of 'smart cities').

We see two distinctive expressions of collective politics stimulated by sharing. The first is the cumulative engendering of civic engagement arising through repeated sharing practices within and across cultural boundaries. The second is the more disruptive form of activist protest, characterized by the Occupy movement and its precursors such as Las Indignadas in Spain. These movements, typically rejecting conventional politics not just the existing parties, and often motivated by concern over the capture of politics by commercial inter-ests, have generated new sharing institutions including alternative currencies and integrated cooperatives, and boosted existing ones such as credit unions. They have adopted sharing platforms and tools to assist refugees arriving from Africa and the Middle East. In some cases they have stimulated new political expres-sions of sharing and solidarity, notably in the growth of Podemos in Spain and Syriza in Greece, although such parties often remain controversial in the movements.

For cities a systemic focus on sharing can help establish a virtuous cycle – it can shift values and norms towards trust and collaboration; enable both civic engagement and political activism; and rebuild a shared urban commons as a venue for political activity. Perversely, though, sharing's potential is so great because it is not purely a doctrine of resistance or resilience, but one whose immediate benefits (more efficient use of resources, workforce flexibility and so on) can appeal even to powerful elites, yet in practice rebuild values and norms that could transform existing power relations, when expressed politically. It is not just economically disruptive but also politically subversive.

Communal sharing, whether led by public authorities, civil society organiza-tions (or even companies) rebuilds civic virtues; and challenges the individualist, post-political, technocratic vision of neoliberalism, currently reproduced in 'smart city' discourses. Moreover, as the public square of collective politics, community activism, and non-traditional political participation is strengthened, so are investments in sustainability and sharing infrastructures more easily agreed (Portney & Berry, 2010), and those investments in turn can generate more sharing and even stronger social capital. In losing sight of the shared nature of such urban commons, cities have devalued them and thus also undermined their potential to support creative and productive economies. This means that cities have been forced to engage in a 'race-to-the-bottom' in social standards and environmental protection – because they focus on the sections of their economies vulnerable to international competition, instead of on the common foundations of the core economy. Sadly, this misdirection of effort is also being aided and abetted by the marketing and discourses of the 'smart city'.

As promoted by companies such as IBM and Siemens, smart cities discourses presume that there is a single technological path to the future, and that countries and cities must compete to race along it as quickly as possible. They therefore subscribe to the neoliberal ideologies of privatization and enclosure, using openness only strategically and instrumentally; and often find common cause with advocates of a 'post-political' reliance on technology as a solution to inherently political challenges. So-called 'sharing' businesses that seek to monetize our every possession and every moment of our time can fit the corporatist smart city model: but approaches to sharing that focus on capabilities, learning, and the reconstruction of community, will struggle to find a place. At their worst, in the built from scratch stand-alone model of Masdar, smart cities promise exclusive private services only for the rich, enabling elite flight from the megacities. Genuinely smart plans for smart cities cannot be economy-driven and technology-led, but socially driven and ethically led. The city and the technologies must be shaped around the people, not vice versa.

Building the sharing city

In this concluding section, we outline some of the practical steps necessary to build genuinely smart and sustainable sharing cities, putting the sharing paradigm into practice.

As cities face the growth of mediated, commercial sharing approaches, we suggest five key principles to make the engagement actively transformative – to shape the norms, regulations, and finance that guides sharing activities. First, the programme, spaces, and platforms involved should be designed in ways that help to build trust and empathy, collectively or individually, and to enable users to obtain and signal their trustworthiness and reputation. Second, utilizing and stimulating intrinsic motivations is generally more effective for rebuilding communities through sharing than focusing on extrinsic (monetary) rewards or sanctions. Third, systems must empower users both to control whether and how much they participate, and to influence the overall design and rules of the system. Fourth, systems must achieve high standards of civil liberties, protection of privacy, security of personal data, and enable anonymity wherever appropriate. Fifth, and most importantly, systems must be designed from the outset for justice and inclusion in intercultural societies. They must be equally accessible and attractive to those from different groups and cultures – especially those otherwise disadvantaged.

These principles seek to reflect a balance between strategic purpose – rooted in a clear social mission and direction; and participatory emergence – recognizing the diversity of urban settings. These guidelines apply generally as cities broaden their engagement with and understanding of sharing. So getting the rules, norms, and finance right to enable squatting of genuinely empty property is as important as getting them right for Airbnb; for public transit and safe streets for walking and cycling, as much as for ride-sharing; for credit unions as well as crowd-finance; for food-banks and community gardens as much as for supper clubs; for student oriented learning environments as well as massive online courses; for libraries as well as reuse markets like Craigslist; and generally, for cooperatives and unions not just online platforms.

What might this imply in practice? An aspiring Sharing City will actively invest in public services and enable co-production in city-led services, protecting and enhancing public common resources, infrastructures, and services, paid for through taxation or insurance. It will support education and skill development that can build confidence and practice in sharing. It will engage the public in governance, for example, through participatory budgeting. It will also invest in the public realm in ways that enable participation and create physical, virtual, and psychological spaces for insurgent counter-cultures and interculturalism. A Sharing City will also enable collaborative economy operations in the city, reforming policy across areas such as taxation, planning, and licensing; and investing its own capital, land, and resources. It will regulate to ensure inclusion and appropriate social protections for participants, especially against labour casualization. It will directly support non-profit, communal sharing as a direct or enabling intermediary or facilitator. And it will act as a sharing hub, perhaps aggregating and guaranteeing reputation for its citizens, underpinned by enabling open, affordable high-speed (mobile) internet access for all residents. Sharing cities will also network with other sharing cities, enabling both local customization and effective interoperability of sharing platforms.

The Sharing City is a new paradigm for cities, opening a genuine third way between state and market. But unlike many past efforts at social emancipation and transformation it works with both the current zeitgeist and our inherited humanity. Sharing is a critical defining characteristic of what it means to be human. Only by expressing our sharing nature more fully can we hope to flourish in the 'age of humanity'. By adopting the principles and policies suggested here, sharing cities offer a truly just and genuinely sustainable pathway into our uncertain post-urban future.

References

Agyeman, J., Bullard, R. D., & Evans, B. (Eds.). (2003). *Just sustainabilities: Development in an unequal world.* Cambridge, MA: MIT Press.

Allport, G. W. (1954). *The nature of prejudice.* Cambridge, MA: Addison-Wesley.

Bernal, P. (2014). *Internet privacy rights: Rights to protect autonomy* (No. 24). Cambridge, UK: Cambridge University Press.

Botsman, R., & Rogers, R. (2010). *What's mine is yours: The rise of collaborative consumption.* London: Harper Business.

Christ, O., Schmid, K., Lolliot, S., Swart, H., Stolle, D., Tausch, N., ... & Hewstone, M. (2014). Contextual effect of positive intergroup contact on outgroup prejudice. *Proceedings of the National Academy of Sciences, 111*(11), 3996–4000.

Cova, B., Kozinets, R. V., & Shankar, A. (Eds.). (2007). *Consumer tribes*. London: Routledge.

Ellen MacArthur Foundation. (2012). *Toward the circular economy: Economic and business rationale for an accelerated transition*. Retrieved 6 July 2017, from www.ellenmacarthur-foundation.org/publications/towards-a-circular-economy-business-rationale-for-an-accelerated-transition.

Freston, T. (2013). You are now leaving the European Union. *Vanity Fair, 9*(12). Retrieved 6 July 2017, from www.vanityfair.com/politics/2013/09/christiana-forty-years-copenhagen.

The Korean. (2008, April 25). Super special Korean emotions? *Ask a Korean*, Blogspot. Retrieved 6 July 2017, from http://askakorean.blogspot.co.uk/2008/04/super-special-korean-emotions.html.

Lee, J.-H., & Hancock, M. G. (2012). *Toward a framework for smart cities: A comparison of Seoul, San Francisco & Amsterdam*. Yonsei University. Seoul: Korea and Stanford Program on Regions of Innovation and Entrepreneurship. Retrieved 6 July 2017, from http://iisdb.stanford.edu/evnts/7239/Jung_Hoon_Lee_final.pdf.

Martinez, M. (2014, May 13). Squatting for justice, bringing life to the city. *ROARMAG*. Retrieved 6 July 2017, from http://roarmag.org/2014/05/squatting-urban-justice-commons/.

McLaren, D., & Agyeman, J. (2015). *Sharing cities: A case for truly smart and sustainable cities*. Cambridge, MA: MIT Press.

Nussbaum, M. (2011). *Creating capabilities: The human development approach*. Cambridge, MA: Harvard University Press.

Ozanne, L., & Ballantine, P. W. (2010). Sharing as a form of anti-consumption? An examination of toy library users. *Journal of Consumer Behaviour, 9*(6), 485–498.

Pagel, M. (2012). *Wired for culture: The natural history of human cooperation*. London: Allen Lane.

Portney, K. E., & Berry, J. M. (2010). Participation and the pursuit of sustainability in U.S. cities. *Urban Affairs Review, 46*(1), 119–139.

Putnam, R. D. (2000). *Bowling alone: The collapse and revival of American community*. New York: Simon & Schuster.

Sassen, S. (2001). *The global city: New York, London, Tokyo*. Princeton, NJ: Princeton University Press.

Sen, A. (2009). *The idea of justice*. London: Allen Lane.

Sennett, R. (2013). *Together: The rituals, pleasures and politics of cooperation*. London: Penguin.

Index

Page numbers in *italics* denote tables, those in **bold** denote figures.

youth 131, 153; American 139n1; in northern Mediterranean cities and towns 294; outmigration 293; programs 246; unemployment *191*; upper-middle-class 133–4; working-class 133–4

Zhang, F. 164, 171
Zhangjiang High-Tech Park 171
Zhang, L. 164, 166
Zhu, J. 159, 166

Taylor & Francis eBooks

Helping you to choose the right eBooks for your Library

Add Routledge titles to your library's digital collection today. Taylor and Francis ebooks contains over 50,000 titles in the Humanities, Social Sciences, Behavioural Sciences, Built Environment and Law.

Choose from a range of subject packages or create your own!

Benefits for you

» Free MARC records
» COUNTER-compliant usage statistics
» Flexible purchase and pricing options
» All titles DRM-free.

Benefits for your user

» Off-site, anytime access via Athens or referring URL
» Print or copy pages or chapters
» Full content search
» Bookmark, highlight and annotate text
» Access to thousands of pages of quality research at the click of a button.

 REQUEST YOUR FREE INSTITUTIONAL TRIAL TODAY | **Free Trials Available** We offer free trials to qualifying academic, corporate and government customers.

eCollections – Choose from over 30 subject eCollections, including:

Archaeology	Language Learning
Architecture	Law
Asian Studies	Literature
Business & Management	Media & Communication
Classical Studies	Middle East Studies
Construction	Music
Creative & Media Arts	Philosophy
Criminology & Criminal Justice	Planning
Economics	Politics
Education	Psychology & Mental Health
Energy	Religion
Engineering	Security
English Language & Linguistics	Social Work
Environment & Sustainability	Sociology
Geography	Sport
Health Studies	Theatre & Performance
History	Tourism, Hospitality & Events

For more information, pricing enquiries or to order a free trial, please contact your local sales team:
www.tandfebooks.com/page/sales

 Routledge
Taylor & Francis Group | The home of Routledge books | **www.tandfebooks.com**